INTRODUCTION TO
SOCIAL WORK

INTRODUCTION TO
SOCIAL WORK

SOCIAL WORKERS EFFECTING
CHANGE IN OUR WORLD

Jessica A. Ritter

cognella®
SAN DIEGO

Bassim Hamadeh, CEO and Publisher
Amy Smith, Senior Project Editor
Alia Bales, Production Manager
Emely Villavicencio, Senior Graphic Designer
Kylie Bartolome, Licensing Associate
Stephanie Adams, Senior Marketing Program Manager
Natalie Piccotti, Director of Marketing
Kassie Graves, Senior Vice President, Editorial
Jamie Giganti, Director of Academic Publishing

Cover image copyright © 2021 iStockphoto LP/Dewin ' Indew.

Printed in the United States of America.

cognella® | ACADEMIC PUBLISHING
320 South Cedros Ave., Ste. 400, Solana Beach, CA 92075

Brief Contents

Detailed Contents

CHAPTER 3

An Introduction to Generalist Social Work Practice   58

CHAPTER 4

Social Justice, Equity, Diversity, and Inclusion in Social Work   **90**

Julie Clockston

Social Work With Children and Their Families   243

CHAPTER 12

International Social Work and Human Rights   326

CHAPTER 13

Social Work Practice in Substance Abuse and Addiction   357

Preface

Vision

Introduction to Social Work has always been one of my favorite classes to teach as I have the opportunity to introduce the core concepts, history, and values of social work to students and to help them sort through whether this might be the right career path for them. I have a special passion for introductory social work texts because, when done well, they can help recruit students into the profession and introduce them to the most critical foundational concepts of the social work discipline.

My goal with this book is to provide an intro-level social work text that is engaging and inspiring for students to read, that teaches them the most important foundational concepts in the social work discipline, and introduces them to the wide array of career paths in social work. While there are a number of introductory social work texts available, this one is unique in that it introduces students to the three major domains of social work practice—practice, policy, and research—and gives equal coverage to micro social work and macro social work. My coauthors and I have also been very intentional in embedding material related to social justice, equity, diversity, and inclusivity into every chapter of this book, including the contributions of Black, Indigenous, and people of color (BIPOC) social workers who are often neglected, discussing the impact of racism within the profession, and highlighting current social justice issues and social movements that impact communities of color.

Framework of the Book

This book is framed in a way that is unique since it introduces students to the three major domains of social work practice—practice, policy, and research—so that students are prepared for their other required classes as they move through their social work program.

Unique features of the book:

- Highlights the three major domains of social work: practice, policy, and research. (Note: In most introductory social work texts, students are not adequately introduced to policy and research.)
- Strong focus on social justice, equity, diversity, and inclusivity (SJEDI)—material embedded throughout book
- BIPOC social workers' contributions included in multiple chapters in this book
- Showcases the strengths of the social work profession as well as its failures and missteps, particularly with regard to the impact of racism within the profession
- Equal coverage of micro and macro levels of social work
- Grounded in the current social challenges facing our country—systemic racism, coronavirus pandemic, economic inequality, environmental justice, current political climate, and political divisions
- Fresh, up-to-date material in the topical chapters regarding current social problems
- Career path options in social work heavily emphasized
- Enhances critical thinking skills of students using practice activities and critical thinking discussion questions

Part I includes five chapters that provide an introduction to social work in the United States. Chapter 1 sets the stage by defining social work, exploring myths and misconceptions, providing a professional outlook for social work, introducing the National Association of Social Workers (NASW) code of ethics, and providing an overview of social work education. Chapter 2 tells the story of how the social work profession and social welfare system developed in the United States and provides a comprehensive overview of the current social welfare system. Chapter 3 delineates generalist social work practice, the phases of the planned change process, and some of the major theorical frameworks used in social work. Chapter 4 is a pivotal chapter that covers social justice, equity, diversity, and inclusivity in social work. Macro social work gets its own focus in Chapter 5 because it is the overlooked and more hidden side of the profession.

Part II has eight chapters that are the topical chapters of the book to highlight the broad fields of practice that are available to people with a social work degree and the social problems that social workers address in our society. The topical areas covered include poverty and housing insecurity, mental health, health care, children and families, older adults, criminal justice, international social work and human rights, and substance abuse/addiction. Each of these topical chapters includes a social worker spotlight, case study, social justice spotlight, content on diversity, equity and inclusivity, practice activities, and discussion questions.

The final chapter of the book, Chapter 14, provides a look toward the future by highlighting critical social issues on the horizon that are of interest to the social work profession. Chapter 14 also provides an important discussion of current social work trends and workplace issues as well as content to help students assess whether social work is the profession for them.

This book lays important groundwork and prepares students for what is to come in all their future courses in the three major domains of social work—practice, policy, and research. It is an inspiring and engaging read that enhances students' critical thinking skills and introduces them to the wide array of career paths in social work.

An Introduction to the Social Work Profession

There is perhaps no more relevant and exciting time to join the social work profession than today. On the positive side, social workers are employed in diverse workplaces across this country, using evidence-based interventions to help individuals and families facing an array of personal challenges. Additionally, there are social workers working at the macro level to address some of the nation's most pressing social problems, some even deciding to run for public office. On the negative side, unfortunately social workers are desperately needed in this country due to serious social problems that affect many millions of Americans such as poverty, systemic racism, the coronavirus pandemic, stark political divisions, child maltreatment, mental health disorders including substance abuse, climate change, and lack of access to health care, just to name a few. When a national crisis like the coronavirus pandemic happens, social workers have to be creative and nimble in order to continue to serve their clients. One example of this is the proliferation of telemental health by mental health providers who are able to provide their services virtually using various forms of technology. See Chapter 7 for more on this exciting development!

IMG 1.1

When undergraduate students enroll in an Introduction to Social Work course at their college or university, they are often trying to determine whether they are well suited for a career as a social worker. The purpose of this book is to provide a comprehensive and current overview of social work to help students answer this important question. However, other students enroll in an intro class simply to learn more about social work since they plan to enter a field that will likely collaborate with social workers. Social work is not for everyone, but for those who do decide to enter this career of service to others, it promises to be both personally fulfilling and challenging. A career in social work often leads to personal and professional growth, a skill set focused on facilitating a planned change process, and lifelong learning regarding the personal human struggles and social problems that exist in this country and around the world.

Common Myths/Misperceptions About the Social Work Profession

Unfortunately, social work is often misunderstood, and there are many **myths** and **misperceptions** surrounding the social work profession. One common myth is that anyone can call themselves a social worker in the workplace if they are doing work that is helping others. In fact, only those with an undergraduate or graduate degree in social work can call themselves a social worker, and in some states, you also must be licensed to use the title of social worker. Another common myth is that social work is a narrow field and that most social workers work in child protection. This could not be further from the truth as there are literally hundreds of career paths for social workers in a broad array of fields including health care, mental health, school social work, international social work, criminal justice, and work in the political arena, just to name a few. Social workers work in government, nonprofit, and for-profit work settings.

There is a common misperception that all social workers are poorly compensated. While some social workers are not compensated as well as they should be, it is incorrect to say that this is true for all social workers. According to the U.S. Bureau of Labor Statistics (BLS, 2021), the median salary for social workers in 2020 was $51,760, meaning that half of social workers were below this and half were above this. Social workers in certain positions are paid quite well, such as those in medical social work, mental health, and when social workers advance into administrative positions.

Another common myth about the social work profession is that social work only involves micro social work, or helping people at the individual level. This is false due to the profession's mission of social justice and the fact that many social workers are working to address systemic change at the macro level. Finally, social workers are often portrayed on television and in the movies as burned out and uncaring people. Social workers are trained to be caring and empathetic, and to treat clients with dignity and respect. Social workers who are burned out or experiencing compassion fatigue should take a break or leave the profession so that they do not cause harm to those they are there to serve. On the flipside, it is also important to note that social workers are not there to be saviors and to "save" others. They are there to assist other people in making changes in their life by providing them with needed tools and support.

▌ What Is Social Work?

There are several influential social work organizations that provide a definition of social work. The **International Federation of Social Workers (IFSW)** and the **International Association of Schools of Social Work (IASSW)** are international organizations that focus on social work in a global context. They define social work as

> a practice-based profession and an academic discipline that promotes social change and development, social cohesion, and the empowerment and liberation of people. Principles of social justice, human rights, collective responsibility, and respect for diversities are central to social work. Underpinned by theories of social work, social sciences, humanities and indigenous knowledges, social work engages people and structures to address life challenges and enhance wellbeing. The above definition may be amplified at national and/or regional levels. (IFSW, 2014).

A U.S.-based organization, the **National Association of Social Workers** (NASW) was founded in 1955 and is the largest group of professional social workers in the world. The NASW is an incredibly influential organization when it comes to helping people understand the mission and goals of the social work profession. The NASW works to enhance the professional growth and development of social workers, and one way that they work to achieve this is by developing a code of ethics that all social workers should follow to ensure that they are engaging in ethical behavior (and not causing harm) with the clients they serve. The NASW code of ethics summarizes the **mission of the social work profession**. According to the NASW (2021):

> The primary mission of the social work profession is to enhance human well-being and help meet the basic human needs of all people, with particular attention to the needs and empowerment of people who are vulnerable, oppressed, and living in poverty. A historic and defining feature of social work is the profession's dual focus on individual well-being in a social context and the well-being of society. Fundamental to social work is attention to the environmental forces that create, contribute to, and address problems in living. ... The mission of the social work profession is rooted in a set of core values: service, social justice, dignity and worth of the person, importance of human relationships, integrity, and competence.

The Three Domains of Social Work

An important framework of this book is to highlight the three major domains of social work—**practice**, **policy**, and **research**. Most people are familiar with social work *practice*, but less aware of the *policy* and *research* side of the social work profession. Social workers are educated and trained to be change agents. One way that they effect change is in their direct practice work with individuals, families, and communities by using evidence-based interventions at the micro, mezzo, and macro level. A few prominent examples of social work practice are case management, crisis intervention, therapeutic

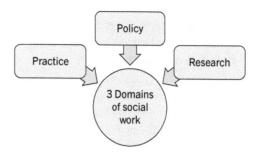

FIGURE 1.1   Three Domains of Social Work

interventions, administration, and program planning. A second way that social workers impact lives is by being involved in policy work at the local, state, and federal level, as well as within the organizations where they work. Social workers do this by working directly for lawmakers, working as lobbyists, being employed in advocacy organizations, and holding administrative positions where they help create policies within their place of work. Finally, social workers effect change by producing research that helps to guide the interventions that social workers use. Social worker researchers, the majority with doctorate degrees, conduct important research studies to help those working in the field better intervene with those they serve. This practice-policy research domain framework will be infused throughout this book. The example that follows illustrates how social workers in the health care field might carry out their work in each of these three domains.

SOCIAL WORK IN THE HEALTH CARE FIELD

Practice: Many social workers with a strong desire to work in the medical or health care field are employed in medical clinics or hospital settings. They serve patients and their families in these settings by providing psychosocial assessments, crisis intervention services, grief counseling, emotional support, case management and care coordination, patient advocacy, and discharge planning. Medical social workers work with an interdisciplinary team of health care professionals to carry out this work. Some medical social workers choose to specialize in areas such as emergency room medicine, oncology, pediatrics, gerontology, or neonatal care.

Policy: Other social workers who focus on health care choose to work in the policy arena in order to influence legislation at the state or federal level. We can find social workers like this employed in health policy advocacy organizations at the state and federal level. Social workers in advocacy organizations might work to pass legislation that would increase people's access to health care and health insurance by making it more affordable, bring down the cost of prescription drugs, or perhaps require cultural competence training for health care workers who work with patients from incredibly diverse backgrounds.

Research: Social workers who become researchers in the health care field might study a variety of interventions to help determine which ones should be considered best practices by those working in the field. For example, they might evaluate interventions that are used by social workers who work with older adults with dementia, study individual and group therapy approaches for parents of children with terminal illnesses, and evaluate treatment approaches used in settings that serve patients with traumatic brain injury. Researchers publish their findings in academic journals and make presentations at academic conferences.

What Is the Difference Between Micro, Mezzo, and Macro Social Work?

One of the most unique features of the social work profession is that social workers can practice at the **micro**, **mezzo**, and/or **macro** level. It is not unusual for social workers to work across these three levels over the course of their social work career. What differentiates these three levels is who the "client" is that the social worker is attempting to create change with:

Micro: Individuals and families

Mezzo: Small groups and organizations

Macro: Communities; large systems; society at large

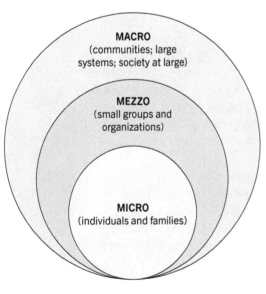

When most people envision the work of a social worker, they likely think about the micro side of the social work profession where social workers intervene directly with individuals and families. Examples of common tasks performed by social workers working at the **micro level** include case management, biopsychosocial assessments, counseling/therapy, crisis intervention, and connecting clients to services in the community. For example, school social workers in a high school work one-on-one with the students in that school who are at risk of dropping out, having mental health struggles, or experiencing problems at home.

FIGURE 1.2   Three Levels of Social Work

At the **mezzo level**, the client shifts to being a small group or organization. Social workers working at the mezzo level might do group therapy or work in an administrative position where the focus is on helping the organization perform well. A school social worker might facilitate a group with students who are struggling with their mental health or provide training to school personnel on issues such as bullying, how to create a safe learning environment for LGBTQ students, or how to support students who are undocumented.

Finally, when social workers work at the **macro level**, they are trying to effect change with communities, large systems (e.g., criminal justice system; child welfare system), and/or society at large. A school social worker with many years of experience might later move into an administrative position within the school district, or the U.S. Department of Education, or may have a job where they attempt to pass legislation at the state or federal level to improve schools' capacity to help students learn and thrive. For example, they might advocate for legislation that would provide funding to support students who are at risk of dropping out or who need mental health support.

SOCIAL WORKER SPOTLIGHT:
Social Work at the Micro, Mezzo, and Macro Level
Jessica A. Ritter, Ph.D., MSSW

Jessica Ritter, the author of this book, is a good example of how social workers often perform work across the three levels of social work practice over the course of a career—micro, mezzo, and macro. Jessica began her career in the field of child welfare as she was extremely passionate about working with children and families who are impacted by various problems that can lead to child maltreatment such as poverty, family violence, substance abuse, and mental illness.

After completing her BSSW internship at Children's Protective Services in Austin, Texas, Jessica felt ready to begin work as a child protection caseworker (**micro-level social work**). In this role, she was assigned a caseload of families where the child had to be removed from their home due to very high risk to their health and/or safety. Her job was to find a temporary placement for the child (e.g., foster home, relative placement), to set up services for the children on her caseload (e.g., therapy, health care), and to set up services for the parents—most of whom were working to have their children returned to their care. A big part of her job was to work with other professionals involved in the case and to keep the court updated on the progress of the family. Her ultimate aim was to secure a safe and loving permanent placement for the children on her caseload. The first goal was to make attempts to reunify children with their parents, and if that was not possible another permanency plan would need to be made, such as permanent placement with a relative caregiver. According to Jessica, "This was one of the most stressful and challenging jobs I have ever had, but also one of the most rewarding. Every day, I learned more and more about the risk factors that lead to child maltreatment and how I could best support the children and families in my care."

After working in the child protection field for several years, Jessica accepted a new position in the state agency that administers child protection services in the state of Texas, the Texas Department of Family and Protective Services. This was a thrilling career change as she now had the opportunity to impact clients by helping the organization perform its best on behalf of the children and families they were serving every day (**mezzo social work**). She was assigned a range of administrative projects to help the agency run efficiently and to improve its programs and policies. It was very exciting to learn new skills in program planning and administration!

Finally, Jessica had the opportunity to effect change at the **macro level** when she served as a board member for an advocacy organization called Children First for Oregon (CFFO). The mission of CFFO was to work for legislative change at the state level that would improve the lives of vulnerable children in Oregon with a special focus on children in poverty and those served by the child welfare system. It was exhilarating to work with a team of people who had a very strong passion for improving conditions for children in the state of Oregon. In this role, she was able to help CFFO carry out its mission by evaluating the fiscal health of the organization and weighing in on the priorities of the organization and the various public policies that the organization would focus on. CFFO advocated on a range of bills that ended up being passed into law, including a few that directly impacted youth in the foster care system. In her role at CFFO (and also her work with the state chapter of NASW), Jessica was able to provide testimony on a number of bills before the Oregon State Legislature and to advocate on behalf of vulnerable children and families in the state.

One of the most important features of social work practice is that sometimes the target of intervention is the individual, when we are trying to help individuals better adapt to their social environment, and other times the target of intervention is the larger social environment so that it can better support individuals and families. Both strategies are crucial. Some social workers have a strong preference for working at one of these levels and feel that their skills and passions are best suited for micro, mezzo, or macro practice. However, other social workers like the challenge of working at each of these levels over the course of their social work career. It is common for some social workers to begin working at the micro and mezzo level and then move into macro level work after getting some valuable direct experience under their belt. Over the years, criticisms have been leveled at the social work profession for prioritizing micro social work over macro social work, and this is discussed in more detail in Chapter 5.

Where Do Social Workers Work?

Let's begin with a question: When you envision a social worker—what they are like, where twork, and the kinds of things they do at their job—what comes to mind for you? Take a minute to write this down. You may have imagined someone working with children and families who have come to the attention of the child protection system. Or perhaps, someone who provides mental health therapy to individuals with a mental health disorder. Or maybe you thought of someone who assists people who live below the poverty line and are struggling to get their basic needs met. If these images came to mind for you, you would not be wrong, but this barely scratches the surface when it comes to all the ways that social workers operate in our world. Social work is often compared to other helping professions such as psychology, counseling, and health care, and students often wonder how social work is unique. One of the most distinctive features of social work is the incredibly broad array of **fields of practice** that social workers can choose from once they earn a degree in social work.

Even though the social work profession has been in existence for over 100 years in the United States, many Americans have a narrow conception of what social

IMG 1.2

workers actually do. Many are oblivious of the broad array of career paths that are available to social workers, social work's mission of social justice, that there is a micro side and a macro side to this profession, and the significant contributions that social workers make every day to individuals, families, and communities across this nation, and around the globe.

There is a book titled *101 Careers in Social Work* (Ritter et al., 2020), which provides a thorough overview of the incredibly diverse array of career options for those who earn an undergraduate and/or graduate degree in social work. It is perhaps one of the biggest draws for those who decide to enter the profession because of the opportunity to work in multiple fields or work settings over the course of one's career, an option not possible for those in many other professions. In *101 Careers in Social Work,* the following chapters are covered, and numerous job titles are profiled under each of these fields of practice:

- Careers in Child Welfare
- School-Based Social Work
- Social Work With Older Adults
- Social Work in Health Care
- Social Work in Mental Health and Addiction
- Careers in Crisis Intervention
- Careers in Criminal Justice and the Legal Arena
- Careers in International Social Work and Human Rights
- Social Work Careers in the Field of Poverty
- Careers in Advocacy and the Political Arena
- Careers in Community Practice
- Leadership in Human Services Organizations
- Careers in Research and Academia
- "Out-of-the-Box" Social Work Careers

This book will cover all the major fields of practice for social workers, so read on! Some social workers choose to spend their entire career in one field in which they have a strong passion (e.g., school-based social worker), while others choose to change the setting where they work to keep things interesting and to learn and grow in different fields of practice. It would not be unusual, for example, for a social worker to begin their career in child welfare and then later move into other fields such as medical social work, clinical social work, or political advocacy work, or even earn their doctorate in social work to work in academia. Social workers work in nonprofit organizations, government agencies, and for-profit organizations. There really is no "typical" career path trajectory for a social worker.

What Is the Professional Outlook for Professional Social Workers in the Coming Years?

Students often want to know whether the demand for social workers will continue, and the answer is a resounding "yes." Table 1.1 includes data from the BLS on the number of social workers in the U.S., median wages in various fields of practice, and projected growth through 2030. According to the BLS (2021), the employment of social workers is expected to grow 12% from 2020–2030, and this is "faster than the average for all occupations." When the BLS breaks this growth down into three specific categories, it shows that the employment of social workers in the mental health and addictions fields will have the most growth at 15%. The employment of social workers in health care is projected to grow 13%, and this is the same for school social workers and those who work with children and families (BLS, 2021).

| 1.1 | PRACTICE ACTIVITY |

Now that you have learned more about the career options for those who earn a degree in social work, please reflect on the following questions:

1. What social problems are you most passionate about tackling?

2. What fields of social work practice are currently most interesting to you? Why do you think this is the case?

3. Do you think you would most enjoy working at the micro, mezzo, or macro level? Can you see yourself working in policy or research? Why or why not?

According to the BLS (2021), social workers in the United States held roughly 715,600 jobs in 2020, and they were distributed as follows, along with median annual wages (i.e., half earned more than this amount and half earned less).

TABLE 1.1   Overview of the Social Work Workforce in the United States

	Number of social workers (2020)	Median annual wages (2020)	Percent growth (2020–2030)
Child, family, and school social workers	335,300	$48,430	13%
Health care social workers	184,900	$57,630	13%
Mental health and substance abuse social workers	124,000	$48,720	15%
Social workers, all other	71,400	$64,210	6%

An Overview of Social Work Education

Formal social work programs have been in existence in the United States since 1889 when Columbia University began offering its first courses in social work. Since this, social work programs have proliferated. According to the **Council on Social Work Education** (CSWE, n.d.), as of October 2022, there were 538 accredited baccalaureate social work programs and 313 accredited Master of Social Work programs in the United States. Students are strongly encouraged to attend a social work program that is accredited by the CSWE since they set the standards that social work programs should follow to provide a rigorous and robust social work education to its students. Students who do not attend an accredited social work program may be limited when it comes to finding employment and obtaining licensure. Anyone who has a goal to become a practicing social worker will need to earn a bachelor's or master's degree in social work.

- **Bachelor's in Social Work (BSW) degree:** Undergraduate students who earn a BSW degree are prepared to be "generalists." This means that students gain knowledge, values, and skills that enable them to work in a variety of entry-level positions as a social worker. Most students earn their undergraduate degree in social work in 4–5 years unless they are attending college on a part-time basis.

- **Master's in Social Work (MSW) degree:** Graduate students who earn an MSW degree are prepared to be "specialists." They receive advanced training

IMG 1.3

and often choose a concentration in their MSW program such as clinical social work, macro practice, or children, youth, and families. Obtaining an MSW degree is necessary for anyone who wishes to work as a licensed clinical social worker (LCSW). It is important to know that some jobs in social work require an MSW degree (e.g., medical social work, mental health), and these jobs typically pay higher salaries. Students who have earned their BSW can apply for an advanced standing MSW program option and earn their MSW in 1 year. For everyone else, an MSW degree is a 2-year program.

- **Doctoral degree in social work:** There are two options for those who are interested in pursuing doctoral studies in social work—a PhD (Doctor of Philosophy) in social work or a DSW (Doctor of Social Work). Those who pursue a PhD in social work are prepared to work in academia so that they can conduct research and teach social work in a university. Others might choose to pursue work as a researcher in a setting outside of academia. Earning a PhD consists of advanced coursework, training as a researcher, and the completion of a dissertation study. Earning a doctorate in social work takes roughly 4–6 years on average, though some PhD students take longer. A DSW on the other hand, is less about being trained as a researcher and is more of a practice doctorate with advanced studies in clinical practice, teaching, and/or leadership and administration. Those with a DSW can obtain a job inside or outside of academia, depending on their career goals.

- **Social work licensure:** In most states, licensure is required for practicing social workers and for anyone who wants to call themself a "social worker." Requirements for licensure typically involve paying a licensing fee, passing an exam, and completing a certain number of continuing education hours each year, particularly in ethics. Social work licensing boards are charged with conducting investigations into complaints against licensed social workers. Licensure protects consumers because if a social worker is accused of doing something unethical, their license can be taken away.

The delivery of social work education has changed dramatically over the years, and there are more options than ever before to respond to the diverse needs of prospective students. For example, many social work programs today offer face-to-face, fully online, or hybrid course options (classes that are a blend of face-to-face and online). Some programs offer the option to complete the program part-time to accommodate students who need to work while attending school. Social work programs focus on the transmission of **knowledge**, **values**, and **skills** when educating students who want to become social workers.

What Knowledge Do Social Workers Need?

There is important knowledge that needs to be obtained for social workers to be proficient and competent in their future career. Social work faculty spend a lot of time thinking about what they want students to learn and how they can best learn it. Guided by the CSWE, social work programs are very intentional in deciding what courses to offer, what content to offer in their curriculum, and the best way to deliver this content to students. There are a number of courses that are commonly offered in social work programs to help students meet these competencies:

- Introduction to Social Work
- Generalist Social Work Practice With Individuals and Families
- Generalist Social Work Practice With Groups
- Generalist Social Work Practice With Organizations and Communities
- Social Welfare Policy
- Social Work Policy Practice
- Research Methods
- Theories of Human Behavior and the Social Environment (HBSE)
- Power, Privilege, and Oppression
- Social Work Electives on a range of topics (e.g., child maltreatment, health care, clinical social work, school social work, antiracist social work practice, social work with immigrants and refugees, international social work, social work in criminal justice settings, grief and loss, trauma-informed social work practice, etc.)
- Field Seminar (for students who are completing their internship)

As you can see from these two lists, the three major domains of social work practice are covered—practice, policy, and research.

What Skills Do Social Workers Need?

Another unique feature in social work education is that students are offered a combination of traditional coursework and required field work. It is common for select social work courses to require a certain number of community service hours to provide students the opportunity to gain experience in the field of social work. The CSWE (2022) requires all students in accredited social work programs to complete a **field internship**. BSW students are required to complete a minimum of 400 hours in the field, and MSW students a minimum of 900 hours. Many social work students report that their field experiences are one of the most valuable parts of their social work education since this is where they get firsthand experience in applying what they have learned in the classroom. Internships can also help students clarify which field of social work practice they would like to enter.

Top 10 Social Work Skills

There are many important skills that students need to master to become a competent social worker. Below are the top 10 that social workers need to cultivate and hone.

Strong interpersonal and communication skills: Social workers need to have strong "people skills," meaning that they can demonstrate warmth and compassion for others to build a positive, authentic, and trusting relationship with their clients. Being fully present when interacting with your clients is also important. Many employers prefer to hire social workers because they are known to have strong communication skills. This involves verbal communication skills, written communication skills, and skills in active listening. Written documentation is a significant part of most social workers' job responsibilities, so they must be able to write clearly, professionally, and without errors. Active listening involves body language and other methods to demonstrate to a client that you are listening and hearing what they are saying (e.g., clarifying questions, paraphrasing, summarizing).

Assessment and critical thinking skills: Social workers must have the ability to gather important data, such as previous history, and detailed information about the client's presenting issues when working with individuals and families in many social work settings. Common assessment tools used by social workers include biopsychosocial assessments, risk assessments used in child welfare, and risk assessments involving suicidal ideation. Social workers are often referred to as "problem-solvers," and this requires being able to gather good data about a person, their social environment, and their presenting issues, and being smart and creative when coming up with potential solutions and interventions. Finally, employers often comment that they like how social workers are trained to think systemically. This means that instead of viewing their clients in a vacuum, they understand the "bigger picture" (i.e., the social systems and social environment that clients are impacted by).

Professionalism: Professional behavior in the workplace is very broad but encompasses being on time, being prepared, being dependable, dressing professionally, dealing with conflict appropriately, being a collaborative member of a team, and treating those in the workplace with dignity and respect. Being competent in the workplace involves cultivating strong organizational skills in order to prioritize tasks and meet deadlines. Professional social workers must keep a calendar to keep track of their meetings and deadlines. Finally, professionalism involves ethical behavior and following the NASW code of ethics (more on this later in the chapter).

Compassion and empathy: There are a number of scholars who study empathy. According to Wiseman (1996), there are four components to empathy: seeing the world as others see it, being nonjudgmental, understanding another's feelings, and communicating your understanding of that person's feelings. Because social workers work with individuals who are struggling and are sometimes in distress, it is important to put aside one's own perspective to try to see the world through another person's eyes. Social workers who experience compassion fatigue have lost the ability to feel empathy or compassion for their clients.

Self-reflection: Because social workers often work with people who are vulnerable, it is important for them to constantly reflect on their own practice and to become aware of their strengths as well as those areas where they need to improve. Being self-reflective involves being aware of your personal biases to prevent them from negatively impact your clients. There are many ways for social workers to get feedback on their practice such as gathering feedback from clients, colleagues, and supervisors as well as taking the time to honestly reflect on their work. The only way we can grow is to be honest with ourselves and make a commitment to work on those areas that need further development.

Conflict-resolution skills: Being able to manage conflict is an important skill for social workers, particularly for social workers who work in settings where they are serving involuntary clients who have not chosen to work with a social worker (e.g., child welfare, criminal justice). Resistance is a normal part of the change process, so social workers must become comfortable with this aspect of the work. Conflict resolution is an area where social workers must work to improve their skills since social workers are helpful people and dealing with conflict can be uncomfortable for many of them. But, with some practice and training, social workers can become competent in deescalating angry or hostile clients and building a good relationship with involuntary clients.

Self-care and resilience: Because social work is a profession that often takes an emotional toll, it is of vital importance that social workers create enough space in their lives to take care of their emotional health and well-being to avoid experiencing burnout or compassion fatigue. When social workers are overworked or get emotionally depleted, it can be difficult to feel empathy or compassion for their clients, and that can be dangerous when working with vulnerable clients. Social workers are advised to find employment in settings where employers are sensitive to the well-being of their employees and support their needs for self-care and a healthy work–life balance.

Ability to work with diverse populations: Social workers work with an incredibly broad array of individuals, families, and communities from diverse backgrounds and cultures. Diversity includes age, race/ethnicity, culture, gender and gender identity, sexual orientation, religion and spirituality, disability status, immigration status, and socioeconomic status. Social workers are trained to be culturally competent and to operate from a framework of embracing cultural humility. See Chapter 4 for more on these terms.

Even though social work is a wonderfully noble profession, it does need to be committed to **anti-oppressive practice** so that it does not replicate the oppressive practices of the larger society. Critics of the social work profession, including some historians, have noted that social workers have at times operated as agents of social control instead of agents of social liberation, particularly social workers who work in large systems such as the child welfare system, the criminal justice system, and the nation's vast social welfare system. Today more and more social work programs are including content in their curriculum, and sometimes even whole courses, that is devoted to teaching students how to operate from an anti-oppressive and antiracist lens. This topic will be covered more fully in Chapters 2, 3, and 4.

Advocacy skills: Social workers are often needed to advocate for their clients at both the micro and macro level. At the micro level, they might advocate for clients to make sure they receive services from programs and large systems of care that they are entitled to, and ensure that clients know their rights and are not being taken advantage of. At the macro level, there are social workers who work in the political arena and in advocacy organizations focusing on issues of social and economic justice for groups of people in our society who have historically been marginalized and oppressed. Social workers who engage in "policy practice" work to pass legislation at the local, state, and/or federal level to help various populations that social workers serve.

Leadership: Many social workers end up taking on leadership roles in their organizations. Most begin as entry-level workers, and as they gain experience they advance into supervisory or administrative positions. Being a leader requires a specific skill set and includes things like managing a budget and making important financial decisions, fundraising, program planning, cultivating relationships with important stakeholders outside of the organization, reporting to a board of directors, hiring and evaluating the performance of employees, and developing the policies and procedures of the organization. Social workers who become executive directors of an organization are willing to take on the incredible responsibility of helping employees understand the organization's vision and leading the organization in achieving that vision.

1.2	PRACTICE ACTIVITY

Please reflect on the top 10 skills needed to become a competent social worker and answer the following two questions:

1. Which of these skills are a strength for you? Provide examples.

2. Of the skills, where do you need the most development?

The Nine CSWE Competencies

Social work is no different than other professions in that leaders and experts within the discipline come to a consensus around what skills or competencies are needed to be a competent and effective professional in that field. The CSWE (2022) outlines **nine competencies** that students should be proficient in by the time they graduate from their respective BSW or MSW program, and all accredited social work programs are required to demonstrate that they are preparing their students to meet these competencies. Table 1.2 lists each competency and provides a brief description. In the latest iteration of the CSWE competencies, competency 3 was worded very intentionally to ensure that social work programs focus specifically on preparing students for addressing racism and having strong practice skills related to diversity, equity, and inclusion.

TABLE 1.2   The Nine CSWE Competencies

Competency 1	Demonstrate ethical and professional behavior.	This competency speaks to the idea that social workers need to follow ethical standards (outlined in the NASW code of ethics) and standards of professional behavior in order to ensure that they are not causing harm to the clients they serve. Social workers need to be able to work through ethical dilemmas that arise in the course of their work.
Competency 2	Advance human rights and social, racial, economic, and environmental justice.	A vital part of a social worker's role is to protect the human rights of all people and to promote social justice, economic justice, racial justice, and environmental justice. Social workers work to dismantle racism, oppression, and systemic discrimination with the goal of having a more just and equal society where everyone has the same access to opportunity.
Competency 3	Engage antiracism, diversity, equity, and inclusion (ADEI) in practice.	Social workers understand the importance of identity and diversity and how this impacts people's lived experiences. Social workers are educated to view people's identities through an intersectional lens that includes age, class, color, culture, disability and ability, ethnicity, gender, gender identity and expression, immigration status, marital status, political ideology, race, religion/spirituality, sex, sexual orientation, and tribal sovereign status.

Competency 4	Engage in practice-informed research and research-informed practice.	This competency reflects the understanding that social workers are both consumers of research and producers of research. Practicing social workers should rely on interventions and approaches that are supported by research evidence and should evaluate their practice. Researchers should use their research findings to improve policy, practice, and service delivery.
Competency 5	Engage in policy practice.	Social workers understand the impact that policies have on individuals, families, and communities. They should fight against policies that cause harm and advocate for policies that advance human rights and social, economic, and environmental justice.
Competency 6	Engage with individuals, families, groups, organizations, and communities.	Competencies 6–9 cover the phases of the planned change process, which is covered later in this chapter. Engagement is the first phase of the planned change process, though engagement continues throughout the entire process. Engagement skills include the ability to build a safe and trusting relationship with client systems, which requires strong interpersonal communication skills such as active listening, empathy, and reflection.
Competency 7	Assess individuals, families, groups, organizations, and communities.	This phase of the planned change process involves collecting data on both strengths and needs and using theories of human behavior and the social environment to interpret that data. Doing a thorough and effective assessment is necessary to develop appropriate goals and intervention strategies based on the data gathered during assessment.
Competency 8	Intervene with individuals, families, groups, organizations, and communities.	This phase of the planned change process involves using evidence-based interventions to achieve the goals that were established by the client system. Social workers often work with professionals from other disciplines as members of an interdisciplinary team. It is an ethical principle to use interventions that are culturally responsive and to end services when the goals have been reached.
Competency 9	Evaluate practice with individuals, families, groups, organizations, and communities.	The final phase of the planned change process recognizes the importance of social workers evaluating their practice (using qualitative and quantitative methods) to be able to assess whether the interventions they use are effective and improve service delivery effectiveness over time. It is a strong ethical principle to evaluate one's practice to ensure that interventions help to improve the client's situation and not cause harm.

Value: *Service*

Ethical principle: *Social workers' primary goal is to help people in need and to address social problems.*

Social workers elevate service to others above self-interest. Social workers draw on their knowledge, values, and skills to help people in need and to address social problems. Social workers are encouraged to volunteer some portion of their professional skills with no expectation of significant financial return (pro bono service).

Value: *Social justice*

Ethical principle: *Social workers challenge social injustice.*

Social workers pursue social change, particularly with and on behalf of vulnerable and oppressed individuals and groups of people. Social workers' social change efforts are focused primarily on issues of poverty, unemployment, discrimination, and other forms of social injustice. These activities seek to promote sensitivity to and knowledge about oppression and cultural and ethnic diversity. Social workers strive to ensure access to needed information, services, and resources; equality of opportunity; and meaningful participation in decision-making for all people.

Value: *Dignity and worth of the person*

Ethical principle: *Social workers respect the inherent dignity and worth of the person.*

Social workers treat each person in a caring and respectful fashion, mindful of individual differences and cultural and ethnic diversity. Social workers promote clients' socially responsible self-determination. Social workers seek to enhance clients' capacity and opportunity to change and to address their own needs. Social workers are cognizant of their dual responsibility to clients and to the broader society. They seek to resolve conflicts between clients' interests and the broader society's interests in a socially responsible manner consistent with the values, ethical principles, and ethical standards of the profession.

Value: *Importance of human relationships*

Ethical principle: *Social workers recognize the central importance of human relationships.*

Social workers understand that relationships between and among people are an important vehicle for change. Social workers engage people as partners in the helping process. Social workers seek to strengthen relationships among people in a purposeful effort to promote, restore, maintain, and enhance the well-being of individuals, families, social groups, organizations, and communities.

Value: *Integrity*

Ethical principle: *Social workers behave in a trustworthy manner.*

Social workers are continually aware of the profession's mission, values, ethical principles, and ethical standards and practice in a manner consistent with them. Social workers should take measures to care for themselves professionally and personally. Social workers act honestly and responsibly and promote ethical practices on the part of the organizations with which they are affiliated.

Value: *Competence*

Ethical principle: *Social workers practice within their areas of competence and develop and enhance their professional expertise.*

Social workers continually strive to increase their professional knowledge and skills and to apply them in practice. Social workers should aspire to contribute to the knowledge base of the profession.

Source: Selections from Code of Ethics of the National Association of Social Workers. Copyright © 2021 by National Association of Social Workers, Inc. Reprinted with permission.

What Are the Core Values and Ethical Principles of the Social Work Profession?

Many professions in the United States have a **code of ethics**. The NASW has developed a code of ethics that social workers are urged to follow when carrying out their work. The purpose of the code of ethics is to establish a common set of core values and **ethical standards** that guide social work practice, assist social workers when they are confronted with ethical dilemmas, and hold the social work profession accountable to the public.

Social workers are routinely confronted by **ethical dilemmas** in their practice. An ethical dilemma occurs when a social worker must take a course of action that involves violating an ethical principle. It is also common for social workers to face a situation in their work where two or more ethical principles are in conflict with each other, and the social worker must decide which ethical principle must take precedence. For example, social workers are often faced with the decision of whether to violate a client's confidentiality when they have learned information that someone's health or safety is at risk. In this case, they must decide which should be prioritized—a client's right to confidentiality or a person's right to be protected from harm.

IMG 1.4

The NASW (2021) code of ethics outlines the **six core values of the social work profession** that all social workers should strive to uphold in their practice with client systems of all sizes.

The NASW (2021) code of ethics is a lengthy document that is full of important guidelines to follow to ensure that social workers are treating their clients competently and professionally. Here are just a few select examples.

Privacy and confidentiality: Confidentiality is certainly one of the most important ethical principles within social work practice. Sometimes privacy and confidentiality get confused, but the code of ethics clearly explains each of these concepts and how they are critically important in treating clients with dignity and respect. Social workers should never invade a client's **privacy**. This means that clients do not have to share information with a social worker unless they feel comfortable doing so. Additionally, it is unethical for a social worker to ask personal questions that are not relevant to the client's presenting issues or concerns. Clients also have the **right to confidentiality**, which means that a social worker cannot share information with other parties unless given permission by the client, usually with a written consent form. Social workers need to make serious efforts to safeguard information gathered about their clients to ensure that it is not accessible to others, whether that data is in hard-copy or electronic formats.

However, clients also need to be told about certain **limitations to confidentiality**. For example, social workers are **mandated reporters** and are required by law to report the abuse/neglect/exploitation of children, older adults, and persons with a disability. Additionally, social workers must report any instances where they deem that the health and safety of their client or another person is at risk (e.g., suicidal ideation, threats of harm to someone else). Finally, in some instances a social worker might be obligated to share some client information with the court or other officials in the legal system, so that should be clearly explained to a client.

Self-determination: Social workers are trained about respecting clients' right to self-determination, meaning that they have the right to make decisions about their life, even when a social worker disagrees with those decisions (as long as there is no threat of harm to the client or another person's health and safety). Social workers should never tell a client what they should do, but rather explore options with a client, which can include offering advice about the pros and cons of these various options. However, the client is the expert of their life, and they should be free in most cases to make their own decisions and to live with the consequences of those decisions. This is not easy as social workers often want clients to make a certain decision, but they must let that go and respect a client's right to make their own decisions.

Informed consent: It is highly unethical for a social worker to treat a client without their **consent**. Clients have the right to be informed about the benefits and risks of treatment, the length of treatment, the cost of treatment, and their right to stop treatment when they choose. Clients must give consent if the social worker would like to make any audio or video tape recordings. When a client lacks the ability to give consent (e.g., a minor, a person with an intellectual disability, a person with severe mental illness), the social worker must get permission from the appropriate third party who has legal standing to do so.

Competence: According to the NASW (2021) code of ethics, "Social workers' primary responsibility is to promote the well-being of clients." Clients have the right to be treated by social workers who are competent, meaning they have the requisite knowledge, training, and skills to perform their job well. Social workers who are not competent can cause harm to their clients, something that should be avoided at all costs. Sometimes, a social worker might have a personal problem such as a mental health disorder or a substance abuse disorder that prevents them from providing competent care to their clients. The code of ethics instructs social workers to address this with a colleague and to take appropriate steps to safeguard the health and safety of all clients.

Cultural competence and cultural humility: **Cultural competence** involves having a set of values, behaviors, and practices that enables you to work effectively with people from different cultures. Because social workers work with clients from a broad array of diverse backgrounds and cultures, it is imperative that they are open to learning as much as they can about various groups, appreciate the richness of culture and how this is a significant strength for many people, and use culturally appropriate and antiracist social work practices. Social workers practice cultural humility by understanding their own personal biases; being willing to admit what they do not know; coming to terms with our privilege; understanding the impact of discrimination, oppression, and marginalization on many groups of people in our society; and being advocates and allies to those groups. This is lifelong work that requires serious commitment and intention.

Conflicts of interests and dual relationships: **Dual relationships** occur when a social worker has more than one type of relationship with a client, and this is to be avoided whenever possible. For example, it would be inappropriate to have a professional relationship with a client and then also have a business or social relationship. The code of ethics is explicit in stating that **conflicts of interests** should be avoided since they often result in a client being taken advantage of. For example, if a social worker were to refer clients to the business of their spouse, that would be highly unethical. In short, it is inappropriate and unethical for social workers to use their power and position with clients to personally benefit in some way. Social workers are not "friends" with their clients, and that boundary needs to be very clear between the client and the social worker.

Sexual relationships: The code of ethics strictly forbids sexual activity (in person or through the use of technology) between a social worker and the following individuals: current clients, previous clients, and close friends or family members of a client. It is also forbidden for social workers to treat any client with whom they have had a previous sexual relationship with. Clients often seek the help of a social worker when they are feeling very *vulnerable,* and it is never okay for a social worker to take advantage of this by entering a sexual or romantic relationship with a client. Social workers are also forbidden to engage in the sexual harassment of their clients in the code of ethics.

When social workers engage in **unethical behavior** that can result in **harm** to their clients, there are several possible negative consequences for the social worker. Licensed social workers can be reported to the state licensing board, which can suspend a social worker or permanently take their license away so that they are no longer able to practice. In some extreme cases, social workers

1.3   PRACTICE ACTIVITY

Case Example 1

During a counseling session involving a father, mother, and their 15-year-old daughter, the discussion turns to an incident that happened 4 years ago. Late one evening when the father came home drunk, he entered his daughter's bedroom and started to touch her breasts and genitals. The daughter's cries awakened the mother, and she put a stop to the incident. The next morning, he did not remember what happened. All three state there was no prior or subsequent sexual abuse. They talk openly about the pain this caused in their family. This incident was never reported to Child Protective Services (CPS). They do not feel that any good can come from reporting the incident to CPS now. What would you do? Would you make the report?

Case Example 2

You have a 23-year-old female client who has been in a very abusive relationship with her partner of 3 years, both emotional and physical abuse. She is struggling with whether to continue to work on the relationship. She has been hospitalized on two occasions for serious injuries, but she does not tell the truth about how she received the injuries with health care workers since she does not want her partner to go to jail.

She does worry about her safety if she stays with him, but she also loves him and would ideally like the relationship to work out. He continues to say that he is committed to changing his behavior as he does not want her to leave him. What would you do? Should you urge her to leave him? Are you required to make a report of intimate partner violence if there are no children involved? How can you find out what the law in your state is?

Questions

Please respond to the following questions for both case examples that involve an ethical dilemma:

1. Identify what the ethical dilemma is and which ethical principles are in conflict with each other.

2. Think about what further information you might need to help you make a good decision. Who might you consult with to help you make this decision?

3. Make a list of the potential decisions you could make, the pros and cons of each, and who might benefit and who might be harmed.

4. Finally, which ethical principle must take precedence, in your view? What decision would you make in this case?

can be sued and/or charged criminally. Examples of behavior that can result in a social worker facing these kinds of consequences include fudging their documentation, engaging in sexual activity with a client, failing to make a report of child maltreatment, violating a client's confidentiality, and failing to intervene when a person's health or safety was at risk (e.g., client made a threat of harm against someone). The best policy to protect oneself is to act ethically, document, and seek help from others when in doubt.

Chapter Summary

This chapter provided an introduction and broad overview of the social work profession in the United States, and definitions of social work from three important social work organizations were provided. The three major domains of social work—practice, policy, and research—were outlined. Many are aware of social work practice but less informed about social workers' contributions to public policy and furthering research knowledge. In this chapter, readers learn that the career paths available to those pursuing a degree in social work are expansive and include opportunities to work with clients at the micro, mezzo, and macro levels. Those who want to become a social worker must earn an undergraduate or graduate degree in social work, as well as be competent, meaning they must have the essential knowledge, values, and skills necessary to practice. Social work is misunderstood by many people, and it is important to educate others about what social workers do and how they contribute to our communities every day. Questions were provided in this chapter to help students begin to assess their own goodness of fit with social work as a potential future career path.

Discussion Questions

1. Visit the website of the NASW and read over the code of ethics. Why do you think that having a code of ethics is so important for those who practice social work?

2. The chapter talks about how many people have a very narrow conception of what social workers do and how there are several myths and outdated stereotypes about the profession. What could be done to increase people's knowledge of social work and help them better appreciate the important contributions that social workers make in our society?

3. Come up with a 1–2-minute elevator speech to explain social work to someone who does not know much about it. What would you want to highlight?

4. Visit the website of the CSWE to learn more about how BSW and MSW social work programs get accredited and what standards they must follow. What did you learn? Do you think it is important for social work programs to be accredited—why or why not?

5. What did you learn about the social work profession in this chapter that most surprised you? What are the biggest takeaways for you?

References

U.S. Bureau of Labor Statistics, U.S. Department of Labor. (2022). *Occupational outlook handbook*: *Social workers*. https://www.bls.gov/ooh/community-and-social-service/social-workers.htm

Council on Social Work Education. (n.d.). *Current number of social work programs*. https://www.cswe.org/Accreditation.aspx

Council on Social Work Education. (2022). *2022 educational policy and accreditation standards*. https://www.cswe.org/accreditation/standards/2022-epas/

International Federation of Social Workers. (2014). *Global definition of social work*. https://www.ifsw.org/what-is-social-work/global-definition-of-social-work/

National Association of Social Workers. (2021). *Code of ethics.* https://www.socialworkers.org/About/Ethics/Code-of-Ethics/Code-of-Ethics-English

Ritter, J. A., Obermann, A., & Danhoff, K. (2020). *101 careers in social work* (3rd ed.). Springer.

Wiseman, T. (1996). A concept analysis of empathy. *Journal of Advanced Nursing, 23*(6), 1162–1167.

Credits

CHAPTER 2

The Evolution of Social Work and the Social Welfare System in the United States

Learning Objectives

After reading this chapter, students will be able to do the following:

- Compare and contrast the role and impact of the settlement house movement, Black mutual aid societies, and charity organization societies in the development of the social work profession in the United States

- Compare and contrast the impact and legacy of President FDR's New Deal and President LBJ's Great Society in the development of the U.S. social welfare system

- Explain the CARIN theory of deservingness and how it seeks to explain people's attitudes about who is deserving and not deserving of social services and aid

- Provide examples of the role that racism has played in the development of the social welfare system in the United States and within the social work profession

- Summarize the origins and major historical milestones of the social work profession in the United States

- Identify prominent social workers, including BIPOC (Black, Indigenous, People of Color) social workers, and their contributions to social work and social welfare history

- Provide an overview of the U.S. social welfare system and summarize the various ways that it can be categorized

- Evaluate the controversies and criticisms that have been raised about the social work profession and the ways it has intervened with people and communities over the years

I t is hard to imagine that at one time there was no social work profession, and no formalized social welfare system, where people in need or in crisis could go to access essential resources or services. The United States is sometimes referred to as a "reluctant welfare state" because of its ambivalence over institutionalizing a social safety net and supporting the federal government in having a significant role in providing for the general welfare of its citizens (Ritter, 2022). It was not until the 1930s in the aftermath of the Great Depression when the United States joined other wealthy industrialized nations in becoming an official welfare state, marked by the passage of the Social Security Act of 1935. Social scientists have offered many explanations for this hesitancy, including its strong social societal value of rugged individualism, Americans' fear of a strong federal government, the role of racism and the fact that the United States has a very racially diverse population compared to many other nations, and strong notions about who is deserving of help and who is undeserving.

So, how did we get from there to here? How did Americans' views and ideas about the provision of social welfare services, and the role of the government in providing some form of social safety net change over time? How did social welfare programs such as Social Security, Medicare, Medicaid, public assistance, unemployment insurance, and other important social programs develop and become part of the fabric of U.S. society? And how does the social work profession fit into all of this? This chapter tells this riveting story. It is important for social workers to have a good working knowledge of this history because as the famous astronomer Carl Sagan asserts, "You have to know the past to understand the present."

American Social Values That Have Influenced the U.S. Social Welfare System

Every nation is faced with making decisions around whether and how to assist citizens who find themselves in need or in a time of crisis. Some individuals are born into difficult circumstances that limit their life opportunities, such as living in poverty, and face the daunting tasks of day-to-day survival and rising out of poverty. Other individuals experience various crises in their life such as unemployment, serious illness, or losing their home that results in experiencing economic insecurity for a period of time. Some nations, such as in those in Scandinavia, are known for having a very generous social welfare system, while other nations cannot afford the luxury of providing social welfare programs for their citizens, as is the case in a number of developing nations. The United States has been referred to as a **reluctant welfare state** by some scholars because "the government and the American public have been quite ambivalent when it comes to answering the question, 'Is it the role of the government to help provide for the general welfare of its citizens, and if so, to what extent?'" (Ritter, 2022, p. 25). Social scientists have studied where this ambivalence comes from and have offered the following theories:

- **Rugged individualism:** In the United States, there is a very strong societal value of rugged individualism, meaning that people should "pull themselves up by their bootstraps," be self-sufficient, and not ask for help from others. People who subscribe to this idea believe that people can succeed on their own and should not seek help from the government. From the beginning, there have been concerns and fears by some that social welfare programs promote dependency instead of self-sufficiency. This may have its roots in the early history of this country when the settlers were forced to make their way without much help or support outside of their family or community. There is also a tendency for people to think that their personal successes in life are derived by their individual efforts and not from outside sources of support. Finally, there is a lot of mythology in the United States around the "self-made man" and the idea that people of humble origins can become wildly wealthy and successful.

- **Americans' fear and distrust of a strong federal government:** The United States became a nation after declaring war against Great Britain, declaring independence, and fighting to become its own country. Americans' fear of a strong national government and ruler likely stems from its early experiences with the British king and federal government. As a result, support for state's rights have been a strong value in the United States, and many Americans have resisted the federal government and U.S. president becoming too powerful, including the power to create federal social welfare programs.

- **The role of racism:** There is an interesting, yet depressing, theory that the more homogenous a population is, the easier it will be for them to have social welfare programs that are designed to take care of each other. This stems from the idea that people will support taking care of others in their community or nation when they perceive that they are similar to them racially and culturally. The United States has a very racially diverse population compared to many other nations, and this has likely been a significant barrier to instituting a more generous social welfare system, including universal health care for all, for example, because some Americans are hesitant to pay for and support programs that will benefit people who are "not like them."

- **Capitalism:** The United States is known around the world for its capitalist economic system and for being the wealthiest nation in the world. Even though capitalism and social welfare programs can coexist, and do not need to be viewed in opposition to each other, they often are, particularly by fiscal conservatives. Because government social programs are paid for by taxation, they are political by nature, and there are many debates surrounding who should bear the burden of taxation (e.g., the middle class, the wealthy, corporations) as well as how much Americans are willing to pay to support these programs. The powerful influence that corporations play in U.S. politics means that they are often able to convince lawmakers to keep taxes low, which prevents many social programs from having the impact they could have.

- **Strong notions about who is deserving and undeserving of help**: From the beginning, strong notions about who is deserving of help and who is not deserving of help have permeated the rules around who can and cannot benefit from social welfare programs in the public and private sector. There are certain groups of people who Americans tend to have sympathy for, as they are viewed as experiencing challenges that are beyond their control, (e.g., orphans, widows, people with physical disabilities), while others have not been viewed with that same level of grace and compassion (e.g., able-bodied people who are out of work, those with alcohol and drug addiction). There is a fascinating area of research by social scientists who study theories of deservingness to better understand why some people are viewed as being worthy of help and others are not.

The CARIN Theory of Deservingness

There have been a number of researchers who have chosen to study the concept of **deservingness** and people's attitudes surrounding who is deserving and undeserving of help. And this research has helped us to better understand what influences people's support for various social policies and social programs that serve people in need. According to work that was originated by Van Oorschot and Roosma (2017), people tend to rely heavily on five criteria when they are distinguishing those who are deserving from those who are underserving: control, attitude, reciprocity, identity, and need (CARIN).

- **Control**: People are more likely to support helping those who are perceived as not being responsible for their situation, and when the challenges are caused by external (rather than internal) factors (e.g., a person who got laid off from their job, a person whose spouse passed away and they were the breadwinner).

- **Attitude:** People are more likely to support helping those who express or show gratitude for the assistance they have been given (versus feeling entitled to the help).

- **Reciprocity:** People are more likely to support helping those who are willing to do something in return for the help they have been given or are viewed as someone who has contributed to society in some way (e.g., paid taxes).

- **Identity**: People are more likely to support helping those who are similar to them in terms of social identity (e.g., someone who is in their same in-group).
- **Need**: People are more willing to help when they can determine that the person is truly in need of assistance.

CRITICISMS OF SOCIAL WORK PRACTICE IN THE UNITED STATES

Even though the social work profession has values to the contrary (e.g., social justice, self-determination, dignity and worth of the person), unfortunately social workers have faced criticisms, historically and currently, over the way it has intervened with individuals and communities in need, in particular with POC and those who are low income. As you read this chapter, pay attention to the themes that arise related to these concerns that tend to fall in the following areas:

- The **elevation of micro social work over macro social work**, which some have characterized as a neglect of the social justice mission and its dedication to serving those living in poverty. Social work has been criticized for its heavy focus on changing the individual instead of changing the social environment. Some critics have pointed to the professionalization of social work over the years as one factor that resulted in moving social work further away the mission of the profession and aims that strive to decrease the power differential between social workers and those they serve.

- Social workers are sometimes viewed as **paternalistic**, meaning they make decisions *for* those they serve instead of trusting that people have the experience and expertise to make their own decisions with support. An example of this are social workers who believe their job is to model "middle-class values" for those living in poverty.

- Social workers who act as **agents of social control**. Even though many social workers strive to provide care to people and to promote people's health and well-being, some have been criticized for working in organizations, such as criminal justice and child welfare, that seek to regulate and control people's behaviors and/or punish them when they have violated societal rules and norms.

- Calls on social work to **decolonize the profession**, which has historically operated based on White, Western, Eurocentric practices, frameworks, and values. Connected to this issue is a need to have a more diverse social work workforce that represents the people it serves in terms of race/ethnicity, socioeconomic status, and lived experiences. This movement originated from Indigenous people and scholars and was referred to as Indigenous social work, but over time has generalized to the idea that social workers need to use practices that respect the customs, beliefs, and worldviews of the diverse and non-Western populations they work with, and which create less oppressive ways of delivering services.

- The **role of racism** in social work practice has been highlighted in recent years, as well as the neglect of social work scholars in highlighting the contributions of BIPOC social workers and leaders in their scholarly work. On June 17, 2021, the National Association of Social Workers (NASW, 2021) apologized for its role in racist practices and provided several historical examples (see Chapter 4).

Major Historical Achievements in the Development of the Nation's Social Welfare System

For most of our early history, the U.S. federal government and state governments did not play an active or significant role in assisting Americans in need. Because Americans were very skeptical about the government's role in social welfare provision, Americans who struggled relied on their family members and compassionate community members and organizations, such as faith institutions or philanthropic groups. But when a person had no one to turn to for help, the options were dismal. For example, many who were poor were punished or treated inhumanely using physical violence, (e.g., flogging; branding), forced into indentured servitude, made to leave town, and incarcerated. Many children in poverty-stricken families were forced into child labor or apprenticeships, where they were often mistreated and exploited for their labor.

Over time, the United States turned to **institutionalization** and created a range of institutions when cities became overwhelmed with those in need, and some who were living in poverty were forced into mental health asylums, orphanages, correctional facilities, and workhouses or almshouses, where people could live and eat but were forced to live and labor in unsafe and deplorable living conditions. However, there have been a few important historical periods in which this country made significant progress in how the nation responded to widespread social problems related to poverty and income insecurity.

| 2.1 | **PRACTICE ACTIVITY** |

Review the CARIN theory of deservingness and the criticisms of social work practice in the previous section of this chapter and reflect on the following questions:

1. Do you think that the general attitudes that people have regarding who is deserving of government assistance rings true? Why or why not?

2. Where do you think these attitudes stem from in our culture?

3. Which of these criticisms are most concerning to you and why?

4. What thoughts and feelings come up for you as you learn more about the role of racism within the social work profession?

5. What should today's social workers be doing to address these criticisms and to work toward one that strives toward diversity, equality, and inclusivity?

Origins of the Social Work Profession in the United States

Most scholars of social welfare and social work history point to the late 1800s as the emergence of social work. In 1898, Columbia University offered the first social work program of study in the United States, and social work would continue to professionalize over time and evolve into a discipline embodied by those with a university degree in social work, social work licensure, and a body of research literature to support the way that it intervenes with client systems from the micro to the macro level.

It is no accident that social work emerged during **the progressive era** (1890–1920) in response to massive social problems that were occurring in many large northern cities due to rapid **industrialization** as the country moved away from an agrarian economy to one that was much more reliant on machine-based manufacturing. This period is referred to as the progressive era "because of the work of progressive social reformers who rejected the idea of social Darwinism (e.g., the idea that only the fittest or strongest will survive) and instead worked toward resolving the social and economic problems of the day that were brought on by corporate greed, government corruption, rapid industrialization, and social inequality" (Ritter, 2022, p. 28).

During this time, many cities were overwhelmed by their new inhabitants from the U.S. South and immigrants from Europe and China who relocated to land jobs in various industries such as the railroads and factories where various goods were being manufactured. Historians refer to the millions of Black people who moved away from the South to states in the west, north, and Midwest as **the Great Migration** as it was one of the largest movements of people in U.S. history.

The social problems that emerged during this time period included people living in overcrowded and unsafe tenement buildings; sweatshops where people were exploited for their labor and endured dangerous working conditions; child labor; increasing numbers of children who were orphaned, abandoned, and homeless; large numbers of immigrants who came to the United States from other countries seeking job opportunities but who suffered discrimination and hardship; women and POC who had few rights and were treated as second-class citizens; cities that were riddled with crime and violence; and people who experienced illness and early death due to poor sanitation, communicable diseases, malnutrition, and industrial hazards. This was the era of the urban slum.

In response to these social conditions two different styles of intervention emerged, and both have greatly influenced modern-day social work practice. The micro approach to social work was heavily influenced by the **charity organization societies** (COS), and the macro approach to social work was shaped by the **settlement house movement** (SHM) and **Black mutual aid societies**. According to Finn (2021),

> The COS tended to see social problems as the result of individual deficits, such as lack of moral character, discipline, or personal capacity. They sought to intervene through scientific philanthropy, that is, a systematic effort to identify personal struggles and shortcomings and provide proper support and guidance. The SHM, on the other hand, focused on conditions in the social environment that contributed to poverty and personal strife (p. 73).

Finn (2021) notes that both approaches were influenced by the emerging disciplines of psychology, sociology, psychiatry, and public health and that this work provided an opportunity for young, educated White women to "enter the helping professions and engage in social investigation, education, and reform" (p. 73). Both the COS and the SHM had origins in Britain, and these ideas were borrowed by social reformers in the United States. As will be explained, the Black mutual aid societies developed in part because they were excluded by many White social workers and reformers in both the COS and SHM.

HISTORICAL MILESTONES FOR THE SOCIAL WORK PROFESSION

- 1780, first Black mutual aid society formed by free Blacks—the African Union Society in Newport, Rhode Island

- 1877, COS movement launches in the United States

- 1886, SHM begins in the United States in New York City

- 1896, Black women's clubs joined together to form the National Association of Colored Women's Clubs (NACW)

- 1898, Columbia University offers the first social work class in the United States

- 1908, Chicago School of Civics and Philanthropy offers a full social work curriculum (today it is the University of Chicago School of Social Service Administration)

- 1931, Social worker Jane Addams receives the Nobel Peace Prize, the first woman in the United States to do so

- 1935, Social Security Act of 1935 passes into law, creating the nation's first significant federal social safety net programs thanks in part to the tireless advocacy and efforts of social worker Frances Perkins

- 1952, the Council on Social Work Education is founded

- 1955, the NASW is founded

- 1964–1965, Civil Rights Act of 1964 and Voting Rights Act of 1964 passed into law; social workers Dorothy Height and Whitney Young are leaders in the civil rights movement

- 2021, the Department of Labor reports that there are 708,100 social workers in the United States

- 2022, the Council on Social Work Education reports that there are 538 accredited baccalaureate programs in social work and 313 accredited master's programs in social work

Charity Organization Societies

COS workers were engaged in charitable work and their primary goal was to "fix the poor and make them independent, responsible, and self-reliant" (Finn, 2021, p. 73). A key feature of this model of intervention was the use of **friendly visitors**, White, privileged women who made home visits to assess the level of need and worthiness of receiving aid. They viewed their role as helping to improve the moral character of those they were visiting by being an example and teaching them important values of hard work and thrift as well as nutrition and household management (Finn, 2021). Although it is easy to be critical of these early social workers, it is important to note that their ideas about human problems did evolve over time as they came to have a more sophisticated understanding of the causes of poverty.

COS workers such as **Mary Richmond** helped to further professionalize social work in the United States by calling on schools to train professional social workers in how to diagnose and intervene with individuals while honoring their dignity, worth, and uniqueness. The publication of her book *Social Diagnosis* (1917) laid the groundwork for casework in social work practice and "presented the casework method as a systematic approach to investigation that considers individual experience in a broader social and environmental context, thus foreshadowing the person-in-environment approach that remains central to social work today" (Finn, 2021, p. 74). A major criticism of the COS was its failure to offer needed support to the growing numbers of African Americans migrating to the northern United States for job opportunities.

Settlement House Movement and Black Mutual Aid Societies

The **settlement houses** served newly arriving immigrants, the majority from European nations, and offered a holistic array of supportive programs and services. Many of the settlement house workers were middle- and upper-class White women from privileged backgrounds, and they were among the first women in the United States to go to college and earn advanced degrees. One of the hallmarks of this movement was their strong belief that, in addition to direct work with people, macro-level change efforts were needed to improve conditions for people, and they did this work in part by engaging in political advocacy efforts focused on issues impacting women, children, and workers.

The SHM workers argued that people cannot be successful when the physical and social environment (i.e., their neighborhood) creates serious systemic barriers that are designed to set them up for failure. Progressive social reformers during this period began to advocate for changes in society that would reduce poverty and provide increased access to opportunity by groups who had been historically excluded. Examples of some of the programs and policies that these reformers advocated for included the following:

- Women's rights, including suffrage and access to birth control
- The abolition of child labor and support for programs that would provide support to vulnerable children (e.g., mandatory education, public assistance, a juvenile justice system)
- Rights for workers (e.g., right to unionize, 40-hour work week, safe working conditions, minimum wage)
- Safe housing
- Improving neighborhood conditions (e.g., public health funding to make cities cleaner and safer places to live, community recreation such as playgrounds, addressing sanitation and industrial hazards)
- Funding for social programs such as Social Security, unemployment insurance, worker's compensation, and health care insurance.

By 1910, there were more than 400 settlement houses in the United States. The first settlement house in the United States, and perhaps the most famous one was **Chicago's Hull House**, which was founded by **Jane Addams** and **Ellen Gates Starr** in 1889. Jane Addams became an admired and well-known figure and was the first U.S. woman to be awarded the Nobel Peace Prize. There were several important principles that guided the work of the settlement house workers at Hull House: "It was important to live in the community alongside those they were assisting; individuals should be treated with dignity and respect, and their culture and customs should be honored; the goal would be to help people to help themselves; and finally, there was a strong belief that poverty, lack of opportunity, and economic desperation were the cause of people's problems, not some moral flaw in one's character" (Ritter, 2022, pp. 29–30). Many settlement house workers used research methods to gather data to document conditions in their community in order to change the policies and practices of the day.

The SHM had an indelible impact on social service provision in the United States. Though many of the laws that these social reformers advocated for did not come to pass until years later (many during the Franklin Delano Roosevelt administration), they laid the groundwork and raised awareness about the importance of

FIGURE 2.1   Jane Addams, Founder of Hull House

changing the larger social environment and eliminating structural societal barriers so that people are able to succeed and thrive. They also strongly influenced the idea that the social work profession should have a dual focus on both micro- and macro-level change efforts.

However, despite the valuable work and achievements of the U.S. SHM, it is important to highlight some important criticisms. Despite the fact that they rejected the charity model embraced by the CPS and sought to work with people in a spirit of partnership, they were still impacted by race and class privilege. Finn (2021) notes that "despite their altruistic intentions, implicit moral judgments and notions of immigrants as *other* still filtered into their work" (p. 77). Additionally, according to historians, the major settlement houses excluded African Americans, and settlement houses were segregated by race. It is disappointing and heartbreaking to learn about the **role of racism** that led many of the major settlement houses of the day to choose to serve White immigrant communities from Europe and to exclude African Americans who were also moving to these large urban cities in the north seeking job opportunities—and desperately needed that same level of support and assistance.

Black Mutual Aid Societies

Black mutual aid societies took different forms and played an invaluable role in proving support to Black people at the micro and macro level, who were suffering from the legacy of slavery and extreme societal racism and oppression. Because Black people were excluded from many social service and charitable organizations of the day, they formed their own organizations. Black churches were a source of support and community for many Black people. In the late 1700s, mutual aid societies were formed by free Black people, the first being the **African Union Society** in Newport, Rhode Island, in 1780, led by freed slaves **Newport Gardner** and **Pompe (Zingo) Stevens** (Barga, n.d.). These societies provided a range of support to their members, providing such things as cultural centers; financial support for families experiencing illness and death; burials for the dead; education and job training; recording of births, deaths, and marriages of people in the community; providing loans to support Black purchase of property; and supporting efforts to end slavery in the United States.

Black Women's Clubs are another notable part of this history. Though many of these clubs focused on similar issues that were addressed by White women's clubs (e.g., health and sanitation, women's suffrage, education), they were also inspired by efforts to end lynching in the United States (National Women's History Museum, n.d.), led by women such as Ida B. Wells-Barnett. In 1896, Black women's clubs

joined together to form the National Association of Colored Women's Clubs (NACW) under the leadership of women such as **Mary Church**

Terrell and **Harriet Tubman**. The motto of the NACW was *Lifting as We Climb*. One of the most effective Black women's clubs was the Neighborhood Union in Atlanta, run by **Lugenia Burns Hope**. The Neighborhood Union divided the city into districts and zones, thus effectively reaching almost every black American in Atlanta" (National Women's History Museum, n.d., para. 2.)

They spoke out about the racism, violence, and humiliation that Black people were subjected to, and they advocated for policy changes, such as ending discrimination in transportation, an end to lynching, ending racist practices in child welfare, and creating protections for Black domestic workers (Finn, 2021).

According to Finn (2021), "Black women's clubs took the lead in establishing settlement houses to support, educate, and empower African Americans facing everyday challenges of urban industrial life in the context of racial oppression" (p. 78). There have been several social work scholars who have recently published articles to highlight the achievements of Black women in our social justice and social welfare history. These scholars argue that they have been ignored by White scholars and left out of the historical record.

FIGURE 2.2   Ida B. Wells-Barnett

Shepherd and Pritzker (2021) highlight the achievements of two Black women who made major contributions to the U.S. SHM, notably **Ida B. Wells-Barnett**, who created a settlement house for Black men in Chicago, and **Victoria Earl Matthews**, whose settlement house in New York supported Black women and children who migrated to New York from the U.S. South. Wells-Barnett was politically active in a number of organizations that focused on racial justice for African Americans, and she engaged in antilynching activism and supported legislative efforts to address these horrific acts of violence. According to Shepherd and Pritzker (2021) "She was a renowned leader in ensuring African Americans participated in democracy and had their voices heard because she understood that the survival of the race depended on it" (p. 244). Victoria Matthews was equally impressive and "provided education, self-help trainings, and services while organizing residents into political engagement and unions. She advocated for the preservation of African American history and facilitated the social uplift of African American women through political awareness and engagement" (p. 245).

Lee and Dieser (2020) bring attention to the achievement of **Ada McKinley**, a Black woman who headed up the South Side Settlement House in Chicago, which was located 4 miles from Hull House, and by 1927 had provided social services to over 25,000 African Americans in the community who were not able to receive services from other settlement house due to their race. Lee and Dieser assert that "the history of African American social reformers and their settlement houses has received little to no attention, not only from leisure scholars but also from the broader academic community. These omissions are troubling because the existing narratives can perpetuate Whiteness in leisure scholarship and continue to marginalize the history of people of color" (p. 2).

President Franklin Delano Roosevelt and the New Deal

One of the most pivotal periods of U.S. history with regard to social welfare provision occurred during the presidential administration of **Franklin Delano Roosevelt (FDR)** who was president between 1933 and 1945, when he died while serving his fourth term in office. FDR was elected in the aftermath of the **Stock Market Crash of 1929** and the **Great Depression** (1929–1939) when the country was terrified and suffering due to the national economic catastrophe that Americans experienced firsthand. It is somewhat ironic that Roosevelt championed policies that benefitted Americans who struggled when he came from such a wealthy and privileged background, even being related to a former U.S. president, Theodore Roosevelt. Some historians attribute his level of empathy for those who suffer in our society in part due to his having the experience of living with a disability after contracting polio at age 39 years and spending much of his life in a wheelchair. He is widely considered to be one of the best U.S. presidents to serve in this role.

It is difficult to comprehend the level of economic hardship and uncertainty that occurred for many people during this time. One in four people were out of work. Long lines of people stood in line for food. Millions of people were thrown into poverty. Americans were desperate and looked for help from the government, and they chose to elect a president who reassured them and told them that the federal government would act. In his inaugural address to the nation, FDR told Americans that "the only thing we have to fear is fear itself."

Before the Great Depression, most Americans believed that **poverty was an individual failing** and that the federal government should play a very limited role in social welfare provision and protecting people from poverty. But this crisis changed attitudes dramatically as many saw, perhaps for the first time, that events can happen (e.g., the economy collapsing) that are beyond any individual's control and that there are structural causes to poverty. FDR came into office ready to act, with three goals guiding these efforts—relief, recovery, and reform. The theme of Roosevelt's administration was the **New Deal**, which focused on providing immediate relief to those who were suffering, reforming the financial system to prevent future economic catastrophes, and passing legislation to create a social safety net for all Americans.

The passage of New Deal programs and policies, such as the Social Security Act of 1935, marked the moment in U.S. history when the United States joined many of its peer nations in Europe in forming a welfare state. When a nation becomes a welfare state, it commits to providing a basic level of economic security for its citizens, typically through the use of social programs, to protect them from the economic risks associated with old age, illness, disability, and unemployment. Highlights of some of the most remarkable policy achievements that came out of the New Deal are as follows:

- **Work relief programs**: One of the more creative strategies of the New Deal was to create programs, such as the **Works Progress Administration** (WPA) and the **Civilian Conservation Corps** (CCC), that focus on giving unemployed people a job. This was a win-win strategy, as it provided workers with needed jobs and helped the country by investing in needed improvements to the nation's infrastructure. Workers in these programs were paid by the government to work on various public works projects across the country, which included roads, dams, bridges, hospitals, airports, parks, public utilities, schools, and even employed artists for public art projects, including paintings, murals, and sculptures. Famous examples of these projects include the Hoover Dam, LaGuardia Airport, the San Francisco-Oakland Bay Bridge, the Lincoln Tunnel, and the Great Smokey Mountain National Park.

- **The Social Security Act of 1935**: This act is one of the most important social welfare policies passed into law in the United States and is an historic achievement. Most people are aware that the Social Security Act of 1935 created the nation's social security program, but it also created two other important social programs—the **unemployment compensation program** and the nation's **public assistance program** that today is named Temporary Assistance for Needy Families, or TANF. According Ritter (2022),

  > The Social Security Act of 1935 attempted to protect those most vulnerable in society, including older adults, the unemployed, the poor, the disabled, widows, and children. The act would create a combination of social insurance programs (for those participating in the workforce) and public assistance programs (for nonworking and dependent individuals). The key program would be social security, a program that would insure people against poverty in old age" (p. 32).

The social security program is one of the most enduring, supported, and successful social programs in existence in the United States today.

- **The Fair Labor Standards Act of 1938**: This piece of legislation was meant to address many problems workers of the day faced, many of whom labored under unsafe and unfair working conditions and did not receive fair compensation for their labor. Before this law, there was little protection provided to workers, and they could be asked to work in sweatshop conditions for long hours and oppressively low wages. This law **abolished child labor** and set the age of workforce entry at 16. It also established a **minimum wage** and a **maximum work week** of 40 hours. In sum, the Fair Labor Standards Act was a worker's rights bill that was focused on improving labor standards in the workplace and leveling the playing field between employers, who hold the power, and their employees.

- **The G.I. bill**: The Servicemen's Readjustment Act, better known as the G.I. Bill, is considered one of the most impactful pieces of legislation in U.S. history. Signed into law by President Franklin D. Roosevelt in 1944, the bill focused on supporting returning World War II veterans by giving them funding for unemployment compensation, low-interest home and business loans, and expenses for job training programs and higher education. The G.I. bill is lauded for helping millions of veterans move into the middle class as they were able to access home ownership and a college education—opportunities that previously would have been unattainable for many. According to Altschuler and Blumin (2009), 78% of veterans (12.4 million) who returned to civilian life benefitted directly from the G.I. bill, and three quarters reported on surveys that the bill changed their life. The G.I. bill has been extended and amended several times over the years and is still in existence today.

Social Workers Frances Perkins and Harry Hopkins

There are two remarkable social workers who contributed greatly to the New Deal policies and programs and worked directly for the FDR administration—**Frances Perkins** and **Harry Hopkins**. Even though FDR deservedly gets much of the credit for getting the New Deal policies passed into law, these two social workers were incredibly influential to his thinking and to the success of these policies and resulting programs. After a very successful career in public service as a social worker, Harry Hopkins was hired by FDR when he was governor of New York to run a relief program for the state as a result of the Great Depression. This marked the beginning of their relationship, and Hopkins later became one of FDR's closest confidants and advisors. When FDR became president, he hired Hopkins to be

FIGURE 2.3   Social worker Harry Hopkins with President Franklin Delano Roosevelt

FIGURE 2.4   Social worker Frances Perkins watching President Roosevelt signing the Social Security Act into law

the nation's federal relief administrator and to oversee several federal agencies that were focused on creating work relief programs for the unemployed during the Great Depression.

Frances Perkins is an extraordinary American who made an enduring impact on the country, though many Americans have never heard of her and her accomplishments. She had a successful career as a social worker and focused primarily on the rights and conditions for women, children, and workers. Watching workers jump to their death to escape the fire that broke out in the infamous **Triangle Shirtwaist Fire of 1911** impacted her greatly and motivated her to work for the rights of workers to labor under safe and just working conditions. Like Hopkins, she worked for FDR when he was governor of New York—though she was responsible for the state's labor department. Then FDR hired her to work in his presidential administration as his secretary of labor. This was a remarkable achievement as she was the first women in U.S. history to serve in a presidential administration at this level, thus breaking major barriers for women at the highest levels of government. According to the Frances Perkins Center (n.d.),

> When, in February 1933, President-elect Roosevelt asked Frances Perkins to serve in his cabinet as Secretary of Labor, she outlined for him a set of policy priorities she would pursue: a 40-hour work week; a minimum wage; unemployment compensation; worker's compensation; abolition of child labor; direct federal aid to the states for unemployment relief; Social Security; a revitalized federal employment service; and universal health insurance. She made it clear to Roosevelt that his agreement with these priorities was a condition of her joining his cabinet. Roosevelt said he endorsed them all, and Frances Perkins became the first woman in the nation to serve in a Presidential cabinet. (para. 23)

Although FDR is credited in the history books with passing the Social Security Act of 1935, in reality Perkins was one of the chief architects and driving forces of the Social Security Act, as documented in many books and writings about her life and professional work. After its passage, she spoke about the capacity of the social security program to provide economic security for the individual as well as the nation.

Criticisms of the New Deal

Though the New Deal programs and policies provided a new level of economic security for millions of people and radically transformed U.S. society for the better, it is also important to examine the criticisms and how many low-income individuals and POC were not treated fairly during this time. Women and ethnic minorities who sought equal participation in these programs often faced discrimination. For example, certain groups of people were excluded from receiving benefits from the Social Security Act of 1935, such as farmworkers, domestic workers, and many POC. And the legislation continued to support societal notions about who is worthy and unworthy of assistance because the income restrictions required by the public assistance programs gave welfare staff significant discretion in deciding who would be provided aid. According to Ritter (2022),

> Perhaps one of Roosevelt's greatest failings was not fighting harder for civil rights for African Americans. Historians note that he needed the support of southern white Democrats to get his New Deal legislation passed so he chose not to antagonize them when it came to civil rights. As a result, some New Deal programs discriminated against Blacks by excluding them from certain benefits or paying them lower wages than Whites. Though he privately supported anti-lynching legislation and opposed the poll tax, Roosevelt did not spend his political capital on these issues for risk of losing the political support that he needed in the South. Other historians argue that some New Deal programs, such as the WPA, were especially helpful to African Americans in providing jobs. (p. 32)

Americans elected FDR president four times—clear evidence of his popularity and the public's confidence in his leadership during this turbulent time. It also illustrates how the public responded to his optimism, charisma, and ability to take action, as well as the confidence they had in his leadership during this turbulent time. The United States later amended the U.S. Constitution to limit U.S. presidents to serving only two terms in office.

President Lyndon B. Johnson's Great Society and War on Poverty

Another pivotal historical period that all social workers should be familiar with occurred during the presidential administration of **Lyndon B. Johnson (LBJ)** during the 1960s. President Johnson came into office during an incredibly turbulent time in U.S. history after President John. F. Kennedy was assassinated. LBJ was vice president at the time, and the nation needed a president who would restore some sense of stability. This period is notable for its social unrest, thriving social movements, and many Americans' demands for more social and economic equality for groups of people who experienced societal oppression and marginalization. Social movements during this time included the **Black civil rights movement**, the **women's movement**, the **gay liberation movement**, and the **antiwar movement** in response to the war in Vietnam.

There were also a number of high-profile national figures who were assassinated during this time, such as President John F. Kennedy, his brother Bobby Kennedy who was running to be president, and the famous civil rights leaders Dr. Martin Luther King, Jr. and Malcolm X. To say that the 1960s were a time of great social

FIGURE 2.5   Vice President Lyndon Johnson being sworn in as President of the United States after President John F. Kennedy was assassinated

change and transformation would be an understatement. President Johnson did what many great leaders do and used the many crises that occurred as an opportunity to make needed social change, and the theme of his administration was **"The Great Society."** LBJ was an ambitious man, and one of his political heroes was FDR. However, compared to his hero and many others in public office, LBJ did not grow up privileged. He grew up in rural Texas, where he saw poverty all around him and his own family experienced periods of economic hardship. Ritter (2022) explains that "early in his career he was a teacher in a public elementary school in Cotulla, Texas, where he taught Mexican American children, most of whom were from very poor families … [and] this experience seemed to make a large impression on him and how he viewed the importance of education in order to rise above poverty" (p. 37).

However, from an early age, LBJ had dreams of being a successful politician and of being president of the United States. He lived and breathed politics, and he is known to be one of the most successful lawmakers of all time due to his ability to get a voluminous amount of legislation passed. He is one of only a few U.S. presidents who held office as a congressman, U.S. senator, vice president, and president. And after a lifetime of opposing civil rights legislation, after he became president, he became a champion of civil rights and worked closely with civil rights leaders such as Dr. King to get landmark civil rights legislation passed into law.

But Johnson was most passionate about addressing poverty in the country and increasing access to education and opportunity in society for the many groups of people who had previously not had access to it. One of his most remarkable achievements as president occurred when LBJ declared a **war on poverty**, as he sincerely believed that poverty could be eradicated through the creation of federal and community-based social programs that were designed to help people rise out of poverty and move into the middle class. According to Ritter (2022),

> This was the first and last time that a sitting U.S. president devoted such a focus to addressing poverty in this country. In terms of passing progressive social welfare legislation, few U.S. presidents have surpassed Johnson; the number of bills passed by the Johnson administration is truly astounding by any measure. The focus of the Great Society was to remove barriers for the disadvantaged and to create a plethora of social programs that would provide them with the opportunity to rise out of poverty and into the middle class. (p. 37)

Highlights of some of the most remarkable policy achievements that came out of the Great Society are as follows:

- **Civil rights**: The Civil Rights Act of 1964 and the Voting Rights Act of 1965 and considered two of the most important pieces of federal legislation ever passed by the U.S. Congress. The **Civil Rights Act of 1964** made discrimination based on race, color, religion, sex, or national origin illegal, and the **Voting Rights Act of 1965** outlawed discriminatory voting practices used in many states to prevent African Americans from voting, such as poll taxes, literacy tests, harassment, intimidation, and violence, and empowered the federal government to oversee voter registration and elections. Though LBJ's support for these policies was instrumental to their passage, they would not have been passed without the tireless advocacy efforts by civil rights leaders and the millions of Americans who were part of the civil rights movement and pushed the president and the U.S. Congress for action.

- **Health care**: The creation of the **Medicare** and **Medicaid** programs created by legislation during this time was a major achievement for the LBJ administration as it expanded health care coverage for many Americans who previously could not access it. The Medicare program was designed to be a social insurance program that would provide health care coverage for those older than 65 years, and for those with disabilities, on Social Security. In contrast, the Medicaid program was designed to be a public assistance health care program for those living in poverty and has income restrictions for eligibility.

- **Poverty and hunger**: One of the hallmarks of LBJ's presidency was the passage of the Economic Opportunity Act of 1964, which was used to fight the administration's war on poverty. It established the Office of Economic Opportunity (OEO) that was charged with directing and coordinating antipoverty programs focused on education, job training, and employment for those in poverty and POC. It supported the creation of thousands of **community action agencies** across the country that offered an array of programs designed to address the causes of poverty. This legislation created the Head Start Program, the Vista Program, and the Job Corps. Finally, the **Food Stamp Act of 1964** was passed to make this a permanent program to address hunger and malnutrition among low-income Americans living in poverty.

- **Federal aid for education**: A number of bills were passed, such as the Elementary and Secondary Education Act of 1965 and Higher Education Act of 1965, to funnel federal funding to states to support students in K–12 schools and those attending higher education as a mechanism to improve social mobility and access to opportunity in the United States. Examples include the College Work Study Program, Upward Bound Program, Head Start Program, and Pell Grant Program.

Historians, such as Robert Caro and Doris Kearns Goodwin, have debated both the successes and failures of LBJ's presidency, though many agree that few U.S. presidents were able to pass more domestic legislation than LBJ. Though poverty was not completely eradicated by the Great Society programs and war on poverty, the poverty rate was reduced significantly, particularly for older Americans and African Americans, who were able to access many of the social programs that were instituted during this time. Perhaps LBJ's biggest failure was allowing funding for his beloved Great Society programs to get overtaken by the funding required to support the unpopular Vietnam War. However, LBJ would be pleased to know that many of the programs that his administration created are still with us today, such as Head Start, Medicaid, Medicare, the Food Stamp Program (now called the Supplemental Nutrition Assistance Program), federal funding for public and higher education, and AmeriCorps. LBJ died 4 years after leaving office.

Social Workers Dorothy Height and Whitney Young

There were a number of social workers with distinguished and impactful careers, particularly Black social workers who were active in the movement for civil rights.

Prominent social workers during this time included **Whitney Young** and **Dorothy Height**. Whitney Young was the executive director of the National Urban League and president of NASW. He was involved in civil rights work at the highest levels, as seen in Figure 2.6 of him in the oval office strategizing with Dr. King and President Johnson over how to pass historic civil rights legislation. He was awarded the Presidential Medal of Freedom by President Johnson for his civil rights accomplishments. Dorothy Height was a civil rights leader and a champion of women's rights, and she served as president of the National Council of Negro Women for 40 years. She passed away in April 2010, and President Obama delivered a eulogy at her funeral service. (Learn more about Dorothy Height and Whitney Young in Chapter 4.)

FIGURE 2.6   Social worker Dorothy Height with Speaker of the House Nancy Pelosi

FIGURE 2.7   Social worker Whitney Young in the oval office with President Lyndon Johnson and Dr. Martin Luther King, Jr.

This chapter profiles an incredible array of inspirational social workers from the progressive, New Deal, and Great Society periods of U.S. history. Select one of these social workers you feel most drawn to in order to learn more about them, their life, and their accomplishments. Then answer the following questions:

1.   What do you find most inspiring about this person?

2.   What do you view as their most important contributions? What drove them to fight for change in our society?

3.   What kinds of barriers and challenges did they have to face as they went about their work?

4.   What did you learn about their personal life that surprised you?

5.   What personal and environmental characteristics helped them to be successful?

Overview of Today's U.S. Social Welfare System

It is hard to imagine that at one time there was no formalized social welfare system through which people in need or in crisis could go to access essential resources or services. It is incredible to think about how this extensive system evolved and emerged over time, developed by leaders and other professionals who were committed to responding to human well-being and need. Wealthy nations are often analyzed and judged by the extent that they are willing to invest in the social welfare of their citizens via a strong, expansive welfare system that is supported by government taxation.

The **social welfare system** in the United States refers to our nation's complex set of programs and services that address the health, social, economic, and educational needs of its citizens. A vast array of social welfare programs are offered across all sectors of the U.S. economy—government, nonprofit, and for profit—at the local, state, and federal levels. The social welfare system can be grouped broadly into the following five categories: education and workforce development, health care, income support, nutrition, and shelter/housing.

Education and Workforce Development

Government programs that focus on education and/or preparing people for being prepared to enter the workforce are as follows:

- **Early Childhood Education**, such as the Head Start program and Early Head Start program, which are funded by the federal government. These are preschool programs for children that are below the poverty line and are designed to promote school readiness by the time they come to kindergarten.

- **K–12 childhood education** is tax funded so that all students can attend school without cost. This is what we refer to as free "public education."

- **The Child Care Development Fund** (CCDF) uses federal funding to provide financial assistance to low-income families to access childcare while they work.

- **College student loan and grant programs** use state and federal funding for college students to help them attend college such as the Federal Pell Grant Program, Federal Student Loan Program, and work- study programs. There are also loan forgiveness programs to help students who engage in some form of public service employment.

- **Job training and workforce development programs**: Most of these programs are under the umbrella of the Workforce Innovation and Opportunity Act (WIOA) and are designed to find employment for people, including youth, with significant barriers to employment. These programs help job seekers access employment, education, training, and support services to succeed in the labor market and to match employers with skilled workers.

2.3   PRACTICE ACTIVITY

Select two to three of the social programs listed that are of interest to you to learn more about them. In your research pay attention to the following questions:

1. When was the program started, and how did it begin? Who was instrumental in getting this program off the ground?

2. What are the eligibility requirements of this program, and who does it serve?

3. What benefits does it provide?

4. How is the program funded? Is it a public, nonprofit, or for-profit organization (see Table 2.1)?

5. Is it a public assistance or social insurance program (see Table 2.2)?

6. Is it curative, preventive, or alleviative (see Table 2.2)?

7. What are the societal attitudes about this program?

8. What are the biggest successes of this program?

9. What improvements are needed to make this a more successful program?

Health Care

Government programs that focus on providing varuous groups of people with access to healthcare are as follows:

- **Medicare program**: The government's social insurance health care program for people age 65 and older and people with serious disabilities who have contributed to this program via the Medicare payroll tax.

- **Medicaid program:** The nation's health care program for low-income people who live in poverty and meet the income restrictions set by the government. It is jointly funded by states and the federal government.

- **Veteran's Health Administration (VA):** This federally funded government program is the nation's health care system for veterans and includes medical centers and outpatient facilities.

- **Children's Health Insurance program (CHIP):** This government program covers children who live in families who are not eligible for the Medicaid program but who are unable to afford other types of health care coverage. It is jointly funded by states and the federal government.

- **Affordable Care Act (ACA):** The ACA, passed during the Obama administration, expanded health care coverage to millions of Americans by requiring that Americans have health coverage, expanding the Medicaid program to more low-income people, reforming the health insurance industry (e.g., preventing them from excluding those with preexisting conditions; requiring them to offer free preventative care), and creating new health insurance marketplaces to make it more affordable for many people to purchase health insurance.

- **Government-funded mental health services:** Both states and the federal government provide significant funding for mental health treatment and services. Medicaid is the single largest funder of mental health services in the country. The federal government also provides mental health block grants (MHBG) that support states in developing and operating their community mental health services. Finally, many people receive mental health treatment while they serve time in correctional facilities, such as jails and prisons.

Income Assistance

Government programs that focus on poverty and income insecurity by supporting various groups of people with financial assistance are as follows:

- **Temporary Assistance for Needy Families Program (TANF):** The nation's federal public assistance program for families with children who are living below the poverty line. This cash-assistance program is jointly funded by states and the federal government. Many states have work requirements, and there is a time limit on the number of years that people can receive services from this program.

- **Social Security program:** This is a social insurance program that is meant to insure workers against their own poverty after they leave the workforce. The program is funded by a payroll tax that is paid by employees and employers, and then after people retire they receive a monthly check. This program also supports some people with disabilities that limit their ability to work, as well as some survivors (spouses and dependent children) of retired, disabled, and deceased workers.

- **Supplemental Security program (SSI):** The SSI program is a federal program that provides cash benefits to people who are very poor and who suffer from serious disabilities, the majority of whom were unable to pay into, and thus benefit from, the social security program.

- **Unemployment insurance program:** This program provides cash benefits to those who have lost their job through no fault of their own while they search for a new job. It is jointly funded by states and the federal government, though states play a much more significant role as they tax employers to fund the program and determine benefit levels and number of weeks that people are eligible to receive benefits.

- **Tax credits for low-income workers:** There are two tax credits that low-middle income workers have access to—the Earned Income Tax Credit (EITC) and the Child Tax Credit, which allow eligible workers to receive a wage supplement from the government when they file their taxes. The EITC in particular has been touted as one of the most effective antipoverty measures currently in existence in the United States.

- **Workers' compensation program:** Almost all states require employers to offer workers' compensation insurance to their employees in case they become ill, injured, or disabled as a result of their job. Benefits include wage replacement and payment for medical care, including health rehabilitation. This is an example of a government-mandated program.

Nutrition

Programs in the public and private sector that focus on hunger and food insecurity are as follows:

- **Supplemental Nutrition Assistance Program (SNAP):** The SNAP program is commonly referred to as the "food stamp" program, which refers to an earlier time when the program gave people stamps to purchase their food. Today, people are provided with a debit card to make their food purchases. The program is funded by the federal government, though it is administered by states, and people have to meet income restrictions in order to receive monthly benefits that vary by state.

- **Nutrition programs for children:** There are a few government-funded programs that focus on serving children to help ensure that their nutritional needs are met. The Women, Infants and Children program, or WIC program, provides monthly food vouchers to women who are pregnant and nursing, as well as children under age 5. Additionally, the National School Lunch Program and School Breakfast Program provide free or reduced-priced school meals to children who live in eligible low-income families. There are income restrictions to receive services in these federal programs.

- **Other nutrition programs:** Across this country there are countless numbers of soup kitchens and food banks that are funded and administered by various nonprofit and faith-based organizations. These are invaluable resources to many people who experience food insecurity by accessing support in their local community.

Shelter/Housing

Programs in the public and private sector that focus on homelessness and housing insecurity are as follows:

- **Government housing assistance programs:** There are two main programs that are set up to assist people who find it challenging to afford housing—(a) the Housing Choice Voucher Program (i.e., Section 8), which provides housing vouchers to landlords who will accept them, and (b) public housing, which provides designated housing where they are able to live at a reduced rental rate. Unfortunately, there are long wait lists, and many eligible people are not able to get access to these programs.

- **Other housing programs:** In many cities and communities across the nation there are nonprofit and faith-based organizations that are set up to serve those who find themselves experiencing homelessness or housing insecurity, such as homeless shelters, emergency shelters, and family violence shelters.

Though many people think primarily about government-funded social welfare programs, there are many **private organizations** that assist people with social service needs in the United States (e.g., faith-based organizations, nonprofit organizations, and for-profit organizations). The following tables summarize the various ways that the social welfare system in the United States can be categorized.

TABLE 2.1   Social Welfare Programs by Sector

Sector	Funding	Examples
Public/government	Funding provided by local, state, and/or federal funds (e.g., taxes)	Medicare program; Medicaid program; Social Security program; VA system; Temporary Assistance for Needy Families; Public health departments; child protection agencies
Nonprofit	Funded by a combination of private and corporate donations as well as government grants	American Red Cross; Planned Parenthood; advocacy organizations such as the Human Rights Campaign; United Way; Salvations Army; faith-based organizations such as Catholic charities; American Cancer Society; homeless shelters; domestic violence agencies
For profit	Funding from bank loans and funds generated from the sales of products or services	Private hospitals; private substance abuse treatment centers; privately funded prisons; mental health clinicians in private practice

TABLE 2.2   Social Welfare Programs by Type of Benefits, Eligibility, and Purpose

Type of Benefits	Eligibility	Purpose
Cash assistance—The program offers cash benefits (e.g., Social Security; Temporary Assistance for Needy Families)	**Public assistance programs**—The program has income restrictions, and you can only receive benefits when you are below a certain income level (e.g., Medicaid; Temporary Assistance for Needy Families; public housing programs)	**Preventive**—Programs that are designed to prevent poverty from occurring in the first place and that are universal and available to all citizens regardless of income status (e.g., social insurance programs such as Social Security; universal health care programs)
In-kind benefits—The program offers vouchers or some type of service (e.g., housing vouchers; health care services; SNAP program)	**Social insurance programs**—Government programs in which workers and sometimes their employers pay taxes into the program while they are working and then they receive benefits when they become eligible (e.g., Social Security benefits; unemployment Insurance; Medicare)	**Curative**—Programs that try to help cure the problem after it has happened; many of these programs target the individual by helping to give them skills and tools to be self-sufficient (e.g., job training programs)
		Alleviative—Programs that seek to ease people's suffering and get them through a rough patch, but they do not cure or prevent the problem from occurring (e.g., Medicaid; Temporary Assistance for Needy Families; SNAP program)

Chapter Summary

The story of how the social work profession and the social welfare system developed in the United States is a fascinating one—one that is full of both inspiration and important lessons. It is important that we understand the strengths of the system that has been designed to assist people who are struggling and in need as well as the failures, including the role that racism has played. It is healthy for any profession or discipline to engage in this level of self-reflection and to take accountability so that mistakes of the past are not repeated. This chapter highlights important historical moments that the country made significant improvements in how it responded to people and need due to both individual and structural causes such as the SHM, the Black mutual aid societies, and the many policies and social programs that came out of the New Deal and Great Society periods in U.S. history. These important moments in history marked the country's journey toward becoming a welfare state. It also highlights the impressive role and accomplishments of social workers in these historic achievements. Finally, the chapter provides a high-level overview of the current social welfare system in the United States and important social programs that are in existence today that cover the five areas of education and workforce development, health, income support, nutrition, and shelter/housing. Social workers at the macro level are needed to ensure that the policies that govern social welfare programming at the local, state, and national levels are grounded in important social work values, such as dignity and worth of the person, self-determination, and compassion.

Discussion Questions

1. How well do you think the CARIN theory of deservingness explains attitudes that Americans have regarding who is deserving/worthy of assistance and who is not worthy/deserving of assistance? What common American social values come into play here? What role has racism played?

2. Why do you believe that the United States was so reluctant to become a welfare state and develop a social safety net? Would this have happened without the crisis of the Great Depression in the 1930s?

3. What were the biggest accomplishments that came out of the New Deal period of U.S. history regarding the development of the social welfare system and which famous social workers had a pivotal role?

4. What were the biggest accomplishments that came out of the Great Society period of U.S. history regarding the development of the social welfare system, and which famous social workers had a pivotal role?

5. Why do you think it is so rare for a U.S. president to declare a war on poverty, like President Johnson did? Is the goal of most of our social welfare programs to be alleviative, curative, or preventive?

References

Altschuler, G. C., & Blumin, S. M. (2009). *The G.I. bill: A new deal for veterans*. Oxford University Press.

Barga, M. (n.d.). *African Union Society*. VCU Libraries Social History Project. https://social-welfare.library.vcu.edu/religious/african-union-society/#:~:text=Background%3A%20Mutual%20aid%20societies%20were,communities%20in%20conjunction%20with%20churches.

Finn, J. L. (2021). *Just practice: A social justice approach to social work*. Oxford University Press.

Frances Perkins Center. (n.d.). *Her life: The woman behind the New Deal*. https://francesperkinscenter.org/life-new/

Lee, K. J., & Dieser, R. B. (2020). Ada S. McKinley: A hidden history of African American settlement house in Chicago. *Leisure Sciences, 45*(4), 351–367. https://doi.org/10.1080/01490400.2020.1830904

National Association of Social Workers. (2021). *NASW apologizes for racist practices in American social work*. https://www.socialworkers.org/News/News-Releases/ID/2331/NASW-apologizes-for-racist-practices-in-American-social-work

National Women's History Museum. (n.d.). *African American reformers: The club movement*. https://www.womenshistory.org/resources/general/african-american-reformers

Richmond, M. E. (1917). *Social diagnosis*. New York: Russell Sage Foundation.

Ritter, J. A. (2022). *Social work policy practice: Changing our community, nation, and the world* (3rd ed.). Cognella.

Shepherd, D., & Pritzker, S. (2021). Political advocacy without a choice: Highlighting African American political social workers. *Advances in Social Work, 21*(2/3), 241–258.

Van Oorschot, W., & Roosma, F. (2017). The social legitimacy of targeted welfare and welfare deservingness. In W. Van Oorschot, F. Roosma, B. Meuleman, & T. Reeskens (Eds.), *The social legitimacy of targeted welfare: Attitudes to welfare deservingness* (pp. 3–36). Edward Elgar.

Credits

CHAPTER 3

An Introduction to Generalist Social Work Practice

Learning Objectives

After reading this chapter, students will be able to do the following:

- Define generalist social work practice

- Summarize the five phases of the planned change process and the purpose of each

- Differentiate between the various roles that social workers can take on at the micro, mezzo, and macro level and evaluate their own goodness of fit with these roles

- Identify at least three interventions that are commonly carried out by social workers

- Provide examples of attending skills and explain why this skill is crucial throughout the phases of the planned change process

- Explain how theory informs social work practice and critique theoretical frameworks and practice models that are used by social workers

When you think about the terms *professional* and *professionalism,* what comes up for you? Chang et al. (2018) describe a **professional** as "a person who has specialized training for a particular career and who acts in conscientious, appropriate ways in the workplace" (p. 74). Chang and colleagues outline a number of important aspects of professionalism, including how you speak and present yourself, using professional values and ethics, dressing appropriately, being organized and timely, being prepared for meetings, using appropriate communication skills with both colleagues and clients, and operating with honesty and integrity.

It is important to explore *how* social workers conduct their work and what guides them when they intervene with client systems of various sizes. In other words, what does social work with clients look like, and how do they know what to do when working with a wide range of clients experiencing a wide range of life challenges? It may be helpful to think about social workers having a **"tool-box" of skills, techniques, and frameworks** that they use in their work. The practice of social work involves knowing which of these tools to use depending on the client and the circumstances.

What Is Generalist Social Work Practice?

Students who are enrolled in undergraduate social work programs are being prepared for **generalist social work practice**, while graduate programs in social work prepare students for advanced, and more specialized, practice. So, what is generalist social work practice exactly? There are three major components of generalist practice—knowledge, values, and skills—which were covered in Chapter 1 of this book.

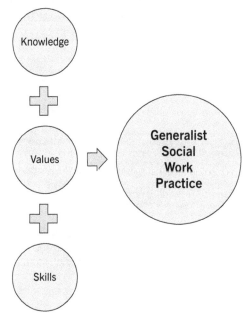

FIGURE 3.1   Visual diagram of generalist social work practice at the BSW level.

The Council on Social Work Education (CSWE, 2022) defines **generalist social work practice** as follows:

> The descriptions of the nine social work competencies presented in the EPAS identify the knowledge, values, skills, and cognitive and affective processes that are subsequently demonstrated in students' observable behaviors indicative of competence at a generalist level of practice. Generalist practice is grounded in the liberal arts and the person-in-environment framework. To promote human and social well-being, generalist practitioners use a range of prevention and intervention methods in their practice with diverse individuals, families, groups, organizations, and communities, based on scientific inquiry and best practices. The generalist practitioner identifies with the social work profession and applies ethical principles and critical thinking in practice at the micro, mezzo, and macro levels. Generalist practitioners engage diversity in their practice and advocate for human rights and social, racial, economic, and environmental justice. They recognize, support, and build on the strengths and resiliency of all human beings. They engage in research informed practice and are proactive in responding to the impact of context on professional practice. (p. 17)

The Nine CSWE Competencies

Chapter 1 provided an overview of the Council on Social Work Education's (CSWE, 2022) nine competencies that students should be proficient in by the time they graduate from their respective BSW or MSW program, and they are included in Table 3.1 as a review.

TABLE 3.1   **CSWE Competencies**

Competency 1	Demonstrate ethical and professional behavior.	This competency speaks to the idea that social workers need to follow ethical standards (outlined in the NASW Code of Ethics) and standards of professional behavior in order to ensure that they are not causing harm to the clients they serve. Social workers need to be able to work through ethical dilemmas that arise in the course of their work.
Competency 2	Advance human rights and social, racial, economic, and environmental justice.	A vital part of a social worker's role is to protect the human rights of all people and to promote social justice, economic justice, racial justice, and environmental justice. Social workers work to dismantle racism, oppression, and systemic discrimination with the goal of having a more just and equal society in which everyone has the same access to opportunity.

Competency 3	Engage antiracism, diversity, equity, and inclusion (ADEI) in practice.	Social workers understand the importance of identity and diversity and how this impacts people's lived experiences. Social workers are educated to view people's identities in through an intersectional lens that includes age, class, color, culture, disability and ability, ethnicity, gender, gender identity and expression, immigration status, marital status, political ideology, race, religion/spirituality, sex, sexual orientation, and tribal sovereign status.
Competency 4	Engage in practice-informed research and research-informed practice.	This competency reflects the understanding that social workers are both consumers of research and producers of research. Practicing social workers should rely on interventions and approaches that are supported by research evidence and should evaluate their practice. Researchers should use their research findings to improve policy, practice, and service delivery.
Competency 5	Engage in policy practice.	Social workers understand the impact that policies have on individuals, families, and communities. They should fight against policies that cause harm and advocate for policies that advance human rights and social, economic, and environmental justice.
Competency 6	Engage with individuals, families, groups, organizations, and communities.	Competencies 6–9 cover the phases of the planned change process, which is covered later in this chapter. Engagement is the first phase of the planned change process, though engagement continues throughout the entire process. Engagement skills include the ability to build a safe and trusting relationship with client systems, which requires strong interpersonal communication skills such as active listening, empathy, and reflection.
Competency 7	Assess individuals, families, groups, organizations, and communities.	This phase of the planned change process involves collecting data on both strengths and needs and using theories of human behavior and the social environment to interpret that data. Doing a thorough and effective assessment is necessary to develop appropriate goals and intervention strategies based on the data gathered during assessment.
Competency 8	Intervene with individuals, families, groups, organizations, and communities.	This phase of the planned change process involves using evidence-based interventions to achieve the goals that were established by the client system. Social workers often work with professionals from other disciplines as members of an interdisciplinary team. It is an ethical principle to use interventions that are culturally responsive and to end services when the goals have been reached.
Competency 9	Evaluate practice with individuals, families, groups, organizations, and communities.	The final phase of the planned change process recognizes the importance of social workers evaluating their practice (using qualitative and quantitative methods) to be able to assess whether the interventions they use are effective and improve service delivery effectiveness over time. It is a strong ethical principle to evaluate one's practice to ensure that interventions help to improve the client's situation and do not cause harm.

Overview of the Planned Change Process

The **planned change process**, also referred to as the **generalist intervention model**, is the heart of social work practice as it shows the process of how social workers intervene with client systems of all sizes from beginning to end. It does not matter whether the client is an individual, family, group, organization, or community; the planned change process is a practice framework that is used by social workers to effect change at the micro, mezzo, and macro level. There are **five phases of the planned change process**: engagement, assessment and planning, intervention, termination, and evaluation (see Figure 3.2). It is important to keep in mind that "although these phases are described here in a linear fashion, the social worker and client frequently loop back and forth between phases as necessary" (Birkenmaier & Berg-Weger, 2017, p. 8).

The Planned Change Process

FIGURE 3.2   The planned change process used in social work.

Engagement

The first phase of the planned change process is focused on how we engage with our clients, or rather how we **build rapport** with a client and begin to build a good working relationship built on trust, collaboration, and open communication. It is always important for social workers to keep in mind how intimidating it can be for clients to share their personal stories with a helping professional. For many clients this requires a great deal of courage and vulnerability. The engagement phase is so crucial because it is the first meeting in which important first impressions are made. Mistakes that happen during engagement can negatively impact later phases of the work.

Helping professionals spend a lot of time thinking through their professional **"use of self."** They think about the personal qualities that wish to bring to their work with clients, how they will present themselves, and how they will behave in their professional working relationships The core interpersonal qualities that are necessary during this phase are **warmth**, **empathy**, **respect for diversity** in all of its forms, **genuineness**, and **unconditional positive regard** (i.e., non-judgmental acceptance) for your client (Birkenmaier & Berg-Weger, 2017; Chang et al., 2018). One of the biggest mistakes to avoid during this phase is offering advice, since there has not been sufficient time to get to know the client and their presenting issues and to collaborate with the client in goal setting (Chang et al., 2018).

Depending on the setting, social workers work may work with **voluntary clients** or **involuntary clients**. Voluntary clients are often easier to engage and build a relationship with than involuntary clients since voluntary clients have chosen to work seek the support of a social worker. Social workers who work in child welfare, criminal justice settings, and some mental health settings often work with those who are not there willingly. Building trust with involuntary clients takes skill, empathy, and patience, but it is possible to build a good working relationship. Social workers trained in motivational interviewing understand that **resistance** is a normal part of the change process and should not be viewed too negatively by a practitioner.

There are a number of important skills that are important for social workers to use during the engagement phase, and these can be viewed as vital "building blocks" of the helping relationship. Social workers who are able to master these engagement skills will excel in their field. **Attending skills** are critically important during the engagement phase, as these are the skills that we use to "attend" to our client and demonstrate that we are listening to them and are fully present. It may sound easy to be a good listener and to be fully present to someone, but for many who are addicted to their technology (e.g., smartphones, social media, email, etc.), honing these skills requires constant vigilance and intentionality.

Attending skills include both **nonverbal and communication skills**. Social workers are trained to think carefully about their nonverbal communication with clients such as using an appropriate amount of eye contact, using an open body position, nodding while someone is speaking, and using their facial expressions

IMG 3.2

to convey warmth and empathy. For verbal communication, the use of **active listening** can be very effective. Active listening "involves fully focusing on what the other person is attempting to communicate" and "requires conscious effort to understand the speaker" (Chang et al., 2018, p. 110). Active listening includes the skills of **reflecting content** and **reflecting feelings** back to a client for the purposes of clarity and demonstrating that you hear them. Social workers can paraphrase and/or summarize what they heard a client saying, or what they appear to be feeling, and then end with something like, "Did I get that right?"

3.1   PRACTICE ACTIVITY

Assess Your Listening Skills

Having strong listening skills is crucial for those who wish to be an effective social worker. Even though some people are naturally good listeners, this is a skill that can be improved significantly with some intentional practice. Social workers show clients they are listening with both their verbal and nonverbal communication. Reflect on your own listening skills by answering the following questions.

Reflection Questions

1. Are you generally more comfortable listening or talking when in a conversation with someone?

2. How challenging is it for you to put your technology, or other distractions, away when with others so you can be fully present?

3. How do you use your body language to convey to someone that you are listening to them?

4. Do you tend to interrupt others when they are talking?

5. The use of silence can be useful when talking with clients. Are you comfortable when there is a lull in a conversation, or do you rush to fill it?

6. How often do you reflect back to someone what you heard them saying (by paraphrasing or summarizing)?

7. What are your strengths when it comes to being a good listener, and where would you like to improve?

Assessment and Planning

This phase of the planned change process is often referred to as the "data gathering" and "goal setting" phase. When social workers work with a new client they want to gather as much information as possible about the client, their background and history, their strengths, and the challenges they are experiencing.

The **assessment and planning phase** is a "collaborative process by which clients can partner with a professional to make informed decisions about the work they can do together" (Birkenmaier & Berg-Weger, 2017, p. 107). It is important that the assessment is done thoughtfully and thoroughly because it lays the groundwork for determining the interventions that will be used in the next phase—the intervention phase.

In many organizations, a formal assessment tool is utilized so that social workers are guided on the important information they need to gather about the clients they meet with. These are sometimes referred to as a **biopsychosocial assessment**, which means the social worker gathers important information related to the client's medical, psychological, and social history (see Chapter 8 for a more detailed description). It is important that the social worker continues using strong engagement skills (e.g., empathy, warmth, active listening, etc.) during the assessment phase since clients need to feel safe sharing very personal important information about their lives.

A critical skill is working with clients is the ability to **ask good questions**, and this is especially true during the assessment phase. Social workers ask questions to gather relevant information about the client's background and history, their strengths, and the challenges they are experiencing and wish to change. Social workers use both **closed-ended** and **open-ended questions** to learn more about the client and should think carefully about how to best use both types of questions. Closed-ended questions (e.g., "Where were you born?") usually elicit one- or two-word answers, while open-ended questions allow a client to have more freedom in how they answer and to provide more depth and details in their answer (e.g., "Can you tell me what it was like to grow up in Houston?"). Both types of questions are useful depending on the type of information the social worker is seeking.

Sample questions that can be used to explore the client's challenges:

- When did the problem begin? (Gather a history or timeline of the problem.)
- What are the causes of this problem, in your view?
- What happened that led you to decide to seek help now?
- What kinds of things have you tried to try to resolve the problem?
- Can you tell me a little more about how this problem is impacting you (e.g., anxiety, depression, sleep, appetite, irritability, quality of relationships, etc.)?
- On a scale of 1 to 10, with 1 being no problem and 10 being the worst problem you have ever faced, what number would you give it?

Sample questions that can be used to explore the client's strengths:

- What is going well in your life?
- Who can you rely on for help and support when you need it? Who can you count on?
- What do you do well? What do you value about yourself?
- What would your friends or family say are your strengths?
- When are you at your best or most happy?
- What past challenges have you overcome in your life?
- How did you resolve previous challenges in your life?
- What past accomplishments are you most proud of?

Mistakes to avoid when asking questions:

- Asking leading questions
- Asking more than one question at a time (i.e., double-barreled questions)
- Asking so many questions that a client feels interrogated
- Using "why questions" since they can make people feel defensive

Tools such as ecomaps and genograms can also be used to gather useful information about the client during the assessment and planning phase. An **ecomap** is a visual representation of a client's social world to help the client evaluate the quality of their relationships, including their sources of support and those areas that cause them stress or where there is a lack of social support. A **genogram** is a visual representation of a client's family tree and can be very helpful in gathering a family history, including important information about genetics, health

history, and family relationships. You can find wonderful resources and examples of these tools by doing a google search on the internet.

Goal setting is another crucial part of this phase of the planned change process. During this phase, social workers support their clients in identifying what they hope to achieve in their work together and "the client's vision of what life would be like if their problems were solved" (Chang et al., 2018, p. 236). Clients are supported in ascertaining their hopes, dreams,

IMG 3.3

and preferred reality in order to develop a picture of "what could be." It is very important that goals are mutually established and that the social worker is not choosing goals for the client (Chang et al., 2018).

Social workers often support clients in identifying goals using the **SMART** method. Goals that meet these criteria are **s**pecific, **m**easurable, **a**chievable, **r**elevant, and **t**imely (has a timeframe).

IMG 3.4

SMART Goal Examples

- Sarah will meet with a therapist for 1 hour once a week for 6 months for cognitive behavioral therapy to learn new techniques for coping with and reducing her level of anxiety.

- Albert will submit four job applications per week for the next 3 months to work toward the goal of landing a full-time position by May 1st.

- Jose will complete a 12-week parenting class at Positive Parenting and earn his certificate of completion by August 15th.

Supporting a client in identifying the goals they want to work on and prioritizing those goals is an important part of a social worker's role during the planned change process. The goals should be frequently reviewed to assess progress, and they can be modified over time as needed. When the helping relationship comes to an end (i.e., during the termination phase), the client and social worker will review the goals to assess the level of progress that was made.

Checking in About Terminology

Client versus Participant

Social workers spend a lot of time thinking about terminology and using language that is sensitive to those we serve. Throughout this book, the words *client* and *client system* are frequently used to refer to the individuals who social workers support in their work. However, there are different opinions about the best word to use and some who prefer a word other than *client*. Depending on the social worker and the work setting, there are a whole host of different terms that are used to describe the individuals who are served by social workers: *client, consumer, customer, service recipient, service user, participant*, and many more. *Client* is most commonly used by practicing social workers today. Morgaine and Capous-Desyllas (2015) explain that some of these terms, including *client*, are criticized as they imply a hierarchical relationship in which the social worker is the powerful expert and the client is in a passive role. They recommend the word *participant* and feel that it is better grounded in anti-oppressive practice and a spirit of partnership between the social worker and the individual they are serving. What do you think? Which of these terms feels better to you?

Intervention

One of the most exciting and unique aspects of social work is the broad array of work settings in which social workers can apply their skills. However, another way that social work offers variety in the work has to do with the different roles they can play from the micro to the macro level. For example, a social worker who works in the field of child welfare can change their role in this field over time such as caseworker, therapist, supervisor, administrator, researcher, and policy advocate.

The **intervention phase** is often referred to as the "working stage" as this is where the actual intervention(s) is carried out. The intervention should directly reflect the goals and priorities that were identified and agreed on in the assessment and planning phase. According to Birkenmaier and Berg-Weger (2017), "The goal of all social work interventions is to empower clients to make changes to enhance the quality of their lives and ability to function within their environments" (p. 184). The types of interventions that social workers employ with clients depend on the presenting issues and the services that are offered in a given organization. The most common type of interventions used by social workers are summarized in Table 3.2.

TABLE 3.2   Types of Social Work Interventions and Roles

Type of Intervention	Social Work Professional Roles
Therapy/counseling	Clinician/therapist/counselor
Case management	Caseworker/collaborator/case manager
Interdisciplinary practice	Team member/collaborator
Case referral to other services	Broker/collaborator/caseworker
Advocacy	Client advocate/policy advocate/lobbyist
Crisis intervention	Mental health clinician/all social workers
Education/skills development	Teacher/educator/trainer/professor
Research and evaluation	Researcher/program evaluator
Administration and planning	Leader/administrator/program director/supervisor

Therapy/Counseling

The vast majority of social workers who perform counseling and therapy services with clients are **licensed clinical social workers**, or LCSWs, who have their MSW, their clinical license, and advanced training in mental health therapies and diagnoses. Job titles varies greatly and can include LCSW, psychotherapist, mental health practitioner, counselor, therapist, and mental health clinician. Mental health clinicians can do **therapy with individuals, couples, and groups**. While some therapists are generalists and see a range of clients with various challenges, other therapists choose to specialize in areas such as marriage and family therapy, severe trauma, grief, addictions, play therapy with children and youth, animal-assisted therapy, cognitive behavioral therapy, solution-focused brief therapy, and so on. **Group therapy** involves one of more therapists working with several people at the same time who are there to get support around a specific issue they are all experiencing. Support groups and skills development groups are common examples.

LCSWs must continue to get training each year in order to keep their license up to date. Because they are working with vulnerable clients, they must closely follow the NASW Code of Ethics, which includes important guidelines related to things such as client confidentiality, self-determination, informed consent, and cultural competence. LCSWs can work in a variety of settings such as their own private practice, mental health centers, and hospitals. Chapter 7 includes an overview of social work in mental health, including the proliferation of **telemental health**, which refers to the practice of using videoconferencing technology to provide mental health services (e.g., Zoom).

Case Management

Many social workers in the United States are employed as caseworkers and/or case managers, and these terms will be used interchangeably in this section. The case management role of social workers dates to the beginning of the profession. **Caseworkers** often have an assigned caseload of clients, individuals or families, with whom they are supporting by setting up, coordinating, and monitoring a range of services for each client. The case manager is the central person who does the coordination work and can thus see the bigger picture. The National Association of Social Workers (NASW, 2013) defines **case management** as "a process to plan, seek, advocate for, and monitor services from different social services or health care organizations and staff on behalf of a client. The process enables social workers in an organization, or in different organizations, to coordinate their efforts to serve a given client through professional teamwork, thus expanding the range of needed services offered.

The NASW (2013) lists the following as the core functions of case management in social work:

- engagement with clients
- assessment of client priorities, strengths, and challenges
- development and implementation of a care plan
- monitoring of service delivery
- evaluation of outcomes
- closure (including termination or transition follow-up) (pp. 18–19)

Case managers work in a wide range of settings and the job titles can include caseworker, case manager, care coordinator, health care/patient navigator, and service coordinator. One good example of case management is a child welfare caseworker since they are assigned a caseload of families for which they coordinate a range of services such as therapy, parenting classes, psychological evaluation, substance abuse treatment, housing and employment support, and so on. Often, these services are outlined in a family service plan, a helpful way to document the services provided, an explanation of roles (i.e., who will do what), and target dates for completion.

Interdisciplinary Practice

Social workers routinely work with professionals from other disciplines in the course of their work with clients. **Interdisciplinary practice** "involves professionals from different professions integrating their professional knowledge to work together, in a single intervention, toward a common goal. An **interprofessional practice approach** involves regular communication and coordination of services" (Birkenmaier & Berg-Weger, 2017, pp. 211–212). Social workers commonly work with professionals in health care, mental health, criminal justice/legal settings, and educational settings.

When social workers work in a **host setting**, this means that they are a social worker in a setting where they are in the minority in terms of their professional background. Two good examples of this are school social work and medical social work where the social worker is working predominantly with teachers and health care professionals, respectively. Working in a host setting has its benefits and challenges. It can be very exciting to work collaboratively with professionals who bring different perspectives and skill sets. However, this can also present challenges at times due to values conflicts, hierarchy, turf battles, and different opinions on the "best way" to approach the work. A crucial skill for social workers who are members of an interdisciplinary team is the ability to build strong partnerships and collaborative relationships with others on the team while still holding onto their social work values and perspective.

Case Referral to Other Services

One of the skills that social workers are known for is their vast **knowledge of community resources** and their ability to refer clients to needed services that are outside of the social worker's place of employment. Social workers who perform this role are referred to as **brokers**, which means linking clients to needed services or resources. It is important for social workers to build positive working relationships with other social service organizations in the community. It can be helpful to conceptualize the social services in a community as a large network where reciprocal relationships exist as agencies in a community refer clients to each other. The more a social worker understands the eligibility requirements and services provided in other community organizations, the better their clients will benefit from that knowledge.

Social workers who do **discharge planning** in hospitals are charged with linking up their patients with needed follow-up care after they leave the hospital, which can include home health care, placement in a rehabilitation facility, hospice and palliative care, mental health therapy, support groups, physical therapy, occupational therapy, speech therapy, and so forth. In order to perform the broker role well, there are several important steps involved. First, the social worker must be able to evaluate what services the client needs. Next, the social worker sifts through their knowledge of available community resources to match and refer the client to the services that are most appropriate for that specific client. Finally, the social worker will follow up to ensure that the client was able to access the services needed. If there were obstacles that prevented this, the social worker might move into an advocacy role to assist the client in gaining access to needed services that they have a right to receive.

Advocacy

Social workers are natural advocates for their clients. Guided by social justice and human rights principles, social workers often step in to advocate for their client's basic human rights at the micro and macro level. Section 6.04 of the NASW (2021) Code of Ethics explains this ethical obligation as follows: "Social workers should engage in social and political action that seeks to ensure that all people have equal access to the resources, employment, services, and opportunities they require to meet their basic human needs and to develop fully. Social workers should be aware of the impact of the political arena on practice and should advocate for changes in policy and legislation to improve social conditions in order to meet basic human needs and promote social justice."

It can be helpful to distinguish between case advocacy and cause advocacy. **Case advocacy** is performed at the micro level and "occurs when a social worker represents the interests of or defends the rights of *an individual or family*" (Ritter, 2022, p. 10). For example, social workers who work in the fields of intimate partner violence and victim's rights organizations often advocate for their clients within the court system. **Cause advocacy** on the other hand is performed by social workers working at the macro level. Cause advocacy is "when a social worker is representing the interests of or defending the rights of *groups of people*" (Ritter, 2022, p. 11), and this typically occurs in the political arena at the local, state, or federal level. Social workers who work in advocacy organizations, or as lobbyists, work to pass legislation that benefits the client population they represent, which is referred to as policy practice.

Policy practice is defined as "efforts to change policies in legislative, agency, and community settings, whether by establishing new policies, improving existing ones or defeating the policy initiatives of other people" (Jansson, 2008, p. 14). This role is covered heavily in Chapter 5.

Crisis Intervention

No matter the work setting, the vast majority of social workers will work with a client in crisis at some point in their career and thus need to cultivate **strong crisis-intervention skills** in order to support clients through a traumatic time in their life. Because social workers work with so many clients who have experienced trauma in their lives, many social workers work with clients from a trauma-informed care perspective (covered later in this chapter). According to Roberts and

IMG 3.5

Ottens (2005), "The main cause of a crisis is an intensely stressful, traumatic, or hazardous event, but two other conditions are also necessary: (1) the individual's perception of the event as the cause of considerable upset and/or disruption; and (2) the individual's inability to resolve the disruption by previously used coping mechanisms" (p. 331).

Examples of Crisis Situations

- A client who is feeling suicidal
- A family dealing with a family member who is dying from a critical illness
- A family that has lost their housing
- A parent suddenly unemployed
- A family dealing with a family member who is experiencing severe mental illness
- A child who has been removed from their home due to child maltreatment
- A client who has been a victim of a violent crime
- A child with a parent who has just been incarcerated
- A family that is going through a separation or divorce

When working with someone in crisis it is important to remember that the client is overwhelmed and cannot take in too much information. Their equilibrium has been disrupted, and they may be experiencing a range of emotions such as shock, intense grief, fear, hopelessness, and confusion. It is imperative for social workers to get good training on how to respond when a client experiences **suicidal ideation**, as this is a very specific type of crisis that requires very careful and deliberate intervention.

The American Psychological Association (n.d.a.) defines **crisis intervention** as "the brief ameliorative, rather than specifically curative, use of psychotherapy or counseling to aid individuals, families, and groups who have undergone a highly disruptive experience, such as an unexpected bereavement or a disaster. Crisis intervention may prevent more serious consequences of the experience, such as posttraumatic stress disorder."

One well known model, **Roberts's seven stage crisis intervention model** (Roberts & Ottens, 2005) provides one example for how social workers can support clients who are going through a crisis:

1. Plan and conduct a thorough biopsychosocial and lethality/imminent danger assessment;

2. Make psychological contact and rapidly establish the collaborative relationship;

3. Identify the major problems, including crisis precipitants;

4. Encourage an exploration of feelings and emotions;

5. Generate and explore alternatives and new coping strategies;

6. Restore functioning through implementation of an action plan;

7. Plan follow-up and booster sessions. (pp. 332–333)

In some social work settings, such as hospital emergency rooms, family violence shelters, and psychiatric facilities, working with clients in crisis is a routine part of the job. When first learning to be a social worker, working with clients in crisis feels like a daunting task, but with practice and experience, this is a skill that can be mastered like any other social work skill.

Education/Skills Development

There are many examples of social workers who are **educators** or **teachers** as part of their professional role. Social workers who have experience in a given field have accumulated knowledge and expertise to share with various client systems at the micro, mezzo, and macro level. Social workers who are very experienced are often hired as **trainers** within various organizations (e.g., train newly hired child welfare caseworkers). Some social workers teach college classes in a university social work program as a way of helping to prepare students to become future social workers (MSW or doctoral degree required).

- **Individual level**: Social workers can share information and teach specific skills to their clients (e.g., how to fill out a job application, stages of child development, job interviewing skills, social skills development, parenting skills, relaxation skills, mindfulness, etc.). Social workers often "role-play" various situations with clients to give them some practice with a specific skill (e.g., interviewing for a job, talking to an employer about a problem in the workplace).

- **Family level**: Social workers can share information with families about effective communication skills, how to resolve conflicts, how to manage the family budget, healthy cooking skills, how to navigate through a divorce, and so forth.

- **Group level**: Social workers often conduct trainings with groups of people in an organization (e.g., how to implement trauma-informed care approaches in school settings, the importance of using anti-oppressive social work practices), and they also conduct skills training in a group therapy format (e.g., social skills, ways to manage grief, anger management skills, etc.).

- **Community/societal level:** Social workers who work in advocacy organizations work diligently to raise people's awareness about a social issue in order to create social and policy change (e.g., the need to address police brutality in a given community, the need for gun control legislation in the United States, the need for affordable housing in a given city; the need for additional funding for mental health in the United States, etc.). Social workers also share their expertise with lawmakers when weighing in on various policy issues.

Research and Evaluation

It may sound intimidating to step into the role of **researcher or program evaluator** as a social worker. But social workers are expected to use research to inform their practice, use practices that are supported by research evidence, and contribute to research and evaluation activities, which leads to the development of new knowledge in the social work discipline. The **four primary purposes of research** are as follows:

1. Promoting science as a way of acquiring knowledge in our field
2. Increasing accountability (i.e., how we evaluate our own effectiveness)
3. Communicating with others about our work (using research findings and data)
4. Enhancing access to scarce funding resources (funders will provide funding to those who are able to demonstrate their effectiveness) (Krysik, 2018, pp. 6–7)

It is an ethical principle to evaluate your own practice to ensure that you are being effective and not causing harm to your clients. Social workers can work as researchers and program evaluators in various settings such as universities, government agencies, and research organizations. Social workers who are skilled in program evaluation are in high demand as all organizations are required to evaluate their programs for program effectiveness and report to funders and other external stakeholders for accountability purposes. The research and evaluation role is covered more extensively in Chapter 5.

Administration and Planning

Social workers with good experience, a proven track record of strong performance, and strong leadership skills are often promoted into administrative and/or managerial roles in an organization. Job titles vary but can include executive director, program director, program manager, or supervisor. This role is covered more extensively in Chapter 5.

3.2   PRACTICE ACTIVITY

Self-Assessment Activity

Review the "Social Work Interventions and Roles" in Table 3.2 and the content that followed that explained each one in more detail; then answer the following questions.

1. Which social work interventions/roles are most appealing to you and why?

2. Which social work interventions/roles are least appealing to you and why?

3. Which of these would you like to explore more in your social work internship experiences?

Termination

The **termination stage** is all about endings and how to end a working relationship with a client in the most sensitive and professional way possible. Please reflect on a few questions: When you have ended a relationship and it did not end well, what did that look like? When you ended a relationship and it did end well, what was happening to make this feel like "a good ending?" When any relationship ends it can bring up a range of emotions for people, such as sadness, grief, abandonment, anger, happiness, and relief—and this is true of a relationship between a client and a social worker as well. An important part of the termination phase involves allowing both parties to share their feelings about the relationship ending.

A competent social worker understands that the termination phase should be carefully planned and discussed from the very beginning so that it does not come as a surprise when it is time to end the work. When working with children and youth, it is important to talk about this in a way that they can understand since their comprehension of time can vary based on the child's age. For example, the social worker can use a calendar to show how long they will work together and can cross off the weeks as they go. They can also plan how they want to spend their last day together and allow the child to have input.

It is an ethical obligation (outlined in Section 1.17 of the NASW [2021] Code of Ethics) that social workers "should terminate services to clients and professional relationships with them when such services and relationships are no longer required or no longer serve the clients' needs or interests." It is highly unethical to continue serving a client when they no longer need services. **Terminations** can occur in a variety of ways: the client abruptly stops attending, the social worker leaves the organization, the social worker believes the client would be better served by another professional and refers the client, the client and social worker agree that the client is ready to stop services, or the services are time-limited and must end after a specific period of time. There are a series of steps that are important to cover in the termination phase (Birkenmaier & Berg-Weger, 2017):

-   Negotiate the timing of the termination
-   Review the agreement for the work

- Process successes and shortcomings
- Develop and clarify plan for termination and maintenance of change
- Share responses to ending
- Practice cultural humility (p. 223)

During the termination phase, it is critical to discuss how the client plans to maintain their progress, and there are a range of possibilities here. Some clients have made tremendous progress and do not feel a need for any further services. In other cases, the social worker might refer the client to other supportive services to continue some other aspect of the work that the client still wishes to do. The social worker should help their client develop a plan for how they will deal with any setbacks and how they will utilize both formal and informal resources that can support them. Finally, the social worker should discuss whether a continued professional relationship would be appropriate should the client wish to come back for services, and under what circumstances.

A Personal Termination Story

By Jessica Ritter

When I was a BSW intern in child welfare, I was assigned the case of an 8-year-old boy who was removed from his home due to allegations that he was sexually abused by his stepfather. I instantly adored this little boy, though he was very hard to build a relationship with since he was not very trusting of people. He was placed in a residential center where he was receiving intensive therapy, and I would see him weekly when I supervised visits between him and his mother, who did not believe that the abuse had occurred. Over the course of the year, we did end up building a good relationship, and it felt like a significant accomplishment when I realized that he did indeed like and trust me! In May, I would have to leave his case because my BSW internship was ending. I felt very sad about this because I had come to care about him a lot.

With good advice from my supervisor, I did all the things that I was supposed to do to prepare for the termination phase: I talked to him about it and explained why I would have to leave his case, we used a calendar and I constantly reminded him of how long we would be working together, and we planned our last day together with his input—miniature golf and a meal at McDonald's. Finally, our last day arrived, and I felt a range of emotions—excited for our day yet not sure how to handle saying goodbye, not knowing how he would react. Our day went beautifully, and we had so much fun playing miniature golf. As we drove back to his placement, I started to feel a bit anxious, but I kept my feelings to myself. I imagined that we would get out of the car, and he would give me a big hug and thank me for everything. I would tell him how much I was going to miss him, and then I would drive happily away. This did not happen.

When I put my car in park, I got out of the car and went over to help him out. He got out, did not look at me, and stomped away into his temporary home without even looking back. I was absolutely stunned. My lack of experience did not prepare me for this reaction on his part, though today it makes perfect sense. I got in my car and cried all the way home, dealing with incredible feelings of guilt. I thought about how I was just one more person to leave him and let him down. That was a hard lesson to learn, but now I can find some comfort in the idea that he might remember me as someone who cared about him and treated him with kindness during a turbulent time in his young life.

Evaluation

The final phase of the planned change process is **evaluation**, which helps social workers focus on the important step of **evaluating their effectiveness** as a social work professional. At the conclusion of our work with clients, there are generally three possibilities: (a) The client is better off, (b) there is no change in the client, or (c) the client is worse off than when they came in for services. But we will not know this unless we take the time to evaluate our work with clients so that we can have good data on what works and what does not work in terms of our interventions. Even though evaluation is often viewed as the final stage of the planned change process, evaluation should be conducted throughout. This is one way that social workers ensure that they are assessing their effectiveness with client systems of all sizes. Evaluating policies, programs, and practice interventions is an ethical principle that is outlined in the NASW Code of Ethics. There are a few ways for social workers to engage in evaluation work:

- Evaluate their work with clients on an individual basis.

- Engage in program evaluation work to help an organization evaluate its program effectiveness.

- Work on research projects (as a researcher or research assistant) that have the potential for publication and to further knowledge in the social work discipline.

Major Theoretical Perspectives and Practice Models Used in Social Work

When social work majors earn their degree, they learn about the importance of theories and how they should inform one's social work practice. What is a theory or a theoretical perspective? A **theory** can be defined as "a generalized set of ideas that describe and explain our knowledge of the world in an organized way" (Payne, 2014, p. 3), while a **perspective** is "a view or lens through which to observe and interpret the world" (Birkenmaier & Berg-Weger, 2017, p. 24). Theories help social workers work by providing them with a framework or a lens for how to approach their work with clients. **Theorizing** is something that all humans engage in to understand and make sense of human behavior and the phenomena we encounter in our daily lives. People have theories about all kinds of things such as health and weight loss, how to make a romantic relationship work, the best way to raise children, what makes an effective leader, and so on. Established theories that are used within disciplines like social work are supported by empirical research evidence; thus, they evolve over time as new knowledge develops.

Social work **practice models** are how social workers implement theories. For example, crisis intervention practice models are informed by crisis intervention theory, which has been evaluated and validated by empirical research. Social work has its own theories and relies on theories from other disciplines such as sociology, psychology, biology, ecology, and anthropology. It is import-

IMG 3.6

ant to keep in mind that all theoretical approaches have their strengths and weaknesses. The complete list of social work theoretical perspectives and practice models used by social workers is too lengthy to include them all here. Because theory is covered in depth in other social work courses, the theories and models included in Table 3.3 are meant to serve as an overview and introduction.

TABLE 3.3   Summary of Theoretical/Practice Models used in Social Work

Theory/Practice Models	Major Focus
Problem-solving model	Uses a logical approach to cases that involve identifying the problem, deciding on a plan of action, implementing the action plan, and modifying the plan as needed
Solution-focused approaches	A future-oriented approach that focuses heavily on assisting clients identify the goals they would like to achieve and the strengths and resources they possess to achieve those goals
Strengths perspective	Rather than placing problems and deficits at the center of the helping process, argues that social workers should focus heavily on clients' strengths, resources, and capacities to motivate clients and facilitate change
Empowerment perspective	Focused on helping marginalized individuals, groups, and communities gain the personal and political power they need to improve their lives
Person-in-environment perspective	Instead of viewing clients in a vacuum, views clients within their larger social environment and strongly endorse the theory that there is a dynamic and reciprocal relationship in which (a) clients have an impact on their social environment and (b) the larger social environment has an impact on clients
General systems theory	Based on the idea that systems are made up of interrelated parts that dynamically influence each other and has enabled social workers to understand families and organizations as systems
Ecological systems perspective	Outlines numerous concepts that are useful for social workers in understanding the relationship between people and their environment such as adaptation, life stressors, coping mechanisms, power dynamics, and human relatedness (i.e., a person's ability to develop relationships and attachments)
Life span development theories	Attempts to explain how humans develop and evolve over the course of their life from birth through old age and the challenges that arise during specific developmental stages
Trauma-informed care approach	Appreciates how common trauma is and that violence and victimization can affect psychosocial development and lifelong coping strategies; emphasizes client strengths instead of focusing on pathology; works on building healthy skills rather than simply addressing symptoms
Social justice and human rights perspectives	Strives to end discrimination, oppression, poverty, and other forms of social injustice and engage in antiracism work; asks us to commit to the idea that all human beings have basic human rights, no matter what part of the world they live in.
Anti-oppressive practice approaches	Using a macro lens, asks social workers to provide services to clients in a way that is highly sensitive and egalitarian while also committing to work that seeks to change oppressive practices and systems and reduce structural inequalities in our society

From the Problem-Solving Model to Solution-Focused Approaches

Despite its criticisms, the **medical model** has been central to social work practice since the founding of the profession. The medical model "is an umbrella term for a range of theoretical and therapeutic approaches that focus on problems, symptoms, or deficits of the individual and their possibilities of amelioration through treatment aimed at the individual" (Finn, 2021, p. 153). It does not take the impact of the larger social environment into consideration, and it places the social worker or psychotherapist into the role of sole expert. However, Payne (2021) argues that this approach does have value as "a diagnosis can be very helpful in giving meaning to one's experience of suffering" and "the process of treatment and recovery can lead to profound life changes" (p. 153).

Social work educator **Helen Perlman** is credited with laying a strong foundation for social casework with clients by outlining an approach called the **problem-solving model** in her famous book *Social Casework: A Problem-Solving Process*, published in 1957. Her approach helped social workers to use a logical approach to their cases that involves identifying the problem, deciding on a plan of action, implementing the action plan, and modifying the plan as needed. Perlman's theories

> stood apart from the leading theories of the day, which typically focused on long-term psychotherapy. She argued that in-depth study wasn't always necessary and could even impede progress. The core idea of her approach was that success could be achieved by partializing—or separating into manageable segments—a client's intertwined problems and focusing on one specific issue the client and social worker agreed needed to be resolved at a given time (Deutsch, n.d., para. 6 & 7).

Perlman's problem-solving model laid the groundwork for later practice models such as the **solution-focused approach**, which has gained popularity in recent years within the social work profession. Like the problem-solving approach, one of the tenets of solution-focused approaches is that many clients can achieve progress in a relatively brief amount of time and do not need to be in long-term therapy. However, this approach differs in that the focus is on strengths instead of weaknesses and solutions instead of problems. It is a future-oriented approach that focuses heavily on assisting clients identify the goals they would like to achieve and the strengths and resources they possess to achieve those goals. The **miracle question** can be helpful in helping a client identify their goals: "Suppose while you are sleeping tonight a miracle happens. The miracle is that the problem that has you here talking to me is somehow solved. Only you don't know that because you are asleep. What will you notice different tomorrow morning that will tell you that a miracle has happened?" Solution-focused therapy was founded by two psychotherapists, Steve de Shazer and Insoo Kim Berg in the late 1970s.

The Strengths Perspective and Empowerment Perspective

One of the hallmarks of social work practice is its emphasis on working with client systems using the **strengths perspective**. The founder of the strengths perspective is social work academic **Dennis Saleebey**, author of the book *The Strengths Perspective in Social Work Practice,* which has been published in many editions. Rather than placing problems and deficits at the center of the helping process, the strengths-based approach argues that social workers should focus heavily on clients' strengths, resources, and capacities to motivate clients and facilitate change. The role of the social worker is to **collaborate** with their clients and not be the sole expert. The following principles are important to understanding the strengths perspective (Saleebey, 2013):

- Every individual, family, group, and community has strengths and is resilient.
- Though clients face serious challenges (e.g., trauma, abuse, illness, struggle), these challenges may also present opportunities for growth and change.
- We should assume that we do not know the upper limits of clients' abilities to grow and change and take their aspirations seriously.
- Social workers best serve clients by collaborating with them; clients are experts of their own lives.
- Every environment has resources that can be tapped into.

The **empowerment perspective** relies on many principles that are embedded in the strengths perspective but is primarily focused on helping marginalized individuals, groups, and communities gain the personal and political power they need to improve their lives. Some clients who deal with internalized and/or externalized oppression (or a lack of agency) need support in developing a strong sense of self-efficacy, meaning a belief in their ability to succeed in particular situations. This perspective can be particularly useful when working with people from communities of color who have faced serious oppression in our society due to racial or other forms of discrimination.

Person-in-Environment and Ecosystems Perspectives

Another hallmark of social work practice is its **person-in-environment perspective**. Instead of viewing clients in a vacuum, social workers view clients within their larger social environment and strongly endorse the theory that there is a dynamic and reciprocal relationship where (a) clients have an impact on their social environment and (b) the larger social environment has an impact on clients. This theoretical perspective allows social workers to assess a client's **goodness of fit with their social environment**. It also helps social workers to assess when the target of intervention is the client (e.g., client is in need of therapeutic services) and when the target of intervention is the client's social and/or physical environment (e.g., poverty, lack of resources).

It is fascinating to see how theories develop and build on each other over time. The **ecological systems perspective** was developed by social work academic **Carel Germain** based on two earlier theories—general systems theory and a theory of the ecological environment. **General systems theory** was developed by a biologist, **Ludwig von Bertalanaffy.** This theory is based on the idea that systems are made up of interrelated parts that dynamically influence each other and has enabled social workers to understand families and organizations as systems, for example. A psychologist, **Urie Bronfenbrenner**, developed a theory of the **ecological environment**, which is the idea that human development must be viewed within the context of the individual's relationship with the environment.

Germain combined these two theories and adapted them for the social work profession with her theory of the ecological systems perspective. In 1991, she published a book titled *Human Behavior in the Social Environment: An Ecological View,* in which she describes the nature of relationships between systems as "reciprocal exchanges between entities, or between their elements, in which each changes or otherwise influences the other over time" (p. 16). Germain's theory outlines numerous concepts that are useful for social workers in understanding the relationship between people and their environment such as adaptation, life stressors, coping mechanisms, power dynamics, and human relatedness (i.e., a person's ability to develop relationships and attachments).

Psychological Theories of Life Span Development

It can be very helpful to have a developmental perspective when working with clients and to consider which developmental stage they are in when you are working with them. **Life span development** is "the scientific study of the ways in which people change, as well as stay the same, from conception to death" (Lally & Valentine-French, 2019, p. 9). In other words, life span development theories attempt to explain how humans develop and evolve over the course of their life from birth through old age and the challenges that arise during specific developmental stages.

According to developmental psychologists, development is lifelong and has three major domains—physical (i.e., changes to the physical body), cognitive (i.e., changes in thinking, memory, intelligence, language, etc.), and psychosocial (i.e., changes in emotion, self-perception, and relationships with others; Lally & Valentine-French, 2019, p. 10). The periods of development are typically broken down as follows:

- Prenatal (conception to birth)

- Infancy and toddlerhood (birth to 2 years)

- Early childhood (age 2–6)

- Middle and late childhood (age 6 through puberty)
- Adolescence (onset of puberty to age 18)
- Emerging adulthood (age 18–25)
- Early adulthood (age 25 to 40–45)
- Middle adulthood (age 40–45 to 65)
- Late adulthood (age 65 and over)

Famous developmental theorists include **Jean Piaget**, who developed a theory that includes four stages of cognitive development and **Erik Erikson's** famous theory that includes eight stages of **psychosocial development**, each one with a psychosocial crisis that each person must face.

Trauma-Informed Care

In recent years, the social work profession has elevated the importance of working with clients using a **trauma-informed lens** and using trauma-informed care (TIC) approaches in their work with clients who have a history of trauma. The American Psychological Association (n.d.b.) defines **trauma** as "any disturbing experience that results in significant fear, helplessness, dissociation, confusion, or other disruptive feelings intense enough to have a long-lasting negative effect on a person's attitudes, behavior, and other aspects of functioning. **Traumatic events** include those caused by human behavior (e.g., rape, war, industrial accidents) as well as by nature (e.g., earthquakes) and often challenge an individual's view of the world as a just, safe, and predictable place" (para. 1).

Today's social workers are encouraged to get training on **trauma-informed care practice approaches**, and many social work programs offer coursework on this topic. Levenson (2017) explains that "trauma-informed social workers appreciate how common trauma is, and that violence and victimization can affect psychosocial development and lifelong coping strategies; they emphasize client strengths instead of focusing on pathology, and they work on building healthy skills rather than simply addressing symptoms. TIC delivers services in a manner that recognizes the emotional vulnerability of trauma survivors, and most important, the worker avoids inadvertently repeating dynamics of abusive interactions in the helping relationship" (pp. 106–107). This topic is also covered in Chapter 7.

Social Justice and Human Rights Perspectives

When social workers work with clients with their "macro hat" on, they often use a social justice and human rights lens. As explained in Chapter 1, social justice is one of the six core values of the social work profession and is embedded in the NASW Code of Ethics. **Social justice** has to do with the level of fairness and equality that exists in a society and whether all groups of people have the ability to realize their potential. It also looks at how fairly society distributes resources such as material goods, income and wealth, opportunities, rights, and protections. Chapter 5 is focused on macro-level social work in which social workers are involved in social and policy change work with the goal of advancing social and economic justice. This involves striving "to end discrimination, oppression, poverty, and other forms of social injustice" and engaging in anti-racism work (Preamble, NASW, 2021).

The **human rights perspective** asks us to commit to the idea that all human beings have basic human rights, no matter what part of the world they live in. These are universal freedoms and rights. Much of our thinking about human rights derives from the United Nations (UN) and the world-famous international document, the Universal Declaration of Human Rights, adopted by the UN General Assembly in 1948, after the end of World War II and the genocide of over 6 million Jewish people. The Declaration of Human Rights is the most translated document in the world and outlines two broad categories of human rights:

Economic, social, and cultural rights

- adequate standard of living
- education
- health care
- housing
- water, food, and sanitation
- social security
- decent work, fair wage, and safe working conditions
- taking part in cultural life and enjoying one's culture

Civil and political rights

- right to a life free from torture, slavery, forced labor, or cruel or degrading treatment
- freedom of movement
- liberty and privacy
- equal treatment before the law, fair trial, and presumption of innocence
- freedom of thought, opinion, and expression
- freedom of religion

- freedom from discrimination
- freedom of association and peaceful assembly
- right to vote and participate in public and civic life

Anti-Oppressive Social Work Practice

Anti-oppressive practice (AOP) has gained more prominence in recent years, though according to Morgaine and Capous-Desyllas (2015), the U.S. is late in adopting this approach compared to other European nations such as the United Kingdom, Canada, Australia, and New Zealand. This practice approach is informed by numerous theories such as radical theory, antiracist theory, feminist theory, queer and transgender theory, critical race theory, intersectionality, and structural social work theory (Morgaine & Capous-Desyllas, 2015). One of the criticisms of social work practice, historically and currently, is that it sometimes (intentionally or unintentionally) replicates oppressive practices against marginalized populations and communities of color that are found in larger society. **Oppression** has been defined in various ways by social justice scholars. Mullaly (2010) defines it as occurring when "individuals are denied access to opportunities for self-development or survival; excluded from participating in society; assigned an inferior status based on their social group membership or identity; or lack rights that members of a privileged group take for granted" (as cited in Morgaine and Capous-Desyllas, 2015, p. 19).

Using a macro lens, this model asks social workers to provide services to clients in a way that is highly sensitive and egalitarian while also committing to work that seeks to change oppressive practices and systems and reduce structural inequalities in our society. This approach asks social workers to be more engaged in macro-level social work practice and to promote social justice. Morgaine and Capous-Desyllas (2015) outline five key concepts of AOP:

- Engaging in **critical self-reflection** on issues related to one's various intersectional social identities, privileges associated with one's identities, power dynamics, and biases

- **Assessing client's experience of oppression** (e.g., listening and understanding client's lived experiences with oppression)

- **Empowering participants** with "the tools and skills to address cultural, structural, and personal barriers that prevent them from gaining control over their lives" (p. 25)

- **Working in partnership** with clients in the change process (social workers as collaborator, not expert)

- **Maintaining minimal intervention** and not engaging in practices that are overly intrusive or coercive; social workers should not serve as agents of social control

Chapter Summary

Generalist social work practice includes a generalized set of knowledge, values, and skills or competencies that can be applied by social workers across a wide variety of work settings and client populations from the micro to the macro level. Students who are enrolled in undergraduate social work programs are being prepared for generalist social work practice, while graduate programs in social work prepare students for advanced, and more specialized, practice. Chapter 3 outlines the nice competencies or skills that social workers must have (according to the CSWE) and the various roles that social workers take on at the micro, mezzo, and macro level. The heart of social work practice is the planned change process, which has five phases: engagement, assessment and planning, intervention, termination, and evaluation. It is crucial for social workers to gain competency in each of these phases since they are all critical to working successfully with client systems. While in school, social work students are taught that theory should inform their social work practice. Theories help social workers work by providing them with a framework or a lens for how to approach their work with clients. Social work practice models are how social workers implement theories. The theories that social workers rely on in their practice vary by the field and work setting. There are some general theories (e.g., strengths perspective, ecological systems, social justice) that most social workers rely on regardless of the practice setting, while other theories tend to be used by social workers in certain specializations (e.g., psychodynamic theories used by social Morgaine and Capous-Desyllas workers in clinical practice).

Discussion Questions

1. A major focus of this chapter is to understand generalist social work practice. How would you explain this to someone else using the three major components?

2. The five phases of the planned change process are engagement, assessment and planning, intervention, termination, and evaluation. Which of these phases can you see yourself doing competently and which ones seem intimidating? Why is this the case?

3. The second phase of the planned change process is assessment and planning, which has a strong focus on goal setting. Think about a goal you would like to set for yourself and practice writing it using the SMART model.

4. Google ecomaps to learn more about how they are used in social work practice. Then make your own ecomap. What takeaways do you have about your social world as it looks currently? Do you think this can be a useful assessment tool when working with clients during the assessment and planning phase of the planned change process?

5. This chapter explained why theories are used to inform social work practice. Select one of the theories or practice models described in this chapter. What are the strengths and weaknesses of this theory as you imagine applying it to a client?

References

American Psychological Association (n.d.a.). *Definition of crisis intervention*. APA Dictionary of Psychology. https://dictionary.apa.org/crisis-intervention

American Psychological Association (n.d.b.). *Definition of trauma*. APA Dictionary of Psychology. https://dictionary.apa.org/trauma

Birkenmaier, J., & Berg-Weger, M. (2017). *The practice of generalist social work*. Routledge.

Chang, V. N., Decker, C. L., & Scott, S. T. (2018). *Developing helping skills: A step-by-step approach to competency* (3rd ed.). Cengage.

Council on Social Work Education. (2022). *2022 educational policy and accreditation standards.* https://www.cswe.org/accreditation/standards/2022-epas/

Deutsch, S. (n.d.). *Helen Harris Perlman*. http://ssacentennial.uchicago.edu/features/features-perlman.shtml

Finn, J. L. (2021). *Just practice: A social justice approach to social work*. Oxford University Press.

Germain, C. B. (1991). *Human behavior in the social environment: An ecological view*. Columbia University Press.

Jansson, B. S. (2008). *Becoming an effective policy advocate: From policy practice to social justice* (5th ed.). Brooks/Cole.

Krysik, J. L. (2018). *Research for effective social work practice*. New York: Routledge.

Lally, M., & Valentine-French, S. (2019). *Lifespan development: A psychological perspective* (2nd ed.). http://dept.clcillinois.edu/psy/LifespanDevelopment.pdf

Levenson, J. (2017). Trauma-informed social work practice. *Social Work, 62*(2), 105–113.

Morgaine, K., & Capous-Desyllas, M. (2015). *Anti-oppressive social work practice: Putting theory into action*. SAGE.

National Association of Social Workers. (2013). *Standards for social work case management.* https://www.socialworkers.org/LinkClick.aspx?fileticket=acrzqmEfhlo%3D&portalid=0

National Association of Social Workers. (2021). *Code of Ethics of the National Association of Social Workers.* https://www.socialworkers.org/About/Ethics/Code-of-Ethics/Code-of-Ethics-English/Social-Workers-Ethical-Responsibilities-to-Clients

Payne, M. (2014). *Modern social work theory* (4th ed). Lyceum Books.

Perlman, H. H. (1957). *Social casework: A problem-solving process.* Chicago: The University of Chicago Press.

Ritter, J. A. (2022). *Social work policy practice: Changing our community, nation, and the world* (3rd ed.). Cognella.

Roberts, A. R., & Ottens, A. J. (2005). The seven-stage crisis intervention model: A road map to goal attainment, problem solving, and crisis resolution. *Brief Treatment and Crisis Intervention, 5*(4), 329–339.

Saleebey, D. (2013). *The strengths perspective in social work practice* (6th ed). Allyn and Bacon.

United Nations. (1948). *Universal Declaration of Human Rights.* https://www.un.org/en/about-us/universal-declaration-of-human-rights

Credits

CHAPTER 4

Social Justice, Equity, Diversity, and Inclusion in Social Work

Julie Clockston

Learning Objectives

After reading this chapter, students will be able to understand and/or define the following:

- Social justice, equity, diversity, and inclusion (SJEDI)
- The current political climate surrounding issues of racism and SJEDI in the United States
- The contributions of important BIPOC (Black, Indigenous, People of Color) leaders within social work
- Standards set by the National Association of Social Workers (NASW) and the Council on Social Work Education (CSWE) that relate to SJEDI within social work practice
- Social identities and intersectionality
- The different forms of power and privilege in our society
- Microaggressions, discrimination, marginalization, and oppression
- Cultural competence and cultural humility
- Anti-oppressive social work practice
- Culturally responsive social work practice

Students should also understand the discrimination and oppression that individuals and some groups face based on their social identities such as the following:

- Race/ethnicity (racism)
- Socioeconomic status (classism)

- Gender and gender identity (sexism or sex-based discrimination, transphobia)

- Sexual orientation (homophobia)

- Age (ageism)

- Disability status (ableism)

- Immigration status (xenophobia)

- Religion and spirituality (religious discrimination)

SOCIAL WORKER SPOTLIGHT:
Julie Clockston, DSW, LCSW, Cert Ed

My name is Julie Clockston, I am a licensed clinical social worker (LCSW) and assistant professor in the Social Work Department at the Metropolitan State University of Denver, where I am an alumnae of the Bachelor of Science in Social Work (BSSW) program and the Masters of Social Work (MSW) program. I am an adjunct professor, doctoral mentor, and curriculum designer in the summer social work program at Smith College in Northampton, Massachusetts. I love being a social work professional. I want to share with you that social work is a very diverse profession, and there is a place in social work for you.

At MSU Denver, I am the social work department's DEI co-coordinator and Colorado Child Welfare Scholars Consortium BSSW Faculty Representative. I work with students from diverse backgrounds in the BSSW and MSW programs. I am a former president of the NASW Colorado chapter 2019–2022. At the end of this chapter, you will find my author's positionality statement, in which I discuss my social location and intersectional identities. This year is my 30th year working in public service and leadership. Throughout my career, I have worked in a variety of professional trades, human service, and social work positions. I have focused on cosmetology, early childhood education, therapeutic foster care, real estate, adult education, and the mental health and disabilities community. I absolutely love being a professor and bringing social work values and ethics to education.

Regardless of where my career lands, I find that I am doing the work of a social worker. My passion is what I call "my heart-set." I have an affinity for the disability community. For over 3 decades, I have worked with individuals living with cognitive or developmental disabilities, also known as intellectual disabilities (DD/ID). Some of my clients and patients have had more than one disability diagnosis simultaneously. This is called a comorbid diagnosis. I have worked through the years in many capacities with the disability community. I have worked as an employment coach to help individuals with disabilities maintain their employment. I have worked as a supportive living service consultant to help individuals with disabilities maintain various aspects of independence. I have worked as a residential service professional to help individuals and families with housing and deinstitutionalized community-based types of living. I have also been a strong advocate and disabilities specialist. One of the niche areas of disabilities I am passionate about distinctively is parents with disabilities, more specifically cognitive, developmental, and intellectual disabilities characteristics and diagnosis. I have worked as an advocate, educator, professional trainer, and family preservationist doing competency-based parent assessments for parents with cognitive disabilities and their families struggling to maintain parenting rights and family unification.

The disability community is often under-researched or examined through an ableist worldview. It is important to recognize that research has documented that many parents with cognitive disabilities interconnect with professionals such as social workers, educators, and human service professionals, who lack knowledge in disabilities and parents with disabilities. Social work warrants an increase in knowledge. One of the areas I am most excited about is my connection with The Association for Successful Parenting (TASP), for which I was the president from 2019–2022. In addition, I worked with the education committee to develop training for professionals who work with parents with cognitive disabilities. At MSU Denver, I have had the great opportunity to develop disabilities courses for both the BSSW and MSW programs.

Gaining knowledge in this area can help to increase effective practice and policy. Through my research, I have gained an understanding of the educational and training needs of the social work and human service professionals who work with individuals diagnosed with DD/ID. It has helped in designing educational courses and professional development to bring disability awareness, illuminate ableism and disablism, and in turn equip individuals diagnosed with cognitive disabilities with better parenting skills. Learning that individuals can parent with appropriate support and services brought awareness to me as a social worker. It changed my perception and understanding about the disproportionate overrepresentation of parents with disabilities in the legal system, child protective services, and poverty if disablism is combated and ableism is dismantled.

I am a mental health and disability normalizer. For me, this means that I strive to dismantle mental health and disability stigmas. People with disabilities are not the problem. Ableism, disablism, and barriers created by society are the issue. As a normalizer, I have chosen to be vulnerable and share that I am diagnosed with primarily unseen disabilities. I consider myself blessed that my parents instilled in me the value of education, information, and learning when I was growing up. I realize that not everyone has the same support system that I just described. In high school, my guidance counselor advised me that I was not college material and should pursue a trade. When I asked what steps I needed to take to attend college, her reply was "Nothing, you're not college material; pick a trade." My high school counselor's behavior is an example of racism and ableism. Regardless of her intention, the impact was a direct attempt to devalue me, and it succeeded for a while. For a time, I accepted what she said. The notion of being incompetent that was implanted in my mind confounded my self-esteem and became a significant challenge. However, I overcame the challenges and achieved every academic level that I set my intention to complete.

IMG 4.1

The United States is one of the most racially and ethnically diverse nations on earth; thus, social workers need to have a strong skill set in working with people who with different backgrounds, lived experiences, and social identities. Recent data from the U.S. Census Bureau showed that roughly four of 10 Americans identify with a race or ethnic group other than White and that the 2010 to 2020 decade is the first time in U.S. history in which the White population declined in numbers (Frey, 2020). Demographers predict that this trend will continue over the next several decades and that Whites will be in the minority in the coming years, perhaps by 2045 or 2050. A writer for the Brookings Institution notes, "Racial and ethnic diversity will be an essential ingredient of America's future. The mostly white baby boomer culture that defined the last half of the 20th century is giving way to a more multihued, multicultural nation" (Frey, 2020, para. 24).

Individuals decide to study social work for a plethora of reasons. Often it is a personal quest to understand oneself and the desire to help others flows from the springs of passion within their souls. Sometimes students enter social work with a strong desire to be a part of the change process, to improve the lives of others, and sometimes it is out of love. However, Day (2009) discusses love and argues that "love is not enough. Social welfare and the profession of social work are much more complex, and we must not let fairy tales blind us" (p. 1). When students first enter social work, they are typically determined to help people at the **micro (individual)** level of social work, where it is essential to be culturally competent and to operate from a place of cultural humility. But students quickly understand how critical it is to engage at the **mezzo** and **macro** levels of social work, which includes social and policy change efforts. Social workers are called to advocate and to work to enact change for marginalized populations, and a fundamental ethical obligation of all social workers is to work toward social justice. Chapter 5 highlights a number of important recent social movements focused on racial justice (e.g., systemic racism, police brutality), LGBTQ+ rights (e.g., same-sex marriage, hate crimes), and women's rights (e.g., sexual harassment in the workplace, sexual violence). These social movements have been incredibly successful in elevating these issues into the national discourse.

 Power, **privilege**, and **oppression** are embedded in our social, economic, and political institutions, and the social profession is no exception. Power can be weaponized as love's evil side. When the social work profession fails to use anti-oppressive and antiracist practices intentionally, it has the power to dominate members of vulnerable groups and replicate the oppressive practices of the wider society. The social work profession is currently being called on to address racism both inside and outside the profession and to reckon with its history of using methods of social exclusion and social control, which is highlighted in Chapter 2 of this book. As a social worker, empowerment is an action that brings about strength. When incorporated with anti-oppressive and antiracist practices, it works to move individuals and groups toward **liberation**. It is important for social workers, regardless of where one's career is positioned in the system, to be social justice activists.

Social Justice, Equity, Diversity, and Inclusion Defined

Social justice, equity, diversity, and inclusion (SJEDI) in the context of social work are foundational concepts crucial for advancing social work practice and societal progress. **Social justice** is a multilayered and dense term. Despite its importance in for those engaged in DEI work and social work, much of it has a Western developmental context (Morgaine & Capous-Desyllas, 2020). Social workers need to apply social justice frameworks through a critically and culturally aware point of view. NASW (2021a) defines social justice as social change and the equitable distribution of wealth, opportunities, and privileges within a society "on issues of poverty, unemployment, discrimination, and other forms of social injustice" (para.19). It is an underlying value in social work. Ethical principles are fundamental to social work (NASW, 2021a). **Equity** is a multifaceted concept rooted in distributive justice, ensuring equitable access to opportunities and resources while considering the privileges or hurdles that any individual may have and removing systemic privileges and barriers. (O'Brien, 2011). Togioka et al. (2022), published in the National Institutes of Health (NIH,) describe **diversity** as "varied race, ethnicity, gender, disability, social class, socioeconomic status, sexual orientation, gender identity, primary spoken language, and geographic region" (p. 1). Diversity is also age, physical ability or attributes, religious or ethical value system, national origin, and political beliefs. Finally, **inclusion** is focused on operationalizing action through the steps taken to recognize, acknowledge, and make the most of each person's distinctive identities and viewpoints to make everyone feel included, valued, and supported (Brooks-LaSure, 2022).

The social and political climate in the United States is complex and complicated. The policy decisions of yesterday and today have created a set of systems that are often harmful to many groups living in the United States. Many individuals believe these systems to be dysfunctional and the fallout to be unintentional, but the systems in operation were set up in a way that often thwart SJEDI for all. Any type of harmful or discriminatory behavior, whether intentional or unintentional, will have an impact. When harmful actions are based on the skin color, race, or ethnicity of individuals or groups of people, the result is individual and institutional racism (Randall, 2007). Social workers need to be aware of the standards set by the NASW and the Council on Social Work Education (CSWE) that relate to SJEDI within social work practice.

NASW Code of Ethics

NASW is the profession's largest organized membership organization of social workers globally. According to the NASW's (2021a) Code of Ethics, social workers are charged with advancing social justice, as stated in ethical standard 6.01:

> Promote the general welfare of society, from local to global levels, and the development of people, their communities, and their environments. Social workers should advocate for living conditions conducive to the fulfillment of basic human needs and should promote social, economic, political, and cultural values and institutions that are compatible with the realization of *social justice*.

The NASW Code of Ethics clearly outlines that social workers have an ethical obligation to engage in social and political action. It is the business of social workers to pursue policy, procedures, and systemic change to uphold betterment for *all* people. The goal should be for social workers to strive to ensure equality and access to necessary resources. Social workers are called on to dismantle policies that are barriers and prevent unequal access to employment and other opportunities essential for humans to have their basic needs met. Following the Code of Ethics is no light call. Action steps can take place in various ways to enhance and support changes in legislative lawmaking and the advancement of social justice (NASW, 2021).

In the third section of the NASW (2021a) Code of Ethics, titled "Ethical Principles Value: Social Justice," social workers are called on to challenge social injustice:

> Social workers pursue social change, particularly with and on behalf of vulnerable and oppressed individuals and groups of people. Social workers' social change efforts are focused primarily on issues of poverty, unemployment, discrimination, and other forms of social injustice. These activities seek to promote sensitivity to and knowledge about oppression and cultural and ethnic diversity. Social workers strive to ensure access to needed information, services, and resources; equality of opportunity; and meaningful participation in decision-making for all people.

It is noteworthy that on June 17, 2021, NASW apologized for its role in racist practices and provided several historical examples such as progressive-era social workers who ran segregated settlement houses; social workers who worked for women's suffrage but blocked efforts to grant Black people the right to vote; social workers who removed Native American children from their homes and placed them into boarding schools; and social workers who were involved with the Japanese internment camps during World War II. NASW (2021b) shared their action plan and outlined its commitment to

> ending racism in the social work field and working with strong coalition partners to dismantle oppressive and racist policies, systems, and practices across our country. Social workers are called by our Code of Ethics to fight injustice in all its forms and to honor the dignity and worth of all people. While we at times have fallen short of this ideal, our profession has recently reinvigorated and expanded its racial equity mandate (p. 1).

CSWE Education Policy and Accreditation Standards

The Council on Social Work Education (CSWE) is the sole accrediting agency in the United States and supports social work by setting quality standards for social work education programs in higher education. The latest CSWE (2022) Educational Policy and Accreditation Standards include an important section titled "Anti-Racism, Diversity, Equity, and Inclusion (ADEI)," in which social work programs are being asked to include ADEI content in their curriculum very intentionally in order to prepare students for practice:

> Social work programs integrate anti-racism, diversity, equity, and inclusion (ADEI) approaches across the curriculum. Programs provide the context through which students learn about their positionality, power,

privilege, and difference and develop a commitment to dismantling systems of oppression, such as racism, that affect diverse populations. Programs recognize the pervasive impact of White supremacy and privilege and prepare students to have the knowledge, awareness, and skills necessary to engage in anti-racist practice. The dimensions of diversity, equity, and inclusion are understood as the intersectionality of multiple factors including but not limited to age, caste, class, color, culture, disability and ability, ethnicity, gender, gender identity and expression, generational status, immigration status, legal status, marital status, political ideology, race, nationality, religion/spirituality, sex, sexual orientation, and tribal sovereign status. (p. 16)

▎ The Role of Identity and Intersectionality

Merriam-Webster's (n.d) defines *identity* as "the distinguishing character or personality of an individual, the relation established by psychological identification." It is important for the social worker to pause in the spirit of cultural humility and reflect upon the deep suffering to many groups of people caused by oppression. A significant number of individuals and groups in society suffer oppression and abuse because of their social location and intersectional social identities. Social workers are asked to reflect on their social location as well as the social location of their clients. **Social location** can be defined as "the combination of factors including gender, race, social class, age, ability, religion, sexual orientation, and geographic location" (National Council on Family Relations, 2019). When intersecting identities overlap, individuals and groups are known as doubly or triply vulnerable (Clockston, 2019). Some identities that we hold afford us privilege (e.g., being male, White, heterosexual), while other identities place us in the nonprivileged category (e.g., being female, person of color, LGBTQ+; see section on "Power and Privilege" later in this chapter).

Over 30 years ago, Kimberlé Crenshaw, a professor, policy and legal scholar at Columbia Law School, and cofounder of the African American Policy Forum, coined the term **intersectionality**. She initially used this term as a method of explaining the oppression that African American Black women face. Intersectionality is a lens used to see where power intersects, clashes, and interconnects. It takes into account that individuals are not typically affected by one issue, but as multidimensional identities intersect, people may experience issues of racism, gender, and class. Today, in its 3rd decade, intersectionality has broadened and is widely used by many to explain the various parts of self and how systems of oppression intersect to generate unique distinguishable experiences for those with various personal and social identities.

Crenshaw describes the term as identifying overlapping patterns of benefits and drawbacks that will vary depending on the situation. The idea that racism and discrimination look the same for all people flattens our conception of how people experience discrimination. People often believe that Black women and Black men both experience racism the same, or that Latina and White women experience sexism the same. But their experience will not be the same due to the way that race and gender intersect. Intersection is not a number of different dynamics; it is about the human experience that results from the intersections one holds (Crenshaw, 1989, 2017).

4.1   PRACTICE ACTIVITY

What Is Your Intersectional Identity?

One of the most important skills that social workers must learn to engage with is self-awareness on a deeper level. Often, social workers want to support individuals, groups, and families across the micro-, mezzo-, and macrosystem levels, but it is essential that social work professionals get to know themselves. This exercise aims to help you think through your intersectional identity and in which areas you are privileged. It will also help illuminate in which areas you are in the nonprivileged categories.

*Trigger warning: Some of these questions may seem simple on the surface. However, for many, they will be thought-provoking and may evoke emotions. Please understand that you may not have the answers to all of these questions for a variety of reasons. The number of unanswered questions is not in any way indicative of you or your self-worth. Please take care of yourself. Seek the mental, emotional, physical, and spiritual support that is necessary for you.

Please review Figure 4.1 and answer the following reflection questions:

1. Where do you come from? Who are your people?

2. What does it mean to claim your race, class, gender, and sexual orientation? Are there risks?

3. Which parts of your identity do you emphasize, and which parts do you underemphasize? Why?

4. Whose ancestral land do you currently occupy?

   o This map of Native Land is one of the more comprehensive maps available: https://native-land.ca/.

   o The Native Languages site offers a breakdown by state, with contact information for local tribes: http:// www.native-languages.org/.

5. For how many generations has your family been in the country you live in now? By what circumstances did the first relative in your family arrive? When did they become citizens? Was this difficult or easy?

6. Is your citizenship important to you? Why or why not?

7. How did the place you grew up come into existence? Where do you live now?

8. Do you maintain your family's culture and history of origin? If so, why? If not, why not?

9. Using categories listed under social identity, how do your social locators provide you with privilege? How do they deny you privilege?

10. What relationships do you have with persons who are marginalized/targeted through social location?

11. Look in your phone and note the identities of the first 10 people you have in your texts and/or calls. What patterns do you notice?

12. Look at photos you have of yourself with friends and family; what patterns emerge here?

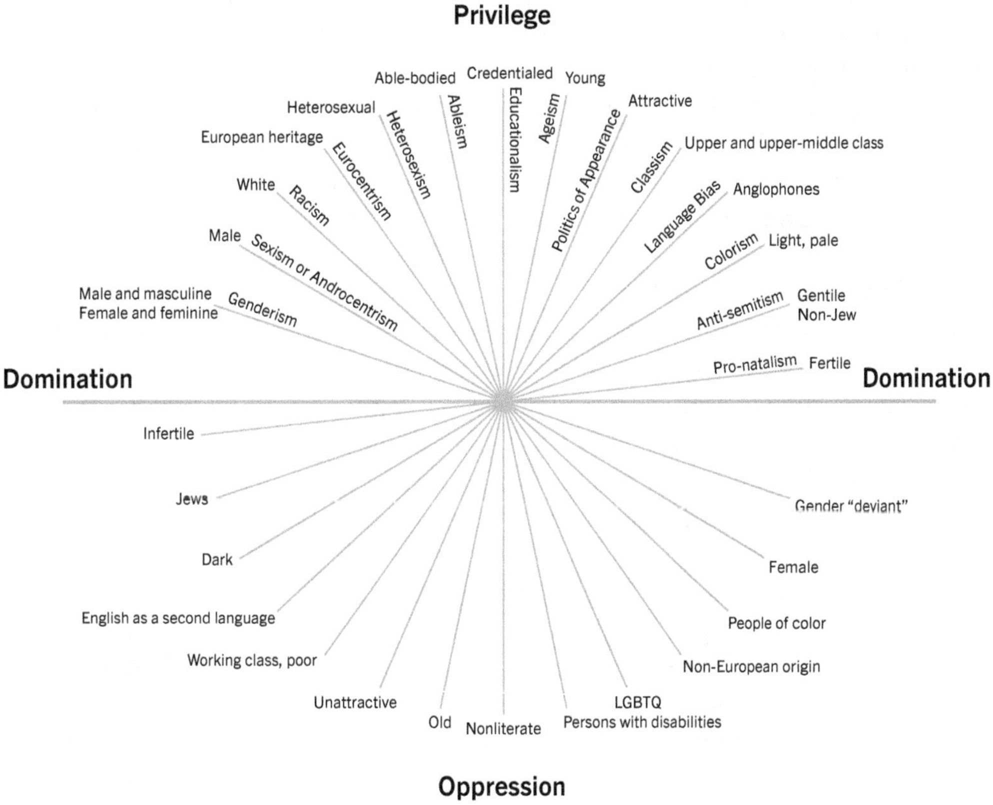

FIGURE 4.1   Intersectionality.

▌ Power and Privilege

The systemic issues that marginalized populations face often result from fully operational and intentional systems. These systems uplift power and privilege while simultaneously oppressing. The concept of *power* is not inherently negative. It is a multifaceted term with a force that typically comes in one form: *power over, power to, and power from* (Kloos et al., 2012). **Power over** is the capacity to dominate, govern, command orders, influence, coerce, and control resources. This form of power runs hand in hand with dominant forms of privilege. Dominant identities that benefit the most from "power-over" are White-identified, nondisabled, cisgender men, Christian religion, middle to upper class, and property- and asset-owning individuals. They include middle-aged and English language speakers and are individuals and groups granted a higher status of privilege when they have one or more of the identifiers mentioned (Jason et al., 2019; McIntosh, 2020).

There are multiple types of privileges in society. Most people have some form of privilege, but the individuals and groups with the most power in our society tend to hold *White privilege, male privilege, nondisabled privilege, and wealth privilege.* These are **unearned privileges** that society gives to those with certain social identities, and people benefit whether they agree to or not. People with substantial amounts of privilege do not have to think about the inequities and inequalities pervasive across all areas of society. According to the critical race theory (CRT) perspective in the legal literature, racial preferences and prejudices are ingrained in current law and policy. Many social workers are fully aware of a tendency of harsher punishments for the same offense among Black people compared to White people in terms of criminal justice.

Deeply rooted, **White privilege** is enmeshed in the fabric of society. Regardless of how awful one may believe *White supremacy* is, *White privilege* coexists and is often accepted without consciousness. For example, many White-identified people believe that racism and discrimination have been eradicated by law and that this translates to equal rights for all people (Desmond & Emirbayer, 2010; Gallagher, 2009; Hudson, 2020; Marson & Dovyak, 2022). The ideas that underpin this presumption are privileged blindness, color-blindness, and oppression blindness. Some people refuse or block accepting that oppression is real. It is almost as if they cannot see beyond their own privileges. Privilege, color-blindness, and oppression blindness are pervasive in society (Bonilla-Silva, 2006; Collins, 2004, 2019; Roberts et al., 2020).

Male privilege is defined as the patriarchal ideology that being a male affords one or more opportunities to socioeconomic power, political power, women's bodies, and work opportunities in some societies (Myers, 2013). It is essential to understand that not all men are allowed the same privilege based on the other intersecting identities that they hold, such as marginalized race, ethnicity, physical appearance, class, socioeconomic status, and disability (Johnson, 2018).

In American society and many other societies, nondisabled privilege results in ableism. **Nondisabled privilege** refers to the unearned benefits afforded to individuals who are not disability identified or enabled. Nondisabled privilege stems from societal assumptions. The first assumption is that normal is right. A normal person is identified as someone who can verbally speak, hear, see, and walk without substantial physical, cognitive, social, emotional, or neurodivergence. The second assumption is that a disability is an issue or problem because it is not what society perceives as normal and, therefore, cannot meet the expectations that society has deemed normal. Ableism is rooted in racism that stems from White supremacist ideologies, which shows up as systemic and structural racism. (Collins, 2023; Kres-Nash, 2016). Some people have disabilities that are visible and others have disabilities that are not as easily seen by others. It is important to note that some individuals, due to barriers and discrimination in society, may experience **disability oppression**.

For many individuals and communities, wealth gaps are pervasive and create a deficit in access to privilege. **Wealth privilege**, also known as financial, economic, money, or rich privileged, is defined as having a level of wealth that gives people advantages that others may not have. Individuals with low- to middle-defined incomes hit what is called a wealth ceiling. This ceiling tends to pigeon-hole people into certain class structures within society. In theory, people classified as poor or persons of color are thought to have the same human rights, legal protections, and opportunities as those with high wealth and class status. However, in practice, it is often unattainable because they have no means to exercise those rights (Bridges, 2019). Wealth privilege is often a byproduct of White supremacist systemic and institutionalized oppressive structures of power. Individuals often face oppressive barriers to obtaining wealth. Historically, family privilege affords privileges to those in White, cisgender, dominant Eurocentric societies (Letiecq, 2019). Every aspect of life is impacted by wealth privilege, including one's capacity to accumulate assets and how one is viewed by one's peers.

What Are the Barriers and Obstacles to SJEDI?

Because social work has a mission of social justice, and social workers are called on to engage in advancing social justice and equality for all groups of people in society, it is important to understand the many barriers that get in the way of having a fair and just society so that all people have the same access to opportunity. It is important to understand the differences and connections between the role of microaggressions, discrimination, marginalization, and oppression that negatively impact many people in society. Finally, it is vital to understand the various forms of oppression that exist in society such as racism, xenophobia, ageism, sexism, homophobia, classism, ableism, and religious discrimination.

Microaggressions

In 1970, Chester Pierce, a Harvard Medical School psychiatrist, coined the term **microaggression** to characterize the subliminal slurs he saw exchanged from White students to their African American/Black counterparts. In 2007, Columbia University psychologist Derald Wing Sue illuminated the concept in his published works, and the phrase experienced a rebirth (Sue et al., 2007). The construct has since sparked much discussion, investigation, and argument (Tulshyan, 2022). Experts argue that there is nothing *micro* about the damage that microaggressions do to the souls of those they target nor the reinforcement of evils on the mind, whether conscious or unconscious. In addition, microaggressions often reinforce the implicit and conscious biases of those who deliver a microaggression.

Some microaggressions are unspoken, such as a BIPOC person being followed around a store because of an implicit bias that they will steal or the use of facial expressions and eye-rolling to shut down or discount BIPOC or marginalized people who express feelings or correct their gender pronouns. The silent treatment is a control tactic that is often used by turning to avoiding someone or excluding and avoiding them altogether—scheduling meetings or events that conflict with religious observances or obligations with no exception—not making an effort to consider the dietary restrictions of others. Excluding certain people from work on front-facing projects is another example, as is not hiring a physically disabled person to report front and center on television but use their work behind the scenes.

Microaggressions are insidious and so pervasive in society that they are psychologically and emotionally abusive. Under the term *microaggression*, there is a spectrum of abuses. One common abuse is **micro-invalidation**. This is best described as an effort to belittle or dismiss the experiences of someone who belongs to a marginalized group. Micro-invalidation, for instance, occurs when you refute what a BIPOC peer has expressed by interrupting to emphasize that their experience wasn't discrimination or by centering your own experiences. In addition, microaggressions convey the message that you aren't good enough. What can be even more hurtful and destructive is when the deliverer of the aggression is made aware of the harm they caused and they refuse to accept that there is a better way to do it.

Author's Personal Experience with Microaggressions

I'll speak for myself as a Black woman. Microaggressions send and reinforce the message of "othering." They are really a whole mind trip. Microaggressions are sometimes hard to explain and can be hard to pinpoint because they are so widely accepted and watered down to be palatable. For me, as a Black woman, they are a teardown and contribute to imposter syndrome, fear of failure, and a host of other harmful thoughts and emotions. I have experienced countless microaggressive cases of abuse in my lifetime. They are like tentacles stretched to my psyche, my soul. While working on my doctoral degree, I had a T-shirt expressing self-encouragement. The inscription said, "Striving to be Dr. Julie Clockston, LCSW." I wore this shirt on days that were good and days that I struggled. One day in particular, a few months before I completed my dissertation research, an individual in line at the store turned around, read my shirt, and asked me if I bought it at "The Goodwill." Two things intersected for me at this moment. My race and my disability are both stigmatized and marginalized.

What is a microaggression that you have experienced, witnessed, or said to someone? Check in with yourself. How are you thinking and feeling? What are your internal beliefs? How can dynamic change take place to dismantle the pervasiveness of these forms of aggression?

Discrimination

In daily life, **discrimination** and **discriminatory practices** are a reality. Discrimination is unjust, prejudicial treatment toward individuals and groups based on many categories and characteristics of race, physical and mental ability or disabilities, gender, age, class, sexual orientation, socioeconomic status, and education. Values are placed on categories and quantify the measure of worth that individuals and groups of people hold. One of the most common forms of discrimination occurs in the workplace when POC, women, or LGBTQ individuals are not treated fairly and are either not hired or fired because of their identity. Many laws are there to mitigate and prevent discrimination (e.g., Civil Rights Act of 1964); however, due to societal power, oppression, and privilege dynamics, discrimination continues to happen (American Psychological Association, 2022).

Marginalization and Oppression

Marginalization is a concept that describes the treatment of an individual or group in society as worthless, insignificant, and social shunning or exclusion by systemic oppression that results in **othering**. It is an act of denial toward some groups from inclusion in certain areas of society or access to information and areas of society that dominant populations have access to (Buzzanell, 2015; Gibson

& Martin, 2019). We may think about certain groups of people in society who have been historically, and currently, *pushed to the margins* and not allowed to enjoy the same rights and privileges as other groups of people.

Oppression can be described as a trap or cage: a system of interconnected institutional barriers that make escape impossible. While every person may encounter isolated cases of prejudice or discrimination, oppression refers to this network of limitations that reinforces itself (Frye, 2003). Systemic oppression is the systematic undercutting and devaluation of individuals and groups of marginalized people that disadvantage and disproportionately affect individuals. It keeps people from receiving and accessing resources necessary to survive and thrive in life and society (Coates et al., 2021). In the poem by the late social justice activist Audre Lorde, she advised society that it is critical not to play what is known as **"Oppression Olympics,"** in that one oppression carries more weight than another. She taught that "there is no hierarchy of oppression" (p. 9). Avoiding the Oppression Olympics can support social workers in their efforts to create a just and equitable society (Aouragh, 2019; Bhopal, 2020; Coaston, 2019; Hampton, 2021; Lorde, 1983; Rogers et al., 2021).

IMG 4.2

White Supremacy and Racism

The ideology of **white supremacy** has been a part of the United States since the very founding of the nation, and the nation continues to grapple with it today. White supremacy has led to a number of horrific and tragic events in U.S. history such as the slavery of Black people, the genocide of Native/Indigenous peoples, the internment of Japanese Americans during World War II, the Jim Crow laws in the South that allowed racial segregation between White and Black people, and laws that have oppressed many who have immigrated to the United States, particularly those from Latin America and Asia. On the positive side, there have been many policy change efforts aimed at protecting the rights of these groups due to the valiant efforts of social movements pushing for change and support from lawmakers with a strong moral compass to help the country move toward equality for all.

According to Marson and Dovyak (2022),

> *White supremacy* is a socio-political reality that sustains variant streams of social injustice to allow innumerable types of oppression. It is founded on a sociopolitical history of projecting biological determinates for which there is no known genetic basis. Social psychology and psychiatry might further trace through the Nuremberg Trials how societies interact to sustain the dynamics of domination and oppression. In fact, the biological and anthropological evidence suggests that racial superiority simply does NOT exist. (p. 5)

Racism encompasses a wide range of actions, beliefs, and social connections. It is a system in which one race maintains power, privilege, and oppression over another through perpetual social structures supporting **racial hierarchy**. Racism is a systemically structured phenomenon that results in dis-equity and dis-equality. Racism manifests through superiority for those who are not racially marginalized and is operational in a variety of forms (Cole, 2019; Love, 2000). Racism shows up in multiple ways, and where there is one form, typically, another form is in operation simultaneously. According to Cole (2019), there are seven coexisting yet distinctive types of racism.

- *Racism in representation* includes widely held cultural beliefs and mainstream and other types of media that frequently depict racial stereotypes. Historically BIPOC people have been portrayed as criminals and victims.

- *Ideology-based racism* relates to stereotypes rooted in racist ideologies and biased societal viewpoints, racial attitudes, mind-sets, world views, and biases.

- *Linguistic racism* is racism that is expressed in the form of coded words with racialized meanings. These words link up with a race of people and perpetuate the degradation of individuals and groups. Some such words are negatively associated with BIPOC individuals and groups such as "ghetto," "thug," and "gangsta."

- *Racism in interaction* is the way in which humans interact with one another and can be harmful on a race-based level. Verbal or physical **hate crimes** are a form of interactional racism. When non-BIPOC individuals call the police on BIPOC people for being in a neighborhood that they don't believe a BIPOC person should be in, this is interactional racism. When a doctor makes the assumption that a patient doesn't have insurance solely on their skin color or race, this is interactional racism.

- *Structural racism*: Historically, racism has plagued society for many generations. Structural racism is a conglomerate of multiple types of racism constructs. This type of racism shows up in every way possible. It is rooted in systems of medical, social, educational, environmental, and other public health and social aspects of society.

- *Systemic racism*: The entire system and process of establishing the United States of America are rooted in colonization and systemic racist worldviews and supremacist values. Systemic racism affects policy, procedures, and law. It is ingrained into the fabric of society. This type of racism is in perpetual operation and necessitates a micro-, mezzo-, and macrosystem-wide movement.

- *The sum of racism:* Racism is prevalent in many ways. It is important for social workers to be aware that racism will not always be easy to detect. Sometimes racism is in operation through covert tactics and methods and can be expressed in tone-deaf or color-blind laws, policies, and decisions that impact BIPOC individuals and communities and cause harm. Racism is often a difficult yet necessary conversation to be had. It begins with having curious, critically reflective conversations to move society toward a more just and equitable society for all.

Xenophobia

When people are prejudiced against people from other countries, it is referred to as xenophobia. The term **immigration status** describes a person's legal standing in the country. Immigrants often give up so much of their lives to find safety, shelter, food, and water and to increase their quality of life, only to arrive at a place of continued oppression. There is often a distinction made between those who are in the United States with legal status and those who are here without legal status. The word *illegal immigrant* is derogatory, degrading, and unacceptable. It is a microaggression that dehumanizes and declassifies certain individuals and groups in U.S. society. Examples of immigrant statuses include U.S. citizenship and legal permanent resident (LPR; "green card holder"). LPR immigration status is garnered through a variety of petitions (i.e., family, employment and self-petition under the violence against women act for all genders, asylee or refugee). The last two are based on conditions in the individual's home country due to human rights violations. Some people have a nonimmigrant status and are allowed to be in the United States on a visa for a designated timeframe, such as attending school or working temporarily. Many individuals live undocumented in the United States, and these individuals are generally under constant oppression. Undocumented individuals live with the vulnerability of experiencing increased hate crimes. They are not in a position of power to obtain services and support for basic needs, and they do not have privileges afforded to them. These individuals suffer from multiple barriers, such as the fear of deportation and separation from family, lack of medical attention, lack of government support or services, and mistreatment when working. They are often taken advantage of with no option for legal recourse.

Author's Note

Despite having origins that go back much further than the United States, Indigenous people did not receive U.S. citizenship until Congress passed the Indian Citizenship Act in 1924 (it would take longer for them to gain the right to vote). Grassroots efforts and coalitions helped to bring about change.

Ageism

Age is a period or length of time that represents how long a person has been alive. In our visual world, it is regularly seen as a set of human developmental characteristics often used to identify and classify people. **Ageism** is real, and it is pervasive in our society. It can negatively impact people across all age ranges. Adults often treat children with a lack of respect due to their age. Older people endure the effects of ageism at a rate of one person in two. Often, ageism presents for older people through their work life. Many are discriminated against in employment, and some are pushed out of their long-term jobs to be replaced by those who are younger. Many implicit bias stereotypes lead to prejudiced ideologies and discriminatory acts against older adults. We know the problem is prevalent, yet it is often hard to pinpoint. Social workers are in continuous need to help combat ageism at the macro level. Policies need activism and research for stakeholders to change the narratives and the devastation of this discriminatory practice.

Sex-Based Discrimination (Including Transphobia)

It is important for social workers to understand the difference between sex, gender, and gender identity as our understanding in this area has advanced greatly in recent years. **Sex** is a binary social construct designed by heteronormative standards and is typically defined by physiological and biological characteristics that differentiate the male sex from the female sex (Russell et al., 2022). According to Russell et al. (2022), biological sex is comprised of "anatomy, chromosomes, hormones" (p. 50). The socially constructed features of men, women, girls, and boys, on the other hand, are considered **gender**. This covers interpersonal connections, standards, mannerisms, and roles. Gender is a social construct that differs from culture to culture and can evolve. Historically, we have viewed gender in a very binary way, meaning that there are only two categories—men and women, boys and girls. Today, gender is considered much more **fluid**.

Historically and currently, women face many barriers and societal challenges such as sexual violence, intimate partner violence, unequal pay in the workplace, and the glass ceiling, which prevents many from moving into higher positions in the workplace, creates under-representation in government, and often results in rights that restrict women's reproductive choices and freedom.

A person's firmly held, internal, and unique experience of gender is referred to as **gender identity**. This experience may or may not line up with the person's physiology or the sex they were assigned at birth. It can be fluid and or evolve. When someone describes themselves as **cisgender**, this means that their gender identity is the same as their assigned sex at birth. People who identify as different from heteronormative or cisgender face oppression. **Transgender** and **gender-nonconforming** individuals face many vulnerabilities and challenges, and it is important for social workers to gain a comprehensive awareness and knowledge about the unique issues impacting this community. Often discriminatory practices are in operation and further stigmatize and create barriers. It is important that social workers are sensitive to using the gender pronouns that people prefer to use such as she/her/hers; he/him/his; or they/them.

Some of the challenges that transgender and gender-nonconforming people face are increased violence, pay disparities, interpersonal and societal harms, and identity discrimination. For individuals in the transgender and gender-nonconforming population, there are staggering data sets that indicate high rates of harassment at over 75%, and close to 25% of physical attacks took place during elementary and secondary educational years. This population is often double or triple marginalized. The intersection between gender-based discrimination and other forms of prejudice includes, but is not limited to, ethnicity, socioeconomic status, disability, age, and residence in terms of neighborhood, state, or country (Austin & Papciak, 2022; Coleman et al., 2022).

IMG 4.3

Homophobia

Sexual orientation is not the same as gender or gender identity, although these concepts are often confused. Who you are attracted to in a sexual, nonplatonic, or romantically emotional way is a matter of sexual orientation, and it differs from gender identity. Accordingly, being transgender is distinct from being gay, lesbian, or bisexual since it involves feeling as though your assigned sex at birth is different from the gender with which you identify. Who you want to *be with* depends on your sexual orientation. One's *sense of self* is referred to as gender identity. The most common ways that people use to describe their sexual orientation are gay, lesbian, queer, straight/heterosexual, bisexual, asexual, questioning, and pansexual. Even though we have come a long way as a society in honoring and valuing those who are LGBTQ+, many challenges remain. LGBTQ+ individuals still face discrimination in many domains of society such as the workplace and are at risk of violence and hate crimes, such as the recent mass shooting incident in Colorado Springs, Colorado, when a gunman entered a gay nightclub in 2022, killing five people and injuring 17 others.

Classism

According to the American Psychiatric Association (2022), **socioeconomic status** (SES) is a term used to describe the point at which a person or group of people land on the socioeconomic scale. This position is based on a variety of social and economic factors, including income, level and type of education, type and reputation of employment, location of residence, and in some societies or subcultures ethnicity or religion (APA, 2022). Worthy et al. (2020) define it as the measurement of an individual's financial and social status in comparison to others based on factors such as "income, education, and employment" (p. 310). In the book *Caste*, Pulitzer Prize–winning author Isabel Wilkerson (2020) describes the term **caste**, which is similar to classism, as a way to assign value to "entire swaths of humankind" (p. 18). **Classism** is not independent of racism and is not synonymous with racism either. Classism drives the division of humans and goes back centuries. It is driven by power and wealth to determine individual groups' and populations' status. Often people with low income are blamed for their SES and are viewed as lazy, lacking intellect, and not working hard enough. Rather, individuals in low-income brackets are often there due to circumstances that have systemically and historically oppressed their ancestors and have continued to pigeon-hole them and limit their social mobility (see Chapter 6). The vast majority of low-income people are employed, though many struggle financially due to poor benefits and low wages.

Ableism

Individuals with disabilities are one of the largest marginalized groups in the world. Disabilities are generally categorized as physical, sensory, cognitive, developmental, intellectual, and unseen disabilities. Disabilities also include long-term and some short-term health issues, mental health illnesses or conditions, and other conditions not listed here (Bogart & Dunn, 2019). One in four adults in the United States lives with some form of disability, and that number only includes individuals who are adults and reported. A **disability** is any physical, biological, or psychological condition that causes impairment. Even though the impairment creates challenges for people with a disability, the barriers they face as a result are the real issue. Very few things in society are created with specific intentions for people with disabilities. There are many types of disabilities, and people with disabilities are not a monolith, even if they have the same diagnosis. Society often lumps people with disabilities into one group and refers to individuals with disabilities as a single population. Still, it is vital to learn and understand that people with disabilities are diverse people with a wide range of needs. Some disabilities may be less visible, but the barriers that disabled people face can profoundly impact their lives (Centers for Disease Control and Prevention, 2020).

Ableism is pervasive discrimination, bias, and social prejudice against individuals and communities of people living with disabilities. The persistent dominant societal attitude places limitations and barriers before individuals with disabilities and devalues their worth. Every person living with a disability has other intersectional identities; thus, it is important for social workers to understand that a person's disability is only one part of the individual. Beyond any other intersections that may marginalize a person with disabilities, they are at increased risk of facing many inequities (Havercamp & Bonardi, 2022).

Disabled individuals live with ableism in a plethora of ways, such as lack of employment, transportation barriers, access to fundamental needs such as housing, food, medical and mental health care, and social-emotional engagement. Interconnected systems of oppression are insidious prevalent problems that work in synch to oppress those with disabilities and maintain privilege for nondisabled people (Singer & Bacon, 2020). Social workers working with individuals living with **cognitive or developmental disabilities**, also known as intellectual disabilities (DD/ID), provide essential work in society. Some individuals who are clients and patients have more than one disability diagnosis simultaneously. This is called a **comorbid diagnosis**. Regardless of what population you serve in your professional career, social workers will likely work with an individual or group of individuals living with one or more disabilities as a part of their intersectional identity. Since social workers are policy advocates and the legislators influence the funding for the programs that increase support and services to the DD/ID population, they need to recognize the service gaps in the local system of care for individuals with DD/ID (Braddock et al., 2008; Jackson-Clockston, 2019).

Religious Discrimination

Regardless of our faith, spiritual beliefs, or nonbeliefs, it is a vital aspect of life for many individuals and groups. For many ethnic and racial groups, **religion** can be a strength-based aspect of life. It will be important for us to examine ourselves for any internal or implicit bias surrounding religion and spirituality, particularly when our beliefs may differ from that of the individual or group we are working with. We often have experiential gaps in knowledge, which make it essential for you to listen to your client and do your "self-work" to increase awareness and competence in order to meet and support your clients where they are. Some religious people face **discrimination** and **religious persecution** for being a member of a particular religion. For example, after 9/11, many Muslim Americans, whose religion is Islam, experienced a rise in hate crimes in the United States.

Spirituality, for many, is a protective factor that encourages resilience in individuals, groups, and communities. It can empower people to achieve posttraumatic growth and to find meaning and purpose, grounding and fulfillment, for example after challenging or traumatic experiences. It is important to recognize that children, youth, and families often have a bond or need a connection to their cultural, ethnic, religious, and spiritual practices. For many, their Indigenous ways and their need or desire for religion or spirituality should not be discounted. For many people with various identities, such as a marginalized race, ethnicity, disability, or gender identity, religion is a point of intersection. Religion and spirituality can vary greatly and widely amongst a variety of cultures. As social workers, it is equally important to understand that one's relationship with religion and spirituality may be complicated for some individuals. Many individuals and groups have experienced oppression through spiritual abuse and religious practices. Never should a person be forced to find strength in the areas that have harmed them.

Highlighting BIPOC Leaders Within Social Work

The representation of BIPOC leaders in social work is essential because, historically, the social work profession has functioned in Whiteness, although many of the communities and populations served are BIPOC. Representation matters because it allows people to feel included. It is like being invited to a party and asked to dance. When BIPOC people are represented, they may feel less out of place, have a sense of belonging, and feel appreciated. As professionals in social work, their lived experience and the social location that their lens comes from may connect with BIPOC clients and help fill the gap and provide culturally responsive support. BIPOC leaders are past and present incredibly active civil rights activists. Many BIPOC leaders have broken down obstacles and become actual leaders in important U.S. government social service organizations. Millions of individuals worldwide have benefited from their efforts, which helped create the momentum needed for societal advancement. The social workers highlighted are far from all-encompassing. The intention is to be aware that BIPOC lives in social work have paved many ways. Chapter 2 also highlights a number of prominent BIPOC social workers and the impact they have made on the social work profession as well as our society at large.

Mary Church Terrell

Born in 1863, the late Mary Church Terrell was the daughter of enslaved parents who later became small business owners. She was a great social service pioneer for Black women. Terrell was one of the first Black women to earn a bachelor's degree. She was the first Black woman appointed to a school board and the first African American admitted to the Washington DC, Branch of the American Association of University Women.

She eventually cofounded the National Association of Colored Women and joined the National Association for the Advancement of Colored People (NAACP) as a founder member. She became an ancestor in 1954 (Social Welfare History Project, 2012).

Edward Franklin Frazier

On September 24, 1894, the late Edward Franklin Frazier was born. He was born in Baltimore, Maryland, and attended "Colored High School," where he graduated. Frazier received a scholarship to continue his education at the Historically Black College and University (HBCU) Howard University. He became an educator in high schools in a number of U.S. states. After making his mark with high school youth, he became a New York School of social work research fellow. Edward Franklin Frazier traveled out of the country with his work, and upon his return to the United States, he taught sociology in Atlanta at Morehouse College, an HCBU. The Atlanta School of Social Work guided his direction and focus, and he initiated his writings on the Black family. His publication "The Pathology of Race Prejudice" was considered controversial and ultimately caused him to leave his teaching position at Morehouse College.

His impact on institutions and practices to embrace African Americans' aspirations for economic, political, and social equality in American society has earned him a spot among the most influential African Americans. The E. Franklin Frazier Research Center was established by the Howard University School of Social Work for his efforts and contributions to the university (Semmes, 2001; Thompson, 2000).

Dorothy Irene Height

In 2010, NASW recognized the late Dorothy Height with the honor of Lifetime Achievement Award. Height contributed to civil rights and social justice for almost

50 years. She was indeed a leader who impacted human rights and an anchor to uplift equality. Height was born in 1912 in Richmond, Virginia. She earned her bachelor's degree in education, master's in educational psychology, and completed postgraduate work in New York at Columbia University in the School of Social Work.

Height was a government and social service organization leader, and she collaborated with other Black civil rights pioneers. Before passing on to ancestry, she collaborated with civil rights giants such as Mary McLeod Bethune, who was appointed by President Franklin D. Roosevelt as the first Black woman head of the federal department as the director of the Division of Negro Affairs for the National Youth Administration (NYA) and Dr. Martin Luther King, Jr., whom she worked with to coordinate the 1963 civil rights March on Washington. Height worked tirelessly in community organizations such as the Young Women's Christian Association (YWCA), the oldest and largest multicultural women's organization worldwide. In 1970, the YWCA National Convention adopted the "One Imperative": "To thrust our collective power towards the elimination of racism, wherever it exists by any means necessary." Height was the first director of the YWCA's Center for Racial Justice (NASW Foundation, 2004).

Whitney Moore Young Jr.

In 1921, the late Whitney Moore Young Jr., a Black man, was born in Louisville, Kentucky. He attended Kentucky State University, where he graduated in 1941 as valedictorian with a bachelor's degree in social work. Young Jr. was trained as an electrical engineer during World War II and served in the military. Despite the tensions he endured between the mistreatment from White military superiors and his Black military crewmembers, he became a social justice advocate. Post-World War II, Young Jr., went to graduate school for social work. He later worked in society as a social work civil rights activist for many notable organizations (i.e., the National Urban League and the National Association for the Advancement of Colored People [NAACP]). Young Jr. worked closely with King Jr. to organize the historic civil rights March on Washington. In social work education, Young Jr. became the dean of the School of Social Work at Atlanta University, which is now Clark Atlanta University (CAU) in Atlanta, Georgia, when he worked at the area's only accredited social work program. Young Jr. is credited for his leadership. Today, more social workers can get their graduate-level degree. However, there are still disproportionate barriers for BIPOC social workers to earn their master's in social work (MSW, MSSW) degrees. During his tenure as dean, elevated numbers in student enrollment took place, and with that growth came expansion. The social work program he led offered social work continuing education (CEUs) to support community-based social workers without MSWs (Peebles-Wilkins, 1995).

4.2 PRACTICE ACTIVITY

BIPOC Leaders in Social Work

Following is a list of noted BIPOC leaders in social work. Many more are not mentioned here and are not prominent in the literature. Nonetheless, they are giants in our society. Next is a small but important call of action for you. I am asking you to do what I call your "self-work." Search the internet, Google Scholar, public library, and your amazing school library for information about the following influential and dynamic BIPOC leaders. Learn about where they started, what era they were born in, their race, ethnicity, and culture, what trajectory they followed in education and work, and what their social work professional work entailed. Now think about what you want to do to be a social work professional. If you are BIPOC, look at what these greats have done! You can do what you are called to do too! If you are not BIPOC, what can you do to center the experiences of BIPOC leaders and support your peers and colleagues in becoming respected social work professionals too? How do you think centering BIPOC leaders increases support in society?

- Mildred "Mit" C. Joyner
- Ronald G. Lewis
- Hilary Noel Weaver
- Hermila Anzaldua
- Diana Ming Chan
- Peter C. Y. Lee
- Sindhutai Sapkal
- Aroti Dutt

Now that you have done your "self-work" researching and learning about a few BIPOC social work leaders, I invite you to journal about what you have discovered. I hope you will realize it is essential for social work students and professionals from all races and ethnic groups to learn and to understand the importance of uplifting and centering the contributions of BIPOC social workers. The profession must include respect for BIPOC social workers as community builders, social justice activists, educators, and social work professionals in their own right.

Tools and Practices to Advance SJEDI Within Social Work

Now that we have learned about the many barriers to SJEDI, we can focus on what tools social workers can use to engage in this important work as change agents at the micro, mezzo, and macro levels. You might be asking, "What can we do, and where should we begin?"

The Importance of Self-Work

As we learn and live out our human experience, we are sometimes left fatigued from the surmounting social issues and challenges in our lives, families, neighborhoods, communities, schools, and workplaces. One option is to be truth seekers. Truth seekers are open to learning new and sometimes uncomfortable and challenging information. Learning information and truth about ourselves is often the best place to begin, including examining our own implicit biases. A **bias** is a prejudicial attitude, behavior, or action that favors or disparages one individual or group over another. **Implicit bias** is a type of prejudice that influences our judgments, decisions, and actions and happens spontaneously and *unknowingly*. Thus, it is important to examine the answers to these questions: What are our biases and implicit biases? How were we socialized? What is our social location? What are our personal identities, and how do they intersect?

Racism is embedded in the fabric of society, and this includes social work practice (NASW, 2020). It is pervasive and free flowing without restriction across all areas of society. Racism is in operation at the micro-, mezzo-, and macrosystems levels. For social workers to mitigate racism in the systems in which we perform professional duties with the client populations we serve, we are challenged with the opportunity to "do our own self-work." Self-work means having the chance to face one's own internalized racial bias toward self and others by reflecting on racial episodes we have encountered, keeping in mind one's own history of power and privilege, and looking for possibilities for change.

It is critical to understand that **antiracism** is an action word that must be operationalized in order to create change. Ibram X. Kendi (2019), race theory scholar and author of *How to Be an Antiracist*, offers this antiracism definition: "I define an antiracist as someone who is expressing an antiracist idea or supporting an antiracist policy with their actions. And I define an antiracist idea as any idea that says the racial groups are equal" (Social Work License Map, 2022, p. 13). Social workers are charged with social justice activities that lead to being actively antiracist. Some ways that social workers can practice antiracism is to interrogate their own racism. Social work is 60% demographically White. This means that inherent White privilege is present, and active compassion and empathy are important when working with non-White clients. Recognize the importance of collaborative efforts that focus on structural changes. Advocate for anti-oppressive and antiracist laws to be changed and for actively antiracist policies to be implemented. This may require working with legislators to fill gaps. Learn about the communities that you serve and recognize that there are barriers restricting equity all around you (NASW, 2020).

IMG 4.4

Anti-Oppressive and Culturally Responsive Social Work Practice

Today social workers across the nation are being trained to engage in anti-oppressive social work practice and on the importance of using practices that are culturally sensitive and responsive to those they are serving. **Anti-oppressive practice (AOP)** in social work is a framework for centering our clients and is strengths-based and empowering. Social workers are obligated to respect their clients and honor their lived experiences. When we think of strengths-based perspectives, we learn that social workers agree to appreciate their clients' autonomy, self-determination, and abilities as humans. Social workers approach their clients as life experts with unique experiences that have influenced, shaped, and molded their personhood. We must actively work to understand and be aware of our intersectional identities, individual subjective beliefs, and world philosophy. Self-examination and exploration of our social location (where we show up in society) can help prevent our clients from enduring disempowerment. It is vital that social workers use evidence-based interventions that are culturally sensitive and relevant to those they are serving instead of assuming that one intervention can work for every group and culture.

AOP social work creates critical awareness and opens partitioners up to a deeper level of consciousness so that we can dismantle immediate micro-level and systemic structures of oppression and inequity created by unequal power differentials and hierarchical operations.

To move the needle in SJEDI work, we must take the often-uncomfortable stance of "getting into good trouble" (a phrase used frequently by the late Honorable Representative John Lewis). In social work, we are platformed to take political stances, follow the NASW Code of Ethics, and uphold the values that support decolonization and liberation from the White supremacists' power structures at the foundations of our society, both locally and globally.

As social workers, we must remember that AOP is not practiced with neutrality. It calls for us to engage in a practice involving controversial spaces. We are called to oppose the oppression of human and nonhuman animals and to be aware that suffering results from oppression. AOP illuminates large systems of power that operate in ways that uphold barriers to the distribution of resources and decenter the voices of BIPOC and other marginalized groups. Social workers must commit to working to change macrosystems such as legislative entities, government laws, policies and procedures, justice systems, health care systems, educational systems, and nongovernment-run entities such as places of worship. This involves gaining important skills in the macro realm of social work such as working to change policies, working as leaders and administrators, and being a part of social movements that are demanding change.

Cultural Humility

Before social work students and new graduates embark upon their work and career, it is critical that they adopt an ongoing heart-set and embrace a practice of **cultural humility. Cultural competency** askes social workers to gain as much knowledge as possible about the backgrounds and lived experiences of their clients, while cultural humility asks social workers to embrace "not knowing" and being willing to learn from the clients we work with you are experts of their own lives. Foronda et al. (2015) explain that before we can know what cultural humility is, we can examine what it isn't: "prejudice, oppression, intolerance, discrimination, stereotyping, exclusion, stigma, inequity, marginalization, misconceptions, labeling, mistrust, hostility, misunderstandings, cultural imposition, judgmental, undermining, and bullying" (p. 213). Cultural humility in the context of social work practice is a framework that began in the biological medical profession. Cultural humility fits together with participatory, relational, and anti-oppressive social work methods. This type of humility is a driving force that moves social workers toward introspection and to consider their own social position: Where are you located in this White supremacist society we all find ourselves? What is your social location? How do your identities influence your perceptions about what is "OK," "good," "natural," "appropriate," "proper," "healthy," "moral?"

Cultural humility challenges us to prioritize our clients' experience over our Western standards and beliefs. It asks us to center marginalized experiences and deconstruct power differentials that fuel disparities and perpetuate implicit bias in micro, mezzo, and macro structural systemic hierarchal and racist ideologies. The implications of power oppression and privilege dynamics have a significant effect on both clients and social work professionals (Gottlieb, 2020; Morgaine &

Capous-Desyllas, 2020). At the root of cultural humility, we will find ourselves striving to be humble and in perpetual operation with respect, kindness, and grace. Be prepared to leave this chapter with more questions than answers and accept that the journey toward understanding SJEDI is an ongoing, never-ending process.

Chapter Summary

SJEDI in the context of social work are foundational concepts crucial for advancing practice and societal progress. This chapter discusses critical information that is applicable to every social worker. Social work presents opportunities daily for engagement in SJEDI work. Microaggressions, discrimination, marginalization, and oppression operate in tandem, and it is imperative that students and professionals engage in working actively to be anti-oppressive and antiracist. For social workers to build skills that are helpful to diverse populations, it is essential to work toward culturally responsive practices that are strengthened through social workers' intentional application of cultural humility. Understanding and respect for intersectional identity of self and others is paramount. The focus of this chapter covered many SJEDI concepts and included discussion about the discrimination and oppression that some individuals and groups face based on their social identities. BIPOC and marginalized individuals are doubly and triply vulnerable to the oppressions of racism, classism, sexism, sex-based discrimination, transphobia, homophobia, ageism, ableism, xenophobia, and religious discrimination. Research conducted by diverse social work professionals is critical to gain insight from those who represent BIPOC communities. It is imperative to be mindful that not everyone in diverse communities is identical; people are not monolithic.

Discussion Questions

1. An established body of literature suggests that earning more might only increase an individual's sense of happiness and accomplishment if it improves their social rank. Researchers have found evidence suggesting that for many U.S. adults "their level of happiness depends on how much they have financially, compared to those around them." Reflect on your perception of wealth privilege. Describe how the dynamics between wealth, privilege and social status/rank might influence someone's quality of life. What are your attitudes and beliefs related to wealth status and privilege?

2. This chapter highlighted the concept of marginalization. Locate essential social services where you live or around where you live. Are there disparities

that exist? What do these look like? What is the overlap between social service availability and proximity to marginalized communities?

3. Understanding the social dynamics of your community is important as a social worker. Regardless of what population we work with, or the system level, micro, mezzo, or macro, social justice is influenced by equity and diversity. What is the racial makeup of your state and local leadership?

4. Social workers are essential workers in society. They strive to break barriers and to dismantle power and oppression. Social workers strive to enhance equality for marginalized individuals and groups. All individuals are influenced by White supremacy. Although some benefit more than others, it is a harmful system of power for all. Where are you at in your understanding of your own relationship with White supremacy?

5. How will the information in this chapter inform your social work education and professional career?

Author Positionality Statement

I come into this work as a Black person from the African diaspora. Although I am not part of a monolith, my social location and Black lens will be present in my written work and research. I live with pervasive hidden and unseen disabilities. I was socialized under the same oppressive and racist systems of White supremacy that many, if not all, of us in the United States were taught to believe. My social location in these systems of power, privilege, and oppression taught me to fear and to internalize racism and oppression. I was raised to love and to accept all people, but I was warned that one day I would see mistreatment. That does not mean that I am without the implicit bias that all humans carry. I am a survivor of many things, and police brutality is one of them. I began working toward social justice and equity when I was 20. My soul grieves when people hurt, and my authentic self operates in a nonmilitant manner, which has often caused me to question my ability to do social justice work boldly. Through the years, I have learned to navigate my way through systemic blatant and covert injustices at the micro, mezzo, and macro levels. I have a solid ability to code-switch, which I consider both a tragedy and a triumph because it calls for affirming oneself that they are authentically "OK" regardless of acceptance. My lived experiences, education, training, and work have shaped my understanding of how systems are accustomed to operating in hierarchical, patriarchal structures. I am also a woman who identifies as asexual. I, like most, was raised with specific expectations surrounding my performance of gender. I consistently performed to these expectations.

Although it is expected and important to be academically professional, it is important for me to share with you that this chapter is written through the lens and the voice of a Black individual who is accustomed to African American vernacular when speaking and often when writing. I must also speak my truth. Although I use the term BIPOC throughout my writing for readability and understanding, it is important for me to share that BIPOC is a term that doesn't encapsulate people's unique experiences in the acronym and leaves some non-White races and ethnicities out, subjecting people to monoliths.

In addition to these identities, I am also an able-body and neuro-divergent person. I come from a low-income class upbringing; however, I was not keenly aware of how much our family struggled, and therefore I have a great deal of privilege. During my adult life, I have found myself vacillating between a low socioeconomic class to middle class, and when I work three jobs, I can be upper middle class. Although I consider this a privileged and economic comfort, I also see it as a biological, psychological, and sociological detriment. I have acquired multiple certifications and degrees up to the doctoral level.

In my authenticity, it is my choice to share with you that I can relate to many of your hopes and fears on your academic and life's journey.

Acknowledgments: The author would like to acknowledge Jessica A. Ritter and esteemed colleagues at MSU Denver for their continued support on my academic journey. Past and present students, you are valued—my children Sydney, Raeven, Mark Jr., and Jayden, who are everything.

> *Calling-in engages in debates with words and actions of healing and restoration, and without the self-indulgence of drama.*
>
> —Loretta Ross

References

American Psychological Association. (2022, October 31). *Discrimination: What it is and how to cope.* https://www.apa.org/topics/racism-bias-discrimination/types-stress

Aouragh, M. (2019). "White privilege" and shortcuts to anti-racism. *Race & Class, 61*(2), 3–26.

Austin, A., & Papciak, R. (2022). Practice with transgender and gender diverse clients. In M. P. Dentato (Ed.), *Social work practice with the LGBTQ+ community: The intersection of history, health, mental health, and policy factors* (2nd ed., pp. 449–476). Oxford University Press.

Bhopal, K. (2020). Confronting White privilege: The importance of intersectionality in the sociology of education. *British Journal of Sociology of Education, 41*(6), 807–816.

Bogart, K. R., & Dunn, D. S. (2019). Ableism special issue introduction. *Journal of Social Issues, 75*(3), 650–664.

Bonilla-Silva, E. (2006). *Racism without racists: Color-blind racism and the persistence of racial inequality in the United States.* Rowman & Littlefield.

Braddock, D., Hemp, R., Rizzolo, M. C., Haffer, L., Tanis, E. S., & Wu, J. (2008). *The state of the states in developmental disabilities* (Vol. 444). American Association on Intellectual and Developmental Disabilities.

Bridges, K. M. (2019). White privilege and white disadvantage. *Virginia Law Review Association, 105,* 449.

Brooks-LaSure, C. (2022, September 15). *Diversity, equity, and inclusion.* CMS. https://www.cms.gov/about-cms/careers-cms/diversity-equity-and-inclusion

Centers for Disease Control and Prevention. (2020, September 16). *Disability and health overview.* https://www.cdc.gov/ncbddd/disabilityandhealth/disability.html

Clockston, J. M. J. (2019). *Perceptions of Human Service Professionals and Parents with Intellectual Disabilities: Action Research* (Doctoral dissertation, Capella University).

Coaston, J. (2019). The intersectionality wars. *Vox.* Intersectionality, explained: meet Kimberlé Crenshaw, who coined the term - Vox

Coates, R. D., Ferber, A. L., & Brunsma, D. L. (2021). *The matrix of race: Social construction, intersectionality, and inequality.* SAGE.

Cole, N. L. (2019, July 14). *Defining racism beyond its dictionary meaning.* ThoughtCo. https://www.thoughtco.com/racism-definition-3026511

Coleman, E., Radix, A. E., Bouman, W.P., Brown, G.R., de Vries, A. L. C., Deutsch, M. B., Ettner, R., Fraser, L., Goodman, M., Green, J., Hancock, A. B., Johnson, T. W., Karasic, D. H., Knudson, G. A., Leibowitz, S. F., Meyer-Bahlburg, H. F.L., Monstrey, S. J., Motmans, J., Nahata, L., … Arcelus, J. (2022). Standards of Care for the Health of Transgender and Gender Diverse People, Version 8. *International Journal of Transgender Health, 23*(S1), S1-S260. https://doi.org/10.1080/26895269.2022.2100644

Collins, P. H. (2004). *Black sexual politics: African Americans, gender, and the new racism.* Routledge.

Collins, P. H. (2019). *Intersectionality as critical social theory.* Duke University Press.

Collins, S. (2023, January 9). *Anti-oppression: Anti-ableism.* https://simmons.libguides.com/anti-oppression/anti-ableism

Council on Social Work Education. (2022, June 9). *2022 EPAS.* https://www.cswe.org/accreditation/standards/2022-epas/

Crenshaw, K. (1989). Demarginalizing the intersection of race and sex: A Black feminist critique of antidiscrimination doctrine, feminist theory and antiracist politics. *University of Chicago Legal Forum,* 1989(1), 139–167.

Crenshaw, K. (2017, June 8). *Kimberlé Crenshaw on intersectionality, more than two decades later.* Columbia Law School. https://www.law.columbia.edu/news/archive/kimberle-crenshaw-intersectionality-more-two-decades-later

Day, P. J.(2009). *A new history of social welfare.* Pearson.

Desmond, M., & Emirbayer, M. (2010). *Racial domination, racial progress: The sociology of race in America* . McGraw-Hill.

Foronda, C., Baptiste, D.-L., Reinholdt, M. M., & Ousman, K. (2015). Cultural humility. *Journal of Transcultural Nursing, 27*(3), 210–217. https://doi.org/10.1177/1043659615592677

Frazier, E. F. (1927). The Pathology of Race Prejudice. *Forum* , 856–851.

Frey, W. H. (2020). *The nation is diversifying even faster than predicted, according to new Census data*. Brookings. https://www.brookings.edu/research/new-census-data-shows-the-nation-is-diversifying-even-faster-than-predicted/

Frye, M. (2003). Oppression. In M. Kimmel, & A. L. Ferber (Eds.), *Privilege: A reader* (pp. 13–20). Westview Press.

Gallagher, C. (2009). Color-blinded America or how the media and politics have made racism and racial inequality yesterday's social problem. In A. Ferber, C. Jiménez, A. O'Reilly Herrera, & D. Samuels (Eds.), *The matrix reader: Examining the dynamics of oppression and privilege* (pp. 548–551). McGraw-Hill.

Gibson, A. N., & Martin, J. D. (2019). Re-situating information poverty: Information marginalization and parents of individuals with disabilities. *Journal of the Association for Information Science and Technology, 70*(5), 476–487. https://doi.org/10.1002/asi.24128

Gottlieb, M. (2020). The case for a cultural humility framework in social work practice. *Journal of Ethnic & Cultural Diversity in Social Work, 30*(6), 1–19. https://doi.org/10.1080/15313204.2020.1753615

Hampton, L. M. (2021). Black feminist musings on algorithmic oppression. In *Proceedings of the 2021 ACM conference on fairness, accountability, and transparency* (pp.1–1). https://doi. org/10.1145/3442188.3445929

Havercamp, S. M., & Bonardi, A. (2022). Special issue introduction: Addressing healthcare inequities in intellectual disability and developmental disabilities. *Intellectual and Developmental Disabilities, 60*(6), 449–452.

Hudson, N. J. (2020). An in-depth look at a comprehensive diversity training program for faculty. *International Journal for the Scholarship of Teaching and Learning, 14*(1), 3.

Jason, L. A., Glantsman, O., O'Brien, J. F., & Ramian, K. N. (2019). Introduction to the field of community psychology. *Introduction to Community Psychology*. Rebus Community.

Johnson, T. H. (2018). Challenging the myth of Black male privilege. *Spectrum: A Journal on Black Men, 6*(2), 21–42.

Kendi, I. X. (2023). *How to be an antiracist*. One World.

Kloos, B., Hill, J., Thomas, E., Wandersman, A., Elias, M., & Dalton, J., (2012). *Community psychology: linking individuals and communities*. Cengage.

Kres-Nash, I. (2016, November 10). *Racism and ableism*. AAPD. https://www.aapd.com/racism-and-ableism/

Letiecq, B. L. (2019). Surfacing family privilege and supremacy in family science: Toward justice for all. *Journal of Family Theory & Review, 11*(3), 398–411.

Lorde, A. (1983). There is no hierarchy of oppressions. *Bulletin: Homophobia and Education, 14*(3/4), 9.

Love, B. J. (2000). Developing a liberatory consciousness. *Readings for Diversity and Social Justice, 2*, 470–474.

Marson, S. M., & Dovyak, P. (2022). Exposing White privilege by two White guys. *International Journal of Social Work Values and Ethics, 19*(1), 4–17.

Merriam-Webster. (n.d.). *Identity.* https://www.merriam-webster.com/dictionary/identity

McIntosh, P. (2020). White privilege and male privilege: A personal account of coming to see correspondences through work. *Privilege and Prejudice: Twenty years with the invisible knapsack,* (pp. 7–18). Routledge.

Morgaine, K., & Capous-Desyllas, M. (2020). *Anti-oppressive social work practice: Putting theory into action.* SAGE.

Myers, J. (2013). *Historical dictionary of the lesbian and gay liberation movements.* Scarecrow Press.

National Association of Social Work. (2020, August 21). *Social workers must help dismantle systems of oppression and fight racism within social work profession.* https://www.socialworkers.org/News/News-Releases/ID/2219/Social-Workers-Must-Help-Dismantle-Systems-of-Oppression-and-Fight-Racism-Within-Social-Work-Profession

National Association of Social Work. (2021a, February 19). *Read the code of ethics.* https://www.socialworkers.org/About/Ethics/Code-of-Ethics/Code-of-Ethics-English

National Association of Social Work. (2021b, June). *Undoing racism through social work* [Report to the Profession of Racial Justice Priorities and Actions]. https://www.socialworkers.org/LinkClick.aspx?fileticket=29AYH9qAdXc%3d&portalid=0

National Association of Social Work Foundation. (2004). *Dorothy Irene Height (1912–2010)—Social worker and civil rights activist.* Social Welfare History Project. https://socialwelfare.library.vcu.edu/social-work/height-dorothy-irene/

National Association of Social Work Foundation. (2009). *Our work.* NASW Social Workers Pioneers Bio Index. https://www.naswfoundation.org/Our-Work/NASW-Social-Workers-Pioneers/NASW-Social-Workers-Pioneers-Listing.aspx?id=678

National Council on Family Relations. (2019). *Inclusion and diversity committee report: What's your social location?* https://www.ncfr.org/ncfr-report/spring-2019/inclusion-and-diversity-social-location#:~:text=An%20individual's%20social%20location%20is,same%20for%20any%20two%20individuals.

Peebles-Wilkins, W. (1995). "Young, Whitney Moore Jr." In R. L. Edwards (Ed.), *Encyclopedia of social work* (19th ed., Vol. 3, pp. 2618–2619). NASW Press.

Randall, V. R. (2007). Eliminating racial discrimination in healthcare: A call for state healthcare anti-discrimination law. *Eliminating Healthcare Disparities in America: Beyond the IOM Report,* 179–196.

Roberts, S. O., Bareket-Shavit, C., Dollins, F. A., Goldie, P. D., & Mortenson, E. (2020). Racial inequality in psychological research: Trends of the past and recommendations for the future. *Perspectives on Psychological Science, 15*(6), 1295–1309.

Rogers, L. O., Niwa, E. Y., Chung, K., Yip, T., & Chae, D. (2021). M(ai)cro: Centering the macrosystem in human development. *Human Development, 65*(5–6), 270–292.

Russell, E. B., Viggiani, P. A., & Sippel, B. A. (2022). Understanding differences from oppression to sexual health and practice. In M. P. Dentato (Ed.), *Social work practice with the LGBTQ+ community: The intersection of history, health, mental health, and policy factors* (2nd ed., pp. 39–83). Oxford University Press.

Semmes, C. E. (2001). E. Franklin Frazier's theory of the Black family: Vindication and sociological insight. *Journal of Sociology & Social Welfare, 28*(2), 3–21.

Singer, S., & Bacon, J. (2020). Ableism in the academy: A series about disability oppression and resistance in higher education. *Critical Education, 11*(14), 1–13.

Social Welfare History Project. (2012). *Mary Church Terrell (1863–1954): Educator, writer, civil rights activist.* https://socialwelfare.library.vcu.edu/eras/terrell-mary-church/

Social Work License Map. (2022, July 6). *Practicing anti-racism in social work: A guide.* https://socialworklicensemap.com/social-work-resources/anti-racism-guide/

Sue, D. W., Capodilupo, C. M., Torino, G. C., Bucceri, J. M., Holder, A. M. B., Nadal, K. L., & Esquilin, M. (2007). Racial microaggressions in everyday life: Implications for clinical practice. *American Psychologist, 62*(4), 271–286.

Thompson, A. (2000, May 24). *E. Franklin Frazier.* Black History Month - Influential Social Workers - National Association of Social Workers - Pennsylvania Chapter (nasw-pa.org)

Togioka, B. M., Duvivier, D., & Young, E. (2022). *Diversity and discrimination in healthcare.* StatPearls. Diversity and Discrimination In Healthcare - PubMed (nih.gov)

Tulshyan, R. (2022, March 8). We need to retire the term "microaggressions." *Harvard Business Review.* https://hbr.org/2022/03/we-need-to-retire-the-term-microaggressions

Wilkerson, I. (2020). *Caste: The origins of our discontents.* Random House.

Worthy, L. D., Lavigne, T., & Romero, F. (2020). Self and culture. *Culture and Psychology.* MMOER. Culture and Psychology – Simple Book Publishing (maricopa.edu)

Credits

CHAPTER 5

Macro Social Work

The Hidden Side of Social Work

Learning Objectives

After reading this chapter, students will be able to do the following:

- Explain the history of macro social work in the United States and the tensions that exist within the profession regarding a perceived imbalance between micro- and macro-level social work

- Differentiate macro-level social work from micro- and mezzo-level social work, including who the "client" is

- Summarize the skills that are needed to engage in macro-level social work

- Identify at least three major career path options for social workers who want to work at the macro level as a social worker

- Provide examples of social justice issues and movements of interest to the social work profession

- Summarize social workers' ethical obligation to engage in social and political action according to the National Association of Social Work (NASW) Code of Ethics

- Evaluate their own goodness of fit with macro-level social work practice as a potential future career option

SOCIAL WORKER SPOTLIGHT:
Jennifer Miles, MSW

My name is Jennifer Miles, and I am a social worker and a lobbyist. Many people do not think you can be both, but I believe social workers are uniquely suited to be great lobbyists.

When I applied to the Master's in Social Work program at the University of Denver, I knew I was interested in nonprofits and programs that provide direct service in communities. I had a degree in sociology and political science from Tulane University in New Orleans. I realized during my 1st-year field placement that I wanted to focus more on the policy issues; by the time I saw the 10th person with the same problem, I wanted to know if I could do something about the problem. That led me down the path of choosing the "indirect practice" track (today called "community practice") in my master's program in which I learned about policy issues from a social work perspective. Yet my 2nd-year field placement was far removed from the community and what was happening in my state. I learned a lot about research, policy analysis, and writing, but I also learned that I wanted to be closer to the action.

After finishing my MSW, I went to work my state's association of Community Health Centers, where I worked for 9 years, eventually as the policy director. I was responsible for the state and federal policy advocacy for the association and started spending more and more time at the State Capitol and would travel to Washington, DC several times each year. I learned a lot from the contract lobbyist the association hired and many others I met over those years. Then I took the bold step of starting my own lobbying firm, opening a business owned by a woman and a social worker! With my experience in health policy, I was soon able to expand my business to a add a number of nonprofit clients working on health and human services issues. Today I get to lobby our state legislature for clients I am proud to represent. I even lobby for social workers as the NASW state chapter lobbyist.

I am now an accomplished lobbyist with over 25 years of experience. My lobbying firm employed two other social worker lobbyists who have now launched their own lobbying firms. My firm employs one other social worker lobbyist still today. We are starting a movement here in Colorado! I have had the privilege of working to advance policy issues related to a variety of topics, including the following:

- Taxes from tobacco, vaping, and marijuana

- Medicaid and CHIP benefits, eligibility, enrollment, and reimbursement

- Colorado Clean Indoor Air Act (indoor smoke free law)

- Safety net health care provider reimbursement, funding, and operations

- Health care and mental health professional workforce issues, including training and loan forgiveness programs

- Health insurance benefits and costs

- Oral health, public health, environmental health, maternal and child health, and women's health

- Substance use disorder (SUD) services reimbursement, funding, and operations

- Affordable housing, food supports, and public benefits

- Early childhood education and childcare improvements

- Colorado's Equal Pay for Equal Work Act

If you are interested in the policies of our country or your state that lead to poverty, racial inequity, behavioral health disorders, or so many other issues impacting social workers and our clients, I encourage you to consider lobbying and policy advocacy as part of your career. Even if you are not a full-time lobbyist like me, you will undoubtedly find yourself lobbying for your clients, the agency where you work, or the programs and funding that support both.

IMG 5.-

Chapter 1 explained the difference between micro-level social work, mezzo-level social work, and macro-level social work. It may surprise you to know that most social workers will work at *all* three of these levels over the course of their social work career. But this chapter will delve more deeply into the macro side of social work and highlight career options for those who wish to engage in macro-level social work. When social workers put their "macro hat" on, their focus shifts from individual problems to social problems. **Macro social work** involves efforts to facilitate change and improve conditions in communities, large systems, and society at large. The author of this text chose to have an entire chapter devoted to macro social work because it tends to be the "hidden side" of social work and less visible than other forms of social work practice in the United States. For example, many Americans would be surprised to learn that some social workers work in the political arena in efforts to get legislation passed that would be helpful to the various populations that social workers serve. And despite the fact that the social work profession has a rich history of being involved in macro-level change efforts (see Chapter 2), it has been criticized by those inside and outside the profession for prioritizing micro-level practice over macro-level practice. The career options profiled in this chapter include policy practice, community practice, administration and leadership, and social work research.

The general public is often unaware that there is a macro side to the social work profession and that some social workers prefer to work at the macro level in order to effect **macro-level change**. Being a social worker requires an understanding of the larger social problems that exist in society; how they impact individuals, families, and communities; and working toward solutions for those social problems. In recent years, social workers have been focused on a number of important social issues such as the coronavirus pandemic, environmental justice, poverty and income inequality, rights for women and LGBTQ+ individuals, and systemic racism, many of which have been brought to the forefront by thriving social movements in this country. Social workers become experts in their fields and thus have a unique role to play when it comes to social and political change efforts. One of the most special and unique features of social work is its dual focus on the individual and the larger social environment, often referred to as the **person-in-environment perspective**. Thus, sometimes the target of intervention is the individual, while other times it makes more sense to focus change efforts on improving the larger social environment so that individuals have what they need to thrive and succeed.

Social Work's Mission of Social Justice

Social workers performing macro-level work are often trying to impact social change and/or political change. According to Ritter (2022), "Social and political action often go hand in hand, and both are critical to advancing the health and welfare of oppressed groups. **Social action** involves promoting social change by advocating for the rights of marginalized or oppressed groups. A strong component of this work involves educating the public, raising awareness about important social problems, and working to change societal attitudes. **Political action** typically involves a range of activities that are designed to (1) pass legislation on behalf of a particular group and (2) elect legislators who support an organization's mission and political agenda" (p. 20). Advocacy organizations are often trying to impact both social change (changing hearts) and political change (changing our laws and policies).

Compared to other professions in the United States, social work is fairly unique in including **social justice** in its mission as a profession and as one of its core values. Social justice, and the idea that social work involves concerted efforts to effect change at the macro level, is imbedded throughout various sections of the NASW Code of Ethics:

- "A historic and defining feature of social work is the profession's dual focus on individual well-being in a social context **and the well-being of society** (Preamble, NASW, 2021).

- "Social workers **promote social justice and social change** with and on behalf of clients" (Preamble, NASW, 2021).

- "Social workers are sensitive to cultural and ethnic diversity and **strive to end discrimination, oppression, poverty, and other forms of social injustice**" (Preamble, NASW, 2021).

- "Fundamental to social work is **attention to the environmental forces** that create, contribute to, and address problems in living" (Preamble, NASW, 2021).

- "Social workers also seek to **promote the responsiveness of organizations, communities, and other social institutions** to individuals' needs and social problems" (Preamble, NASW, 2021).

- "Social workers **pursue social change,** particularly with and on behalf of vulnerable and oppressed individuals and groups of people. Social workers' social change efforts are focused primarily on issues of poverty, unemployment, discrimination, and other **forms of social injustice**" (Ethical Principles, NASW, 2021).

- "Social workers should advocate for living conditions conducive to the fulfillment of basic human needs and should promote social, economic, political, and cultural values and institutions that are **compatible with the realization of social justice**" (Section 6.01, NASW, 2021).

- "Social workers **should engage in social and political action** that seeks to ensure that all people have equal access to the resources, employment, services, and opportunities they require to meet their basic human needs and to develop fully. Social workers should be aware of the impact of the political arena on practice and **should advocate for changes in policy and legislation to improve social conditions in order to meet basic human needs and promote social justice**" (Section 6.04 , NASW, 2021).

While some social workers believe that the social work profession should be neutral politically and stay above the political fray, others argue that having a mission of social justice means that the profession is inherently political. Since the beginning of our nation's history, numerous groups have had to fight for social equality. Historically, groups that have faced serious oppression and marginalization in U.S. society include Black, Indigenous, and People of Color (BIPOC); women; those who are LGBTQ+; persons with disabilities; children; those living in poverty; older adults; and immigrants. **Social justice** is a multifaceted social construct that can be conceptualized and defined in a number of ways:

- The distribution of wealth, opportunities, and privileges within a society
- The ability people have to realize their potential in the society in which they live
- Promoting a just society by challenging social injustice
- Equal access to opportunity in a society
- Having the same rights as others to participate fully in all realms of private and public life
- The right to be treated equally under the law
- Justice as fairness

Micro—Macro Tensions Within the Social Work Profession

One of the biggest strengths of the social work profession is the fact that it has both a micro and a macro side and can impact change at *both* of these levels. However, since the beginning of the social work profession, there has been a healthy tension and debate between the "micro-changers" and the "macro-changers" concerning whether both have been embraced equally. Some scholars of social work have argued that over the years micro social work has been valued and prioritized more as social work became increasingly professionalized and sought to compete with related disciplines such as psychology and counseling professions.

Specht and Courtney's (1994) thought-provoking book *Unfaithful Angels* argued that social work has abandoned its historic social justice mission to the disenfranchised and those living in poverty in favor of popular psychotherapies for the middle class. They argued that social work is at risk of being undifferentiated from other mental health professions. Social work has been criticized by those outside of the profession as well. In 1945, the famous community organizer **Saul Alinsky** shared his views about social workers and how they approach their work:

They come to the people of the slums not to help them rebel and fight their way out of the muck. … Most social work does not even reach the submerged masses. Social work is largely a middle class activity and guided by a middle class psychology. In the rare instances where it reaches the slum dwellers it seeks to get them adjusted to their environment so they will live in hell and like it. A higher form of treason would be difficult to conceive. (as cited in Homan, 2016, p. 5)

Despite these criticisms, as was covered in Chapter 2, there have been a few time periods in U.S. history that social workers were heavily active in macro-level change efforts, including major social movements. During the progressive era, social workers worked in settlement houses and worked to pass laws that would improve the social and health conditions of cities that were rapidly moving toward industrialization. These early social workers are credited with influencing the development of the macro side of social work and the idea that social workers should focus on impacting individuals' social environment. During the Great Depression, social workers advocated for major changes to the nation's social welfare system, which resulted in historic legislation being passed into law that created the nation's social safety net such as the Social Security Act of 1935 and the Fair Labor Standards Act of 1938. And many social workers were part of the thriving social movements in the 1960s and 1970s, such as the civil rights movement, the women's movement, and the gay liberation movement. Others threw themselves into the community practice and community organizing work that was popular during this time.

In recent years, efforts have been made to address the imbalance between micro social work and macro social work by social work leaders, academics, and practitioners, which led to the creation of the **Special Commission to Advance Macro Practice in Social Work** in 2013. According to the commission, they "seek to promote the visibility and importance of macro practice in the social work profession" by increasing the enrollment of MSW students in macro-specialized concentrations and ensuring that BSW and MSW programs "include a more equitable balance of macro and micro content" ("About the Special Commission," Association for Community Organization and Social Action, n.d.).

What Is Macro Social Work Exactly?

Since more people tend to be aware of social worker's work at the micro level, it is easier for them to grasp the work that social workers carry out when the client is an individual or a family. Understanding macro social work requires thinking a bit differently about *who* the client is. In macro-level social work, the client is a community, a large organization or system, or the larger society in which the social worker is trying to impact change (see Figure 5.1).

- **Communities:** When social workers are trying to impact change with a community, they might do this by creating and developing programs that can help a community thrive such as affordable daycare, after-school programs for youth, job training programs, healthy food access, and affordable health care clinics. They might also engage in work with communities of people that are not bound by geography (e.g., undocumented youth; LGBTQ+ individuals).

- **Large organizations or systems:** Social workers are trained to develop "systems thinking" and to understand how systems work. Many large systems such as child welfare systems, education systems, and criminal justice systems require strong leadership to ensure that they are not using practices that are racist or oppressive. Social workers can effect change by working "within the system" (e.g., as an employee of the organization) or "outside of the system" (e.g., advocating changes from the outside).

- **Society at large:** There are social workers across the country who work in advocacy organizations that have a mission to educate the general public about a social issue, raise awareness, change societal attitudes, and pass new policies and laws (e.g., equal rights for LGBTQ Americans and BIPOC people; reduce mental health stigma; raise awareness and pass laws that address sexual violence against women).

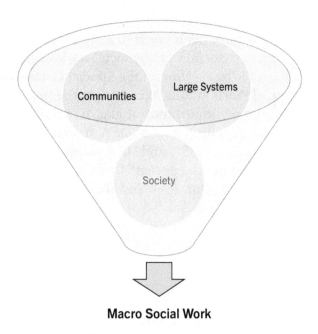

Macro Social Work

FIGURE 5.1   Macro social work: Effecting change with communities, large systems, and society at large.

Recent Social Movements in the United States

In recent years, Americans have witnessed a number of social movements rise up to address the needs of groups who are fighting for social equality and/or to urge lawmakers to address an urgent social problem. Because of the social work profession's mission of social justice, the NASW and many social workers across the nation have supported and sometimes joined in with these social movements working for social and policy change.

Black Lives Matter (#BlackLivesMatter and #SayHerName)

The Black Lives Matter movement (**#BlackLivesMatter**) began in response to a number of high profile shootings of primarily unarmed Black men across the United States by police, almost all of whom were later acquitted in court. The hashtag was coined by activists Alicia Garza, Opal Tometi, and Patrisse Cullors in 2013 after the acquittal of private citizen George Zimmerman who shot and killed Trayvon Martin. And the movement continued to gain momentum after the police shooting of Michael Brown in Ferguson, Missouri, the death of Eric Garner in Staten Island, New York, after police used a chokehold that resulted in his death, and the horrific murder of George Floyd in Minneapolis, Minnesota, by a police officer who held his knee on Floyd's neck for over 8 minutes as three other police officers watched and failed to intervene. The Black Lives Matter movement has been incredibly successful in focusing the nation's, and the world's, attention on the issue of police brutality against communities of color as well as the unequal treatment of people of color by the U.S. criminal justice system.

In 2014, the #SayHerName campaign was created by the African American Policy Forum (AAPF, n.d.). In 2020, Breonna Taylor (26 years old) was shot multiple times and killed by police during a botched raid of her apartment using a no-knock warrant for arrest that police obtained using false and misleading information in. their case against her ex-boyfriend. In 2015, Sandra Bland was arrested after a minor traffic stop and died in police custody 3 days later. The hashtag's purpose is to bring awareness, recognition, and uplift the often unknown and forgotten Black girls and women police have killed but have not received as much media attention compared to others who have been killed by police officers. According to AAPF (n.d., para. 2):

> Black women and girls as young as 7 and as old as 93 have been killed by the police, though we rarely hear their names. Knowing their names is a necessary but not a sufficient condition for lifting up their stories which in turn provides a much clearer view of the wide-ranging circumstances that make Black women's bodies disproportionately subject to police violence. To lift up their stories, and illuminate police violence against Black women, we need to know who they are, how they lived, and why they suffered at the hands of police.[1]

A Revived Women's Movement (#MeToo)

The #MeToo movement was coined in 2006 by Tarana Burke, a victim of sexual assault herself, who was working with young women and girls of color who had experienced sexual violence. This movement, that began on social media, gained serious momentum after a series of high-profile cases of sexual misconduct and sexual violence against women emerged in the media (e.g., Bill Cosby, Harvey Weinstein, President Trump, Matt Lauer) and women across the country began to share their personal stories of sexual harassment and sexual violence. On January 21, 2017 (the day after President Trump was inaugurated), millions of women and men across the country, and around the globe, attended the **Women's March** in almost every major U.S. city, including a massive one in the nation's capital, to protest Trump's election. Millions of women were disheartened when Trump defeated Hillary Clinton, who was poised to be the first woman president of the United States. And many were disgusted by allegations of sexual misconduct toward the new president and the remarks that he made in a now infamous videotape with Access Hollywood where he stated that "When you're a star … you can do anything … Grab 'em by the [expletive]." At the Women's March, many women wore handcrafted pink hats that came to symbolize Trump's vulgar remark.

The #MeToo movement sparked a new national (and even global) conversation about sexual harassment and sexual violence against women and men in the workplace. And a number of accused high-profile men from various occupations, including Hollywood, journalism, and corporate America, lost their jobs and social status as a result, some even facing criminal prosecution.

---

1   This section co-authored by Dr. Julie Clockston and Dr. Jessica Ritter

LGBTQ+ Rights and the Battle to Win Same-Sex Marriage

Marriage equality has been a controversial hot-button political issue in the United States for many decades. Gay rights advocates have viewed the right to marry as a civil rights and human rights issue, whereas many religious conservatives argued that it goes against the traditional view of marriage between one man and one woman. After many years of advocacy by prominent gay rights organizations such as the Human Rights Campaign, the U.S. Supreme Court ruled in 2015 that **same-sex marriage** is legal in the United States—a historic change with regard to social justice for LGBTQ+ Americans. Though this was an incredible win for LGBTQ+ people, advocates are still working on other needed legislation such as laws that outlaw workplace discrimination and laws to protect the rights and safety of transgender individuals.

#StopAAPIHate[2]

Asian American Pacific Islander (AAPI) people are a minoritized population of individuals who are not a monolith but comprised of multiple cultures and diverse identities rooted in all areas of Asia and the Pacific Islands. AAPI communities have historically experienced blame for various public health crises and were pegged to be carriers of contagious diseases such as "smallpox, syphilis, bubonic plague and other diseases" (Stop AAPI Hate, 2022b, p. 6). Politicians' rhetoric of blaming China for the COVID-19 epidemic and describing China as an economic threat to the United States has exacerbated the scapegoating of Asian Americans. **Scapegoating** is an insidious and dangerous method of oppression that contributes to discrimination, prejudice, and hate. It is the act of othering individuals and groups by placing unmerited blame on them, resulting in devastating and negative impacts. Since COVID-19 began to rise in 2020, AAPI individuals' reports of experiences of "hate incidents" has topped over 11,000 incidents, but this is believed to be the tip of the iceberg as one nationally representative survey found that one in five Asian Americans and one in five Pacific Islanders experienced a hate incident in 2020 or 2021 (Stop AAPI Hate, 2022a, p. 3).

Gun Control Youth Movement (#NeverAgain)

In February 2018, a new youth-led social movement emerged on the national scene as a response to the mass school shooting at Marjory Stoneman Douglas High School in Parkland, Florida that resulted in 17 casualties. Though there had been previous school shootings, this one prompted youth to demand that state and federal lawmakers pass gun control legislation or be faced with being voted out of office. The Parkland students organized a national school walkout on March 14, 2018, followed by a **March for Our Lives** protest on March 24. Protests were held in every U.S. state,

---

2   This section authored by Dr. Julie Clockston.

and the largest protests were held in Washington, DC and New York City, where they were joined by celebrities and prominent lawmakers. It was reported that this was the largest youth protest since the Vietnam War. In terms of strategies and tactics, it was remarkable to witness youth activists who were very adept at knowing how to use social media as a tool for advocacy and social change.

Career Options as a Macro Social Worker

Social work students who are interested in doing work at the macro level often wonder whether they should begin their career doing micro-level work and then move into macro work, or whether they can jump right into macro-level work. There is no right answer to this question, and both options are possible! For example, some students who have a passion for doing policy work in an advocacy organization can directly follow that passion. Perhaps the more common experience is to begin doing work at the micro/mezzo level before moving into macro work, and this path does have some advantages since it provides the opportunity to gain a deep understanding of the challenges that individuals and families experience. But again, there is no right way to do this. The exciting career options profiled include policy practice, community practice, administration and leadership, and social work research.

Policy Practice

Some social workers have the desire to effect change in the political and/or legislative arena in their chosen field of practice, and this is referred to as **social work policy practice**. Doing advocacy work in the macro realm means representing the interests of or defending the rights of groups of people (e.g., children, those living in poverty, those with mental illness, etc.) in the political arena. According to Ritter (2022), there are a number of reasons social workers need to be at the table engaged in political advocacy work:

- Policies can be an important vehicle for social justice and advance human rights and protections on behalf of groups that have been marginalized and/or oppressed (e.g., Civil Rights Act of 1964; Americans with Disabilities Act; Violence Against Women Act; hate crimes legislation).

- Policies can cause harm to vulnerable populations (e.g., laws that legalized slavery; Jim Crow laws in the South; laws that barred women from voting; laws that prohibited same-sex couples from marrying or adopting children).

- It is important for social workers to share their expertise with lawmakers to help them make informed decisions about the populations that social workers serve.

- Policies impact many aspects of social programs in the United States such as program goals, who is eligible to receive services, and the funding levels of these programs.

- Policies can create new social programs and improve existing ones.

- Social workers are called on to be advocates for those who often have no voice in the political system.

IMG 5.3

Social workers can engage in policy work at the local, state, and federal level. All accredited social work programs in the United States are required to offer courses in social welfare policy to help students meet Competency 5 outlined by the Council on Social Work Education (CSWE), which is to "engage in policy practice." When social workers perform policy practice it is a major part of their job responsibilities to use their skills and knowledge to engage in policy change efforts.

Policy practice is defined as "efforts to change policies in legislative, agency, and community settings, whether by establishing new policies, improving existing ones or defeating the policy initiatives of other people" (Jansson, 2008, p. 14), which are undertaken by social workers as an integral part of their professional activity with the aim of contributing to the well-being of service users (Gal & Weiss-Gal, 2013). Though policy change work in the political arena is heavily emphasized, it is important to know that social workers can also do policy work within the organization that employs them since all organizations have policies that guide the work of the organization. When a social worker believes that a policy in their organization is ineffective or unethical, they should seek to change that policy.

Social workers who work to effect change in the political arena are most often focused on one type of public policy—**social welfare policy**, which includes many topics that are of interest to social workers, such as health, mental health, poverty and homelessness, criminal justice, family violence, civil rights, child welfare, and issues that affect women, older adults, those who are LGBTQ+, and people with disabilities.

There are a variety of work settings for social workers who wish to do this work. One of the most common routes is to work in an advocacy organization that works to pass legislation at the local, state, or federal level. Believe it or not, there is an advocacy organization for almost every population and social problem that social workers focus on (see Practice Activity 5.2). Social workers can hold a variety of positions within an advocacy organization, including working as a lobbyist. Another option is to work directly for a lawmaker as a member of their legislative staff. In this role, social workers provide support to constituents who have a problem in their community, develop expertise in a specific policy area, and support the legislator they work for in passing legislation.

Social workers can also run for and hold public office, perhaps one of the most powerful ways to effect public policy (see spotlight that profiles Jennifer Miles, a social worker who works as a lobbyist for NASW). Finally, social workers who

---

5.1   PRACTICE ACTIVITY

You are a social worker providing case management services to LGBTQ+ youth in a community-based organization, including supportive services to transgender youth and their families. It has just been reported in the news that Republican state lawmakers have introduced a bill that would allow child welfare officials to investigate parents who affirm their child's gender identity by allowing them to access "gender-affirming care"—a model or approach that is used by health care and mental health professionals to help and support transgender individuals as they transition and explore whether to pursue medical, surgical, and mental health services. Please work through the following questions as you think through how you would respond to this proposed legislation:

1. Do some research to understand *both* sides of this debate, including experts such as the American Medical Association, the American Psychiatric Association, NASW, the American Academy of Pediatrics, and the American Psychological Association.

2. How can social work values and the NASW Code of Ethics inform how social workers might position a bill like this?

3. How might social workers get involved to provide some advocacy around this issue as this bill is being debated? What expertise can social workers bring to the table to inform this debate and impact the outcome?

are interested in conducting policy analysis or policy evaluation can find employment in government or nonprofit organizations who do this type of policy work. Policy analysis and evaluation is critical work since it helps to determine the right policies to address certain social problems and helps to assess whether a specific policy is working well.

Common activities that are carried out by social workers engaging in policy change work include deciding how to message or frame a policy issue, lobbying, providing testimony at legislative committee hearings, building a coalition, producing professional advocacy materials (e.g., fact sheets), and conducting policy analysis and evaluation (Ritter, 2022).

Community Practice

Another option for social workers who want to practice at the macro level is called **community practice**, which means thinking about a specific community as the client. Community might seem like an abstract concept, but for many people being a part of a community is a crucial part of the human experience. **Community** provides safety, connection, and belonging for many people. When people live in a community surrounded by people from their same cultural background, it can provide an important space for acceptance and belonging. Communities can be large or small, urban or rural, diverse or homogeneous. Take a moment to reflect on the communities you have been a part of and how they have shaped you, your values, and your lived experience.

Social workers understand very well that in order for individuals and communities to be healthy and thrive, they need to live in communities that are safe and healthy. Unfortunately, there are many communities in the United States that suffer from systemic problems such as poverty, high levels of crime, under-resourced schools, lack of employment opportunities, and a lack of adequate resources that are needed to support families, such as affordable health care and daycare services. Efforts by social workers and others to strengthen a community can yield tremendous benefits for the individuals and families who reside there.

Social workers in community practice often work to increase the **social capital** of the community they are focused on. **Robert Putnam** is one of the gurus of social capital and has written best-selling books on the topic, including *Bowling Alone: The Collapse and Revival of the American Community* (2001) and *Better Together: Restoring the American Community* (2004). Communities with high levels of social capital are healthier communities that consist of established social networks; social connectedness; high levels of civic engagement; a strong value of collaboration, reciprocity, and social trust; and an attitude of "we" rather than "I." In other words, people in the community feel connected to each other, trust each other, and help each other out when community members fall on hard times. In his books, Putnam documents a decrease in social capital in the United States since the 1980s and includes data to show that Americans have become less involved in their communities. For example, fewer people are politically involved, volunteer in their community, attend religious services, and are involved in social activities (e.g., bowling leagues). Investments to enhance the social capital of communities can include community revitalization projects, **community development** projects, and programs that bring people together to improve their community and increase social cohesion.

One important tool for social workers who are doing community practice is the ability to carry out a **community needs assessment**, which is used to gather information on the needs and gaps in services in a community as well as the assets and strengths of that community. Information can be collected in a variety of ways, such as gathering demographic data from Census records, conducting interviews with key informants and key stakeholders in the community, sending out surveys to the community, holding town hall meetings, and conducting focus groups with community members. Results from this assessment can then be used to inform recommendations for policy change or environmental change (e.g., needed community services and resources.

When lawmakers or other decision-makers are not receptive to making changes identified in a community needs assessment, sometimes a **community organizing** effort might be established to create the political pressure that is necessary to prompt decision-makers to take needed action. Community organizing has a long history in the United States, and one of the most famous community organizers is **Saul Alinsky**, who is sometimes referred to as the father of community organizing. Starting in the 1930s and through the 1960s, Alinsky supported a number of low-income and minority communities in advocating for better living and working conditions. His famous book, *Rules for Radicals*, published in 1971, describes his philosophy and methods of community organizing that can be used to shift power so that decision-makers are pressured to respond to the needs of people in a given community. Tactics used by community organizers can include a combination of traditional methods (e.g., lobbying lawmakers) and confrontational methods (e.g., protests and other tactics designed to gain media coverage).

Examples of community organizing efforts might include these:

- Parents in a low-income community demanding increased school funding and drawing attention to the way that school funding is distributed unequally in the state that results in some schools being under-resourced

- Community members advocating for affordable housing

- Community members demanding changes due to incidents of police brutality motivated by racial bias

- Community members advocating for an increase in the minimum wage to address high levels of poverty

- Community members joining together to demand that local lawmakers find solutions to the increasing numbers of people who are homeless

- Community members who come together around the issue of environmental racism to protest dangerous conditions due to unsafe water and hazardous waste sites

- Community members who join in efforts to oust a leader from public office who is viewed as corrupt or is failing to respond to the needs of those in the community

Administration and Leadership

It is very common for social workers to work in leadership roles at various points in their career. Though some social workers choose to stay in direct services roles, others decide they want the challenge of moving into **supervisory and/or administrative roles** in an organization. In many organizations, there are layers of management

5.2   PRACTICE ACTIVITY

There are thousands of advocacy organizations across the United States that work to impact social and political change with regard to a specific vulnerable and/or oppressed population. These organizations work to effect policy change at the local, state, or federal level. Think of a social problem or population of interest that you are passionate about and find an advocacy organization that focuses on that issue in your state or at the federal level. Learn about their mission, what policy issues they focus on, and how they go about their work. What successes have they had as an advocacy organization in recent years? As you learn about their work, pay close attention to whether working for an organization like this feels exciting to you.

IMG 5.4

positions. Some positions are considered "middle management" and may have the title of supervisor, program director, or policy director, just to name a few examples. Then higher up the chain of command, some social workers might work their way into senior management positions, including the role of executive director or chief executive officer (CEO).

These administrative roles come with higher pay due to the increased pressure and responsibilities that are an inherent part of the job. Other ways for social workers to assume leadership positions include serving on a board of directors for a nonprofit organization or a governmental board or commission in which members are appointed by public officials such as a mayor, governor, or even the president of the United States. Finally, social workers can run for public office at the local, state, and/or federal level (see Policy Practice section).

When stepping into a leadership role, it is vital to understand the importance of **leadership development**, meaning that these positions require the careful development of new skills and the ability to engage in critical self-reflection to understand both one's strengths as a leader and those areas that require further development. It can be very helpful to gather anonymous feedback from those under your supervision to learn what is working and not working for those reporting to you. Many people in leadership positions seek out mentors/coaches, attend leadership trainings, and read books and articles about leadership.

Important Leadership Competencies

- Ability to inspire people in an organization to work toward a common vision
- Skills in supervising and leading a team of employees, which can also include hiring and firing
- Budget and resource management, including fundraising and managing a budget
- Program administration, which involves developing and managing programs
- Program evaluation skills to evaluate the effectiveness of the organization
- Developing relationships with external stakeholders
- Conflict management and mediation skills
- Strong team-building skills; ability to build coalitions and bring people together to work toward a common goal
- Ability to think critically and strategically; detail oriented but also able to see the "bigger picture"
- Strong organizational skills and the ability to complete tasks in a timely manner

Social Work Research

The vast majority of social workers who are engaged in conducting research in the United States are those with an earned PhD who work either in academia or research organizations, though it is possible to conduct research with an MSW. However, it should be noted that specialized training is needed to gain the skills necessary to be an effective researcher. Social work researchers are motivated to discover new knowledge by asking a question, figuring out the best way to gather data to answer that question (e.g., methodology), analyzing the data using quantitative and/or qualitative research methods, and then making conclusions based on their findings (see Figure 5.2).

Social work students take research classes at the BSW, MSW, and PhD level to learn about the importance of research in social work and how critical it is that social workers evaluate their effectiveness. Practicing social workers who have a BSW and/or MSW degree often use skills that they learn in research classes, for example when they conduct focus groups and construct surveys to get feedback from clients about the services they received. Some jobs require social workers to help the organization gather data to evaluate its effectiveness. Finally, as part of their job some social workers write and submit grant proposals to attempt to obtain funding to support a specific project or program. In most grant proposals, grant seekers are asked to delineate their project's outcomes and how they will measure the impact of their project's outcomes, which are important research skills.

Ideally, the interventions that social workers use are **evidence-based practices**, meaning that they are supported by scientific evidence and shown to be effective. Students learn how to be both a consumer of research (e.g., knowing how to read research studies that can inform your practice) and a producer of research (e.g., knowing how to carry out a research study). Students also learn about important ethical considerations such as informed consent and confidentiality when conducting research to ensure that researchers do not cause harm to those who participate as research subjects.

The Steps of the Research Process

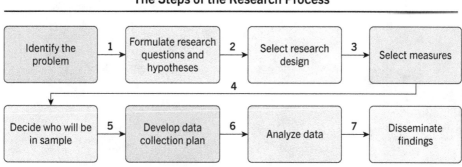

FIGURE 5.2   Overview of the research process.

The primary reason that social work research can be classified as macro-level social work is that the results of social work research should be used to inform policy and/or social work practice. In other words, social work research is used to advance knowledge, and most research studies have implications that should inform the policies that we have and the ways that we practice. For example, when we find that a particular intervention is not effective, we should stop using that intervention. But when we discover that an intervention is effective, we should not only begin using that intervention widely; in some cases we can encourage lawmakers and other funders to support that intervention with state and/or federal dollars.

According to Krysik (2018), there are **four major purposes or functions of social work research**. First, like many other disciplines, this is one of the ways that we acquire knowledge in our field and is based on the scientific method. Second, it is how we are accountable to the public and those we serve since it requires us to evaluate our own effectiveness. Third, it helps us to communicate with the public and with lawmakers about our practice and the evidence behind it. Finally, it can enhance our access to various funding resources (public and private monies) as funders are more likely to fund services and programs that have data to demonstrate their effectiveness.

Brene Brown, social work professor at the University of Houston, has become famous for her qualitative research and has published several books that have become best sellers. Brown studies topics that resonate with many people such as human connection, shame, empathy, and vulnerability. Her TED Talk titled "The Power of Vulnerability" (2010) is one of the most watched Ted Talks of all time.

IMG 5.5

Top 10 Skills Needed for Macro-Level Social Work Practice

To work effectively as a social worker at the macro level, there are a variety of important competencies that are needed to be effective:

- Strong advocacy skills; using one's voice to speak up for others
- Being passionate about addressing larger social problems and issues of social and economic justice
- Ability to frame arguments and be persuasive; find work in the political arena to be important and exciting
- Strong written and oral communication skills, including the ability to communicate to others on social media
- Strong public speaking and presentation skills, including the ability to use software presentation programs such as Microsoft PowerPoint
- Willingness to strive to be cultural competent and embrace cultural humility when working with people and communities that are different from your own
- Strong leadership and managerial/supervisory skills
- Data collection and analysis skills, including the ability to use software programs such as Microsoft Excel
- Self-awareness (constantly self-assessing personal strengths and areas in need of improvement)
- Ability to work with and listen to people with various points of view and to resolve conflicts in a professional manner

Common Myths About Macro-Level Social Work

Some social work students feel hesitant to engage in macro-level work as a social worker and report being more drawn toward micro-level work. The beauty of social work is that social workers get to choose how and where they want to practice based on their skills, passions, and interests. However, there are several misconceptions about the macro realm of social work that keep some social workers from engaging in this work, which is unfortunate (see Table 5.1 for a summary). Some social workers are hesitant because they feel that, compared to micro social work, it takes too long to see change. A good counterargument to this is that it can take just as long to see change at the micro level as some individuals and families face significant life challenges such as addiction that take years to

TABLE 5.1   Top Five Common Myths About Macro Social Work

Macro-level social work is harder and more intimidating than micro-level social work.	Some social workers believe that micro-level social work is "easier" and aligns more easily with their knowledge and skill set. While this may be true for some, the truth is that both micro social work and macro social work require training, experience, and important knowledge to effectively facilitate change. With curiosity and an open mind, social workers can be skilled and competent in both. Social work programs offer many courses in both areas.
Macro-level social work takes longer to see change than micro-level social work.	This is a common myth that is easy to dispel. Once social workers begin working at the micro level, they are able to appreciate that facilitating change at the micro level can take just as long as facilitating change at the macro level. For example, helping a client move out of poverty, secure permanent housing, or overcome a drug addiction can take years. When a macro-level social worker gets a "win" that impacts thousands, or millions of people, that is unbelievably gratifying!
Macro-level social work feels riskier than micro-level social work, particularly work in the political arena. Social workers should be neutral politically.	It is true that doing work in the political arena as a social worker requires putting your political beliefs and positions out there on display, which can feel uncomfortable for some people. The social work profession's mission of social justice demands that we are in involved with policy change efforts that support the populations that we serve.
It is harder to find a job doing macro-level social work.	While it might be true that there are more micro-level jobs than macro-level jobs, it is also true that there are many job opportunities for social workers who wish to work at the macro level. Social workers across the country are working in policy, leadership, research, and administration. Most social workers begin their career at the micro level and then move into macro-level work as they gain more experience.
Macro social work requires special skills and knowledge that social workers may not have.	Social workers definitely have the skills needed for macro-level social work! They have knowledge and expertise in systems theory and policy change, and they have excellent communication skills, people skills, and team-building skills.

make progress. Additionally, some legislative efforts at the local and state level can happen quickly! There is also a myth that social workers should avoid getting involved in policy work as social workers should be politically neutral and stay above the political fray and because politics is a messy and corrupt environment. Many dedicated macro social workers would argue that social work's **mission of social justice** makes it impossible for social work to be neutral politically and that clients depend on social workers to work for needed policy change, despite the fact that the political environment has its challenges.

Finally, some social workers feel that they do not have the knowledge and skills to engage in work at the macro level. Social workers often need to be reminded that this is patently untrue. They need to be reminded that macro social work involves work with organizations, large systems, communities, and policy practice and that they have developed a skill set (e.g., communication and relationship building, advocacy, leadership) and a knowledge base (e.g., theories of power and change) that translate very well to this work. Like anything else, it just takes on the job experience, mentoring, curiosity, and passion.

Chapter Summary

Though it is less visible than micro practice, macro social work practice is a critical component of the social work profession and helps the profession achieve its mission of social justice for vulnerable and oppressed populations. Students in BSW and MSW programs are required to complete coursework that prepares them for practicing at both the micro and macro levels. Macro social work requires a shift in thinking with regard to who the client is that is the target of the intervention—a large system, a community, or society at large. Social workers working in this realm often work to improve conditions in the larger social environment to enhance the well-being of individuals and families. Recent efforts have been made to elevate the macro side of the profession is response to criticisms that it has been neglected and deprioritized. Many social workers will engage in macro-level practice over the course of their social work career and have the option of policy practice, administration and leadership, community practice, and social work research. Social workers who step into leadership roles must be committed to the development of leadership skills in order to be an impactful and effective leader.

Discussion Questions

1. This chapter describes macro-level social work as the "hidden side of social work." Is it problematic that the general public is generally unaware of the macro side of social work? Why or why not?

2. Tensions between micro and macro social work were discussed in this chapter, including various opinions about whether the social work profession should be neutral politically or whether its mission of social justice demands that it take stands on certain policy issues. How do you feel about this debate? Where do you stand?

3. Four major macro roles were described in this chapter—political advocacy, community practice, leadership and administration, and social work research. Which of these macro roles are most and least appealing to you?

Which of the skills that were profiled as important to macro-level work would you need to enhance in order to be effective?

4. Watch Brene Brown's famous TED Talk titled "The Power of Vulnerability." How did watching her talk make you think differently about engaging in research as a social worker? Why do you think that her research resonates with so many people?

5. This chapter listed several recent social movements that have emerged in the United States in recent years. Do you believe it is important for social workers to be engaged with social movements if a movement's goals align with the mission and values of the social work profession? Defend your answer.

References

African American Policy Forum. (n.d.). *#Say her name.* https://www.aapf.org/sayher-name#:~:text=say%20her%20name.%20Launched%20in%20December%202014%20by,police%20violence%2C%20and%20provides%20support%20to%20their%20families

Alinsky, S. D. (1971). *Rules for radicals: A practical primer for realistic radicals.* Random House.

Association for Community Organization and Social Action. (n.d.). *About the special commission.* https://acosa.clubexpress.com/content.aspx?page_id=22&club_id=789392&module_id=335370

Brown, B. (2010). *The power of vulnerability.* TED. https://www.ted.com/talks/brene_brown_the_power_of_vulnerability?language=en

Gal, J., & Weiss-Gal, I. (2013). *Social workers affecting social policy: An international perspective.* Policy Press.

Homan, M. (2016). *Promoting community change: Making it happen in the real world* (6th ed.). Cengage.

Jansson, B. S. (2008). *Becoming an effective policy advocate: From policy practice to social justice* (5th ed.). Brooks/Cole.

Krysik, J. L. (2018). *Research for effective social work practice* (4th ed). Routledge.

National Association of Social Workers. (2021). *Code of Ethics of the National Association of Social Workers.* https://www.socialworkers.org/About/Ethics/Code-of-Ethics/Code-of-Ethics-English

Putnam, R. D. (2000). *Bowling alone: The collapse and revival of the American community.* Simon & Schuster.

Putnam, R. D. (2004). *Better together: Restoring the American community.* Simon & Schuster.

Ritter, J. A. (2022). *Social work policy practice: Changing our community, nation, and the world* (3rd ed,). Cognella.

Specht, H., & Courtney, M. E. (1994). *Unfaithful angels: How social work has abandoned its mission*. The Free Press.

Stop AAPI Hate. (2022a, July). *Two years and thousands of voices: What community generated data tells us about anti-AAPI hate*. https://stopaapihate.org/wp-content/uploads/2022/07/Stop-AAPI-Hate-Year-2-Report.pdf

Stop AAPI Hate. (2022b, October). *The blame game: How political rhetoric inflames Anti-Asian scapegoating*. https://stopaapihate.org/wp-content/uploads/2022/10/Stop-AA-PI-Hate-Scapegoating-Report.pdf

▐ Credits

CHAPTER 6

Social Work Practice in Poverty and Housing Insecurity

Kristen Atkinson

Learning Objectives

After reading this chapter, students will be able to do the following:

- Summarize key facets of poverty and housing insecurity as social problems and how they were exacerbated during the coronavirus pandemic

- Explain the connections between intersectional social identities (e.g., race/ethnicity, gender; age) and poverty and housing insecurity

- Describe the income assistance and housing support safety net in the United States and the limitations of these systems

- Understand poverty and housing insecurity using a human rights framework

- Explain the goals of the housing as a human rights movement and how it seeks to address systemic oppression

- Evaluate the housing first model as a public policy solution for people experiencing housing insecurity

- Summarize research findings on interventions to interrupt intergenerational poverty

- Identify three major career path options for social workers who want to work for poverty alleviation and housing security

- Evaluate their own goodness of fit with social work practice to alleviate poverty and housing insecurity as a potential future career option

SOCIAL WORKER SPOTLIGHT:
Barbra Evans-Small, MSW, Service Coordinator at the Denver Housing Authority

My personal experience as an African American single mom in 1998 brought me to the social work arena. Being a single mother living in a low-income unit in Denver became a driving factor and motivation to turn my social and economic barriers into building blocks to create a path for a better future for my family. I know what's it like to depend on public transit, to live in a food desert, to rely on Mile High United Way for childcare assistance, and to struggle to keep a roof over my head. My survival to make life-changing decisions daily became my hope for a better life.

I always knew I wanted to help others and give back to those who helped me, but I was unsure of how to make my dream come true. This is why I enrolled in Metro State College of Denver (now called Metropolitan State University of Denver) to advance my education so I could become a role model and provider for my family. Three years into college, I still had not declared a major. I asked a mentor "What should I major in?" and he stated, "Whatever you are willing to do for free. Because when the money is not there, your love and passion for the work you love will keep you going back." I've since learned that what we do for others is not always valued. I immediately answered my mentor, "I will help someone in a heartbeat." He stated, "That is what you should major in, so now go find a career in helping others." Therefore, I chose the Department of Social Work.

While going Metro State, I worked part-time and became involved in the inner-city community because I knew I wanted to create solutions and changes for the under-served. I graduated from Metro State College in 2001 with a Bachelor of Science/Social Work degree.

I'm appreciative for Metro State because I was given an opportunity to face my fears of returning to school after 15 years and for providing me with the hands-on support I needed to believe in myself. In 2002 I enrolled at the University of Denver (DU) to further my study in social work. I was determined to finish school before my first child finished high school, so I enrolled in the 1-year advanced standing MSW program and graduated with a Master of Social Work degree in 2003.

Upon completion from DU in 2003, I was offered a job at Denver Housing Authority. Today I have a 20-year professional career as a social worker/service coordinator at Denver Housing Authority. My current position at Denver Housing Authority gives me the opportunity to provide resources, make referrals, provide advocacy, and bring in community partners to create changes for the low-income senior and disabled residents I serve. I believe that "when you know better, you will do better." This statement motivates me to secure speakers to educate the residents on personal finances, mental health, and healthy living habits.

For 6 years, I was given a chance to serve as an appointee by Mayor Hancock to serve as a Commission on Aging member. It was important to me to shed light on low-income housing, lack of healthy food choices, and medical issues seniors in the city face daily. The unique perspective I bring as a social worker is my ability to meet residents where they are. My goal is to make sure they are given equal opportunities to a better health care system, affordable housing, and equality regardless of their race and background. I personally know that best practice is essential, and everyone should be given an opportunity.

I have pure gratitude for the residents at Denver Housing Authority who inspire me to love what I do and do what I love for the people I love. Social work is the heart of humanity.

One of the core values of the social work profession is to promote **social and economic justice**, and there is perhaps no issue that is more deserving of social workers' attention than the reduction of poverty due to the many negative impacts it has on people's health, well-being, and life opportunities. In fact, the first sentence of the preamble to the NASW (2021) Code of Ethics states, "The primary mission of the social work profession is to enhance human well-being and help meet the *basic human needs* of all people, with particular attention to the needs

IMG 6.1

and empowerment of people who are vulnerable, oppressed, and *living in poverty*" (emphasis added). Most would agree that poverty is not an easy social problem to solve and that historically there has not been the political will to seriously address it in the United States (with the exception of President Lyndon B. Johnson's war on poverty in the 1960s).

What's more, the **COVID-19 pandemic** has had an immediate and striking impact on low-income individuals and families across the country. Unemployment and economic downturn have left many facing housing and food insecurity, with Black and Hispanic households experiencing higher rates of economic burden during this time. According to the National Alliance to End Homelessness, should these disparities continue, they could exacerbate existing racial disproportionality among the unhoused population (Pagaduan, 2021). While federal relief efforts have helped mitigate the economic impact of the pandemic, the long-term outcome of these time-limited financial programs is yet to be determined.

Unfortunately, poverty in the United States has been primarily viewed as an individual failing despite the findings of social scientists who study poverty and highlight the structural causes of it. The strong mythology in the United States around the "self-made man" and the idea that anyone can be successful if they are just willing to work hard enough ignores the significant systemic barriers that many People of Color and low-income individuals face in society. The ability of people to move from a lower to a higher socioeconomic status, referred to as **social mobility**, is possible but often comes with much struggle and through the support of others. To add to this complexity, how we define who is living in poverty in the United States is political and not without controversy. Social workers work with low-income individuals and families every day, and this chapter is focused on various programs, practices, and policies that are designed to support those living in poverty, and in the best-case scenario, to help people move out of poverty.

Overview of Poverty and Housing Insecurity

Poverty is a complex social issue to define. In fact, the U.S. government currently uses two distinct measures of poverty. The **official poverty measure** (OPM) compares pretax cash income with the cost of a minimum food diet that is adjusted for family size. On the other hand, the **supplemental poverty measure** (SPM) provides an alternative view of poverty that attends to contemporary social, economic, and policy considerations. This measure considers complex family compositions such as unmarried partners and unrelated cohabitants, geographic housing costs, costs of goods and expenses beyond food, and noncash benefits (Institute for Research on Poverty, 2023). Even with these additional criteria, both measures of poverty are widely criticized as failing to accurately capture the economic reality of millions. While they may provide some sense of economic deprivation and inadequate living standards, they offer only a limited understanding of the hunger, lack of access to quality educational and medical services, and psychological tool of poverty. Despite these limitations, it is critical that social workers understand the prevalence and impact of poverty on the people and communities they serve.

According to the U.S. Census Bureau's (2022) OPM, 37.9 million people in the United States currently live in poverty; this is a significant 11.6% of the U.S. population. When looking strictly at those under age 18, the rate climbs to 15.3%, or roughly 11.1 million children and youth. Women and children in female-headed households experience higher rates of poverty, at 25.3% of their population rate, sometimes referred to as the **feminization of poverty**. Unemployed individuals and those without a high school diploma also experience high rates of poverty, 30% and 27.2%, respectively. Notably, rates of poverty vary based on racial identity and are highest among American Indian and Alaskan Native (24.3%), Black (19.5%), and Hispanic populations (17.1%; Creamer et al., 2022).

Poverty is often understood as an individual failure: Those who are poor don't work hard enough, aren't educated enough, lack motivation or relevant workplace skills. This individual pathology perspective, however, fails to account for external factors that limit the opportunities available to so many people. **Root causes of poverty** are well established in research and include lack of economic opportunities, quality education, public infrastructure, quality health care, and government support (Brittain & Blackstock, 2015; Rank et al., 2003; Wildsmith & Alvira-Hammond, 2023). For example, Rank et al. (2003) argue that poverty in the United States is, in fact, a structural failure of the labor market to provide enough living-wage jobs with benefits to accommodate the workforce, coupled with the lack of political will to develop a strong system of social supports for those living in poverty. Additional factors influencing poverty in the United States include the high cost of living of many localities, environmental devastation (i.e., wildfires, hurricanes, tornados, etc.), and historical injustices such as the enslavement and forced labor of Africans and the genocide and forced relocation of indigenous peoples.

The myth of **meritocracy**—that we are a land of equal opportunities—ignores how forced, unpaid labor, physical and sexual abuse, denial of citizenship and land ownership rights, and illiteracy has effectively curtailed economic mobility for generations of Black people in the United States. Even into the mid-20th century, employment discrimination and redlining in the housing market worked to prevent the accumulation of wealth among Black families. Similar dynamics are evidenced in the impact of settler colonialism on Indigenous tribes, removed from richly resourced lands, relocated to under-resourced reservations, and made economically dependent on the U.S. government (Brittain & Blackstock, 2015). These early beginnings of our country have undeniably contributed to greater economic privilege for many White people while creating undue burdens on Black, Indigenous, and People of Color (BIPOC) communities that continue today. This phenomenon is known as the **racial wealth gap**, and in 2022, Black families on average possessed just one fourth the wealth of White families (Kent & Ricketts, 2022).

Housing insecurity refers to the safety and quality of a home environment and is widely accepted as a burgeoning social problem in the United States. Housing insecurity is the result of a myriad of factors, including high housing costs relative to income, poor quality of housing, overcrowding, and neighborhood instability. Homelessness, evictions and forced moves, and doubling up to share housing costs are also considered indicators of housing insecurity (Leopold et al., 2016). In 2019, 37.1 million households were **cost burdened**, meaning these households spent more than 30% of their income on housing costs. Housing cost burden, which is twice as likely to impact Black and Hispanic households, can lead to foreclosure and eviction. Poor quality housing, frequent moves, and overcrowding expose people to health, safety, and mental health risks. People reentering community postincarceration face additional systemic barriers, such as discrimination or ineligibility for public housing benefits (U.S. Department of Health and Human Services, n.d.). In its most extreme form, housing insecurity becomes **homelessness**. A single-night count in January 2022 revealed 582,462 people were experiencing homelessness at that point in time. Individuals with disabilities and those who identify as Black or Indigenous continue to be overrepresented among the unhoused (U.S. Department of Housing and Urban Development, 2022).

As we will explore in this chapter, poverty and housing insecurity are undoubtedly **social determinants of health**, or factors that impact the health and development of individuals and communities. Economic factors such as un- or underemployment influence stress; exposure to violence and environmental toxins; access to services and resources; physical, mental, and behavioral health; high-risk behavior; and ultimately mortality. Households contending with housing cost burden often struggle to obtain the necessities of life (food, clothing, utilities, and health care; U.S. Department of Health and Human Services, n.d.). Housing instability may also further social exclusion, or the sense of belonging an individual has to their community (Community Toolbox, 2023). When considered from intersectional and systemic perspectives, our understanding of poverty must move beyond single-factor explanations and acknowledge the complex and multifaceted lived experience of poverty; likewise, as we will see in our exploration of antipoverty policy, practice, and research, our efforts to ameliorate it must confront this complexity.

Social Welfare Responses to Poverty and Housing Insecurity

The practice of promoting financial and housing stability has a long history within the field of social work. In fact, some of our country's oldest social supports include policies and programs to alleviate poverty. During the progressive era, for example, 40 states enacted laws to provide economic support to "needy widowed mothers" (Skocpol, 1995). These gendered pension laws allowed children to remain home with their mothers despite the lack of paternal support. Social welfare provisions further expanded during the Great Depression with the passage of the **Social Security Act of 1935**. This act established programs such as **Old-Age Assistance** and **Aid to the Blind**, which helped meet the needs of older adults and disabled individuals experiencing loss of life savings and employment opportunities. The Social Security program is one of the most successful antipoverty programs in the United States as it is designed to insure people against poverty after they leave the workforce and retire by providing a monthly financial benefit. The Social Security Act also provided federal grants to states to support the health and welfare of mothers and their children, known as **Aid to Families With Dependent Children** (AFDC; Social Security Administration [SSA], n.d.). It must be noted that, although these early poverty-relief efforts established an important foundation of social support, their implementation reflects racist and sexist notions of "deserving," "moral," and "suitable" motherhood. Unwed mothers, Black mothers, and low-wage mothers (e.g., domestic and farm workers) were depicted as undeserving of aid, while White widowed mothers were viewed as deserving caretakers (Center for Budget & Policy Priorities, 2022).

Thirty years later, the Social Security Act was extended to include **Medicaid**, a medical assistance program for low-income people. Additional poverty-relief efforts at this time addressed nutritional needs (the Food Stamp Act, Special Supplemental Food Program for Women, Infants, and Children, and free school meals), home energy assistance, and public or subsidized housing (SSA, n.d.). Versions of these social programs remain today, although many contain restrictions and limitations rooted in systemic racism and capitalism that hamper our individual and collective efforts to overcome poverty.

As Ritter (2022) describes, there are three primary strategies that nations can use to address poverty and income security when designing their social welfare system. The **alleviative approach** relies on programs that ease the suffering of the poor but do not ameliorate the causes of poverty (e.g., public assistance programs such as the Food Stamp Program and Temporary Assistance for Needy Families [TANF]). This approach relies on **means-tested programs** that only allow people to access them when they fall below a certain income level. The **preventive**

approach attempts to prevent poverty from occurring and often employs social insurance strategies (e.g., Social Security, Medicare, the unemployment insurance program). The **curative approach** targets the root causes of poverty and involves structural changes in society that would result in low levels of poverty (e.g., high taxation and redistribution of wealth similar to the social welfare systems used in Scandinavian nations). Instead of using means-tested programs, the preventive and curative approaches rely on social welfare benefits that are **universal**, meaning that every citizen receives them regardless of their income. Even though the United States uses all three of these approaches, we do not rely as much on the curative approach. The Scandinavian nations are known for relying heavily on this approach, and as a result they have the lowest poverty rates in the world.

Income Assistance Programs in the United States

Temporary Aid to Needy Families Program

Today when people in the United States refer to the nation's welfare program and those who are "on welfare," they are referring to the TANF program. One of the largest revisions to the public safety net was enacted in 1996 with the **Personal Responsibility and Work Opportunity Reconciliation Act** when the AFDC program became the TANF program. The legislation replaced the cash benefits of AFDC with time-limited assistance to families with children under the new TANF program. The controversial new law included a new lifetime limit in that families can only receive financial benefits for a total of 5 years. Through this act, the federal government provides grants to states for distribution as cash benefits and programs that promote family stability and job readiness (U.S. Department of Health & Human Services, 2019). Unfortunately, TANF has reduced the level of cash assistance low-income children and families receive, effectively undermining the potential stability income supports offer those experiencing poverty. In fiscal year (FY) 2020, only 22% of total TANF spending was allocated to basic assistance; the remaining funds supported education and training (10%), work and supportive services (2%), childcare (17%), tax credits (9%), prekindergarten/Head Start (9%), child welfare (8%), program

> **6.1   PRACTICE ACTIVITY**
>
> So far, this chapter has focused on providing an overview of poverty and housing insecurity, including the causes, and how the United States has responded to this social problem.
>
> 1. When most Americans think about people who live below the poverty line, what images do you think come to mind for them? How do most view the causes of poverty (e.g., individual versus societal causes)?
>
> 2. When you think about working in an agency that is designed to help address poverty in your community and to support people in moving out of poverty, what thoughts and feelings come up for you?
>
> 3. Do you support the United States using an alleviative, preventive, or curative approach to poverty? What are the pros and cons of each approach? Defend your answer.

management (10%), and other expenses (13%; Center for Budget & Policy Priorities [CBPP], 2022a). According to research from the CBPP (2022a),

> TANF benefit levels are low and are not sufficient for families to meet all their basic needs...In July 2021, the maximum TANF benefit that a family of three could receive ranged from $204 in Arkansas (11 percent of the poverty line) to $1,098 in New Hampshire (60 percent of the poverty line), with a median of $498 (27 percent of the poverty line). (para. 9)

While the financial assistance established by TANF is critical to the welfare of our nation's poorest, these figures demonstrate that the benefits provided are insufficient to meet basic family needs. Moreover, since its creation in 1996, the number of families enrolled in the program has steadily declined. Today, only 21% of families experiencing poverty will receive TANF benefits. Given geographic population trends, Black children and families are more likely to live in states with lower rates of cash assistance, underscoring the differential impact of poverty relief programs (CBPP, 2022a).

Like its predecessors, aspects of this policy reflect gendered and racialized narratives of motherhood, sexual behavior, and workforce participation (Floyd, et al., 2021). Provisions to immigrants are heavily restricted in most states, with complete bans on eligibility for those who are undocumented. Many states have enacted full or partial restrictions for people with felony drug convictions, as well as "family caps," which deny additional cash support to families who have another child while receiving benefits. Some states collect child support payment from the noncustodial parents as reimbursement for the cash assistance rather than pass this support to the child (CBPP, 2022a).

The Social Security Program

The Social Security program is one of the best antipoverty programs in existence. It is a social insurance program that is meant to insure workers against their own poverty after they leave the workforce and retire. According to the CBPP (2022b), roughly 22 million adults and children would be poor if we did not have this program. In 2020, 9% of older adults were living in poverty, but if they did not have Social Security benefits, a shocking 37.8% would be living in poverty (CBPP, 2022b). The program is funded by a payroll tax that is paid by employees and employers, and then after people retire they receive a monthly check from the program based on their lifetime earnings. This program also supports some people with disabilities that limits their ability to work as well as some survivors (spouses and dependent children) of retired, disabled, and deceased workers. In 2023, the average monthly benefit was $1,827, while the maximum benefit $3,627.

The Supplemental Security Program

The Supplemental Security (SSI) program is another major income assistance program funded by the federal government that is set up to provide a monthly cash benefit to people who are very low income and who suffer from **serious disabilities or blindness**, the majority of whom are unable to pay into, and thus benefit from, the Social Security program. However, some people who are over 65 and do not have a disability are also eligible if they meet certain income requirements. In 2023, the monthly maximum federal payment amount was $914 for an eligible individual, $1,371 for an eligible individual with an eligible spouse, and $458 for an essential person (i.e., someone who lives with an SSI beneficiary and provides essential care to them).

Unemployment Insurance Program

This program, overseen by the Department of Labor, is designed to prevent financial hardship to those who have lost their job until they can find a new one. It provides cash benefits to those who have lost their job through no fault of their own while they are searching for a new job. It is jointly funded by states and the federal government, though states play a much more significant role as they tax employers to fund the program and determine benefit levels and number of weeks that people are eligible to receive benefits. Most states provide up to 26 weeks of benefits to unemployed workers, replacing about half of their previous wages, up to a maximum benefit amount. Just before the start of the COVID-19 recession in February 2020, average weekly benefits were about $387 nationwide but ranged from a low of $215 in Mississippi to $550 in Massachusetts (CBPP, 2021).

Tax Credits for Low-Income Workers

The **Earned Income Tax Credit (EITC)** allows eligible low-income workers to receive a wage supplement from the government when they file their taxes. Only people who are working can claim this benefit; thus, it is meant to reward people with children who work and provide for their family. In 2022, the tax credit was $3,733 for families with one child; $6164 for families with two children; and $6935 for families with three or more children. The EITC has been touted as one of the most effective antipoverty measures currently in existence in the United States.

Programs That Address Hunger and Food Insecurity

There are a few important social programs that are set up to address hunger and food insecurity for low-income individuals and families who struggle to have enough money for food. Child welfare advocates and medical professionals have educated lawmakers over the years about the negative impact to children and their developing brain when they lack the nutrition they need. In the private sector, there are countless numbers of soup kitchens and food banks across the country that are funded and administered by various nonprofit and faith-based organizations.

The federal government also plays an important role in addressing food insecurity. A well-known program in the United States is the **Supplemental Nutrition Assistance Program**, or **SNAP**, which is more commonly referred to as the "food stamp" program. The Food Stamp Act was passed in 1964 as part of President Lyndon B. Johnson's war on poverty. This program provides a monthly financial benefit for those with very low incomes, including older adults and people with disabilities, to purchase food. There are strict eligibility requirements that people must meet in the areas of gross monthly income, net monthly income, and assets. The CBPP (2022c) reports that in 2021, 41 million Americans received help from the SNAP program, two thirds were in families with children, and the average monthly benefit per person was $127 per month plus an additional $92 a month in temporary pandemic-related benefits that will expire in 2023. The monthly benefit that families receive varies based on family size.

Other important food assistance programs are the **Special Supplemental Food Program for Women, Infants, and Children** (or **WIC**) and programs that provide meals to low-income children in schools. The WIC program, established in 1975, provides nutritious food as well as nutrition education and counseling to women who are pregnant and breastfeeding and children younger than 5 years. The

IMG 6.2

School Breakfast Program and the **National School Lunch Program** provide free or low-cost meals to eligible children at school. The National School Lunch program was created by the National School Lunch Act of 1946, and the breakfast program became a permanent program in 1975.

The Housing Safety Net

There are many examples of people who find themselves at risk of being without housing due to a variety of circumstances such as these:

- A youth who has been kicked out of their home due to being LGBTQ+

- The provider of a family who has lost their job and can no longer pay the rent

- A woman who has left an abusive partner and needs to seek emergency shelter at a family violence agency

- A youth who has aged out of the foster care system and is in need of transitional housing

- A person who has lost their income due to a serious chronic illness and/or mental illness

- A young adult living in a city where the rent has become unaffordable

- A veteran with a substance abuse addiction who is living on the street

- A man who has just been released from prison and is in need of support with housing until he is able to obtain employment

In the private sector, there are nonprofit and faith-based organizations in many cities and communities across the nation that are set up to serve those who find themselves experiencing homelessness or housing insecurity, such as **homeless shelters**, **emergency shelters**, and **family violence shelters**. Additionally, the federal government provides several supportive services to improve the housing security of people in the United States, including rental assistance, home ownership supports, and fair housing programs. Housing assistance provided by the federal government, via the U.S. Department of Housing and Urban Development, or HUD, is often referred to as "Section 8" because the Section 8 housing program was created in 1974 to provide rental subsidies to low-income families who could not afford the rent in their neighborhood or community. Today's **housing choice voucher program** is intended to assist low-income families, older adults, and people with disabilities find and keep safe, quality housing. Participation in the program is based on meeting income requirements established by local housing authorities. Home ownership programs include low down payments for first-time buyers, incentives for certain categories of public servants (teachers, firefighters, etc.) to buy in designated revitalization areas, and loan guarantees for American

Indians, Alaskan Natives, and Native Hawaiians. Emergency rental assistance and eviction assistance programs, as established during the COVID-19 pandemic, provide crucial emergency supports for communities facing disproportionate risk of housing insecurity, including youth and BIPOC. Specialized services are also offered for veterans, survivors of violence, youth and older adults at risk of homelessness, and people living with mental health or substance use disorders. These services may include emergency shelters, supportive housing, transitional housing, and independent living programs.

As an example, the **Runaway and Homeless Youth Act** was enacted by Congress to address the impact of youth homelessness on personal health and well-being, as well as its social impact on community welfare. This policy acknowledges the important supports and opportunities unhoused youth need to survive and thrive as they transition to adulthood, including safety and structure, sense of belonging, self-worth and social contribution, self-efficacy, supportive relationships, educational options, and employment skill development. It establishes a developmentally relevant continuum of care ranging from temporary to transitional housing, access to food, clothing and medical care, therapeutic services, recreational programs, life skills programs, educational supports, and job counseling and placement (Interagency Working Group on Youth Programs, n.d.).

While critical to survival for poor individuals and families, constraints within the U.S. housing safety net keep many people vulnerable. A history of substance use or criminal system involvement can result in ineligibility for services. Immigration status, especially that of undocumented, is another significant barrier to services and supports. Long waiting lists for housing, lack of available beds or affordable units, underfunded subsidies, and restrictive agency policies may dissuade those in need. Not to mention, gender-based programs—which are common within shelter systems—may fail to offer welcoming, inclusive spaces for transgender and nonbinary people.

Contemporary Challenges in the Housing Safety Net

In the United States, we continue to grapple with increasing income disparity simultaneous to an increasing cost of living. As mentioned earlier, this reality is compounded by the complexity and intersectionality of how poverty and housing insecurity are experienced. Race, gender identity, family composition, immigration status, mental illness and substance use, system involvement, age, and disability all impact how these issues are navigated by individuals, families, and communities. What's more, experiences of trauma—such as intimate partner violence—can contribute to poverty and housing insecurity; conversely, poverty, homelessness, and housing insecurity can be sources of trauma (Klest, 2012).

Gender-Affirming Services

Contemporary challenges in housing stability are often rooted in accessibility issues. As mentioned earlier, discrimination against marginalized groups creates housing insecurity for many, while strict housing program requirements reinforce vulnerability. For example, programs that serve gender-specific populations complicate access for transgender and nonbinary people. Gender-specific shelters may misclassify people's gender identity and fail to provide the safety and privacy transgender people deserve. The risk of violence and harassment—verbal, physical or sexual—is increased in these nonaffirming spaces. Given the rampant discrimination that transgender people experience in employment, education, health care, familial and social spheres, the lack of gender-affirming care in our most basic social safety net is especially troubling. For many, sleeping on the streets, staying with an abusive partner, or engaging in sex work in exchange for a night inside may seem like better alternatives to the physical, emotional, and psychological harm of shelters. Of course, these alternatives carry other potential consequences for trans and nonbinary people, including health and mental health issues, criminalization, or victimization (Mottet & Ohle, 2003).

Gender-affirming services must adopt a stance of respect for individuals' self-identities. This may require agencies to revisit housing policies and practice approaches or to physically improve the safety of sleeping and bathroom facilities. Additionally, it may be necessary to increase staff awareness of legal issues (e.g., changing legal documents to align with self-identification) and medical needs (e.g., safe and effective hormone treatments) impacting the transgender community. Agencies serving trans and nonbinary young people will need to take care in their approach to identity development, dress codes, and emotional validation. Safety and confidentiality, inclusive language, welcoming messages (e.g., posted signs), and policies of respect are critical considerations for all housing residents. What's more, housing programs aiming to provide gender-affirming services would benefit from networking with other agencies providing supportive services to this community (Mottet & Ohle, 2003); education and advocacy with referral partners may be necessary as well.

Policy Focus: Housing First Model

Another contemporary challenge in the field is whether treatment for mental and behavioral health needs must proceed access to housing services. For many years, emergency shelters and transitional housing programs required individuals to move through a linear housing system; people demonstrated "**housing readiness**" through their ongoing participation in supportive, transitional services prior to receiving permanent housing. Within this approach, people actively using drugs or alcohol or opting not to engage in psychiatric treatment may not qualify for services or may be evicted from the housing resource for failing to comply.

6.2   PRACTICE ACTIVITY

Identify a contemporary issue in housing services such as gender-affirming spaces, housing first program models, or emergency shelter for undocumented immigrants. Do some research to understand the issue and identify key service challenges within this arena. Determine the following:

- What are the strengths of this practice approach?

- What resources exist for implementing this approach or serving the target community?

- What, if any, drawbacks exist within this practice approach?

In the 1990s, the **housing first model** emerged as an alternative to the existing system; this model forefronts the provision of permanent housing for individual and families. Support for personal goals such as finishing school, getting a job, or entering recovery are offered to assist people in maintaining their stability but are never required. In these ways, the housing first model both removes barriers to permanent housing and increases personal choice. Housing first has become the dominant paradigm in the field, with federal funding now prioritizing the model.

Initial research into this approach shows promising results, including quicker exits from homelessness, increased housing stability over time and taxpayer cost savings for public services; that said, insufficient evidence exists on how housing first might impact substance use, mental illness, or physical health outcomes (Tsai, 2020), as well as community-level indicators. Additionally, despite the positive potential of this model, Housing first cannot account for structural contributors to housing instability, such as lack of affordable housing, income equality, or access to affordable mental and physical health care.

IMG 6.3

Housing as a Human Right

Economic and housing security are synergistic. While housing insecurity stresses our familial, economic, social, and educational systems, stable housing in supportive neighborhoods empowers individuals and families to live healthy and productive lives. Housing stability, then, provides a foundation for peace, security, and human dignity. This is the basis for housing as a human right. First established in 1948 in the U.N. Declaration of Human Rights and later reaffirmed through the International Covenant on Economic, Social and Cultural Rights of 1966, this framework argues that all people deserve adequate places to live, access to necessary services and opportunities, and the ability to live in a way that reflects their cultural practices. According to the United Nations, the right to housing should be interpreted broadly to include "security of tenure" (i.e., legal protections against forced eviction, threats, and harassment), access to services and infrastructure, affordability, safety and physical protection against the elements, accessibility for marginalized and vulnerable people, freedom from pollution and other hazards, and response to cultural identity (Office of the United Nations High Commissioner for Human Rights, n.d.). Integral to this perspective is the understanding that "human rights are interdependent, indivisible and interrelated" (Office of the United Nations High Commissioner for Human Rights, n.d., p. 9). In other words, adequate housing is essential to realizing many other rights — the right to health, education, privacy, and work, to name a few. Housing as a human right is further elucidated in several international conventions to protect groups at high risk, including women, children, persons with disabilities, unhoused and displaced people, and indigenous people.

While a limited number of countries have adopted this principle through national legislation, without sufficient funding and accountability measures, evidence of its effectiveness remains to be seen (Fallon, 2021). As a member of the United Nations, the United States has signed onto international covenants, including the 2016 New Urban Agenda, which commits us to ending homelessness and realizing adequate housing for all. Major federal entities, including the Departments of Justice and Housing and Urban Development, are now taking steps to prevent and decriminalize homelessness.

As of this writing, the **Housing is a Human Right Act** is still pending in Washington, DC. Introduced in 2021, and backed by numerous legislators and advocacy organizations, this policy would allocate several billion dollars to emerging housing needs, create a grant program to support local infrastructure related to housing and homelessness, and reduce the criminalization of unhoused people by providing evidence-based interventions (Jayapal, 2021). At the state and local levels, momentum for housing rights continues to grow, as evidenced by bills of rights for the unhoused and calls for reparations for the long-term exclusion of BIPOC communities from the housing market (Tars, 2021). Social workers across the nation can support these efforts through coalition building and policy advocacy; our efforts to do so align us with our ethical mandate to work for social and economic justice for all people.

Research Focus: 2Gen Approaches to Ending Intergenerational Poverty

Thus far, this chapter has discussed the evolution of social policy to address poverty and housing insecurity. Sound public policy depends on a nuanced understanding of the social issue, as well as quality data on the impact of potential interventions. Important, emerging research within this service arena spans a wide range of topics—job creation, legal assistance, hunger, education, unplanned pregnancy, juvenile and criminal justice, health equity, economic and community development, and more. Intergenerational poverty, and efforts to interrupt this cycle, are topics deserving attention. **Intergenerational poverty** is defined as "poverty in which two or more successive generations of a family continue in the cycle of poverty" (Utah State Legislature, 2018, para. 1). Childhood poverty is directly connected to the likelihood of experiencing poverty as an adult and is the result of "structural barriers and policies rooted in systemic racism designed to keep certain individuals, families, and communities out of the economic and social mainstream" (Pathak, 2021, para. 1).

Evidence-based interventions aimed at disrupting intergenerational poverty may be child focused (e.g., school-based curriculum and welcoming school climates), family-focused (e.g., supporting the parent–child relationship), health focused (e.g., affordable insurance, nutrition supports, etc.), or intergenerational. **Intergenerational approaches** provide supports for both the caregiver(s) and child(ren) simultaneously, and generally focus on the following six domains: physical and mental health, early childhood education, postsecondary and employment opportunities, economic assets, primary and secondary education, and social capital (Wildsmith & Alvira-Hammond, 2023). Recognizing the stress poverty creates for individuals and family systems, these programs take a holistic, intersectional approach to family well-being. Research over the past decade shows "that programs that raise the level of parents' education, health, income, etc. can have a causal impact on children's development" (Haskins et al., 2014, p. 9).

Initiatives across the nations using the "**2Gen**", or **two-generation approach** illustrate impressive results; for example, one county program using a coaching approach for parents with children in childcare or Head Start showed gains in (a) child educational achievement, (b) preventative health care use, (c) employment rates, and (c) family income (Jefferson County, 2019). Another 2Gen program provides tuition, coaching, and wraparound supports to youth and parents attending college at the same time. As of 2020, 54% of youth and 58% of parents receiving services were continuously enrolled in college; six had successfully completed their degrees (Sommer et al., 2020). In addition to increasing well-being for individuals and families, the integration of services evident in this approach has aligned state and county systems around a shared purpose of equity and efficacy (Mosle & Sims, 2021).

Social Work Practice in Poverty and Housing Insecurity

Social workers are committed to serving the most economically vulnerable people in our society. Doing so requires them to understand the complexity of people's lived experience of poverty and to embrace the framework of health and housing as universal human rights. Given poverty's connection to so many other social ills—health disparities, homelessness, child neglect, to name a few— many will work at the intersection of these issues. They may help low-income survivors of intimate partner violence access emergency shelter services, assist youth experiencing homelessness through free therapy, or enroll older adults in government-sponsored income support programs. These efforts require them to develop in-depth knowledge of relevant social policies, as well as locally available resources and how to access them. By brokering resources and assisting others in navigating these complex systems, they empower individuals to make changes that align with their personal goals. These roles are consistent with that of a **case manager**, **care navigator** or **crisis manager**. They require skills such as negotiation, collaboration, communication, consultation, systems thinking, and educating others (Cesta, 2020). Related social work careers can be found in integrated care settings, community mental health and substance abuse services, agencies serving unhoused people, nonprofits serving foster families, and many others.

Case Manager

A typical day in the life of a **case manager** involves meeting with clients to conduct assessments and establish personal goals. The case manager may research, share, and broker resources on a client's behalf. They work to ensure that clients have adequate information to make informed decisions about their options. They may also coordinate services within an interdisciplinary setting and advocate to ensure needed resources are available to clients. Case managers are also required to complete paperwork and track the progress of clients over time.

Social workers may also provide supportive services in housing and poverty-specific realms, including **homeless shelters**. They may work for local government agencies, such as the county Department of Human Services, assisting low-income people in accessing welfare, housing, and health care benefits. Alternatively, they may work for a nonprofit housing development and connect residents to services and supports for which they qualify. they might serve at

IMG 6.4

a community-based agency advocating on behalf of clients with their land-lords to ensure that their housing meets local safety standards or advocating for home modifications to accommodate disabilities. While these micro-level interventions make an important contribution to individuals' and families' lives, eradicating poverty and housing insecurity requires complementary mezzo- and macro-level work.

Community Organizing

Social workers may work in **community organizing**, bringing people together to actively address social issues. Similarly, within their organizational roles, social workers may join in coalitions to align with other human service providers with shared goals. Many communities have alliances to address homelessness, for example through prevention, intervention, and civil rights advocacy. **Coalitions** allow stakeholders—local leaders, service providers, and those with lived experience—to join in developing community-specific, culturally responsive solutions to pressing issues of poverty and housing insecurity. The skills involved in community organizing and coalition building include community assessment and issue analysis, relationship building, strategic planning, mobilizing others, training and education, facilitation, consensus building, mediating conflicts and power dynamics, and sharing power.

The typical day of a social worker in community organizing involves meeting with community members to hear their concerns and ideas. Organizers seeks to identify common concerns among these stakeholders and bring people together to develop and take action on the identified issues. Community organizers may educate the public about specific concerns, assist with fundraising efforts, plan and facilitate community meetings, lead strategy sessions, and help develop the leadership skills of concerned citizens.

Community Development Work

Affordable housing and **community development work** are other critical practice arenas for mezzo-oriented social workers. They may work in or with urban planning and development offices to create new affordable housing units within communities. This work involves assessing the nature of local need: Is the need for family housing? Transitional housing? Housing for veterans? Seniors? It includes partnerships between government, industry, and community groups to determine incentives and subsides for building affordable housing, approving proposals for new developments, and establishing realistic implementation plans given the long-term, multifaceted nature of real estate development. More broadly, they may partner with community members to create an overall vision for the community that builds on existing strengths and garners new resources to foster positive change. This approach is driven by the community, with social workers serving as facilitators to the work.

Skills necessary within community development efforts include effective listening and communication, research and writing competency, knowledge of the public sector, negotiation and advocacy, creative thinking and problem solving, and the ability to motivate others to action. A typical day as a community developer includes facilitating meetings and capacity-building trainings, building relationships between people with shared interests, and providing research and resources to support the community effort. These positions often include an administrative component such as writing reports, managing program budgets, and coordinator schedules.

However, it is important to note that affordable housing development work, while critical, is not without controversy; in recent years, many communities have struggled with the displacement of long-term residents that may occur when new construction requires low-income people to "temporarily" relocate. When development increases the economic value of an area, low-income people may find it difficult to return to their community (Zuk et al., 2015). The rise in property value may also drive out long-standing local businesses that can no longer afford their rent and whose customer base has vanished. These dynamics can shift the culture of neighborhoods, as well as the racial, ethnic, and economic composition

Explore the work of a local or national coalition that addresses poverty or housing insecurity. Some examples include the National Alliance to End Homelessness, National Low Income Housing Coalition, and the National Coalition for the Homeless. Consider the following:

- Who are the key stakeholders—individuals, organizations and partners—involved in this coalition?

- What project or policies does the coalition advocate?

- How does their work forefront intersectional analysis and systemic solutions?

of residents. Given their unique training in systems thinking and power analysis, and our commitment to justice for vulnerable people, social workers may bring a nuanced perspective to the complex issues of housing and community development and must exercise responsibility with great care when working in this realm so that community development does not become community displacement.

Policy Advocacy Work

Policy advocacy efforts are also imperative for social workers fighting for economic reform and housing rights for all. These efforts gain them a seat at the decision-making table with leaders at all levels of government; they allow them to advise and influence the legislation that elected officials put forth, support, or oppose. The **National Coalition for the Homeless** provides an important example of advocates, activists, service providers, and people with lived experience coming together to inform the collective response to housing insecurity. This network engages in education and advocacy campaigns to improve the lives of unhoused Americans; it raises awareness of how civil rights issues, including voting, violence and criminalization, intersect with housing insecurity and prioritize public policies that affirm the worth and dignity of all people (National Coalition for the Homeless, 2022). Key skills for policy advocacy include research and data analysis, critical and creative thinking, persuasive communication, networking and communication with a broad array of stakeholders, time management and prioritization, and the ability to apply social work ethics within a macro context. The typical day of a policy advocate may include building relationships with legislators and their staff, testifying on behalf of a specific policy, monitoring policy and budget proposals, drafting policy proposals, and sharing information with media, relevant departments and agencies, and other public officials.

Organizations Using an Integrated Framework

Some organizations approach poverty alleviation and housing stability work from an integrated framework. The **National Fund for Workforce Solutions** (NFWS), for example, collaborates with employers, workers, and communities to advance their mission of more prosperous and equitable communities. **At the micro level**, the organization provides support, job connections, and skill development for workers. In 2022 alone, 11,835 job seekers completed training through the organization; another 1,850 workers completed career advancement training, of whom 1,286 advanced in their field. Training opportunities range from basic literacy to career readiness to apprenticeships and 2-/4-year degree programs (NFWS, 2022).

At the mezzo level, it partners with businesses to improve workplace practices that truly value worker engagement and well-being; utilizing their national network, NFWS engages employers in one-on-one coaching and peer learning to align workplaces with research-based job quality practices. Two recent examples of its impact on employment practice include the incorporation of trauma-informed care and worker voice into the design and development of workplace cultures. NFWS (2022) also utilizes its network to pool regional funding sources around a shared vision for local workforce development, thereby creating greater efficiency and impact within communities.

At the macro level, it advocates for systems change to address the broad structural factors contributing to inequities in the workforce and in economic immobility. It does so by sharing promising practices, developing tools and frameworks that foster positive change, connecting leaders across the county willing to support and inspire each other, and funding innovations in workforce practices. In 2020, NFWS (2022) convened the Liberatory Learning Community, a national network to build local leadership around racial and economic justice in the workforce. Additionally, in the last 3 years, it published a series of reports and tools on workplace equity, trauma-informed organizations, and human-centered design within the workforce. Through their integrated approach of developing the resources all workers need to succeed and addressing racial and gender disparities through systems change, NFWS is advancing the economic stability of long-disenfranchised communities. They are a model for holistic, innovative solutions of the complex crisis of poverty.

Workforce Development Case Study

Nehemiah is a social worker in a community center serving refugees relocated to a major urban area in the United States. His role as a job developer is to match the skills and experiences of newly resettled refugees with local employers looking to fill positions. The goal of this program is to foster self-sufficiency and a sense of belonging within the boarder community for refugees as they rebuild their lives in an entirely new country. Nehemiah is working with a mother, Chesa, and her 6-year-old child, Hayma. The family was forced to flee their homeland due to the Myanmar government's persecution of Rohingya Muslims. They fled to a temporary refugee camp in Bangladesh until receiving asylum status in 2020.

Since settling in the United States, Chesa has completed English language training and has secured initial employment in a warehouse. This position provides benefits, regular hours, and a wage of $17/hour. As a single parent, Chesa is hoping to secure a higher paying position now that she has acclimated to the country and established herself as a reliable employee. Chesa has prior experience and training in health care as an assistant in a school-based clinic in Myanmar. She enjoyed this work and found it rewarding to assist students with basic health needs. Transitioning into a health care profession, though, will require more education and a deeper understanding of the U.S. health care system. Chesa is concerned about how she will pay for and obtain additional training and education and the impact this new time commitment might have on her parenting responsibilities.

Over the last 3 years, Chesa has built a social support network of friends and neighbors and is active in a women's group associated with the local mosque. Hayma attends a diverse public school and is engaged both socially and academically. She engages in after-school activities including art and tutoring services provided at the school. Both receive therapeutic services from a local behavioral health nonprofit to help them heal from their traumatic experiences.

Questions

1. What are the strengths in this case?

2. How can the social worker, Nehemiah, assist Chesa at the micro level? Be specific.

3. What macro-level actions might support Chesa and other refugees in similar situations?

4. What cultural considerations will be important to supporting Chesa in a responsive and empowering way?

5. What questions or feelings arise for you as you imagine working with a family in this situation?

▮ Chapter Summary

In this chapter, we defined poverty and housing insecurity as contemporary social problems in the United States. We explored the complex, interconnected dynamics giving rise to these issues such as the lack of economic and educational opportunities, the high cost of social necessities such as health care, the devasting consequences of natural disasters, and the long-lasting impacts of historical atrocities. We also unpacked the ways in which intersectional oppression reinforces present-day poverty and housing insecurity, exploring this nuance through the lens of age, gender, and disability.

We then turned our attention to the role of social work in alleviating poverty and housing insecurity. We considered the historical policy precedents—such as "widows' pensions" and AFDC—that have given rise to TANF and our array of housing supports. We examined this safety net with an eye to contemporary issues of equity and justice, noting important limitations to this system. We then introduced more recent frameworks intended to better address *some* of these systemic inequities: (a) housing as a human right and (b) housing first. We highlighted an emerging area of research on the alleviation of intergenerational poverty through the provision of simultaneous supports for children and their caregivers.

Finally, we highlighted three major career paths for social workers who want to work for poverty alleviation and housing security—case management and resource navigation, housing and community development, and policy advocacy. Within these career options, we discussed the practice skills and settings associated with social work so that students may assess their fit with this area of practice. Within this discussion, we presented an innovative example of an integrated approach to poverty alleviation and concluded by offering a case study for your analysis. The discussion questions that follow are intended to reinforce your learning and prompt critical thinking on the complex nature of our work for housing and economic stability for all.

Discussion Questions

1. Consider the three career paths outlined in this chapter and the skills and settings associated with them. Which path might best align with your existing strengths and passions? What additional learning and growth might be necessary for you to enter this field of practice?

2. Reflect on the societal factors contributing to poverty and housing insecurity. Which factors are best addressed through our current economic and housing safety net? In what ways is our safety net failing to address these contributing factors?

3. Given that poverty and housing insecurity disproportionally impact people with marginalized identities, what additional supports and resources might be necessary to significantly impact these issues?

4. Research the Housing as a Human Right Act. What arguments are advocates of this policy centering? What opposition might they be facing?

5. This chapter highlighted the housing first model as a predominant approach to serving unhoused and housing-insecure people. In what ways does this model align with social work values and ethical principles? What drawbacks to this model might exist?

References

Brittain, M., & Blackstock, C. (2015). *First nations child poverty: A literature review and analysis.* First Nation Children's Action Research and Education Service. https://fncaringsociety.com/sites/default/files/First%20Nations%20Child%20Poverty%20-%20A%20Literature%20Review%20and%20Analysis%202015-3.pdf

Center on Budget and Policy Priorities (2021). *Policy basics: Unemployment insurance.* https://www.cbpp.org/research/economy/unemployment-insurance

Center on Budget and Policy Priorities. (2022a). *Policy basics: Temporary Assistance for Needy Families.* https://www.cbpp.org/research/family-income-support/temporary-assistance-for-needy-families

Center on Budget and Policy Priorities (2022b). *Policy basics: The Supplemental Nutrition Assistance program.* https://www.cbpp.org/research/food-assistance/the-supplemental-nutrition-assistance-program-snap

Center on Budget and Policy Priorities (2022c). *Social Security lifts more people above the poverty line than any other program.* https://www.cbpp.org/research/social-security/social-security-lifts-more-people-above-the-poverty-line-than-any-other#:~:text=Most%20people%20aged%2065%20and,(See%20Figure%201.)

Cesta, T. (2020). *The case manager's toolbox: The essential skills of an effective case manager, part 1.* Relias Media. https://www.reliasmedia.com/articles/145456-the-case-managers-toolbox-the-essential-skills-of-an-effective-case-manager-part-1

Creamer, J., Shrider, E. A., Burns, K. & Chen, F. (2022). *Poverty in the United States: 2021.* U.S. Census Bureau. https://www.census.gov/library/publications/2022/demo/p60-277.html

Community Toolbox. (2023). *Addressing social determinants of health and development.* University of Kansas. https://ctb.ku.edu/en/table-of-contents/analyze/analyze-community-problems-and-solutions/social-determinants-of-health/main

Fallon, K. (2021). *Naming housing as a human right is a first step to solving the housing crisis.* Housing Matters. https://housingmatters.urban.org/articles/naming-housing-human-right-first-step-solving-housing-crisis

Floyd, I., Pavetti, D., Meyer, L., Safawi, A., Schott, L., Bellew, E., & Magnus, A. (2021). *TANF policies reflect racist legacy of cash assistance.* Center for Budget and Policy Priorities. https://www.cbpp.org/research/family-income-support/tanf-policies-reflect-racist-legacy-of-cash-assistance

Haskins, R., Garfinkel, I., & McLanahan, S. (2014). Introduction: Two-generation mechanisms of child development. *The Future of Children*, 3–12.

Kent, A. H., & Ricketts, L. R. (2022). *Racial and ethnic household wealth trends and wealth inequality*. Federal Reserve Bank of St. Louis. https://www.stlouisfed.org/institute-for-economic-equity/the-real-state-of-family-wealth/racial-and-ethnic-household-wealth#:~:text=However%2C%20the%20gaps%20(represented%20by,every%20dollar%20of%20white%20wealth

Klest, B. (2012). Childhood trauma, poverty, and adult victimization. *Psychological Trauma: Theory, Research, Practice, and Policy, 4*(3), 245–251. https://doi.org/10.1037/a0024468

Institute for Research on Poverty. (2023). *How is poverty measured?* University of Wisconsin-Madison. https://www.irp.wisc.edu/resources/how-is-poverty-measured/#:~:text=Poverty%20is%20measured%20in%20the,in%20charge%20of%20measuring%20poverty

Interagency Working Group on Youth Programs. (n.d.). *Federal programs*. https://youth.gov/youth-topics/runaway-and-homeless-youth/federal-programs

Jayapal, P. (2021). *Jayapal and Meng lead lawmakers in introducing the Housing is a Human Right Act*. https://jayapal.house.gov/2021/06/08/housing-is-a-human-right-act/

Jefferson County. (2019). *JeffCo prosperity partners: Breaking the cycle of poverty in Jefferson County*. https://www.jeffco.us/2716/Jeffco-Prosperity-Partners

Leopold, J., Cunningham, M. K., Posey, L. & Manuel, T. (2016*). Improving measures of housing insecurity: A path forward*. Urban Institute & Enterprise Community Partners. https://www.urban.org/research/publication/improving-measures-housing-insecurity-path-forward

Mosle, A., & Sims, M., (2021). *State of the field: Two-generation approaches to family well-being*. Ascend, Aspen Institute. https://ascend.aspeninstitute.org/state-of-the-field-two-generation-approaches-to-family-well-being/

Mottet, L., & Ohle, J. M. (2003). *Transitioning our shelters: A guide to making homeless shelters safer for transgender people*. National Gay & Lesbian Taskforce Policy Institute & National Coalition for the Homeless. https://srlp.org/wp-content/uploads/2012/08/TransitioningOurShelters.pdf

National Association of Social Workers. (2021). *Code of Ethics of the National Association of Social Workers*. https://www.socialworkers.org/About/Ethics/Code-of-Ethics/Code-of-Ethics-English

National Coalition for the Homeless. (2022). *About us*. https://nationalhomeless.org/about-us/who-we-are/

National Fund for Workforce Solutions. (2022). *Impact report 2022*. https://nationalfund.org/our-resources/publications/national-fund-for-workforce-solutions-impact-report-2022/

Office of the United Nations High Commissioner for Human Rights. (n.d.). *The right to adequate housing*. UN Habitat. https://www.ohchr.org/sites/default/files/Documents/Publications/FS21_rev_1_Housing_en.pdf

Pagaduan, J. (2021). *Millions of Americans are housing insecure: Rent relief and eviction assistance continue to be critical.* National Alliance to End Homelessness & Homelessness Research Institute. https://endhomelessness.org/wp-content/uploads/2021/11/HousingInsecurity-Brief-November-2021.pdf

Pathak, A. (2021). *Using holistic, multigenerational strategies to alleviate poverty.* American Progress. https://www.americanprogress.org/article/using-holistic-multigenerational-strategies-alleviate-poverty/

Rank, M. R., Yoon, H., & Hirschl, T. A. (2003). American poverty as structural failing: Evidence and arguments. *Journal of Sociology and Social Welfare, 30*(4), 3–30.

Ritter, J. A. (2022). *Social work policy practice: Changing our community, nation, and the world* (3rd ed.). Cognella.

Skocpol, T. (1995). *Protecting soldiers and mothers: The political origins of social policy in the United States.* Harvard University Press.

Social Security Administration. (n.d.). *Social Security programs in the United States: Historical developments.* https://www.ssa.gov/policy/docs/progdesc/sspus/histdev.pdf

Sommer, T. E., Tighe, L. A., Chase-Lansdale, P. L. (2020). *HOPE Toledo Promise: A model two-generation college scholarship program.* Northwestern University. https://bpb-us-e1.wpmucdn.com/sites.northwestern.edu/dist/6/3833/files/2022/09/HOPE-Toledo-Promise_Northwestern-Implementation-Brief-2020-2022_09.26.22.pdf

Tars, E. (2021). *Housing as a human right.* National Homelessness Law Center. https://nlihc.org/sites/default/files/AG-2021/01-06_Housing-Human-Right.pdf

Tsai, J. (2020). Is the housing first model effective? Different evidence for different outcomes. *AJPH Perspectives, 110*(9), 1376–1377.

U.S. Census Bureau. (2022). *Income, Poverty and Health Insurance Coverage in the United States: 2021.* https://www.census.gov/newsroom/press-releases/2022/income-poverty-health-insurance-coverage.html

U.S. Department of Health and Human Services. (n.d.). *Housing instability.* https://health.gov/healthypeople/priority-areas/social-determinants-health/literature-summaries/housing-instability

U.S. Department of Health & Human Services. (2019). *Major provisions of the Personal Responsibility and Work Opportunity Reconciliation Act of 1996 (P.L. 104-193).* https://www.acf.hhs.gov/ofa/policy-guidance/major-provisions-welfare-law#:~:text=issues%20described%20below.-,The%20Personal%20Responsibility%20and%20Work%20Opportunity%20Reconciliation%20Act%20of%201996,work%20requirements%20for%20most%20recipients

U.S. Department of Housing and Urban Development. (2022). *HUD releases 2022 annual homeless assessment report.* https://www.hud.gov/press/press_releases_media_advisories/HUD_No_22_253

Utah State Legislature. (2018). *Evidence-based Interventions to address intergenerational poverty.* https://le.utah.gov/interim/2018/pdf/00003215.pdf

Wildsmith, E., & Alvira-Hammond, M. (2023, March 1). *Data on families with low incomes across America can inform two-generation approaches.* Child Trends. https://doi.org/10.56417/1147h453i

Zuk, M., Bierbaum, A. H., Chapple, K., Gorska, K., Loukaitou-Sideris, A., Ong, P. & Thomas, T. (2015). Gentrification, displacement, and the role of public investment: A literature review. Federal Reserve Bank of San Francisco. https://www.frbsf.org/community-development/publications/working-papers/2015/august/gentrification-displacement-role-of-public-investment/

Credits

CHAPTER 7

Social Work Practice in Mental Health Settings

Learning Objectives

After reading this chapter, students will be able to do the following:

- Summarize the biggest social problems involving mental health disorders in the United States, including the prevalence of mental illness

- Define mental health and mental illness and differentiate between these two concepts

- Describe the mental health system, including the four main sectors

- Identify three major career path options for social workers who want to work in the mental health field

- Explain why using a trauma-informed care approach is important in mental health practice and summarize the research findings on animal-assisted therapies

- Evaluate a federal policy that seeks to increase access to mental health treatment for Americans with mental health disorders

- Describe current controversies and criticisms that arise in the field of mental health

- Explain why criminalization of those with mental illness is a social justice issue of concern for social workers

- Evaluate their own goodness of fit with mental health as a potential future career option

IMG 7.1

SOCIAL WORKER SPOTLIGHT:
Louise Haimowitz, LCSW

My Journey as a Clinical Social Worker

....

We are presented with many choices in life, and I can say without hesitation that choosing a career as a licensed clinical social worker (LCSW) has been the smartest, most rewarding decision I have ever made. It has allowed me to engage in work that has been meaningful and deeply satisfying and the freedom to practice in a wide range of professional settings while developing multiple clinical specializations. I can also report that I have been gainfully employed as a social work practitioner for the past 3 decades.

As an undergraduate, I double-majored in psychology and sociology as I felt drawn to both the micro and macro perspectives on social problems and targets for change. I chose to pursue a master's degree in social work as I felt strongly aligned with the profession's values rooted in social justice, its person-in-environment assessment lens, and strengths-based approach to treatment. I also chose to become licensed as having an LCSW has opened many doors to employment opportunities, increased my salary range, and allowed me to receive third-party payments as a private practitioner.

I began my career at Mesa State University's Counseling Center, where I maintained a caseload of individuals and treatment groups addressing substance use, eating disorders, relationship difficulties, and mental health struggles. I also had the opportunity to utilize macro practice skills through the development of a wellness and substance abuse prevention program, while serving on the board of directors on the Mesa County Mental Health Center. It was exciting to apply my academic training as a generalist practitioner, engaging in micro, mezzo, and macro interventions in daily work activities.

I developed a curiosity around the treatment of disordered eating, a common struggle among college students, which led me to accept a position as coordinator of a new outpatient eating disorders program at Boulder Memorial Hospital. As an administrator, I collaborated with a multidisciplined team of medical and mental health professionals in designing outpatient programs. I provided supervision to a staff of social workers, counselors, and master's-level interns and continued to hone my clinical skills through maintaining a caseload of individual clients struggling with disordered eating, dual diagnosis/substance use disorders. Again, the separation between micro, mezzo, and macro practice became more diffuse as the needs of the program integrated all forms of practice.

Ten years after earning my MSW, I became a parent and paused to attend to the needs of my family. During this time, I felt both introspective and intrigued by my own birthing and postpartum experiences and was able to integrate this journey into my career path. I became a certified Bradley childbirth instructor and developed a practice of providing childbirth education to groups of pregnant couples. This gave me a deeper glimpse into nuanced dynamics of family transitions around pregnancy, childbirth, postpartum, and the mental health components of the perinatal experience.

Family therapy and parent–infant attachment became new areas of professional interest, and I accepted a position with the Community Infant Program/Mental Health Partners in Boulder as a clinical team supervisor and dyadic/family therapist. This program opened my eyes to the treatment needs of families at risk for child abuse/neglect, parent–child attachment disorders, postpartum depression, failure to thrive, and the treatment of intergenerational trauma. I was also deeply committed to addressing social justice factors (i.e., lack of resources for marginalized families and inaccessibility to therapeutic services). These macro problems became targets for change along with treatment goals of individuals and families.

Expanding on my commitment to strengthening families, I moved into a role of clinical director of Parenting Place, a nonprofit agency in Boulder aimed at reducing the incidence of child neglect and abuse in Boulder County. There, I had the opportunity to once again apply micro, mezzo, and macro skills, developing an evidence-based curriculum of clinical and educational services for diverse families with children aged 0–5. This included the creation and supervision of a clinical team charged with facilitating therapy and support groups for single parents, adopting parents, postpartum mothers, and multicultural families as well as groups for fathers. I also strove to increase accessibility to therapeutic services and the provision of basic needs to vulnerable families through outreach to local human service agencies and resources.

Continuing to follow the path of clinical social work, I bridged the world of community practice with academia when the master's in social work program at Metropolitan State University of Denver began in 2011, first becoming an adjunct instructor and later a full-time faculty member in 2016. I have taught clinical courses and have been delighted to integrate expertise as a psychotherapist into classroom instruction.

Throughout my career as an LCSW, I have maintained a private practice, which has kept me current in new evidence-based clinical practices and alternately provided real world clinical case examples to bring life and authenticity to classroom learning.

Further, being a seasoned clinical practitioner has allowed me to support and mentor workers on the front line with Denver Human Services child welfare programs. As a consultant through the THRIVE grant, I have provided therapeutic group support with the goal of mitigating vicarious trauma among caseworkers.

In conclusion, clinical social work is practiced in a variety of different contexts, addressing a diverse range of social issues. It provides practitioners richly rewarding opportunities to wear many hats in serving as a positive change agent in the world.

Many people can relate to the pain of having a mental health disorder or having a loved one who has suffered with one. **Mental health** is a major field of practice for social workers, and many Americans are surprised to learn that the largest group of mental health providers in the United States are **licensed clinical social workers**, or LCSWs, and that they outnumber other types of mental health clinicians such as psychologists, psychiatrists, and licensed professional counselors. Social workers who wish to become a mental health practitioner must earn their master's degree in social work and then attain their license to become an LCSW—which requires an additional 2 years of supervised clinical social work experience. **Telemental health** (i.e., the use of videoconferencing technology such as Zoom) to provide therapy to clients has become more common and increased even more as a result of the coronavirus pandemic. There have been concerns raised about the impact of the coronavirus pandemic on the mental health of both children and adults, and some early data suggests that Americans are suffering more with anxiety, depression, substance abuse, and suicidal thoughts. However, it will likely take researchers more time to gather good data about the mental health impact of this challenging health crisis.

Due to increased knowledge about the causes and treatment of mental health disorders, there is a new understanding that **mental illness** is a disease of the brain and body, and experts no longer believe that mental health should be viewed separately from physical health. Despite the fact that mental health disorders are very common, with nearly one in five adults living with a mental illness in 2020 (NIMH, n.d.), **stigma** continues to impact those with mental health disorders, which impacts their ability to seek treatment. Historically and currently, it is much harder to access mental health treatment compared to physical illnesses based on the way that mental health services are funded and organized. Ritter (2022) explains, "For decades, committed mental health advocates have fought tirelessly for a system of care that is less fragmented and provides access to quality care for those in need of treatment. Unfortunately, the United States has a long history of stigmatizing mental health disorders and providing inadequate care to those with mental illness, especially as compared to medical care. In many ways, the mental health sector has been treated as the stepchild of the U.S. health care system" (p. 183).

Overview of the Larger Social Problem—Mental Health Disorders in the United States

Before we jump into looking at the social problem of mental health disorders in our society, it is important to explore the concept of **mental health** and differentiate it from **mental illness**. Similar to the way that we think about promoting our physical health in order to keep ourselves physically healthy, many also think about ways to promote positive mental health in order to stay mentally healthy. According to the Centers for Disease Control and Prevention (CDC, n.d.a.), "Mental health includes our emotional, psychological, and social well-being. It affects how we think, feel, and act. It also helps determine how we handle stress, relate to others, and make healthy choices" (para. 1). It is important to understand that someone can have poor mental health and not have a diagnosed mental disorder. In recent years, there has been an increased focus on how to achieve and maintain strong mental health such as keeping one's level of stress low, doing physical exercise, spending time with people who bring you happiness, being out in nature, and engaging in mindfulness and meditation practices, just to name a few.

The Problem of Stigma

According to mental health experts such as the American Psychiatric Association (n.d.a.), despite the progress that has been made, people with mental health disorders still experience **stigma**, **prejudice**, and **discrimination**, and this prevents many people from seeking treatment for fears of losing their job, relationships, or even their livelihood. Not until people feel as comfortable sharing their mental illness with others as readily as with their physical illnesses will we know that

stigma has been completely eradicated. Researchers have identified three types of stigma when it comes to mental illness (American Psychiatric Association, n.d.a.):

- *Social stigma*: Negative attitudes that people in society have about mental illness

- *Self-stigma*: The internalized shame that people with mental disorders have about their condition

- *Institutional stigma*: When organizations have policies and/or practices that limit opportunities for people with mental illness (can be intentional or unintentional)

The **National Alliance on Mental Illness** (NAMI), suggests the following strategies to reduce mental health stigma (Greenstein, 2017):

- Talk openly about mental health

- Educate yourself and others

- Encourage equality between mental and physical illness

- Show compassion for those with mental illness

- Choose empowerment over shame

- Let the media know when they are being stigmatizing
- Don't harbor self-stigma

Prevalence of Mental Health Disorders

Because of the stigma surrounding mental illness, people often conjure up images of people with severe mental illness even though it is not very prevalent in our society. Because mental illnesses vary in the level of severity, the National Institute of Mental Health (NIMH) distinguishes between those with "Any Mental Illness" and those with "Serious Mental Illness," which represent those with the most debilitating forms of mental illness.

Mental illness generally refers collectively to all mental disorders that can be diagnosed in the *Diagnostic and Statistical Manual of Mental Disorders* published by the American Psychiatric Association (APA, 2022). Mental disorders are health conditions that are characterized by alterations in thinking, mood, or behavior (or some combination of these three) associated with impaired functioning and/or distress. The American Psychological Association (n.d.) defines a **mental disorder** as "any condition characterized by cognitive and emotional disturbances, abnormal behaviors, impaired functioning, or any combination of these. Such disorders cannot be accounted for solely by environmental circumstances and may involve physiological, genetic, chemical, social, and other factors" (para. 1). Examples of common mental disorders include these:

- anxiety disorders (e.g., posttraumatic stress disorder [PTSD], phobia, obsessive compulsive disorder)
- mood disorders (e.g., depression, bipolar disorder)
- autism spectrum disorders
- attention deficit hyperactivity disorder (ADHD)
- personality disorders (e.g., borderline personality disorder)
- psychotic disorders (e.g., schizophrenia)
- addiction disorders (e.g., substance use disorder)
- eating disorders
- dual diagnosis or co-occurring disorders (i.e., when someone has both a mental health and substance use disorder)

Collectively, **anxiety disorders** are the most common type of mental disorder experienced by those in the United States.

Adults With Any Mental Illness

According to data reported by the NIMH (n.d.a.), roughly one in five (21%) U.S. adults suffered from a diagnosable mental disorder in 2020 (which represented 52.9 million people). Young adults aged 18 to 25 years had the highest prevalence of mental illness (30.6%) compared to adults aged 26 to 49 years (25.3%) and those aged 50 and older (14.5%). Females had a higher prevalence than males, 25.8% compared to 15.8%. Less than half of those with any mental illness in 2020 (46%) received mental health services in the past year, a concerning piece of data for mental health advocates and organizations (NIMH, n.d.a.).

Adults With Serious Mental Illness

As stated previously, serious mental illness, which describes those on the most severe side of the mental illness continuum, is not as common. **Serious mental illness** is defined as "a mental, behavioral, or emotional disorder resulting in serious functional impairment, which substantially interferes with or limits one or more major life activities (NIMH, n.d.a., para. 4). In 2020, 5.6% of U.S. adults suffer from serious mental illness, which represented 14.2 million adults. Young adults aged 18–25 years had the highest prevalence of SMI (9.7%) compared to adults aged 26–49 years (6.9%) and aged 50 and older (3.4%). About 64% of those with serious mental illness in 2020 received mental health services in the past year (compared to 46% of those with any mental illness; NIMH, n.d.a.).

Children with Mental Health Disorders

Many social workers focus on the well-being of children and adolescents in a holistic way and the best methods to support their social/emotional, cognitive/intellectual, language, and physical development. There has been an increased focus in recent years on the need to better support the **mental health of children and youth**, especially because children are not always able to verbalize or express to others when they are not doing well psychologically. According to the CDC (n.d.b.), the most commonly diagnosed mental health disorders in children are ADHD, anxiety, behavior problems, and depression. During 2016–2019, 9.8% of children (aged 3–17) were diagnosed with ADHD, 9.4% with anxiety disorders, 8.9% with behavior problems, and 4.4% with depression. For adolescents, the biggest concerns are depression and suicide. Data collected during 2018–2019 showed that 36.7% of adolescents aged 12–17 had persistent feelings of sadness or hopelessness, 15.1% had a major depressive episode, 18.8% seriously considered attempting suicide, 15.7% made a suicide plan, and 8.9% attempted suicide (CDC, n.d.b.).

IMG 7.3

A recent study published in *JAMA Pediatrics* (Lebrun-Harris et al., 2022) revealed some troubling data concerning the mental health of U.S. children, including a significant increase in the number of children with a mental health disorder between the years 2016 and 2020. The goals of this study were to analyze trends over these 5 years and to examine the impact of the coronavirus pandemic on the health and well-being of the nation's children. The findings revealed the following:

- Between 2016 and 2020, the number of children ages 3–17 years diagnosed with anxiety grew by 29% and those with depression by 27%.

- From 2019 to 2020, researchers found a 21% increase in children with behavior or conduct problems.

- In 2020, the proportion of children with preventive medical care visits dropped by 9% and the proportion with unmet health care needs grew by 32%.

- Children's physical activity decreased by 18% between 2016 and 2020.

- The number of parents who reported difficulty coping with parenting demands increased significantly from 2019 to 2020. The proportion of young children whose parents quit, declined, or changed jobs due to childcare challenges increased by 34%.

Suicide

It is incredibly tragic when someone is in so much pain and decide that the only way to alleviate their suffering is to end their life. **Suicide** also has a deeply painful impact on the friends and loved ones of those who die by suicide. Death by suicide is a serious social problem in the United States, and there are many organizations at the state and federal level that are dedicated to prevention efforts to help people who are suffering from a mental disorder (e.g., serious depression) that causes some to want to end their life. The NIMH (n.d.b.) defines **suicidal ideation** as thinking about, considering, or planning a suicide, while suicide is as "death caused by self-directed injurious behavior with intent to die as a result of the behavior" (para. 3). The CDC collects data on suicide, which is helpful so that we can know the prevalence of this problem, who is most at risk, as well as trends over time. CDC data (n.d.c.) from 2020 reveals the following:

- Suicide was the 12th leading cause of death in the United States (just under 46,000 people).

- Suicide was the second leading cause of death for people ages 20–34, the third leading cause of death for people ages 10–19, and the fourth leading cause of death for people ages 35–44.

- People aged 85 and older had the highest rates of suicide.

- The racial/ethnic groups with the highest suicide rate were American Indians and non-Hispanic Whites.

- Over 12 million Americans thought seriously about suicide while 1.2 million attempted suicide.

- Men died by suicide four times more often than women.

- Firearms were used in 52.8% of suicides.

- Suicide rates increased 36% between 2000–2018 but then decreased 5% in 2018–2020, which was encouraging to public health experts.

Despite the recent 5% decrease in suicides, public health officials have expressed concern about the **impact of the coronavirus pandemic** on suicide rates, though more time is needed to collect this data. Ehlman et al. (2022) explain:

> As the nation continues to respond to the COVID-19 pandemic and its long-term effects on isolation, stress, economic insecurity, and worsening substance use, mental health, and well-being, prevention is critical. Existing data suggest that suicide rates might be stable or decline during a disaster, only to rise afterwards as the longer-term sequelae unfold in persons, families, and communities, as was the case in New Orleans 2 years after Hurricane Katrina. (para. 12)

According to the CDC, **suicide is preventable** and requires a comprehensive approach that includes "strengthening economic supports (e.g., unemployment benefits), expanding access to and delivery of care (e.g., telehealth), promoting social connectedness, creating protective environments (e.g., safely securing medications and firearms), teaching coping and problem-solving skills, identifying and supporting persons at risk, and lessening harms and preventing future risk (e.g., safe media reporting on suicide)" (Ehlman et al., 2022, para. 13).

Causes of Mental Illness

Mental health researchers and experts have learned over the years that there is **no one single cause of mental health disorders**. Instead, there are a number of **risk factors** that can lead to mental illness, and sometimes it is a combination of multiple risk factors that causes someone to develop a mental health disorder. Researchers have explored various theories, including whether the causes are more nature or nurture, and most experts have come to the conclusion that it is both—and often it is the interaction between the two.

Individual causes of mental illness includes genetics/inherited traits that can make someone susceptible (e.g., tends to run in the family), having negative thoughts, having negative habits (e.g., sleep deprivation, abusing drugs or alcohol), a chronic medical condition, traumatic brain injury, and the neurochemistry of one's brain. **Environmental causes** of mental illness include adversity in one's social and/or physical environment such as childhood trauma; chronic stressors at home or work, including economic hardship; exposure to toxins; experiencing traumatic events; racial (and other forms of) discrimination; and isolation (e.g., having few healthy relationships or a support system).

Overview of the U.S. Mental Health System

Historically, mental health services have not been prioritized within the health care industry, and as a result, treatment has been inaccessible to many patients. Similar to the larger health care system in the United States, the mental health system is often described as a fragmented, loosely coordinated system of care. Because health care in the United States is not viewed as a right and operates largely in a for-profit system in which health insurance companies, pharmaceutical companies, some physicians, and hospital executives are able to reap large profits from their work while those without health insurance, and those who are underinsured, have a difficult time getting access to needed treatment.

History of Mental Health Services in the United States

In order to understand the current mental health care delivery system, it is important to understand the history of the provision of mental health services and how they developed and evolved over time in the United States.

- In our early history, people with mental illness were incarcerated as there was little understanding about mental health disorders. Thanks to social reformers like **Dorothea Dix**, this practice ended when awareness was raised about the abusive treatment that those with mental illness were subjected to in jails and prisons.

- As a result of these advocacy efforts, states began to open **state asylums**, specialized institutions to provide care for those with mental illness. Though this was a step forward, it also presented new challenges as we began to learn about the downside of institutionalization that included overcrowding, inhumane treatment, and by today's standards did not represent a high quality of care.

- In 1946, President Truman signs the **National Mental Health Act** calling for a National Institute of Mental Health to conduct research on mental illness and in 1949, the NIMH was formally established. This marks the first time that the federal government demonstrated the importance of conducting research to better understand the causes and best treatment for mental health disorders.

- The 1960s marked the beginning of **the deinstitutionalization movement**, based on the idea that people should receive care in communities rather than asylums. As a result of increasing criticisms that mental institutions were not the best way to help those with mental illness, in 1963, the **Mental Retardation Facilities and Community Mental Health Centers Construction Act** was signed into law by President Kennedy, the first time the federal government provided funding to support the treatment of mental illnesses. This resulted in the removal of hundreds of thousands of patients from mental institutions with the goal of serving these newly released patients in community-based facilities and mental health centers. The new federal law signed by President Kennedy aimed to shift resources away from large state mental institutions towards community-based mental health centers. Unfortunately, the funding and infrastructure was not adequate to realize these aims, so many become homeless and/or began to be served in the criminal justice system.

- The good news is that there have been many incredible advances regarding how we understand and treat mental health disorders, including both pharmaceutical and therapeutic approaches.

- The bad news is that for many individuals with severe mental illness, **prisons are the new asylums** as this is the only place that many can receive treatment due to a lack of other options. There have been numerous news stories and articles written about this topic and how tragic it is that the United States has gone back in time to incarcerate many people with mental illness (See Social Justice Spotlight).

One of the biggest policy issues in mental health that advocates have focused on is **mental health parity legislation** to ensure that health insurance policies do not provide less generous coverage for mental health services than they do for general health care benefits. This policy issue is covered in more detail later in the chapter. There are four major sectors of the mental health system in which clients in need of help may be served (see Table 7.1).

7.2   PRACTICE ACTIVITY

Reflect on the timeline that shows the criminalization of those with mental illness in early U.S. history and then how we are back to using this practice due to a lack of other options such as community-based mental health centers and psychiatric hospitals.

1. Google "prisons are the new asylums" to see what comes up in your search.

2. What lessons can be learned from the policy failures of the deinstitutionalization movement that had very good intentions but some very bad unintended consequences for those with serious mental illness?

3. What do you think this says about U.S. public policy priorities and how we care for those with serious mental illness? Why do you think this situation has been allowed to occur?

4. What feelings come up for you as you reflect on this situation?

TABLE 7.1   Four Major Sectors of the U.S. Mental Health System

The specialty mental health sector	Consists of specialized mental health professionals such as psychiatrists, psychologists, psychiatric nurses, and licensed clinical social workers who are trained to treat those with mental disorders
The general medical care sector	Consists of health care professionals with training in general medical care such as primary care physicians, pediatricians, nurse practitioners, and social workers in medical settings
Human services organizations	Consists of nonprofit organizations, school-based counseling services, residential programs, criminal justice settings, and faith-based organizations, which employ those who are trained to provide social services
The voluntary support sector	Consists of self-help groups such as 12-step programs and peer counselors; often where people with mental illness and their family members assist others dealing with the same problem

Mental Health Spending

The mental health system includes services that are provided by the **public sector** and the **private sector.** Services provided by the public sector include those directly operated by government agencies (e.g., state and county mental hospitals) and those financed with government resources (e.g., Medicaid, Medicare, Veterans Affairs, Health Resources and Services Administration [HRSA], Substance Abuse and Mental Health Services Administration [SAMHSA]). In contrast, services provided by the private sector include those directly operated by nongovernmental agencies and services that are financed with private resources (e.g., employer-provided insurance, pay out of pocket).

People pay for their care in a variety of ways. Some people access treatment through private health insurance provided by their employer or pay out of pocket. Others access care through funding provided by the government. Historically state and local governments have been the major payers of public mental health services, but since the mid-1960s, state funding has decreased while the role of the federal government has increased through various government programs such as Medicare and Medicaid. In 2019, **mental health spending in the United S**tates was $225 billion, an increase of 52% over the past decade. This represented 5.5% of all health spending. Government funds accounted for the majority (62.7%) of mental health spending at $149.5 billion, while private payers accounted for the remaining $88.9 billion (37.3%; Oss, 2020). In 2022, the Biden administration increased funding to SAMHSA (for a total of $6.5 billion) to better support mental health treatment, substance abuse prevention and treatment, and suicide prevention.

Major Criticisms of the Mental Health Care System

Like many large systems of care, the mental health system in the United States faces its fair share of criticisms that roughly fall into four categories:

- **Quality of care:** There have been calls for the mental health system to provide a higher quality of care for the vulnerable populations that they serve. This would require that mental health clinicians are trained to be compassionate and ethical and to use interventions that are both evidence based and culturally sensitive.

- **Lack of accessibility:** Many people who need treatment and care have historically had a difficult time getting access due to lack of health insurance and the way that it is funded in the United States. People of Color face additional access barriers. There are also workforce shortages that greatly impact people's ability to access care, particularly those in rural areas. Data from the Kaiser Family Foundation (as of September 2021) reveals that just under 130 million Americans live in 5,930 regions designated as having a mental health clinician shortage. Only 28% of the mental health clinician need is met across all health professional shortage areas and would require roughly 6,500 new mental health practitioners to meet the demand.

- **Racial/ethnic disparities**: SAMHSA collects data on racial/ethnic disparities within mental health. A recent report shows that between the years 2015 and 2019, people from ethnic/racial minority groups were less likely to mental health care. For example, among adults with any mental illness, 48% of White adults received mental health services compared to 40% of American Indians/Alaska Natives, 31% of Black adults, 32% of Latinos, and 22% of Asians (Center for Behavioral Health Statistics and Quality, 2021). The American Psychiatric Association (2017) identifies several barriers to care for members of diverse groups such as lack of insurance, mental health stigma, language barriers, lack of culturally competent providers, and lack of diversity among providers.

- **Fragmentation of care**: The mental health system is fragmented and has historically operated separately from the larger health care system despite calls by mental health experts who assert that mental health care should not be viewed separately from physical health care as they are all diseases of the body. Experts recommend that mental health services be well coordinated with general health and social services to ensure a good continuity of care.

- **Funding challenges**: Mental health has historically been viewed as the responsibility of local and state governments; thus, major investments by the federal government have been lacking. Federal funding for research on the brain and mental illness has lagged behind research related to general health conditions, such as cancer research and heart disease.

Mental Health Providers in the United States

The **mental health workforce** is made up of professionals from various disciplines and professional backgrounds, so when students decide they want to work in the field of mental health, they have a number of options with regard to the type of program they attend. Depending on the type of degree, professionals working in mental health vary with regard to their educational training, degree requirements, scope of practice, and licensing requirements (see Table 7.2). However, virtually all disciplines require specialized coursework, state licensure, and supervised clinical training in the field.

For example, to become an LCSW, one needs to earn a Master of Social Work degree, then engage in roughly 3,000 supervised clinical hours over 2 years (number of hours varies by state), and then pass a state licensing exam. Most mental health clinicians can diagnose and treat mental health disorders, though

TABLE 7.2   Types of Mental Health Clinicians in the United States

Type of Mental Health Clinician	Degree Required	Number of Professionals (Dept. of Labor)	Able to Diagnose and Provide Treatment for Mental Health Disorders?	Able to Prescribe Medication for Mental Health Disorders?
LCSWs	Master of Social Work and supervised clinical training	124,000 (in 2022)	Yes	No
Clinical psychologists	Doctoral degree in psychology and supervised clinical training	118,800 (in 2022)	Yes	No
Marriage and family therapists	Master's degree and supervised clinical training	73,200 (in 2020)	Yes	No
Licensed professional counselors (LPCs)	Master of Counseling and supervised clinical training	____	Varies by state	No
Licensed substance abuse/addictions counselors	May require associate's, bachelor's, or master's degree, depending on the state and level of licensure, as well as supervised training	____	Can treat substance abuse disorders	No
Psychiatrists	MD and supervised clinical training	25,520 (in 2021)	Yes	Yes
Psychiatric nurses	Master of Science in Nursing and clinical hours	____	Yes	Yes

only psychiatric nurses and psychiatrists can prescribe medication. Licensed clinical social workers are the largest group of mental health providers in the United States. It is important to work well with people from other disciplines when you work in mental health as you will often be part of an interdisciplinary team of health care providers.

A Controversy Within Social Work Mental Health Practice: The DSM

Those who work in mental health become well acquainted with the **Diagnostic and Statistical Manual of Mental Disorders (DSM)**, published by the APA, with contributions from more than 200 subject matter experts. It is more commonly referred to as "the DSM" and is sometimes referred to as the "psychiatrist's bible." The DMS is used to diagnose people with mental disorders and has been revised a number of times over the years as new mental disorders are added and existing ones are updated or even eliminated. One of the most infamous examples of this was in 1973 when homosexuality was removed from the DSM. The current edition is called the DSM-5-TR (2022) and includes roughly 300 mental disorders. The APA's initial objective was "to establish a nosology of mental disorders that can

IMG 7.4

constitute a common language among clinicians, researchers, health insurance companies, and the pharmaceutical industry" (Khoury et al., 2014, p. 602).

Disorders in the DSM are classified or categorized under headings so that common types of disorders are listed together. For example, one heading is "anxiety disorders," under which various types of anxiety disorders are included such as social anxiety disorder, panic disorder, and agoraphobia. The DSM does not tell clinicians how to treat people with mental disorders—only how to diagnose them. It does this by including a common list of signs and symptoms that tend to occur with various disorders. There are three major parts to the DSM:

- **The diagnostic classification**: This is the part of the DSM that includes a list of mental health disorders, including a common diagnostic code that is used by multiple parties such as providers and agencies for data collection and billing purposes (APA, n.d.b.).

- **The diagnostic criteria sets**: For each disorder included in DSM, "a set of diagnostic criteria indicates symptoms that must be present (and for how long) as well as a list of other symptoms, disorders, and conditions that must first be ruled out to qualify for a particular diagnosis. These criteria help increase diagnostic reliability (i.e., the likelihood that two doctors would come up with the same diagnosis when using DSM to assess a patient; APA, n.d.b.).

- **Descriptive text**: There is text that accompanies each disorder that provides information on a range of topics such as diagnostic features, prevalence, risk factors, and culture-related issues, just to name a few (APA, n.d.b.).

On the positive side, supporters of the DSM argue that it is a diagnostic tool that helps mental health practitioners to have a common understanding of mental disorders, which helps guide goal setting and treatment approaches. They point out that the DSM allows for standardization of diagnosis across different treatment providers, the codes in the DSM allow providers to bill insurance companies, and it helps guide research in mental health enabling researchers to study the same disorder. For some patients, having a diagnosis to understand their symptoms is comforting and empowering and leads to a treatment plan that can help mitigate their symptoms and improve their life.

On the flipside, the DSM is somewhat controversial and has faced a number of criticisms by those in various disciplines, including social work. One major criticism is that mental health diagnoses oversimplify human behavior that is very complex. Others worry that using the DSM can lead to misdiagnosis and overdiagnosis when some people's behaviors fall outside of social norms or people's perceptions of "normal behavior." Others have voiced their concerns about how the DSM leads clinicians to make decisions on what is normal behavior and what is abnormal or pathological behavior, when in some cases, this is not clear-cut based on the complexities of human behavior and cultural differences that have different social norms on what is considered "normal." Khoury et al. (2014) question the validity of the DSM as a diagnostic tool and argue that "named symptoms in the DSM and behaviors are contextually embedded and vary dramatically according to the situation, for example, aggressive behavior can be well-adapted in one context but not in another one. Even if the DSM partially addresses this issue, subtle contextual differences may create several diagnostic biases" (p. 602).

Barsky (2015) warns that using the DSM can raise ethical concerns in the areas of respect for the dignity and worth of all people, empowering clients, practicing within one's professional competence, and owing a primary duty of care to one's clients, unless social workers are careful. He explains that social workers should avoid **labeling people** or reducing them to a diagnosis as this can be **stigmatizing** (e.g., "She is a person with schizophrenia" versus "She is a schizophrenic."). Some have argued "that psychiatric labels serve only the interests of clinicians and their professional associations (e.g., APA) as well as the pharmaceutical industry whereas these labels can have devastating effects of the individuals receiving them" (Khoury et al., 2014, p. 602). Barsky (2015) cautions that the DSM tends to lead clinicians to focus on clients' pathologies and not their strengths and that the role of the clinician as expert can feel disempowering to a client. He recommends that clinicians weigh the risks and benefits of giving a client a diagnosis.

The Criminalization of those With Mental Illness ("Prisons Are the New Asylums")

One of the biggest social justice issues in mental health that is incredibly distressing to mental health experts and advocates, as well as the individuals and families who are impacted, is the current practice of sending people with mental illness to jails and prisons instead of getting them access to needed mental health treatment. This represents one of the biggest failures of social welfare policy. It is distressing that this was normal practice in the early part of U.S. history and that we have returned to this practice, though for very different reasons (see "History of Mental Health Services in the United States"). The **deinstitutionalization movement** occurred in the 1960s and was prompted by calls to close down the state hospitals and other institutional settings for those with mental illness so that they could be served in less restrictive community-based treatment programs. However, the state and federal funding required to create this new infrastructure never came to fruition, and as a result many people with mental illness became homeless and began to populate the jails and prisons because there was nowhere else for them to go. In essence, jails and prisons have become de facto mental health hospitals in the United States, and today more mentally ill people are in jails and prisons than hospitals.

NAMI (n.d.) advocates strongly against this practice and cites data showing that those with mental illness are over-represented in the mental health system and that the majority do not receive adequate mental health services while they are incarcerated. The prevalence of women with mental illness who are incarcerated is much higher than men. Those in charge of running jails and prisons have been outspoken about the fact that they are ill-equipped to serve this population and that this should not be within their domain. Though many states have passed laws to outlaw or limit the practice of **solitary confinement**, this practice is still used and can be very harmful to those with a mental illness. According to the Southern Poverty Law Center (2017), solitary confinement worsens a person's mental illness and can cause mental illness in healthy prisoners.

One positive development in recent years is the advent of **mental health courts**. Today there are hundreds of mental health courts across the country. Mental health courts include judges, prosecutors, defense attorneys, social workers, and other professionals with mental health expertise. These courts generally serve nonviolent offenders who have been diagnosed with a mental illness or co-occurring mental health and substance abuse disorders, and the goal of these courts is to decrease recidivism by providing clients with case management and needed resources such as support with employment, housing, mental health treatment, and other supportive services. It is important for researchers to continue to evaluate the effectiveness of this practice model to assess the impact it has on the lives of these individuals.

▎▌ Social Work Practice in Mental Health Settings

As stated at the beginning of this chapter, the largest group of mental health providers in the United States are LCSWs, and they outnumber other mental health practitioners such as psychologists, psychiatrists, and licensed professional counselors. The U.S. Bureau of Labor Statistics (2022) projects that the employment of social workers in substance and mental health **will grow by 15% between 2020 and 2030** due to increased demand for these services. There are shortages of mental health clinicians in many parts of the country, which needs to be addressed. LCSWs have a wide variety of work settings to choose from and can also choose to specialize in their clinical work (e.g., with older adults, children, adolescents, couples, individuals who have experienced severe trauma, those with severe mental illness, etc.). They can have their own **private practice** or work for an organization in the public or private sector.

Becoming a mental health clinician requires the acquisition of specialized therapeutic knowledge and skills and a strong adherence to the NASW Code of Ethics. Because of this, social workers who wish to become mental health

IMG 7.5

clinicians must complete a few important steps, such as earning their master's degree in social work and then attaining their clinical license to become an LCSW—which requires an additional 2 years of supervised clinical social work experience. Social workers who wish to become an LCSW take courses at the MSW level in clinical social work and work under a clinical supervisor to gain experience in using the **various types of evidence-based mental health therapies** that are used in clinical practice such as cognitive behavioral therapy, play therapy with children, art therapy, animal-assisted therapies (covered in this chapter), motivational interviewing, psychodynamic therapy, group therapy, trauma-focused therapies (covered in this chapter), marriage and family therapy, and many more.

Some clinicians choose to specialize and use a narrower set of therapeutic approaches with their clients, while others use a more **holistic or eclectic approach** and use a wide variety of therapies depending on the client and their needs. Because therapists work with people who are in distress and are quite vulnerable, it is important that they follow many of the **ethical guidelines** included in the NASW Code of Ethics such as ensuring that clients have given informed consent, supporting clients' right to self-determination, providing care that is culturally responsive, not engaging in a sexual relationship with clients, and respecting their right to privacy and confidentiality. The list below highlights the primary settings for social workers who specialize in mental health.

- **Private practice:** Some LCSWs choose to have their own private practice, and they can either do this as a solo practitioner or enter a private practice with other LCSWs. There are some advantages to going into business for yourself such as freedom to decide which clients to serve, setting up your own schedule, and being your own boss. The downside is that since it is your own business, you have to manage the financial side of the organization such as billing clients and working with health insurance companies.

- **Telemental health:** The use of videoconferencing technology (e.g., Zoom) to provide therapy to clients has become increasingly common, especially as a result of the coronavirus pandemic. There are some advantages and drawbacks to this model of providing mental health services. The benefits include convenience and the ability to reach people in underserved areas such as rural parts of the country. The challenges include the access to technology, the quality of the technology, and whether this approach can ensure that clients have the privacy they need to share very sensitive information without violating their confidentiality. Because this is a new and developing practice, more research is needed to assess its efficacy with different mental health disorders and populations.

- **Psychiatric hospitals:** Though the number of psychiatric hospitals has decreased significantly due to the deinstitutionalization movement that began in the 1960s, there are still some hospitals where patients can go to receive care on an inpatient or outpatient basis. These hospitals typically serve those who are experiencing a mental health crisis. These hospitals can be public, operated by a nonprofit organization, or operated by a for-profit organization. Social workers can also work in residential treatment centers, which is a step down from inpatient treatment. Though residents still live on staff, the supervision they are provided is less intense, and it feels less like a hospital and more of a home-like environment.

- **Community mental health centers (CMHCs):** There are roughly 230 CMHCs in the United States that are provided with federal funding to serve those with serious mental illness who do not have access to mental health services either because they are low income or do not have health insurance. CMHCs are set up to provide a range of services including emergency care, rehabilitation, and inpatient and outpatient services.

- **Medical hospitals/primary care:** Many individuals who experience distress due to a mental health condition end up going to their primary doctor or to the emergency room (ER) of a hospital. Additionally, some patients who come in with a physical health condition also have a mental health condition; thus, health professionals must respond to both issues. The degree to which medical hospitals are well equipped to respond to the psychiatric needs of patients varies widely from hospital to hospital. One recent study found that of 4,812 hospitals surveyed, more than 50% of the emergency departments and general hospitals lacked psychiatric services (Ellison et al., 2022). However, many hospitals do employ LCSWs to work with patients and to connect them with needed mental health services in the community.

- **The Military and the Veteran's Administration (VA):** Licensed clinical social workers in mental health who have a strong interest in working with those in the military have a few options. One option is to work as a social worker in one of the branches of the military on a military base to provide mental health services. Therapists can offer individual and family counseling in areas such as intimate partner violence, child maltreatment, substance abuse, and dealing with the trauma of serving in a war zone. Some of these jobs allow a social worker to be a civilian while other positions require military training to become a member of the military. Outside of the military setting, LCSWs can choose to have a clinical practice where they specialize in treating this population. Finally, many LCSWs provide clinical services to veterans who receive services through the VA, which is one of the largest employers of social workers in the nation.

- **Nonprofit and government-funded organizations**: There are number of organizations in the public and private sector that employ LCSWs to provide clinical/therapeutic services, such as jails and prisons, K–12 schools, universities, family violence shelters, residential facilities for older adults, and employee assistance programs for employees of an organization who are struggling with their mental health.

- **Advocacy organizations**: Social workers can work in organizations to try to get legislation passed at the state or federal level to improve support for those with mental health disorders (e.g., NAMI).

Trauma-Informed Care

When you think about the word "**trauma**," what comes up for you? Social workers commonly work with clients who have experienced trauma in their lives, for example being a victim of a violent crime, serving in a war, suicidal ideation, child maltreatment, and losing one's home due to natural disaster. Working with clients using a **trauma-informed care approach** is embraced by many professions, including social work. This framework came about after the realization, by many who work in various helping professions, of the fact that many people experience traumatic events; that some will be adversely impacted by these events, which can include the development of mental health disorders; and that people can overcome these adverse impacts with the right interventions and supports. Experts on trauma-informed care emphasize the need for individual practitioners, organizations, and large systems of care to embrace the philosophy and tenets of this practice framework.

According to SAMHSA (2014), **individual trauma** "results from an event, series of events, or set of circumstances that is experienced by an individual as physically or emotionally harmful or life threatening and that has lasting adverse effects on the individual's functioning and mental, physical, social, emotional, or spiritual well-being" (p. 7). Their concept of trauma includes the three E's, which they consider key to understanding and defining trauma: the traumatic **event**, the individual's **experience** of this traumatic event, and the **effects** of the event.

Because social workers will work with individuals who have experienced trauma in almost every field of practice, it is highly recommended that they get excellent training in how to operate from a trauma-informed care lens. SAMHSA (2014) outlines six key principles of a trauma-informed approach:

- **Safety**: Throughout the organization, staff and those they serve feel physically and psychologically safe.

- **Trustworthiness and transparency**: The organization operates in a transparent way in order to build trust among all of those who are involved with the organization.

- **Peer support:** Mutual self-help (e.g., connecting with others who have the lived experience of trauma) is an important part of healing and recovering

- **Collaboration and mutuality**: There is a strong emphasis on partnership, shared decision making, and moving away from hierarchy and power imbalances since this better promotes healing

- **Empowerment, voice, and choice:** This approach encourages a strong focus on client strengths and resilience. Also, that clients are the experts of their lives and should share in decision-making. Helping clients gain skills in self-advocacy leads to empowerment.

- **Cultural, historical, and gender issues**: The organization recognizes the impact of historical trauma and uses practices that are culturally responsive, gender responsive, and inclusive of those from all backgrounds. (p. 10)

Research Focus: Animal-Assisted Therapies

One intervention that has enjoyed tremendous popularity in recent years is animal-assisted therapies. Social workers who are animal lovers are intrigued with the idea of using animals such as dogs, cats, and horses (referred to as equine-assisted therapy) in their work with clients. One definition of **animal-assisted therapy** (AAT) is "the deliberate use of an animal in a treatment plan" which involves "a credentialed treatment provider who guides interactions between a patient and an animal to realize specific goals" (Nimer & Lundahl, 2015, p. 225). Many mental health providers and social service organizations have adopted this treatment approach, and it is typically used in conjunction with other therapeutic interventions.

There are social work programs that offer coursework, and even specific concentrations, in AAT for students who want to gain expertise in using this treatment approach with clients. AAT is being used in a variety of settings and with a variety of client populations (e.g., older adults and children in mental health settings and to aid in healing and recovery in health care settings, children and adults with disabilities, clients who have experienced trauma, etc.), which has necessitated the need for researchers to evaluate this intervention. As is true with any intervention, it is possible that it is more effective with certain clients than with others.

IMG 7.6

According to Nimer and Lundahl (2015), "The use of an animal in therapy may be beneficial because animals seem to have a natural tendency to create a bond with people. A good therapy animal will seek affection and interaction with the client. Thus, animals may promote a warm and safe atmosphere that can be independently therapeutic and help clients accept interventions offered by the treatment provider. AAT is not generally viewed as a stand-alone treatment. Rather, animals are used as a supplement or in conjunction with other interventions" (p. 226). These authors conducted a meta-analysis to review and summarize the findings of many research studies that have been conducted to evaluate the effectiveness of AAT.

In their review of 49 research articles, they concluded that AAT is a promising intervention that shows some moderate benefits, particularly for those with autism-spectrum symptoms, medical difficulties, and challenges regarding behavioral problems and emotional well-being. However, they also noted that there is a lot of variation in the way that AAT is being used since many times it is used in conjunction with other interventions. Thus, they concluded that in order "to gain further insight into the precise impact of AAT interventions, studies will need to be designed to account or control for the confound of using AAT with other interventions" (p. 235).

Mental Health Case Study

Matthew is a licensed clinical social worker who works in a state prison, and though it is a challenging job he really enjoys working with many of the men who are incarcerated there. In this mental health role, he performs a variety of functions such as assessing new arrivals to the prison, developing treatment and support plans for inmates, providing individual and group therapy, providing referrals for medical or mental health services, and monitoring the progress of inmates in treatment. Matthew is responsible for evaluating inmates for mental illness, including substance abuse. Finally, when inmates are getting ready to be released, he also assists them with discharge planning to plan for successfully reintegrating into the community.

Even though many of these men have caused harm and violence to others, he has the ability to provide care to them and to treat them with dignity and respect. Because of his social work training, he understands the impact of the larger social environment and how many of these men have been impacted by poverty, unstable family lives, violent neighborhoods, and lack of opportunity. Matthew enjoys the challenge of building relationships with men, many of whom have a distrust of helping professionals, such as social workers.

Lately, Matthew has been grappling with a serious ethical issue. Though some states have outlawed the practice of solitary confinement, the state where he works and resides still uses this practice. He has witnessed firsthand the harmful effects that solitary has on the mental health of inmates and has been reading the research on this. One of his clients who struggles with serious mental illness was put into solitary and ended up gauging out his eyes. Even though Matthew is in a clinical role, he knows that he has an ethical obligation to try to change policies and practices that are harmful to clients, particularly those who are vulnerable, such as those with mental illness.

Questions

1. What feelings come up for you as you imagine working as a social worker in a prison like Matthew does?

2. Do you agree that Matthew has an ethical obligation to do something even though he is a clinical (and not a macro) social worker?

3. If you were in this situation, would your goal be to change the policy in the prison or to change the law in your state? Which would impact all prisons in the state? Weigh the pros and cons of both options.

4. What steps could you take to reach this goal? Think creatively!

5. What obstacles would you anticipate facing as you attempt to make changes?

6. What further questions does this case raise for you?

Policy Focus: The Paul Wellstone and Pete Domenici Mental Health Parity and Addiction Equity Act of 2008

At a macro level, Americans are forced to focus on the failings of the U.S. mental health system when examples of untreated mental health disorders result in unspeakable tragedy, such as mass shootings that are committed by someone with an untreated mental health disorder. Even though the vast majority of people with a mental illness are not violent, it still raises questions about who should have access to purchase guns and whether the mental health system in the United States is adequately meeting the needs of its citizens. Social workers working at the macro level in mental health can find work in advocacy organizations that are attempting to get policies passed into law that improve people's access to mental health treatment and the quality of care that is provided by the mental health care system. Prominent examples of organizations doing this work are NAMI and **Mental Health America**.

There are many examples of policies that have been passed into law to improve the lives of those with mental health disorders, but this section will focus on one of the biggest legislative battles in mental health that took 12 years for advocates to get leaders in Washington, DC to pass a strong federal bill to address discrimination against those with mental health disorders who need treatment—mental health parity. Simply put, **mental health parity** is the principle that health insurance plans should have to include equal coverage for medical care and mental health care, when policies cover both.

Before the 2008 law was passed, it was legal for health insurance companies to provide less coverage for mental health care than for the treatment of medical conditions such as cancer or heart disease, and many people were not aware of this inequity until a family member required mental health treatment and was shocked to discover how limited their coverage was. For example, most health insurance plans were much less generous with regard to the number of outpatient visits and hospital days allowed, and mental health benefits were often more costly and had higher copays. Advocates framed this as discrimination against those with mental illness.

The NASW strongly supported this legislation and agreed with experts such as former U.S. Surgeon General David Satcher, who argued against the common misconception that there should be a division between "mental" health and "physical" health based on an overwhelming body of research that shows that mental illnesses have biological causes and are diseases of the brain.

The 2008 legislation outlawed health insurance discrimination by requiring insurance companies to treat mental health on an equal basis with physical illnesses, when policies cover both. It is important to understand that the act does not mandate that group insurance health plans include mental health and addiction, but when mental health is included on a plan it must be on par with medical treatment with regard to the following categories of coverage:

- Copays
- Deductibles
- Inpatient hospital days
- Number of outpatient visits

Change on this issue did not happen overnight, and it took 12 years for advocates to get this bill passed into law at the federal level, proof that it requires patience and perseverance to do work in the legislative arena. However, when an historic bill like this gets passed into law, the payoff is huge as it can improve the lives of millions of Americans. When this 2008 bill was passed, federal officials estimated that the new law would improve mental health coverage for 113 million people and only increase premiums by an average of about two tenths of 1%. Businesses with fewer than 50 employees were exempted from this law.

> **7.3   PRACTICE ACTIVITY**
>
> Visit either the NAMI or Mental Health America websites. What issues are they working to address currently in the policy arena?

Chapter Summary

Mental illness generally refers collectively to all mental disorders that can be diagnosed in the *DSM* (2022), published by the APA. There are a multitude of opportunities for social workers who want to impact change in the field of mental health at the micro, mezzo, and macro levels. LCSWs interested in this field of social work practice can work in a multitude of work settings, and this chapter highlighted private practice, community mental health centers, psychiatric hospitals, medical hospitals, military bases and the VA, public and private organizations such as schools and criminal justice settings, and the rapidly expansive practice of telemental health. Because LCSWs will work with individuals who have experienced trauma, it is highly recommended that they get excellent training in how to infuse trauma-informed care approaches into their clinical work. Social workers who wish to become mental health clinicians must first earn their master's degree in social work and then work to attain their clinical license to become an LCSW—which requires an additional 2 years of supervised clinical social work experience. There is a shortage of mental health clinicians in many areas of the country, and they will continue to be in high demand over the next decade.

Despite the fact that mental health disorders are very prevalent, those who experience a mental health disorder often experience stigma, though this has improved a lot in recent years due to growing understanding and acceptance. The mental health system has faced criticisms in a few key areas such as the quality of care it provides; lack of accessibility for those who need help; fragmentation of care; the way that the system is funded; and the recent trend of criminalizing those with mental illness instead of getting them needed treatment in the community or in a hospital setting. Getting mental health parity legislation passed at the federal level has been an important public policy focus for mental health advocacy organizations, and in 2008 the Paul Wellstone and Pete Domenici Mental Health Parity and Addiction Equity Act of 2008 was made federal law after 12 years of advocacy. This law that requires health insurance companies offer benefits for mental health that are on par with benefits for medical coverage. Research on animal-assisted therapies, an approach that utilizes animals to promote healing among those who have experienced trauma and/or are in emotional distress, is proving to be a promising intervention for some.

Discussion Questions

1. After learning about social work mental health practice and the major career paths outlined in this chapter, which of these settings feel like they could be a good fit for you? Which ones do not feel like a good fit? Why?

2. A number of criticisms of the mental health care system were highlighted in this chapter that result in some serious negative consequences for certain groups. Summarize them here. Which ones concern you the most?

3. In your opinion, how significant was the passage of the Mental Health Parity Act of 2008 in trying to get mental health care and treatment on par with medical care and treatment? Do you agree with the policy advocates that this was an issue of discrimination against those with mental health disorders?

4. The chapter discussed why using the DSM to diagnose clients is controversial within the social work discipline. What ethical concerns are raised? What are the benefits and drawbacks of mental health diagnosis?

5. This chapter highlighted some promising interventions such as animal-assisted therapy, telemental health, and mental health drug courts. How do these approaches align with social work values and ethics? What more would you like to learn about these interventions to have a more informed opinion about them?

References

American Psychiatric Association (n.d.a.). *Stigma, prejudice and discrimination against people with mental illness.* https://www.psychiatry.org/patients-families/stigma-and-discrimination

American Psychiatric Association (n.d.b.). *About DSM-5-TR.* https://www.psychiatry.org/psychiatrists/practice/dsm/about-dsm

American Psychiatric Association. (2017). *Mental health disparities: Diverse populations.* https://www.psychiatry.org/File%20Library/Psychiatrists/Cultural-Competency/Mental-Health-Disparities/Mental-Health-Facts-for-Diverse-Populations.pdf

American Psychiatric Association. (2022). *Diagnostic and statistical manual of mental disorders* (5th ed., text revision).

American Psychological Association. (n.d.). *Mental disorder.* APA Dictionary of Psychology. https://dictionary.apa.org/mental-disorder

Barsky, A. (2015). *DSM 5 and the ethics of diagnosis.* The New Social Worker. https://www.socialworker.com/feature-articles/ethics-articles/dsm-5-and-ethics-of-diagnosis/

Center for Behavioral Health Statistics and Quality. (2021). *Racial/ethnic differences in mental health service use among adults and adolescents (2015–2019)* (Publication No. PEP21-07-01-002). Substance Abuse and Mental Health Services Administration. https://www.samhsa.gov/data/report/racialethnic-differences-mental-health-service-use

Centers for Disease Control and Prevention (n.d.a.). *What is mental health?* https://www.cdc.gov/mentalhealth/learn/index.htm

Centers for Disease Control and Prevention (n.d.b.). *Data and statistics on children's mental health.* https://www.cdc.gov/childrensmentalhealth/data.html

Centers for Disease Control and Prevention (n.d.c.). *Suicide data and statistics.* https://www.cdc.gov/suicide/suicide-data-statistics.html

Ehlman, D. C., Yard, E., Stone, D. M., Jones, C. M., & Mack, K. A. (2022). Changes in suicide rates—United States, 2019 and 2020. *Morbidity & Mortal Weekly Report, 7,* 306–312. https://www.cdc.gov/mmwr/volumes/71/wr/mm7108a5.htm

Ellison, A. G., Jansen, Luc A. W., Nguyen, F, Martina, A., Spencer, J. Wierdsma, A. I., Kathol, R. G., & van Schijndel, M. A. (2022). Specialty psychiatric services in US emergency departments and general hospitals: Results From a nationwide survey. *Mayo Clinic Proceedings, 97*(5), 862–9=870. https://www.mayoclinicproceedings.org/article/S0025-6196(21)00847-8/fulltext#%20

Greenstein, L. (2017). *9 ways to fight mental health stigma.* National Alliance on Mental Illness. https://www.nami.org/blogs/nami-blog/october-2017/9-ways-to-fight-mental-health-stigma

Kaiser Family Foundation. (2021). *Mental health care health professional shortage areas (HPSAs).* https://www.kff.org/other/state-indicator/mental-health-care-health-professional-shortage-areas-hpsas/?currentTimeframe=0&sortModel=%7B%22colId%22:%22Location%22,%22sort%22:%22asc%22%7D

Khoury, B., Langer, E. J., & Pagnini, F. (2014). The DSM: Mindful science or mindless power? A critical review. *Frontiers in Psychology, 5,* 602. https://doi.org/10.3389/fpsyg.2014.00602

Lebrun-Harris, L. A., Ghandour, R. M., Kogan, M. D., & Warren, M. D. (2022). Five-year trends in US children's health and well-being, 2016–2020. *JAMA Pediatrics, 176*(7). https://jamanetwork.com/journals/jamapediatrics/fullarticle/2789946

National Alliance on Mental Illness (n.d.). *Mental health treatment while incarcerated.* https://www.nami.org/Advocacy/Policy-Priorities/Improving-Health/Mental-Health-Treatment-While-Incarcerated

National Institute of Mental Health. (n.d.a.). *Mental illness.* https://www.nimh.nih.gov/health/statistics/mental-illness.shtml

National Institute of Mental Health. (n.d.b.). *Suicide.* https://www.nimh.nih.gov/health/statistics/suicide#:~:text=A%20suicide%20attempt%20might%20not,%2C%20considering%2C%20or%20planning%20suicide

Nimer, J., & Lundahl, B. (2015). Animal-assisted therapy: A meta-analysis. *Anthrozoös, 20*(3), 225–238. https://www.tandfonline.com/doi/abs/10.2752/089279307X224773

Oss, M. E. (2020). Mental health spending now & after the pandemic. *Open Minds.* https://openminds.com/market-intelligence/executive-briefings/mental-health-spending-now-after-the-pandemic/

Ritter, J. A. (2022). *Social work policy practice: Changing our community, nation, and the world* (3rd ed.). Cognella.

Southern Poverty Law Center. (2017). *Solitary confinement can cause mental illness.* https://www.splcenter.org/news/2017/10/16/splc-solitary-confinement-can-cause-mental-illness?gclid=Cj0KCQjw54iXBhCXARIsADWpsG_0LEvnxoHKCJvZLqjKjAC5IAWwll-vOo9M5-57MMi3VZROpOtQXMtYaAnmaEALw_wcB

Substance Abuse and Mental Health Services Association. (2014). *SAMHSA's concept of trauma and guidance for a trauma-informed approach.* https://store.samhsa.gov/product/SAMHSA-s-Concept-of-Trauma-and-Guidance-for-a-Trauma-Informed-Approach/SMA14-4884

U.S. Bureau of Labor Statistics. (n.d.). *Social workers job outlook.* Occupational Outlook Handbook. https://www.bls.gov/ooh/community-and-social-service/social-workers.htm#tab-6

Credits

CHAPTER 8

Social Work in Health Care and Public Health Settings

Jess Retrum

Learning Objectives

After reading this chapter, students will be able to do the following:

- Summarize the biggest social problems we face with the health care system in the United States and why social workers are needed and in demand

- Explain what the role of social work looks like in various health care and public health settings

- Explain the relationship between health disparities and social determinants of health

- Identify three specific health care social work positions in unique health settings

- Explain policy initiatives designed to promote access to health care and insurance for all and to develop an interprofessional health workforce as potential solutions for social work's grand challenge of closing the health gap

- Summarize the major social justice issues in health care and how the Affordable Care Act addressed some of the barriers to accessing care

- Explain the goals of health equity and how it seeks to eradicate health inequalities for future generations with specific application to the United States

- Highlight research on palliative care interventions

- Evaluate goodness of fit with social work practice in health care and public health settings as a potential future career option

SOCIAL WORKER SPOTLIGHT:
Ann Slavkin, MSW, LCSW

My name is Ann Slavkin, and I work as a medical social worker in a large not-for-profit trauma one teaching hospital. The hospital encompasses a burn center, eye center, cancer center, intensive care unit, mom/baby, and a myriad of other services like cardiology, gynecology, stroke, orthopedics, transplant, urology, and so on. You get the picture; pretty much any acute medical need can be seen on any given day. Being able to work on various services and learning the nuances to the individual care needs has given me a broad base of experience in the health care arena.

When I was in high school, my grandfather was in a nursing home, and when one of the volunteers came into my grandfather's room, she always used a "sing-songy" voice and called him by his first name. My grandfather was from a generation in which no one under the age of 40 would call someone of his age by their first name. I saw my aunt and my mom cringe when they heard her talking to my grandfather in a way that seemed disrespectful. When I asked my mom later why they had not advocated for him, my mom said that she had not wanted to cause any issue that might affect my grandfather's care. She was concerned about the aide getting mad and treating my grandfather poorly. I knew then that I wanted to be a support for families and patients who needed help navigating unknown, complex, and sometimes scary systems. I wanted to offer the reassurance that care would not be determined by patients and families' acceptance of the status quo; instead, dignity and respect should be the standard practice.

I took the long route getting into social work. My mom had wanted me to find a lucrative career, one that would provide a high level of financial achievement, which generally, social work does not. Thus, I worked in the corporate realm for 20 years, but I was not happy in the business world. I felt like I was not making a difference for anyone, and it was unfulfilling. I decided to go back to school in my 40s and pursue the passion that had sparked from my grandfather's experience. I had volunteered at hospitals and nursing homes, provided respite foster care, and taught adult literacy, so in many ways, I always had my hand in helping professions. Getting my master's degree in social work seemed a good fit to further my ability to contribute in the supportive roles I desired.

I was surprised to find that school as a "nontraditional student" was much easier than it had been in my youth. I suppose my focus was clearer and my passion was guiding me this time. I spent every Sunday in the library and had study sessions with a fellow kindred spirit who was also a mom and had gone back to school "at our age." We proofed each other's papers and chose each other for the dreaded group assignments. We supported each other and had a mutual understanding of juggling jobs, kids, and family obligations along with school. Finding support systems that aid in getting your needs met is an important skill for social workers while in school and beyond. My focus was on the aging population, and I was able to secure an academic scholarship from the university I attended that was offered to students who worked with this marginalized group. For several years postgraduation, I worked in a clinic serving individuals over the age of 55. Eventually, I transitioned to the hospital, where I was able to expand my scope of practice by working with a broader population.

I found my passion by becoming a social worker. I can support patients and their families during some of the most difficult transitions in their lives. Adjusting to new a diagnosis and shifting roles can challenge even the closest of families. Those with difficult family dynamics often need a neutral party to help process information and validate feelings. I get to use my clinical skills to help families from all walks of life navigate their new realities. As a case manager, I am able to help problem solve and offer tangible solutions to various barriers to care. Providing education to increase people's health literacy allows me to empower others in their health care journey, which enables them to take control of situations in which they often feel powerless. Even sitting and holding space in uncomfortable situations with another human gives me a sense of fulfillment knowing my professional presence makes a positive difference.

Social workers in health care are essential members of most health care teams and are leaders in health care organizations and initiatives across the country in a wide variety of settings. Social work in health care and public health are exciting, expanding, and evolving areas to work. According to the U.S. Census Bureau's 2019 American Community Survey (ACS), 14% of all U.S. workers are in the health care industry, which is one of the largest and fastest growing sectors.

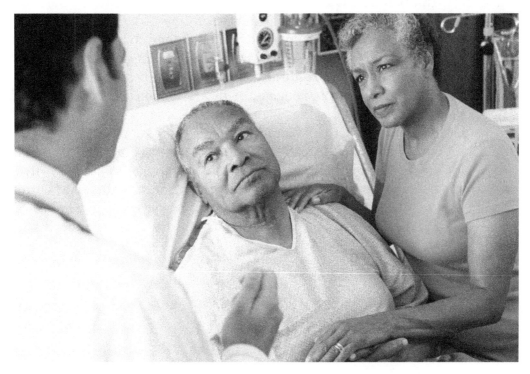

IMG 8.1

Social workers with expertise in health care are employed in various settings across the health care continuum, such as prevention and public health, primary and acute care, rehabilitation, specialty care home health, long-term care, and hospice (National Association of Social Workers [NASW], 2016). According to the U.S. Bureau of Labor Statistics, as of 2020, in the United States there were 708,100 employed social workers. Of those, 179,500 are health care social workers; that's one fourth of all social workers! **Health care social work** is the second largest area of growth for social work, projected to grow by 11% in the next decade (U.S. Bureau of Labor Statistics, 2023). Social workers in the health field work with individuals and families facing significant health challenges, sometimes the most serious matters of their lives. They also get to work alongside a variety of professionals from many disciplines and be part of cutting-edge health interventions. This is an area of social work practice for those interested in meaningful and impactful time with their clients and in work in a high-energy and face-paced environment.

Health and Illness in the United States

The World Health Organization (WHO, 2023) says that "**health** is a state of complete physical, mental, and social well-being and not merely the absence of disease or infirmity" (para. 1). **Illness** is a disease or period of sickness that affects the body or mind and can last for a short or long period of time. Most illnesses we can recover completely from or at least reach a point that they no longer impact our everyday lives. Other illness can be more serious and take longer to recover from and be limiting or terminal. "**Chronic diseases** are defined broadly as conditions that last 1 year or more and require ongoing medical attention or limit activities of daily living or both. Chronic diseases such as heart disease, cancer, and diabetes are the leading causes of death and disability in the United States. They are also leading drivers of the nation's $4.1 trillion in annual health care costs" (National Center for Chronic Disease Prevention and Health Promotion [NCCDPHP], 2023, para. 1). According to the most recent report from the Centers for Disease Control and Prevention (CDC), life expectancy at birth was 76.4 years for the total U.S. population, and the top 10 leading causes of death (and the number of deaths) in the United States are as follows:

1. Heart disease (695,547)
2. Cancer (605,213)
3. COVID-19 (416,893)
4. Accidents (unintentional injuries) (224,935)

5. Stroke (cerebrovascular diseases) (162,890)

6. Chronic lower respiratory diseases (142,342)

7. Alzheimer's disease (119,399)

8. Diabetes (103,294)

9. Chronic liver disease and cirrhosis (56,585)

10. Nephritis, nephrotic syndrome, and nephrosis (54,358; Murphy et al., 2021)

In 2020 and 2021, COVID-19 was the third leading cause of death in the United States. **Infant mortality**, an important measure of the quality of a nation's health, was 5.4 infant deaths per 1,000 live births. Unfortunately, there is considerably higher infant mortality among Black (10.6), Native Hawaiian or Pacifica Islander (8.2), American Indian or Alaska Native (7.9), and Hispanic families (5) when compared with other groups (Ely & Driscoll, 2019). Extensive research has shown that socioeconomic status, race/ethnicity, sex, and other factors play a role in common health and mental health issues. "Many populations in America, whether defined by race, ethnicity, immigrant status, disability, sex, gender, or geography, experience higher rates of certain diseases and more deaths and suffering from them compared with the general population. While the diversity of the American population is one of the nation's greatest assets, one of its greatest challenges is reducing the profound disparity in health status of its racial and ethnic minority, rural, low-income, and other underserved populations" (National Institute on Minority Health and Health Disparities, 20232para. 1). In addition to the biological factors causing disease progression, the National Institute on Minority Health and Health Disparities sharpens the scientific community's focus on nonbiological factors that impact health disparities such as socioeconomics, politics, discrimination, culture, and environment. There is indisputable evidence that that **health inequalities** (or **health disparities**) exist broadly, beyond individual behaviors or isolated communities. These inequities are matter of social injustices as they are often avoidable and due to systemic failures.

Health Equity and Social Determinants of Health

Many who work in the health care and public health fields are concerned about inequalities as some groups of people in our society have better access to getting needed care than others and thus have better health outcomes. **Health disparities** are preventable discrepancies in the frequency, prevalence, mortality, and disease burden that are associated with social, economic, and environmental disadvantage. The social determinants of health are factors that affect a wide range of health and quality-of-life outcomes and are responsible for most health disparities.

Social determinants of health (SDOH) are the nonmedical factors that influence health outcomes. They are the conditions in which people are born, grow, work, live, and age, and the wider set of forces and systems shaping the conditions of daily life (U.S. Department of Health & Human Services, Centers for Disease Control and Prevention, 2022). These considerations include income, housing, education, employment, and access to health services, among others. SDOH are shaped by individuals' and communities' access to money, power, and resources, as well as situations in the environments where people are born, live, learn, work, play, worship, and age that impact a wide range of outcomes and risks related to health, functioning, and quality-of-life. Healthy People 2030 is an initiative charged with the mission to, "promote, strengthen, and evaluate the nation's efforts to improve the health and well-being of all people" (U.S. Department of Health and Human

FIGURE 8.1   Healthy People 2030.

Services, Office of Disease Prevention and Health Promotion, n.d., para. 2; see Figure 8.1). Central to Healthy People 2030 work is to measure and promote ways to impact SDOH by setting ambitious goals, sharing in, and directly supporting multileveled efforts, and tracking outcomes.

Overview of the U.S. Health Care System

The WHO (2017) describes the broader health system as one that includes all institutions, organizations, and resources that have the main purpose of promoting, restoring, and/or maintaining health. Contacts such as a doctor visit, prescription pick-up, or receiving a public health announcement, such as vaccination availability, means contact with the health care system. Health care services in the United States are delivered through various organizations, as seen in Table 8.1 (Knickman & Elbel, 2019).

As you may have experienced personally, health care services are paid for through a combination of ways, such as government-funded health insurance, private health insurance, or out-of-pocket costs to individual households. Health service provider organizations are both for-profit and nonprofit, including government-owned nonprofit, entities. The 91.7% of Americans who have health insurance receive it through private and/or public health insurance programs. The largest portion of health care financing is government funded through

8.1	PRACTICE ACTIVITY

Visit the website of one of Healthy People 2030: https://health.gov/healthypeople/priority-areas/social-determinants-health. Choose and explore one of the five domains and explain in your own words why this area is important to the health of our communities in the United States. What would happen if we accomplished the goal?

TABLE 8.1   Health Care Services in the United States

Health Care Services	Health Care Delivery Organizations
Prevention	Hospitals
Public health, community health, and population	Physician organizations
Health	Ambulatory surgery centers
Primary prevention services	Long-term care organizations
Acute care	Rehabilitation organizations
• Emergency/urgent	Integrated delivery systems
• Prehospital	Emergency medical services
○ Primary, specialty, chronic	Home health organizations
• Tertiary and quaternary	Hospice and palliative care organizations
• Subacute inpatient	Pharmacies
Rehabilitative care	Pharmaceutical companies and medical device
Long-term care	Manufacturers
End-of-life care	Telemedicine services
	Retail clinics

Source: James R. Knickman and Brian Elbel, Jonas and Kovner's Health Care Delivery in the United States. Copyright © 2019 by Springer Nature.

IMG 8.2

public health insurance programs. The main way individuals and families have public health insurance coverage are through **Medicare**, **Medicaid**, and the **Children's Health Insurance Program** (CHIP). Medicare coverage is for those over the age of 65 years, and all individuals above this age have universal access to this benefit. Some individuals with certain chronic illnesses or other conditions may be eligible for this coverage sooner. Medicaid and CHIP are both designed for those considered from low-income households, and CHIP is designed for those under 18 years old. Military veterans received benefits through the U.S. Department of Veteran Affairs (VA). All enrolled veterans receive the VA's (2023) comprehensive medical benefits packages, which includes preventive, primary and specialty care, as well as diagnostic, inpatient, and outpatient care services. Veterans may receive additional benefits, such as dental care, depending on their unique circumstances. **Private health insurance** coverage is available through private companies such as UnitedHealth, Anthem, Kaiser, Centene Corp, and Humana. Most often, employers offer health insurance as a benefit of employment, but other insurance can be purchase by individuals. The individual access to insurance increased with the new health exchanges created by the Affordable Care Act (i.e., Obamacare), which many individuals now take advantage of. Payment systems between health providers, insurance companies, and consumers are complex. It is essential that health social workers are familiarized with how health care financing impacts consumers and their organization.

What Is the Difference Between Public Health and Other Health Care Services?

Public health, community health, and population health are often seen as similar, but they are distinct and different than other health care foci. Public health is often defined as having the focus of created methods and programs that reduce the risk of getting disease, including infectious disease, and decreasing acute and chronic disease burden and injury, and promoting health. Community health is a broader application of public health efforts. "Community health is a multi-sector and multi-disciplinary collaborative enterprise that uses public health science, evidence-based strategies, and other approaches to engage and work with communities, in a culturally appropriate manner, to optimize the health and quality of life of all persons who live, work, or are otherwise active in a defined community or communities" (Goodman et al., 2014, p. 5). Population health is simply defined as health outcomes within specific groups of individuals.

It is a unique time in medical advancement for emerging new medical technologies as well as advanced technologies, such as smartphones, that have an impact on health care service delivery. For instance, advancement in pharmaceuticals, learning from big data, DNA coding, stem cell technologies, and robotic surgeries all pose a new frontier in modernizing the health care system that will improve patient outcomes in ways we've only begin to imagine. They also pose new challenges in health care funding and access to care. Another advancement impacting health care workers, including social workers, over the last decade has seen an emergence and exponential growth of **telehealth interventions**. These interventions have varying degrees of effectiveness and evidence base, and this area is still being developed but is certainly a game changer for several populations who otherwise would not have access to care, such as those who are homebound, restricted by their resources, environment, or health to travel to receive care.

What Are the Major Challenges Facing Our Health Care System?

The biggest problems facing the U.S. health care system relate to health inequities including but not limited to access to care, health care costs, quality and efficiency of care, and the lack of agility and human resources to respond to changing health needs of our populations and environment. Compared to many other nations, the U.S. health care system is by far more complex, advanced, and expensive. However, not all people in the United States have health coverage, and many are under-insured. Being under-insured means even though individuals have some coverage, it doesn't cover enough services they need for them or their families so they must choose between paying out of pocket for health care or paying other bills, such as buying groceries or paying for childcare. One of the biggest political debates between conservatives and liberals concerns whether health care is a right or a privilege. Our country has a long, developmental history of health care services, health and social policy, and private industry, which impacts how accessible our health care system functions. This history contributes to how well the health system serves individuals and communities today and the financial cost for our government entities and taxpayers as well as individuals and families who pay for health care services out of their own pockets.

According to the U.S. Census Bureau (Keisler-Starkey and Bunch, 2021), 8.3% of the population are uninsured, a slight decrease to 8.5% in 2018. The increased coverage is due to increased enrollment in government-sponsored health insurance. Between 2008 and 2013, the average uninsured rate was 15%, a significant improvement, arguably attributed to the Affordable Care Act (ACA) of 2010. Unfortunately, 27 million Americans still do not have health insurance and lack access to health care services. This was a particular problem during the coronavirus (COVID-19) pandemic. According to the Kaiser Family Foundation (Tolbert, Orgera, & Damico, 2020), most uninsured individuals are in low-income households, non-elderly adults, in working families, and six in 10 are people of color. This means lack of health insurance coverage disproportionately impacts people of color. A function of geographic variation in income and the accessibility of public coverage, most uninsured people live in the South or west part of the country. Interestingly, 70% of people who are uninsured are employed full-time or related to someone who is. The reason cited for this is due to either having an employer that does not offer health coverage or a health insurance option that the employee can afford.

Although the United States is one of the wealthiest nations in the world and spends far more per person on health care than any other industrialized nation, the health outlook of our people pales in comparison to other wealthy countries and appears to be worsening. Over the past 3 decades, the U.S. population has poorer health and lower life expectancy throughout the life cycle (birth to death) and has been dying at younger ages than those of the populations in peer nations (Institute of Medicine, 2013). The United States spends far more of its gross domestic product on health care compared to 11 other high-income countries but ranks last overall. "The U.S. ranks last on access to care, administrative efficiency, equity, and health care outcomes, but second on measures of care process" (Schneider et al., 2021).

Health challenges emerge for individuals in diverse ways throughout the human life cycle. Disease type, trajectory, and availability of treatments will all impact an individual's experiences; as you can imagine, health challenges can impact entire family systems. Alternatively, social environments often influence how susceptible people are to developing illnesses and how well individuals can recover from and cope with illness. For all these reasons, social workers are an important part of health systems and health teams serving individuals, or **patients**, in the world of health care.

Medical science upon which our health systems are built has a central focus: to cure illness. Therefore, the diseases of the human body, disease etiology (cause), disease progression, and interventions to treat the illness has been the primary area of study. This approach, often referred to as the **medical model**, has received criticism over the years because it did not centralize the social, psychological, and spiritual aspects of the human experience, which can also have important implications for disease and treatment outcomes. In the past 50 years, health and allied health professionals have learned that a more holistic approach to human health and well-being as well as interdisciplinary models of intervention are more effective in achieving better patient outcomes and in researching disease progression and treatment.

Health Care Policy Focus: The Patient Protection and Affordable Care Act of 2010

Health policy is developed and implemented by government or the private sector to achieve various health goals related to access, costs, quality, and accountability of health care services and systems. In March 2010, the Patient Protection and Affordable Care Act, most often referred to as the Affordable Care Act (ACA), also dubbed Obamacare, the comprehensive health care reform law, was enacted. Three goals of this landmark legislation were (a) to make health insurance more affordable for more people, (b) expand the Medicaid system to cover more adults by making the income eligibility more realistic, and (c) to support new and innovative models of care designed to lower the cost and increase the quality of health care. Social work roles often found in mental and physical health integration, prevention, and public health gained renewed importance under the ACA (NASW, 2016). The continued success of the ACA has led to a long list of advancements of health equity in the United States. Even though health outcomes are not the return on investment we'd hope, with the addition of the ACA, we have seen improved health of all Americans, including women and families, kids, older adults, people with disabilities, LGBTQI+ and individuals, families, and communities of color. Since the enactment of the ACA, millions more Americans have gained health coverage without certain limitations and there are protections in place for people with preexisting conditions. Benefits gained for those who have improved access to care include but are not limited to preventive and rehabilitative care, prescription drugs, wellness visits and contraceptives, mental health and substance use treatment, and more.

The ACA was inspired by innovations that many health policy advocates continue to address that target health care system quality issues. A popular framework for health system from form, called "Triple Aim," emphasizes the importance of implementing new approaches and models that aim to improve all three of these at the same time: (a) the quality and satisfaction of health care, (b) population health, and (c) reduced health care costs. Continued innovations of the health care system aim to improve the quality and efficiency of

8.2   PRACTICE ACTIVITY

Visit the website of the U.S. Department of Health & Human Services fact sheet "Celebrating the Affordable Care Act" https://www.hhs.gov/about/news/2022/03/18/fact-sheet-celebrating-affordable-care-act.html). What are the most remarkable accomplishments from your perspective and why?

health services by improving the models of how care is delivered and have an important place for social work skills, knowledge, and expertise. Many new models are rooted in patient-centered care, integrative care, and prevention-focused concepts. Examples of models currently being tested include patient-centered medical homes, health homes, accountable care organizations, community-based solutions, and integrated health care delivery, which includes different provider–organization relationships.

SOCIAL JUSTICE SPOTLIGHT:
Health Inequities in the United States

Health inequalities in the United States exist, and decades of research indicate several factors, including race, ethnicity, gender, geography, sexual and gender identity, age, disability status, and socioeconomic status (National Institute on Minority Health and Health Disparities [NIMHD], 2022. A recent initiative launched by the American Academy of Social Work & Social Welfare (AASWSW) was designed to hone our social work researchers' attention on 13 of the most pressing problems facing society today: "The **Grand Challenges for Social Work** is a groundbreaking initiative to champion social progress powered by science. It is a call to action for all of us to work together to tackle our nation's toughest social problems" (AASWSW, 2023, para. 1). Among these challenges is to **"close the health gap,"** as millions of Americans facing discrimination, poor living environments, and poverty don't have adequate access to basic health care. As noted, 8.3% of the U.S. population is uninsured (U.S. Census Bureau, 2021), and most uninsured individuals are low income or nonelderly adults, and lack of health insurance coverage disproportionately impacts People of Color (Tolbert et al., 2020). This is due the fact that individuals either have an employer that does not offer health coverage or a health coverage option that the employee cannot afford. This social justice spotlight will focus on two policy recommendations from the most accomplished social work health research scholars in the country.

The most significant health policy in recent history is ACA. The policy was complex and multifaceted, but the overarching intent was to shift health insurance and health policy to incorporate more prevention and primary care strategies. Within the social work grand challenge to close the health gap, policy recommendation 4, "Promote Access to Health Care and Insurance for All," endorses building on the groundwork of the ACA to expand health insurance coverage to all Americans by maximizing enrollment in health insurance, especially for disadvantaged populations who are eligible but have barriers during the enrollment process as well as among vulnerable populations not included in the act's protections. It also recommends policy advocates take on the inequitable access to public insurance programs along racial lines. A second ambitious policy focus, recommendation 5, "Foster Development of an Interprofessional Health Workforce," acknowledges the demand for a social work health care workforce is on the rise and often higher than other disciplines in health, with a 11% increase in the need for health care social workers expected over the next decade. What's more, employment of mental health and substance abuse social workers is projected to grow by 19%. These policy recommendations for social workers lead to integrated initiatives for evidence-based workforce development. With expertise in interdisciplinary communication and systems integration, social workers are well suited to develop competence areas for the emerging health systems.

The National Academies of Science, Engineering, and Medicine (NASEM) issued two reports in the last 5 years recommending better integration of health care and social services and community-based solutions to improve health outcomes (NASEM, 2019, 2021). The AASWSW dares us to take on the ambitious goal of achieving health equity, eradicating health inequalities for future generations, and giving us specific targets to aim for. It identifies "priorities for action include focusing on settings to improve conditions of daily life, advancing community empowerment for sustainable health, cultivating innovation in primary care, promoting full access to health care, generating innovations in research on social determinants of health inequities, fostering interprofessional workforce development, and stimulating multisectoral advocacy to promote health equity policies" (Walters et al., 2016, p.1).

While the ACA has many successes to celebrate, unfortunately, over 8% of Americans remain uninsured, and many continue to be underinsured. A March 2022 issue brief summarized some of the major trend that persist:

- "Efforts to expand health insurance coverage are central to improving health equity and responding to the health and economic challenges of the COVID-19 pandemic. Millions of uninsured individuals are currently eligible for subsidized coverage under the Affordable Care Act (ACA), and this number is anticipated to grow with the provisions of the American Rescue Plan Act of 2021 (ARP).

- Though the national uninsured rate has decreased substantially since the implementation of the ACA, high uninsured rates persist in some states such as Texas and Florida.

- In some areas of the country, large portions of the uninsured population, up to 69 percent, reside in households in which the adults have limited English proficiency.

- Hispanic individuals represent 19 percent of the total U.S. population but account for 29 percent of the uninsured.

- Black individuals comprise approximately 13 percent of the U.S. population but 16 percent of the uninsured.

- Data on the uninsured population can assist with outreach efforts to inform eligible individuals about their health insurance coverage options." (Bosworth et al., 2021, para. 1)

Why Is Social Work an Important Health Profession?

Since the early 20th century, social work has been recognized as having a vital role in health care. During the late 19th century, demographic shifts, recognition of how social contexts impact health, and changing views of illness and public health caused medical institutions and society in general to expand their views of what should be included in health care provision. This was the first step in the development of the medical social work field (Gehlert & Browne, 2019). The Royal Free Hospital of London hired the first social worker (called a "hospital almoner") in 1895. Social workers recognized early on that social determinants such as poverty and lack of education could negatively impact illness, equal access to care, and treatment outcomes. In 1906, the first social services department in the United States was established at Massachusetts General Hospital, and after much success was noted there, Johns Hopkins Hospital hired their first social worker in 1907 (Bartlett, 1988). Social work in health care has evolved in scope and focus over the years and remains an essential member of health care teams and leaders in health care organizations and initiatives across the country, in a wide variety of settings and health foci.

As noted, social work in health care is one of the fastest growing sectors for social work. There are many, many areas in health care in which social workers work, the most common being hospitals, individual and family services, home health, skilled care facilities, integrated behavioral health teams, and outpatient settings. They typically function as part of an **interdisciplinary team**, and their population focus is determined by the health challenges of individuals they serve, the social context and needs of the individuals, how individuals and their supports cope with their illness or disease progression, and the composition of the teams they work with. This chapter features three highly specialized areas of practice that illuminate different health social work career pathways. Two are focused on clinical practice in health settings, chronic disease, and nephrology social workers, and one is focused on community and public health, or macro-level, health social work.

Current Events Spotlight: Implications of the COVID-19 Pandemic

In 2020 and 2021, COVID-19 was the third leading cause of death in the United States. The COVID-19 pandemic has permanently changed the social and health landscape of our country. More than a million people died in the United States alone, and several of our most vulnerable communities, such as older adults, those with compromised immune systems, and communities of color, suffered negative impacts, including long-term effects and death at higher rates. The pandemic illuminated significant weakness in our health care system, including lack of preparedness of the public health system to respond to a public health crisis and lack of stability and agility of the health care system to respond. The pandemic also shifted Americans' mind-sets, triggering deep reflection on what is important in life. A Pew Research survey study found that 26% percent of Americans learned through the pandemic it is more important to protect health, listen to public health officials, and take health precautions than previously thought. Many also had a newfound appreciation and value for social interactions but found it less important to be in large crowds, go out, and socialize in person (Sharpe & Spencer, 2022). While it appears we've pulled through the worst of the pandemic and have moved toward a more stable outlook, the impacts will be with us for years to come in areas such as long-term implications of delayed preventative and primary care, such as later-stage cancer diagnosis, and the long-term effects of COVID survivors. We are also going to be dealing for many years with ancillary affects such as complicated grief and loss and a nationwide mental health crisis that spans across all ages, increasing the need for mental health services.

Our already extended health care workforce in the United States was highly impacted by the COVID-19 pandemic. While we see an increased need in mental health and social services, we are simultaneously experiencing workforce shortages as well as increased health care worker vicarious trauma, burnout, and exhaustion. Prior to COVID-19, there were already workforce shortages, overburdened workers, and inefficiencies contributing to burnout, stress, and mental health problems. During the pandemic, many health care workers were furloughed or laid off, ironically because the demand COVID-19 placed on health care systems needing to cancel and postpone procedures and care due to lack of capacity or safety. Overall employment in the health care industry declined but has gradually begun to recover since the summer of 2020. Federal, state, and local governments took significant action such as supplemental funding from federal relief legislation and easing many regulatory requirements to address the need for prevention and treatment services and disruptions in health care delivery. Since the health care workforce faced challenges even before the pandemic, it is anticipated that it will take quite a while for our systems to recover (U.S. Department of Health and Human Services, 2022).

Health social workers are an important member of the health care workforce and have been impacted significantly by the pandemic. Health social workers were leaned on heavily to support patients while families and friends were forced to stay away from hospitals, long-term care facilities, and clinic settings. Many health social workers were forced to move to a telehealth service delivery method with very little warning, training, or infrastructure in place. A recent analysis of over 256 studies related to social work practice and/or research revealed many innovative approaches were championed by health social workers to address the need of many populations, largely including older people and those with vulnerable health

IMG 8.3

challenges (Cheung, 2022). In their study of the impact of COVID-19 pandemic on U.S. social workers, Holmes et al. (2021) found that more than 25% exhibited symptoms of PTSD, higher than in the health social work population prior to the pandemic, indicating a higher need for emotional support for social workers in this area.

What Does a Health Social Worker Do?

Social workers can be found in all areas of health care, from providing direct clinical practice to leading and supervising units and divisions, to advancing new health policies through research or policy advocacy. In terms of direct practice, health social workers provide individuals, families, and groups with the psychosocial support needed to understand, adapt to, and cope with health issues, including chronic, acute, or terminal illnesses. A new or progressing health diagnosis can create emotional, financial, and social needs, and health social workers are trained to assess and intervene. Services typically include supporting and educating family caregivers. They also frequently serve patients through information, counseling, and providing referrals for other services. They also can engage in case and care management, or interventions designed to promote health and well-being, prevent illness, and address barriers to access to health care (U.S. Bureau of Labor Statistics, 2023). **Population health**– or **public health**–focused social workers engage in community-level interventions and policy advocacy that address the needs of communities who otherwise struggle due to inadequacies of or access to health services. Common roles and responsibilities of social workers in health care settings include the following:

- understanding of common ethical and legal issues in social work practice in health care settings
- biopsychosocial–spiritual assessment
- use of the strengths perspective
- client and family engagement in all aspects of social work intervention
- case/care management/care coordination/health care navigation
- discharge and transition planning
- client concordance with and adherence to the plan of care
- advance care planning
- palliative care, including pain and symptom management
- hospice and end-of-life care
- identification of child/elder/vulnerable adult abuse, trauma, neglect, and exploitation
- crisis intervention
- facilitation of benefits and resource acquisition to assist clients and families, including an understanding of related policies, eligibility requirements, and financial and legal issues
- advocacy with other members of the interdisciplinary team and within the health care institution to promote clients' and families' decision-making and quality of life
- client, family, interdisciplinary, and community education
- family systems issues, including the impact of health care concerns, illness, and disease on family relationship,; life cycles, and caregiving roles and support needs
- participation in research and evaluation of social work practice in health settings (NASW, 2016)

Guiding principles of health social work practice are similar to other areas of social work: honor, self-determination, **cultural competency**, and affirmation of the dignity and worth of all people; seeing the person in their environment; using a strengths perspective; primacy of the client–social worker relationship; the promotion and advocacy of social justice; and valuing the importance of social work research. A quintessential aspect of social work in health care is to practice with a biopsychosocial–spiritual perspective. This approach acknowledges the importance of whole-person care and incorporates a client's physical or medical condition; emotional or psychological state; socioeconomic, sociocultural, and sociopolitical status; and spiritual needs and concerns.

What Is a Biopsychosocial and Spiritual Assessment?

It is important to realize, while social workers are often called on to help people address a health issue or problem they are facing, they must first obtain a clear picture of all the aspects of a person. This includes a close look at what has gone well and is going well prior to the health challenge. All people have strengths and challenges. Strengths are aspects of people and their surroundings that have carried them through each phase of life, helped them accomplish their successes, and overcome obstacles. Challenges are the problems they may face that can originate within their body or mental health or from the social environmental context in which they grew up or are currently living in. To develop an accurate, comprehensive picture of the clues about the best ways to help, social workers need tools to guide them. Regardless of setting a health care social worker is in, an important step is to conduct a **biopsychosocial–spiritual assessment**. The purpose of a biopsychosocial and spiritual assessment is to help determine a holist picture of an individual, their social supports, and their social environment. All of us have a history that includes overcoming challenges and risks. Conducting a thorough assessment will provide indications for the social worker that will help them address the immediate problem or concern. This is often referred to as using a strengths-based or holistic approach for an assessment of needs. The domains of any assessment are broad: personal information, presenting problem or issue, the historical context of the individual, and their social network and environment. Based on these, the social worker can develop their assessment and plan for intervention. The level of detail a social worker needs to assess within these domains or use additional and more specific assessment or diagnostic tools, will vary based on the setting and the specific problem or issues the individual is facing. The following is an example of categories that might be seen in a comprehensive biopsychosocial–spiritual assessment.

I. **Identifying Information**

    a. Demographic information: age, sex, ethnic group, current employment, marital or partner status, physical environment/housing: nature of living circumstances (house, apartment, group home or other shared living arrangement, unhoused), neighborhood

    b. Physical health, psychological or mental health, and cognitive functioning (typical and current), social and spiritual status (typical and current)

    c. Referral information: referral source (self or other), reason for referral; other professionals or indigenous helpers currently involved

    d. Data sources used in writing this assessment: interviews with others involved (list dates and persons), tests performed, other data

II. **Presenting Problem**

    a. Individual's thoughts and feelings about illness, treatment, and care

    b. Description of the problem and situation for which help is sought as stated by the client

    c. What needs to be known about the client and family to give them the best care

    d. How the client and family best receive information

    e. What is most important to the client right now and in the future and if this is different from what they perceive as important to their family

    f. If past experiences are related to the current challenge and how this was handled in the past

III. **Background**

    a. Developmental history: from early life to present (if obtainable)

    b. Family background: description of family of origin and current family; extent of support; family perspective on client and client's perspective on family; family communication patterns; family's influence on client and intergenerational factors

    c. Cultural background

    d. Spiritual and/or religious background

    e. Health care power of attorney and supporting documents

    f. Intimate relationship history

    g. Educational and/or vocational training

    h. Employment history

    i. Military history (if applicable)

    j. Use or misuse of alcohol or drugs, self, and family

    k. Medical history (e.g., birth information, illnesses, accidents, surgery, allergies, disabilities, health problems in family, nutrition, exercise, sleep)

    l. Mental health history (e.g., previous mental health issues and treatment, hospitalizations, outcome of treatment, family mental health issues)

    m. Nodal events, specifically deaths of significant others, serious losses or traumas, significant life achievements

IV. **Assessment**

    a. The key issue or problem from the client's and worker's perspective

    b. How the client and family are functioning

    c. Factors, including thoughts, behaviors, personality, environmental circumstances, stressors, vulnerabilities, and needs, that seem to be contributing to the problem(s); systems theory with the ecological perspective as a framework when identifying these factors

    d. Strengths, sources of meaning, coping ability, and resources that can be mobilized to help the client

    e. Assessment of client's motivation and potential to benefit from intervention

V. **Recommendations/Proposed Intervention**

    a. Short-term and long-term goals

    b. Areas of attention

    c. Interprofessional team involvement or communication

    d. Possible obstacles and approaches

Developing a strong, trusting rapport and assessing an individual facing a health issue or problem is the first step in providing quality care and developing interventions. There are certain strategies on how to assess in greater detail than biopsychosocial–spiritual assessment, depending on the specific area of practice. Examples of these will be provided later in this chapter.

NASW Standards for Social Work Practice in Health Care Settings

NASW (2016) developed the "Standards for Social Work Practice in Health Care Settings," a guide for the essential knowledge and skills health care social workers should have to provide competent and ethical services in today's health care environment. Following are brief highlights of each *standard:*

- *Ethics and values*: Social workers are expected to uphold ethics and values in any setting but are commonly asked to assist their teams with navigating ethical dilemmas, which occur frequently in health care settings. The NASW Code of Ethics and prevailing clinical bioethics provide a foundation for social workers to manage such dilemmas.

- *Qualifications*: Along with the minimum requirements of all social work professionals having a degree from a CSWE-accredited program, if they are in a health setting that requires them to diagnose mental and behavioral health conditions and/or the provision of psychotherapy the social worker must have a master's degree in social work and adhere to licensure requirements.

- *Knowledge*: Work in health settings requires a unique set of knowledge and skills beyond generalist training, such as the interplay between physical (acute, chronic, and life-limiting) illness and social, mental/behavioral, spiritual health; understanding of relevant concepts, theories, and medical terminology; and understanding of health care system delivery issues such as the ins and outs of public and private health insurance, new health care policies, trends, and delivery system models.

- *Cultural and linguistic competence:* Practitioners must obtain cross-cultural knowledge so they can understand that an individual's cultural background and life experience as well as societal oppression and privilege related to cultural and linguistic diversity (e.g., racism, sexism, homophobia, ageism, or xenophobia) can and do affect clients' biopsychosocial–spiritual well-being. It also impacts how individuals, families and supports perceive an experience health, illness, health care treatments, disability, caregiving roles, and death and dying.

- *Screening and assessment*: Screenings specific to needs and/or health issues as well as a comprehensive biopsychosocial–spiritual assessment (see Chapter 10), which allows social workers to build interventions upon a holistic understanding of an individual's health challenges but also who they are to maximize their options and success.

- *Care planning and intervention*: Development and implementation of care plans informed by best practices and centered in client, family, and support systems needs is an essential task of a health social worker. Social workers' unique perspectives position them to apply a biopsychosocial–spiritual lens to planning for a successful medical intervention. This task most resembles what is called case management in social work, also given other titles in various health settings such as care manager, care transition manager, discharge planner, patient navigator, and care coordinator.

- *Advocacy*: Social workers advocate for clients' and client supports within their organizations, whether at the micro level with a specific provider or team or at a systems level with an organization's policies and procedures. This often includes advocating to improve outcomes, access to care, and delivery of services, particularly for marginalized, medically complex, or disadvantaged populations.

8.3   PRACTICE ACTIVITY

Read the "Standards for Social Work Practice in Health Care Settings" (https://www.socialworkers.org/LinkClick.aspx?fileticket=fFnsRHX-4HE%3d&portalid=0). Choose one standard to explore in detail and reflect on what it might feel like to become advanced in this standard.

- *Interdisciplinary and interorganizational collaboration*: Essential to health care quality is effective communication among the health care team serving the patient (client) as well as their family and support systems. Therefore, social workers must be familiar with various interdisciplinary team models, the basics of each discipline's focus with the client, and typical patient–provider communication strategies. This often means providing goal and role clarity for the team and client and good conflict-resolution and professional communications skills. Social workers frequently serve as leaders in team communication and coordination.

- *Practice evaluation and quality improvement*: Social workers practicing in health care settings participate in ongoing formal evaluation of their practice to advance client health and well-being, assess the appropriateness and effectiveness of services and supports, ensure competence, and strengthen practice.

- *Record keeping and confidentiality*: Written communication is also essential in good health care, so social workers must be skilled at the timely documentation of assessments, plans, and communications while upholding appropriate privacy and confidentiality standards.

- *Workload sustainability*: Health care settings can be impacted by limited funding resources, so there is often a risk that health professionals are subject to workloads that are not feasible, preventing social workers from being effective with clients and families. Therefore, they must also advocate for reasonable caseloads appropriate for the level of needs of the clients they are serving.

- *Professional development*: Social workers are obligated to seek continued professional development opportunities relevant to the health care setting they are in and to adhere to licensure or certification requirements.

- *Supervision and leadership*: Health social workers strive for competence in leadership roles in educational, supervisory, administrative, and research efforts within the health system organizations they work in. This includes mentorship of other social workers to provide high-quality services.

The Importance of Diversity, Equity, and Inclusion in Health Care Settings

As noted in NASW standard 4, Cultural and Linguistic Competence, it is essential that health social workers engage diversity in their practice, regardless of what area of health they work in. As such, it is important that social workers are able to do the following:

- Explain critical definitions of culture that recognize how power dynamics and societal structures shape various aspects of identity and oppression and how they can impact health outcomes

- Be vigilant at having introspection in one's own biases and ensure a strengths-based approach at every phase of work with clients, supports, and communities

- Practice with the consciousness that health disparities, injustices, and barriers persist, created by conscious and unconscious bias that can harm individuals, families, groups, and communities based on race/ethnicity, immigrant status, ability, income, sexual orientation, and gender identity expression

- Resist participating in or using one-dimensional notions of identity and strive to see people as intersectional, with various risks for oppression and status or privilege

- Provide interventions that consider social determinants of health (CSWE, 2022)

> **8.4   PRACTICE ACTIVITY**
>
> Visit the NASW page "Diversity, Equity & Inclusion" (https://www. socialworkers.org/About/Diversity-Equity-and-Inclusion). Choose one "Undoing Racism Through Social Work" volume and explore it in detail. Look for where and how many times "health" is mentioned and dig deeper into the connection to diversity, equity, and inclusion.

SOCIAL WORKER SPOTLIGHT:
Mekinzi Douglas, MSW, LCSW

My name is Mekinzi Douglas, and I am a clinical social worker at Children's Hospital Colorado. I received my Master's in Social Work from Metropolitan State University in 2021. I am Woman of Color, social justice advocate, creator, and lifelong learner. My social work story started writing itself long before I chose the profession. I have always been inspired by the strength of families and the resiliency of young children. One of the greatest influences that lead me to working with children and families is my own family. I am the youngest of five children. Growing up, I lived in a household with two brothers and a sister. In my formative teenage years, I was introduced to my oldest sister for the first time. My family is blended, a byproduct of intricacies that have directly impacted me as a person and social worker. I understand that families come in all different forms, whether they are blended, grandparents raising grandchildren, kin having temporary custody, or family members supporting a single parent. Family, regardless of how it is defined, lays a foundation for the start of the human experience.

I started college with the goal of becoming an elementary school teacher. When I completed my internship in my final year, I realized teaching was not for me. At first, this realization felt like a failure. However, after some time and perspective, I was able to see that my true passion was in building relationships, being an advocate, and supporting others. In 2018, I was introduced to the field of social work by my boss at the time. I began doing research, and everything I read fully aligned with my own core values.

During my foundation year at MSU Denver, I completed my internship at the Boys and Girls Club in their PACE program. I developed assessment skills, fostered relationship with young folks, and leaned into my passion of serving people in my community. As I started exploring options for my concentration year field placement, I was drawn toward an internship at Children's Hospital Colorado. From a young age, I have had dreams of becoming a doctor and helping those in need. Throughout the years, that dream morphed, but my passion for helping never changed. My internship at Children's Hospital was fast-paced and exposed me to a wide range of experiences. Although the work was challenging, I felt fulfilled. Following graduation, I started a job as a child and family therapist at a community mental health agency. I enjoyed working one-on-one with children, but I kept turning back to medical social work. In 2022, I decided to return to Children's Hospital as a clinical social worker in the Child Health Clinic.

Working at Children's Hospital I am faced with a variety of situations; no 2 days are the same. I work in a multidisciplinary team to provide **psychosocial support** to patients and families. Interventions include assessing for **psychosocial stressors** that can impact a child's access to care, providing brief emotional support and counseling, child protection and advocacy, and coordinating care with community partners. It is my goal to meet families where they are and empower them to achieve goals for long-term success.

As a professional on the health care frontlines, I have seen the direct impact of health inequity. All the patients and families that walk through our doors come with stories. It is my mission to make sure those who are often overlooked are listened to. I have had many conversations with parents who have shared experiences of racism, discrimination, and being dismissed by providers. I strive to be an advocate and voice for marginalized individuals. As a Woman of Color, I am a proponent of social justice and diversity within our health care system. Families have shared that they have a sense of relief when I come in the door, knowing that they have someone who relates to their experience. It is important that our doctors, nurses, clinical staff, and supervising professionals reflect the population we serve. I hope the "sense of relief" becomes the norm experienced by all individuals and not the luck of the draw.

A Closer Look at Specialized Areas of Health Social Work Practice

The daily tasks and foci of a health social worker are heavily dependent on the setting in which they work. In turn, this often dictates the types of health challenges the individuals and families they serve are facing as well as the health care team

IMG 8.4

members they will work alongside. The health care financing and geographical location of the setting also influence the socioeconomic status of the patients, families, and support systems social workers will serve. The following sections look closer at three specific types of health care social work roles.

Chronic Disease and Social Work

Rates of chronic illness continue to grow in various populations, and psychosocial challenges often come with them. Social workers are often part of the health care teams caring for those who face chronic illness because these health challenges are often complex and long-term. Social workers who support individuals living with chronic illness and disability focus on the psychosocial and physical aspects of these conditions when conducting biopsychosocial assessments, navigating the health care system, and intervening with individuals, families, and communities. Social workers supporting those with chronic illnesses must be prepared to work within interdisciplinary teams to provide expertise and promote sensitivity and understanding of the specific psychosocial impacts related to chronic illness and disability, serious and/or life-threatening illness, and end of life. They must also be familiar with relevant social and health service systems and policies intended to support those with chronic illness and disability and explore ways to provide effective service. Some of the most common chronic illnesses that social workers support are diabetes, heart disease, dementia, HIV/AIDS, and kidney disease.

Nephrology Social Work

It is estimated that more than one in seven adults in the United States, or 37 million Americans, are affected by chronic kidney disease (CKD). "Nearly 786,000 people in the United States are living with End-stage kidney disease (ESKD), also known as end-stage renal disease (ESRD), with 71% on dialysis and 29% with a kidney transplant" (National Institutes of Diabetes, Digestive, and Kidney Diseases 2020, para. 5). Nephrology social work is an example of a specialty area of social work practice with chronic illness. End-stage renal disease (ESRD) is chronic and requires ongoing (lifelong) treatments such as peritoneal dialysis, hemodialysis, or a kidney transplant. There is a Medicare mandate for a master's-prepared social workers to be part of the service provision team. The National Kidney Foundation's Council of Nephrology Social Workers (2021) defines nephrology social work as services that "support and maximize the psychosocial functioning and adjustment of chronic kidney disease patients and their families. These services are provided to improve social and emotional stresses resulting from the interacting physical, social, and psychological concomitants of chronic kidney disease which include shortened life expectancy, altered lifestyle with changes in social, financial, vocational, and sexual functioning, and the demands of a rigorous, time-consuming, and complex treatment regimen" (para.2). Along with other duties performed by health social workers, nephrology social workers often conduct predialysis education and assessment, crisis intervention, and mediation. "The major categories of problems addressed by nephrology social workers include:

- Adjustment to chronic illness and treatment as they relate to the patient's quality of life
- Physical, sexual, and emotional relationship problems
- Educational, vocational, and activity of daily living problems
- Conflict resolution
- Problems related to treatment options and setting transfers
- Resource needs, including finances, living arrangements, and transportation
- Decision making with regard to advance directives" (National Kidney Foundation's Council of Nephrology Social Workers (2014, page 11, para. 3)

Specialized Competencies and Assessment Tools

Due to the unique nature of kidney disease, various stages of progression, various options for treatment, and unique symptoms and care, social work with this population is also unique. The Council of Nephrology Social Workers endorses various ways to develop competencies in this area of practice. Nephrology-focused health care teams often utilize the Teams Comprehensive Interdisciplinary Patient

Assessment (CIPA), which contains example questions and social work–focused criteria. End-stage renal disease is also a serious public health concern. It is another chronic illness that illuminates health inequities. ESRD diagnosis and burden disproportionately impacts those with lower incomes and Black and Latino populations. These same populations are less likely to receive have pre-ESRD medical care. "The rate of ESRD was higher among individuals living in areas with worse [State Disability Insurance] scores regardless of race/ethnicity. However, racial/ethnic differences in the rate of ESRD persisted within SDI categories" (NIDDK, 2021, page 11 para. 3).

Integrated Behavioral Health Worker

An important aspect of the ACA was advancement of integrating mental and physical health care, which has resulted in expanded efforts to integrate behavioral health services as part of primary care across the United States. Not only was this incentivized by the ACA and Medicaid expansion, but it has been acknowledged as having strong potential to decrease health and mental health disparities. Master's-prepared social workers are well suited for the behavioral health provider role on integrated care teams in primary care, and therefore can often be found serving in these positions. With health care rapidly changing, it is important for social workers practicing in health care to stay up-to-date on their understanding of how the system works. A recent article proposes additions to the social work curriculum to revisit how social workers play a significant role in interdisciplinary health care practice in the call for a more integrated health care system (Held et al., 2019).

A behavioral health provider in a primary care clinic provides behavioral health consultation, brief assessment, groups, and preventions and interventions for children, adolescents, and adults during medical visits while also providing traditional therapy and brief therapy. They may also provide leadership to their teams through mentorship of colleagues and interns and development and evaluation of the programming.

Typical primary care behavioral health specialist qualifications and duties include these:

- Expertise with the DSM V-TR and diagnostic techniques

- Knowledge base and ability to do the following:
  - Work on a strength-based and client-centered perspective
  - Conduct mental health screenings utilizing standardized instruments and assess clients to determine appropriate level of treatment in accordance with relevant ethical and legal standards
  - Assess crisis situations and employ appropriate interventions.

o   Assess psychosocial aspects of chronic and acute diseases and sub- stance use, including educating clients and families with prevention and treatment enhancement techniques. Develop treatment plans; monitor treatment progress and follow-up at disposition times

o   Deliver services such as counseling support and other services to indi- viduals, families, as well as groups that are evidence-based, from a trauma-informed and culturally responsive lens, and appropriate to the age and needs of patients

o   Provide case management services to patients as needed

o   Make appropriate referrals to outside community resources and advocate for appropriate services for patients when indicated

o   Provide primary care physician–instructed consultation services that may include differential diagnosis, psychoeducation, brief intervention, and referral for further treatment

o   Consult with and advise other health care team members on the meth- ods of assisting patients and their families in overcoming social and emotional difficulties, which may prevent effective health care

•   Adhere to protocols for electronic health records system to provide accurate and timely clinical documentation consistent with organizational standards

•   Produce written material for patients' psychoeducation that references established, peer-reviewed, and evidenced-based practices

•   Demonstrate cross-systems and multidisciplinary relationship development skills, including a positive approach to communication and problem solving

•   Participate in team meetings, in-services, and supervisory sessions as required

•   Be able to address multiple requests, prioritize work, meet deadlines, exe- cute work plans, and manage caseload independently and with flexibility

Specialized Competencies and Assessment Tools

The U.S. Department of Health and Human Services' Health Resources & Service Administration has invested resources on behavioral health workforce training to promote integrated behavioral health in primary care. As part of this work a set of core competencies considered the gold standard of what needed to deliver inte- grated care include were published, for example "Core Competencies for Integrated Behavioral Health and Primary Care" (Hoge et al., 2014). Specialized assessment tools include instruments geared toward assessing emotional stress and func- tional levels, from depression to anxiety and general functioning, depending on the population being seen. For example, clinics most often use the latest short version of the Patient Health Questionnaire (PH-Q-9), a nine-item self-administered questionnaire to capture the patient's level of depression. Another common assessment tool is the Alcohol Use Disorders Identification Test (AUDIT) to screen and identify people at risk of alcohol problems.

Public Health and Health Policy Advocacy

Public health social work is a type of practice that incorporates public health approaches into practice. Public health practice and generalist social work practice overlap but are different mainly in how public health is rooted in prevention and promoting health and conditions of health. Alternatively, social work practice often focuses on improving human functioning and well-being through addressing problems with interventions. Public health social work can be found as early as the 1900s as it related to maternal and child health. More contemporary public health social workers focus on disaster response, social policy, health care access, and public health crises, such as the COVID-19 pandemic. A public health social worker today might provide technical assistance to health care providers to facilitate behavioral health integration, manage a department of fair housing, or oversee a multisite community-based substance misuse prevention initiative (Ruth et al., 2019).

Specialized Competencies and Assessment Tools

Health policy advocacy requires being well versed in community-based relationship building and research. Social workers in this area must have extensive knowledge of existing policies at the local, state, or federal levels that impact the population and health topic. They must also have strong knowledge of the political and legislative processes that create policy as well as be well versed in developing a health policy advocacy strategy. It is also essential to have good understanding of or access to research methods, particularly those effective with community advocacy and participatory research for applied practice methods. Finally, it is important to have analytical and communication skills. You can access resources and learn more at the U.S. Department of Health and Human Services' Agency for Healthcare Research and Quality. Macro-level social workers are also well suited to become public health directors who organize, plan, direct, and manage programs to improve a population's overall health and well-being. Public health directors ensure that state and federal laws are being adhered to, design and oversee emergency response plans, and hold public meetings on public health issues. NASW often drives public and health policy-related initiatives, organizing and employing many social workers across the country. For example, NASW (n.d., 2022) has shared numerous public policy statements and advocated for social workers and the people they serve during the COVID-19 pandemic.

Health Social Work Case Study

Andrea Hernandez is 49 years old, wife to her husband Reggie, mother of two adult children in their early 20s, and the primary caregiver for her 72-year-old father, who lives with them and is in the early stages of dementia with mild cognitive impairment. Hernandez's father has good functional ability and requires minimal support in all activities of daily living, including dressing, feeding, toileting, and bathing. However, he does require some support with remembering tasks and appointments. Andrea and Reggie each work full-time to support their children, who are in college and live away from home. The health team referred the hospital social worker when Hernandez was diagnosed with chronic kidney disease, which has significant symptoms and is debilitating at times. Andrea has a sister, Alma, who is married and lives in the same neighborhood. Although Alma spends time with her father, she has been adamant she will not become the primary care provider for her father.

Questions

1. What are the strengths of this situation?

2. What are the initial steps the health care social worker would take to better understand Hernandez's needs at the micro or clinical practice level? Be very specific. What are the macro-level needs?

3. How can the health care social worker be culturally responsive in this case?

4. What questions or feelings are raised as you imagine working with this individual and her family?

Research Focus: Palliative Care

Health social work has a very wide scope of areas of research, as many areas as there are types of health social work positions and areas of focus. Social work researchers examine all topics relevant to social work issues, from topics related to public health or social determinants of health to specific clinical interventions and development of evidence-based practice models. In essence social work research should advance the development of knowledge and inform health social work practice through micro and macro levels. The research knowledge base that social work researchers and practitioners utilize is interdisciplinary in nature: analytic reviews of research, theoretical articles pertaining to health social work, evaluation studies, and any research studies that contribute to knowledge about issues and problems relevant to health social work.

Palliative care has grown over the past decade and is being recognized as an important type for care that improves quality of life for patients and families, as well as effectively managing high health care costs. Despite a high need, palliative care is underutilized in skilled nursing facilities (SNFs; Retrum et al., 2015). Research points to a need for more high-quality psychosocial care and testing social work–led interventions that aim to improve quality of life and care goal alignment. Current studies are ongoing to determine the effectiveness of the palliative care social worker–led intervention called ALIGN (Assessing & Listening to Individual Goals and Needs; Fischer et al., 2021). ALIGN is an intervention aimed to improve quality of life and communication and to provide support to patients and caregivers. This is an example of a social work–led intervention implemented within health settings and that has been supported and encouraged by multiple health systems.

Chapter Summary

The health care system contact involves any interface with various health services such as a doctor visit, prescription pick-up, or receiving a public health announcement. Health care services in the United States are delivered through various organizations paid for through public and private means and directly by consumers. The biggest problems facing the U.S. health care system relate to health inequities, including but not limited to access to care, health care costs, quality and efficiency of care, and the lack of agility and human resources to respond to the changing health needs of populations and environment. Our country has a long, developmental history of health care services, health and social policy, and private industry that impact how accessible our health care system functions. Social workers play a vital role at micro and macro levels of the health care system and are in growing demand. Health care social workers must be prepared to develop specialized competencies that are customized for health care systems and the health challenges of the health care teams and communities they serve. There is a vast array of ways health care social workers provide unique assessments and interventions at the micro and macro levels.

Discussion Questions

1. Describe how you have contact with the health care system. Explain how the biggest health care system challenges do or do not impact you and the people you know. Provide examples of how problems in our health care system can negatively impact individuals and families as well as the community and state.

2. Describe the role of health social workers. How are the activities and competencies different and like other social work specialties you are learning about in this book?

3. Explain your values and beliefs about health and illness. How could this impact your approach to people experiencing health challenges and their supports?

4. We are facing new health challenges, which has effects for social workers in the United States and across the world. What are some things micro-level social workers need to think about to prepare? What macro-level approaches are needed?

5. When you read about health inequities and social determinants of health, what was your initial reaction? Were these reactions of fear, curiosity, or frustration? Or something different?

6. What aspects of social work in health care settings in this chapter surprised you? What aspects do you think you may enjoy the most? What aspects are you not so sure of?

References

American Academy of Social Work & Social Welfare. (2018). *Policy recommendations to address the grand challenges for social work.* https://grandchallengesforsocialwork.org/close-the-health-gap/

Bartlett, H. M. (1988). *Analyzing social work practice by fields.* NASW Press.

Bosworth, A., Finegold, K., & Ruhter, J. (2021, March 23). The remaining uninsured: Geographic and demographic variation (Issue Brief No. HP-202106). Office of the Assistant Secretary for Planning and Evaluation, U.S. Department of Health and Human Services. https://aspe.hhs.gov/sites/default/files/private/pdf/265286/Uninsured-Population-Issue-Brief.pdf

Cheung, J. C. S. (2022). Responses to COVID-19 in major social work journals: A systematic review of empirical studies, comments, and editorials. *Research on Social Work Practice, 32*(2), 168–185.

Council on Social Work Education. (2022). *Specialized practice curricular guide for health social work.* https://www.cswe.org/education-resources/2015-epas-curricular-guides/

Dziegielewski, S., & Holliman, D. C. (2019). *The changing face of health care social work: Opportunities and challenges for professional practice* (4th ed.). Springer.

Ely DM, Driscoll AK. Infant mortality in the United States, 2019: Data from the period linked birth/infant death file. National Vital Statistics Reports; vol 70 no 14. Hyattsville, MD: National Center for Health Statistics. 2021. DOI: https://dx.doi.org/10.15620/cdc:111053.

Ewald, B., Golden, R., & Mason, D. J. (2021, December). Promoting health equity by paying for social care. *JAMA Health Forum, 2*(12), e215023.

Fischer, S. M., Tropeano, L., Lahoff, D., Owens, B., Nielsen, E., Retrum, J. J., Jensen, E., Ross, C., Mancuso, M., Drace, M. and Plata, A. & Gozansky, W. (2021). Integrating palliative care social workers into subacute settings: Feasibility of the assessing and listening to individual goals and needs interventiontTrial. *Journal of Palliative Medicine, 24*(6), 830–837.

Gehlert, S., & Browne, T. A. (Eds.). (2019). *Handbook of health social work* (3rd ed.). Wiley.

Goodman, R. A., Bunnell, R., & Posner, S. F. (2014). What is "community health"? Examining the meaning of an evolving field in public health. *Preventive Medicine, 67,* S58–S61.

Held, M. L., Black, D. R., Chaffin, K. M., Mallory, K. C., Milam Diehl, A., & Cummings, S. (2019). Training the future workforce: Social workers in integrated health care settings. *Journal of Social Work Education, 55*(1), 50–63. https://doi.org/10.1080/10437797.2018.1526728

Hoge, M. A., Morris, J. A., Laraia, M., Pomerantz, A., & Farley, T. (2014). *Core competencies for integrated behavioral health and primary care.* SAMHSA, HRSA Center for Integrated Health Solutions. https://www.thenationalcouncil.org/wp-content/uploads/2020/01/Integration_Competencies_Final.pdf

Holmes, M.R., Rentrope, C.R., Korsch-Williams, A. et al. Impact of COVID-19 Pandemic on Posttraumatic Stress, Grief, Burnout, and Secondary Trauma of Social Workers in the United States. Clin Soc Work J 49, 495–504 (2021). https://doi.org/10.1007/s10615-021-00795-y

Institute of Medicine. (2013, January). U.S. health in international perspective: Shorter lives, poorer health (Institute of Medicine Report Brief). Retrieved from http://www.nationalacademies.org/hmd/Reports/2013/US-Health-in-International-Perspective-Shorter-Lives-Poorer-Health.aspx

Knickman, J. R., & Elbel, B. (Eds.). (2019). Jonas and Kovner's health care delivery in the United States (12th ed.). Springer.

Keisler-Starkey, K. and Bunch, L.N. (2021) U.S. Census Bureau, Current Population Reports, P60-278, Health Insurance Coverage in the United States: 2021, U.S. Government Publishing Office, Washington, DC, September 2022.

Murphy, S. L., Kochanek, K. D., Xu, J., & Arias, E. (2021). *Mortality in the United States, 2020.* https://stacks.cdc.gov/view/cdc/112079; https://dx.doi.org/10.15620/cdc:112079

National Academies of Science, Engineering, and Medicine. (2019, September 25). Integrating social care into the delivery of health care: Moving upstream to improve the nation's health. https://www.nationalacademies.org/our-work/integrating-social-needs-care-into-the-delivery-ofhealth-care-to-improve-the-nations-health

National Academies of Science, Engineering, and Medicine. (2021, May 11). The future of nursing 2020–2030: Charting a path to achieve health equity. https://nam.edu/publications/the-future-of-nursing-2020-2030/

National Association of Social Workers. (n.d.). *COVID-19 policy issues.* https://www.socialworkers.org/Advocacy/Policy-Issues/COVID-19-Advocacy

National Association of Social Workers. (2016). *NASW standards for social work practice in health care settings.* https://www.socialworkers.org/LinkClick.aspx?fileticket=fFnsRHX-4HE%3d&portalid=0

National Association of Social Workers. (2022). *Policy issues.* https://www.socialworkers.org/Advocacy/Policy-Issues

National Center for Chronic Disease Prevention and Health Promotion. (2023). *About chronic diseases.* https://www.cdc.gov/chronicdisease/about/index.htm

National Institute on Minority Health and Health Disparities. (2022, September 30). *Minority health and health disparities: Definitions and parameters.* https://www.nimhd.nih.gov/about/overview/

National Institute on Diabetes, Digestive and Kidney Diseases.

National Kidney Foundation's Council of Nephrology Social Workers (2014). *Standards of Practice for Nephrology Social Work* (6th Edition) https://www.kidney.org/sites/default/files/CNSW%20SOP%206th%20Ed_FINAL_July2014.pdf

Retrum, J. H., Gozansky, W. S., Lahoff, D. G., Rosenberg, E. L., Tropeano, L. E., Owens, B. A., & Fischer, S. M. (2015). A need for more palliative focused care: A survey of Colorado skilled care facilities. *Journal of the American Medical Directors Association, 16*(8), 712–713.

Ruth, B., Wachman, M. K., & Marshall, J. (2019). Public health social work. In *Handbook of health social work* Gehlert, S., & Browne, T. (Eds.). (pp. 93–118), John Wiley & Sons.

Schneider, E. C., Shah, A., Doty, M. M., Tikkanen, R., Fields, K., & Williams, R. D. (2021). *Mirror, mirror 2021: Reflecting poorly: Health care in the US compared to other high-income countries.* Commonwealth Fund. https://www.commonwealthfund.org/publications/fund-reports/2021/aug/mirror-mirror-2021-reflecting-poorly

Sharpe, M., & Spencer, A. (2022, August 18). *Many Americans say they have shifted their priorities around health and social activities during COVID-19. Pew Research Center.* https://pewrsr.ch/3QNTEBu

Tolbert, J., Orgera, K., & Damico, A. (2020). *Key facts about the uninsured population.* Kaiser Family Foundation. https://www.kff.org/uninsured/issue-brief/key-facts-about-the-uninsured-population/

U.S. Bureau of Labor Statistics. (2023). *Occupational Outlook Handbook, social workers.* https://www.bls.gov/ooh/community-and-social-service/social-workers.htm

U.S. Census Bureau. (2019). *American Community Survey.* https://www.census.gov/; https://www.census.gov/programs-surveys/acs

U.S. Department of Health and Human Services. (2022). *Impact of the COVID-19 pandemic on the hospital and outpatient clinician workforce* [Issue brief].

U.S. Department of Health & Human Services, Centers for Disease Control and Prevention. (2022). *Social determinants of health at CDC.* https://www.cdc.gov

U.S. Department of Health and Human Services, National Institute of Diabetes and Digestive and Kidney Diseases. (2021). *Annual data report.* https://usrds-adr.niddk.nih.gov/2021

U.S. Department of Health and Human Services, Office of Disease Prevention and Health Promotion. (n.d.). *Healthy People 2030.* https://health.gov/healthypeople

U.S. Department of Veteran Affairs. (n.d.). *About VA health benefits.* https://www.va.gov/health-care/about-va-health-benefits/

Walters, K. L., Spencer, M. S., Smukler, M., Allen, H. L., Andrews, C., Browne, T., & Uehara, E. (2016). *Health equity: Eradicating health inequalities for future generations.* American Academy of Social Work and Social Welfare.

World Health Organization. (2023). *Constitution.* https://www.who.int/about/governance/constitution#:~:text=Health%20is%20a%20state%20of,absence%20of%20disease%20or%20infirmity

Credits

CHAPTER 9

Social Work With Children and Their Families

Learning Objectives

After reading this chapter, students will be able to do the following:

- Summarize the biggest social problems facing children and their families in the United States

- Explain what adverse childhood experiences are and how this relates to social work practice with children

- Describe the child welfare system and how a case moves through the system

- Identify three major career path options for social workers who want to work with children and their families

- Evaluate child allowances as a potential public policy solution for children and families in the United States to alleviate child poverty

- Summarize research findings on home visiting programs, a child maltreatment prevention intervention

- Explain the goals of the upEND movement and how it seeks to address racism in state child welfare systems

- Evaluate goodness of fit with social work practice with children and families as a potential future career option

SOCIAL WORKER SPOTLIGHT:
Eric Lozano-Olivas, MSW, BSSW

My name is Eric Lozano-Olivas, and some of the identities that are part of my narrative are immigrant, Latinx, activist, queer, leader, veteran. My passion for working with children and families stems from the deficits in support that my family and I encountered as new immigrants when we first arrived in the United States in 1999. I belong to a rich ethnic culture that embraces family unity as a way of thriving. My family and I migrated in search of the American dream. Growing up, my family always modeled humility and a sense of giving back to others unconditionally as a way of life. Regardless of the deficit in support my family received as new immigrants, in my process of assimilation in the American culture I felt a greater need to give back to the nation that had taken us in and decided to join the U.S. Army. Enlisting in the military was one of the most privileged opportunities I have come across in my journey as an immigrant. My time in the military gave me a sense of duty to not just serve our country in a time of war as a Purple Heart medal recipient but also allowed me to use my privilege and skills to be part of the process to empower members in my community in their quest toward self-sustainability.

For me it has been a series of events and experiences as an immigrant overcoming adversity requiring me to establish resiliency practices that have steered me in the work of child welfare and work with children and families. I am a firm believer in the saying that it's not you who chooses the profession but rather it's the profession that chooses you. My drive to work and provide support for children and families comes from the love and support I have received from my family. Every family should have that opportunity; therefore, I enjoy working in this field. During my undergraduate program in social work, I had the privilege to receive a financial stipend provided by the Colorado Child Welfare Scholars Consortium in the Social Work program at the Metropolitan State University of Denver to support and train social worker students interested in the field of child welfare. The stipend is a mechanism to support the commitment under Title IV-E of the Social Security Act and the 2018 Family First Prevention Services Act (FFPSA), with the focus of keeping families safely together.

During my academic journey in social work learning about the roots and reform of child welfare and child and youth development, along with the circumstances that lead families to enter the system, it occurred to me that during my youth I had been an at-risk individual myself and was never aware of it. My resiliency taught me to overcome, and if I could overcome, I knew that I could walk alongside others who needed support to overcome. This is what led me to become an intern with the Denver Human Services (DHS) Child Protection Bilingual Unit.

Having a culturally competent diverse workforce of social workers who reflect the diversity in a community is crucial for the health and success of its members. The bilingual unit at DHS serves Spanish-speaking families who lack the ability to communicate in English and find themselves entangled with child welfare services in their community. The opportunity to intern with the bilingual unit has given me meaningful insights about the circumstances that lead families to their engagement with child protection services. As an intern I have had the opportunity to understand the role of the case worker, assess reports of child neglect and abuse, conduct report investigations, address safety findings for children in the home, engage with families, refer families to services, and make plans for how to safely care for children.

The bilingual unit is part of the best practices initiative to better serve the community. Families who don't speak the same language as the dominant culture often have a harder time navigating the many systems that make up our society. This lack of ability to communicate places them at a disadvantage when services aren't tailored to meet the needs of a diverse population, which is a form of oppression. This is something my family and I experienced firsthand when we first arrived as immigrants, and that is a reason I decided to use my privilege to serve and give back to my community.

When you ask social work students why they want to enter the social work profession, a very high percentage will tell you that they want to impact the lives of some of the roughly 73 million children and youth residing in the United States. **Children** represent about 22% of the U.S. population. Indeed, one of the most prevalent areas of social work practice is social work with children and families. It is hard to find a practicing social worker whose work does not impact this population in some way, and many fields of practice serve children and their families, such as health care, mental health care (including addictions), and juvenile justice, just to name a few. However, this chapter will focus primarily on three important fields of practice that have children and their families at the forefront of the work: **child welfare**, **school social work**, and **positive youth development**. Social workers work with many vulnerable populations, and children are considered a vulnerable population because they rely on adult caregivers to provide them with a safe, secure, and loving home living environment. Unfortunately, because of a variety of personal and environmental risk factors, many families struggle to keep their children safe from various adverse child experiences.

What Are Adverse Childhood Experiences (or ACEs)?

Social workers who wish to work with children need to be aware of the growing body of research on **adverse childhood experiences**, or **ACEs**, and how they impact a child's ability to lead a happy, healthy, and successful life. ACEs are traumatic events that children experience directly or that they witness in their social environment, which can impact their sense of safety and stability—and ultimately their physical and mental health. Examples of ACEs include child abuse or neglect; being separated from a parent due to divorce, abandonment, incarceration, or some other reason; witnessing violence in the home or in one's community; the death of a parent; having a parent attempt or die by suicide; and having people

PRACTICE ACTIVITY

Take the ACE Quiz

Visit https://stopabusecampaign.org/take-your-ace-test/ to take the ACE quiz.

1. What was your score, and what takeaways did you have about how ACEs apply to your life? Were you surprised by what you found?

2. Do you think this can be a useful resource when working with clients and as an assessment tool? How would you imagine implementing this in your work as a social worker with clients of different ages?

in the household who were impacted by substance abuse and/or mental health problems (Centers for Disease Control and Prevention [CDC], n.d.b.).

Experts on ACEs report that they can have a detrimental impact on an individual's ability to be successful in their education and future employment as well as their ability to maintain healthy relationships with others. The more ACEs that a child experiences, the more severe the potential impact can be. There are a number of quizzes on the internet people can take to see how many ACEs they experienced in their childhood). On the positive side, social workers can work in **prevention programs** that focus on impacting those protective factors that have the potential to decrease the possibility of children experiencing ACEs. There are individual, family, and community protective factors, and a few examples of each are provided (CDC, n.d.a.):

- *Individual*: Helping children do well in school; helping kids have positive peer relationships; making sure kids have mentors and role models in their life

- *Family*: Families who can meet their basic needs; families who encourage their kids to do well in school; families who can provide their kids with safety and stability and work through conflicts peacefully; families that spend quality time together doing fun activities

- *Community*: Communities in which violence is not tolerated; safe and affordable childcare and after-school programs; employment opportunities; access to health care, including mental health care; safe and affordable housing; high levels of community involvement

Just a few examples of **prevention programs** include employing school social workers in schools; mentoring programs for kids, affordable childcare programs for working parents, early childhood home visitation programs, after-school programs, safe outdoor spaces for recreational activities, family therapy, programs that address food deserts in low-income communities, parenting skills programs, and programs that support parents with seeking and securing employment.

The Changing American Family

It is important to note that there is no "typical" family in the United States and that today's families come in many different shapes, forms, and sizes. At one time, the

IMG 9.1

ideal family was a traditional one with two married opposite-sex parents in their first marriage with two or more children. However, data from the Pew Research Center (2015) shows that there is **no longer one dominant family form** and that families are more diverse than ever. For example, in 1960, 73% of children were living in a two-parent family in their first marriage while by 2014 this percentage had shrunk to 46% (Pew Research Center, 2015). Social workers who want to work with children and their families need to be prepared to work with families from diverse backgrounds in terms of race/ethnicity, culture, and religious differences.

Social workers will work with families who have immigrated to the United States as well as families that are headed by **same-sex couples**. They will work with **kinship families**, meaning children who are being raised by a relative. They will support families with foster youth, adopted youth, and families that have a combination of biological children and children who were adopted. They will work with **blended families** when people have remarried and/or found new partners. Findings from the Pew Research Center (2015) about the nature of the changing American family are as follows:

- There has been a decline of two-parent households and a rise in the numbers of people experiencing divorce, remarriage, and cohabitation; one in six children is living in a **blended family**.

- More people are having children outside of marriage (e.g., rise of single-parent households and those living with nonmarital partner).

- There is an increase in the number of women having biological children with more than one partner, referred to as **multi-partner fertility**.

- Family size is getting smaller as women are having fewer children and having children later in life due to several factors (e.g., higher education, more women in the labor force, fewer getting married, and access to abortion and contraception)

- More mothers have become the primary breadwinners in their family; mothers are older and more educated than they were in the past.

- There has been a decline in the share of mothers who are stay-at-home moms.

What Are the Biggest Problems Facing Children and Their Families in the United States?

Children are a vulnerable population in our society, and some of the biggest problems they face include living below the poverty line, lacking adequate food and nutrition, experiencing child maltreatment, and having challenges at school. Social workers who work with children and their families need to become knowledgeable about these social problems and how they impact children and their physical and social development.

Poverty and Food Insecurity

Child advocates are particularly concerned about the impact of poverty and food insecurity on children due to the impact it has on their life chances and developing brains. Children who live in poverty are at higher risk for health problems, including obesity, low academic achievement, and difficulties related to their social and emotional development.

The United States ranks high in levels of **child poverty** when compared to other wealthy industrialized countries and faces criticism by child welfare advocates for not doing more to decrease child poverty through government spending on family and social benefits.

Data has consistently showed that children are overrepresented among the nation's poor in the United States (Children's Defense Fund [CDF], 2020). In fact, children are one and a half times as likely as adults 65 years and older to live in poverty. Among all children under age 18 in the United States, about one in seven were poor in 2019, which represented 10.4 million children. However, when the data is examined by race, **stark racial disparities** emerge. Roughly 71% of poor children were children of color. In 2019, African American, American Indian/

Alaska Native, and Latinx children were disproportionately poor compared to White and Asian children:

- 7.0% of Asian American children (one in 14)

- 8.3% of White children were poor (one in 12)

- 20.6% of American Indian/Alaska Native children (one in five)

- 20.8% of Latinx children (one in five)

- 26.5% of African American children (one in four)

Additionally, roughly one in seven children experience **food insecurity**, which is defined as living in a home without enough food to eat (CDF, 2020). The ability to have access to health insurance is connected to family income. Roughly 5.7% of children under age 19 (nearly 4.4 million) were **uninsured** in 2019 (CDF, 2020).

Poverty researchers have been closely monitoring the impact of poverty rates on children and families as a result of the **coronavirus pandemic**. Initially poverty rates increased during the pandemic but were then somewhat alleviated by federal spending that was targeted to support families during this global health crisis (e.g., unemployment benefits, stimulus checks, expansion of the child tax credit, etc.).

Child Maltreatment

According to the latest government data from the U.S. Department of Health and Human Services (2021), in 2019, there were 656,000 victims of child abuse and neglect and children, and age 1 and under had the highest rate of victimization. Child neglect is by far the most common type of child maltreatment (74.9%), followed by physical abuse (17.5%) and sexual abuse (9.3%). According to the Child Welfare Information Gateway (2019), **child neglect** occurs when a caregiver does not provide for a child's basic needs and includes the following five categories: physical, emotional, medical, educational, and abandonment. **Child abuse** can take the following forms: physical, sexual, emotional, and parental substance abuse in some states.

IMG 9.2

The vast majority of people who perpetrate abuse and neglect are parents (77.5%). Sadly, 1,840 children died from child maltreatment in 2019 (U.S. Department of Health and Human Services, 2021). In some severe cases, a child may need to removed from their home and enter the custody of the state. According to data reported by the Children's Bureau (2021), in

September 2020, there were roughly 407,000 **children in the foster care system**, the majority being placed in either a relative or nonrelative foster family home. Roughly 117,000 of these children were waiting to be adopted.

The CDC (n.d.a.) explains that there are certain **risk factors**, a combination of individual, family, community, and societal factors that can contribute to the risk of a child being abused and/or neglected. **Parental risk factors** include things such as substance abuse, mental health disorders, intimate partner violence in the home, poverty, high levels of stress, and having a history of being abused or neglected as a child. **Community or societal risk factors** include living in communities with high rates of violence and crime, limited educational and employment opportunities, poverty and food insecurity, and unstable housing (CDC, n.d.a.).

It is important for social workers to understand the risk factors of **child maltreatment** so that they can work on prevention strategies. The child welfare system is currently striving to have a stronger prevention focus than they have in the past to avoid the removal of children from the home when possible. The practice of social workers in the field of child welfare is informed by scientific research that shows the detrimental impact that child maltreatment can have on children's physical and emotional development, particularly when they are young (age 0–5) and their brain is developing.

Educational Success of Children and Youth

When children have access to a high-quality education, it has the power to equalize their chance of success in society regardless of their social class. Unfortunately, due to the way that schools are funded in the United States, students who live in high-poverty neighborhoods are often relegated to schools that do not have adequate funding and resources. Historically, children living in lower income areas do not receive the same **educational opportunities** as those who live in wealthier communities and are forced to attend underfunded schools with fewer resources, larger class sizes, and fewer high-quality teachers. And due to the disruptions that schools experienced **during the coronavirus pandemic**, it appears that this problem has been exacerbated. Research shows that even though *all* children have fallen behind in reading and math since the pandemic, the students who have been most impacted are students who attend low-income schools, which are disproportionately attended by Black and Latinx children (Mervosh, 2021).

Like other social problems affecting children, there are **racial disparities** when it comes to educational achievement in the United States. In 2017, 60% of Black children attended high-poverty schools with a high share of students of color, while fewer than 9% of White children did. Data shows that 14 million children attend schools with police present but lack a counselor, social workers, nurse, or psychologist (CDF, 2020). Additionally, many schools remain **highly segregated**

by race, a social problem that hearkens back to a time in the United States when schools were legally allowed to have separate schools for White and Black children. A report by the CDF (2020) notes that "only 1 in 8 white students attends a school where the majority of students are Black, Hispanic, Asian, or American Indian, whereas nearly 7 in 10 Black children attend such schools" (p. 26). This same report reveals important data showing that children of color and children in low-income families lag behind their peers in academic performance and high school graduation:

- Less than half of children born into household and neighborhood poverty are ready for school at age 5 compared with 78% of their wealthier peers.

- More than 77% of Hispanic and more than 79% of Black fourth- and eight-grade public school students were not proficient in reading or math in 2019, compared with less than 60% of White students.

- During the 2017–2018 school year, 19% of Black, 21% of Hispanic, and more than 26% of American Indian/Alaska Native public school students did not graduate on time compared with only 11% of White students

Social workers working at the macro level have the opportunity to address these racial and income disparities to ensure that all children have access to a high-quality education in the United States, which has been termed by some as **"the great equalizer"** in our society (originally attributed to educator Horace Mann).

Policy Focus: Child Allowance Policies as a Method to Reduce Child Poverty

Social workers working at the macro level can find work in advocacy organizations that attempt to change policies and work on reforms to school and child welfare systems. Prominent examples of organizations doing this work are the CDF, court-appointed special advocates (CASA), Casey family programs, and many organizations at the state level such as Our Children Oregon.

Many social workers who work with children and their families feel frustrated by the fact that children are often not a public policy priority despite lawmakers' rhetoric that "children are our future." Child advocates point to funding disparities between how much the government spends on children versus adults, for example. The two most expensive social programs in the United States are the Medicare and Social Security programs, which serve older adults, and there are no comparable programs that invest in children this robustly. Advocates are perplexed as to why the United States remains the only nation in the world that has failed to ratify the **U.N. Convention on the**

Rights of the Child, an international treaty devoted to the rights and protections of children. Because children are a vulnerable population, they rely on adults to advocate for them in the public policy arena. Some social workers choose to work in child welfare policy right out of the gate, while other social workers may move into policy work after first gaining some experience in direct services.

One of the most famous child welfare policies is the **Child Abuse and Prevention Treatment Act** (CAPTA), which was passed in 1974. CAPTA was the first federal law that provided substantial federal funding to states so they could focus on the prevention, treatment, and investigation of child abuse and neglect. This law includes federal definitions of child abuse and neglect and establishes a role for the federal government to engage in research and evaluation related to child maltreatment. Since CAPTA, there have been a multitude of policies passed into law at the state and federal level to address child maltreatment, including child abuse mandatory reporting laws, safe haven laws that focus on child abandonment, and policies that fund services for youth who age out of the foster care system, just to name a few.

In many developed nations around the world, families with children receive a monthly check from the government, funded by taxes, for each child in the family until age 16 or 18, which is termed a **child allowance** or a **child benefit**. The philosophy behind a child allowance is to help families pay for some of the costs of raising children and to keep children out of poverty since research shows that poverty can impair children's development. It is kind of like a social security program for children. Child allowances policies vary by country in terms of the payment amounts and eligibility requirements. For example, some countries provide the child allowance for every family regardless of income, while some nations only provide them for families below a certain income threshold. And the amount of the child allowance also varies greatly—anywhere from $50 (e.g., United Kingdom) to as high as $550 a month (e.g., Canada).

The United States had never instituted a child allowance as part of its social welfare system until March 2021 when the Biden administration included it as part of its American Rescue Plan to support working families during the coronavirus pandemic. To do this, changes to the **child tax credit** were made so that families would be able to receive a monthly cash payment instead of waiting to receive the payment in one lump sum after they filed their taxes, and the benefit was increased from $2,000 per child per year to $3,000 (age 6–17) or $3600 (age 5 and younger) per child per year. The new policy was expanded to cover roughly 90% of children in the United States who would receive monthly payments of $250–300 a month.

Researchers from the **Columbia University Center on Poverty and Social Policy** found that this new child benefit reduced monthly child poverty by close to 30%

(Parolin & Curran, 2022) and also reduced food insecurity. And a report by the **Center on Budget and Policy Priorities** (Zippel, 2021) found that 90% of families with low incomes used the monthly payments to pay for basic household expenses such as food, clothing, shelter, and utilities. Much to the dismay of child poverty experts and most Democratic lawmakers in the U.S. Congress, the new benefit was not renewed at the end of the year in December 2021 mainly due to opposition from U.S. Senator Joe Manchin (D-West Virginia) over his concerns about the high cost of this new social program. The last payment was sent to eligible families on December 15, 2021.

Social Work Practice With Children and Families

For social workers who wish to work with children and their families, there are plenty of career paths to choose from, and many of them are included throughout this book, such as health care, mental health care (including addictions), family violence, and juvenile justice, just to name a few. However, this chapter will focus primarily on three important fields of practice that have children and their families at the forefront of the work: child welfare, school social work, and positive youth development.

Child Welfare Practice

When a social worker says that they work in the field of **child welfare**, they usually mean that they work in child protection services (CPS). When most people think about the work of social workers, the first job that comes to mind for many are **child protection caseworkers**, and many people think that this is *all* that social workers do, which is a fallacy. However, it is true that child welfare is an important field of practice for social workers—though it is certainly not for everyone due to the stressful and serious nature of the work. Witnessing the varying effects of child maltreatment requires the ability to stay calm and professional while on the job and to take care of oneself when off the clock. Within the field of child welfare there are a wide range of specialties where social workers can gain experience and expertise, so read on!

Overview of the Child Welfare System

The overall mission of state child welfare systems is to protect children from child maltreatment and to enhance the ability of caregivers to provide a safe home for their children. Child welfare work has always been controversial because it requires the government to intervene into the private affairs of the family (which has been viewed as sacred) and assess whether parents or caregivers are causing significant harm to their children. Some believe we should have a system that prioritizes the protection of children above all else while others believe the system should focus more on prevention and putting serious efforts into family preservation so that children do not have to face the trauma of maltreatment and possible family separation. State child protection systems find themselves in a no-win situation because many Americans believe they do not go far enough in protecting the nation's children from abuse and neglect, whereas others believe they are overly intrusive and tear families apart unnecessarily.

Each state operates a **child protection system** that is responsible for investigating reports that are made to the state child abuse hotline by either private citizens or mandatory reporters. **Mandatory reporters** are professionals, such as teachers, social workers, and medical professionals, who have a special obligation to make reports to child protection officials when they have a suspicion that child maltreatment is occurring. The following process is fairly typical in most state child welfare systems:

1. A report is made to children's protective services, usually through a 1-800 hotline.

2. Trained child welfare professionals make as assessment about whether the report meets the criteria to be followed up on. Not all reports are assigned for investigation.

3. If the report is "screened in," it will be assigned for investigation and a child protection caseworker will make contact with the child and the family to gather relevant information about the family in order to assess whether child maltreatment is occurring. When a case is assigned a high priority, a caseworker will need to see the child within 1–2 days.

4. During the investigation, a caseworker will interview the child, the caregivers, anyone else who lives in the home, as well as other people who may know important information about the family (e.g., relatives, medical professionals, school officials, etc.). The caseworker's most important job is to assess the level of risk and safety of the children living in the home. The following are possible outcomes at the end of an investigation:

   - **No significant concerns** were found, and the case is closed.

   - **Some low to moderate concerns** to the child's safety were identified. Services are offered to the family—in some cases they are voluntary and in other cases the services may be court ordered. Case may be transferred to a family preservation unit with caseworkers who specialize in doing "in-home" casework.

- **Very serious concerns** to the child's safety were identified and the only way to remedy the risk is to remove the child from their home, which means they enter the custody of the state. The case is transferred to an "ongoing" unit and assigned a caseworker who specializes in working with families in which the child has been removed from the home. Removing a child from their home is a decision that is not done lightly, as caseworkers understand the trauma that is involved for the child as well as the family with family separation. The first priority for child placement is to find a relative who can provide a safe home, referred to as a kinship care placement. When that is not possible, then a child will be placed with a foster family.

When **a child is removed from their home**, the goal is to find a permanent placement for them as soon as possible. Federal law dictates that all cases be resolved within 12–18 months so that children are not living in limbo. In September 2019, there were roughly 424,000 children in the foster care system (Child Welfare Information Gateway, 2021). **Permanency options** for children who have been removed include (a) returning home to their parents if their parents can provide a safe and stable home; (b) permanent placement with a relative (referred to as "kinship care"); (c) adoption by a family that is not related to the child; or (d) long-term foster care. The vast majority of children removed from their home do achieve permanency, however; some grow up in the foster care system and **"age out" or "emancipate"** from the system after reaching adulthood. Roughly 20,000 children aged out of the foster care system in 2019 (Child Welfare Information Gateway, 2021). There are specialized programs for emancipating youth to help them make the transition to adulthood and live on their own due to the many challenges they face after leaving the child welfare system.

What Does a Day in the Life of a Child Welfare Caseworker Look Like?

Because of the intensive and serious nature of the work, caseworkers must complete extensive training by the state before entering the field as a caseworker. Students who are interested in working in child welfare can complete a BSW or MSW internship while they earn their social work degree, which gives them an easier transition into the job. Some social work programs are able to offer financial stipends to students if they are part of a federal program called the **Child Welfare IV-E program**, which seeks to encourage and prepare social workers to enter the field of child welfare. Many people are surprised to learn that it is not a requirement in many states for child welfare caseworkers to have a social work (or related) degree.

Child welfare caseworkers perform a wide variety of tasks, and each day is varied and different, which keeps the job interesting. Following are a few of the most common duties:

- *Risk assessment and safety planning*: Caseworkers are trained to perform risk assessment and safety assessment using the tools they are provided by their agency. To do this well, caseworkers must have strong interviewing skills.

- *Service planning*: It is common practice for caseworkers to develop service plans for the parents (called a family service plan) and the children (called a child service plan). A service plan outlines all of the services that need to be set up and coordinated for the child and the caregivers, some of which have been ordered by the court. Typical services can include parent–child supervised visitation, individual therapy, group therapy, parenting classes, support finding employment and housing, and substance abuse treatment.

- *Updating the court on the family's progress*: Caseworkers must go to court on a certain time schedule to update the judge on the progress of the case and the permanency plan. It is common for caseworkers to submit a written report to the court in advance of the court hearing.

- *Interdisciplinary work*: Child welfare caseworkers work with a wide variety of professionals such as attorneys, CASA volunteers, judges, law enforcement officers, health professionals, and mental health providers.

- *Permanency planning*: For caseworkers who do "ongoing" work with families in which a child has been removed from the home, a key part of their job is to achieve a permanent plan for the child, and this plan may change over the course of the case depending on the parents' progress. Permanency plans include return to home, permanent placement with a relative, or adoption by a family that is unrelated to the child.

- *Case documentation*: Paperwork is a big part of a caseworker's job, and they must be disciplined to keep up with it. Caseworkers must document all of their interactions with anyone associated with the case in their case notes as well as things such as home visits and supervised visitation v between the child and their parents.

- *Building positive relationships with the family*: Child welfare can be a challenging field to work in because the clients are "involuntary clients" for the most part, meaning that they are not choosing to work with you. Thus, you must have strong skills in gaining the trust of parents who are often angry that you are in your life. However, a strong working relationship is possible to build over time if you are compassionate and tenacious. Caseworkers report really enjoying the time they spend with the children they are working with, whether it be taking them for ice cream, driving them to an appointment, or playing games in their office or at the park.

Job Specializations Within Child Welfare

When most people envision the work of a child welfare caseworker, they usually think about the investigative caseworker who knocks on someone's door to follow up on a report to child protective services. However, it is important to know that a career in child welfare has a wide variety of opportunities, which is important for career longevity:

- *Investigations*: Short-term work with families that ends at the conclusion of the child abuse investigation. The caseworker's role is to gather interview everyone in the family, including people outside of the family, to determine whether child maltreatment is occurring and assess the level of risk to the children in the home. In some extreme situations, the child may need to be removed from the home.

- *Family preservation*: In-home work provided by child welfare caseworkers. Much of this work is geared toward providing a range of supportive services to the family in order to prevent a child removal.

- *Ongoing work*: Caseworkers with a caseload of families in which the child has been removed from their home. The caseworker's role is to work with the family to attempt family reunification is at all possible, and if not to find another permanency plan for the child (e.g., permanent placement with relatives, adoption).

- *Foster care*: Caseworkers who recruit, train, certify, and support those who wish to become foster parents. Foster parents need ongoing support due to the emotional and behavioral difficulties that many children in foster care have due to the trauma of child maltreatment and family separation.

- *Adoption*: Caseworkers who recruit, train, certify, and support those who wish to become adoptive parents to children in the foster care system. They also match children and families and help prepare the child for adoption.

- *Administration and program planning*: Many caseworkers move into management and/or supervisory roles in state child welfare systems after gaining direct experience in the field.

- *Policy/advocacy work*: Some social workers choose to effect change at the macro level in child welfare by working in advocacy organizations (e.g.,

CDF) that attempt to pass legislation at the state or federal level that helps children and families affected by child maltreatment.

- *Related agencies*: Some social workers interested in child welfare choose to work in organizations outside of the formal child welfare system such as CASA; children's advocacy centers (where forensic interviews are conducted with children by trained professionals to gather information pertaining to allegations of child maltreatment); foster care and adoption agencies; and home visiting programs that are designed to support pregnant and new mothers.

Positive Youth Development

There are social workers across the country who work in various programs that focus on helping children and youth thrive and reach their highest potential in life. These can include **mentoring programs**; programs that get young people involved in community service, civic engagement, and leadership experiences; and programs that prepare youth for adulthood (e.g., education and employment). Some of these programs can be specialized to support the needs of specific youth who face significant barriers in society such as LGBTQ youth, youth who are undocumented, foster youth, youth with disabilities, and BIPOC youth, while others include all youth in their program's services.

IMG 9.3

The Interagency Working Group on Youth Programs (Youth.Gov, n.d.) defines **positive youth development** as "an intentional, prosocial approach that engages youth within their communities, schools, organizations, peer groups, and families in a manner that is productive and constructive; recognizes, utilizes, and enhances young people's strengths; and promotes positive outcomes for young people by providing opportunities, fostering positive relationships, and furnishing the support needed to build on their leadership strengths" (para. 2).

It is important to note that **positive youth development is an approach, not a program**. There are several important principles of positive youth development that these programs embrace:

- Positive relationships with caring adults who work as allies and advocates for them

- Strong focus on enhancing the strengths, resiliency, and protective factors of young people (instead of focusing solely on reducing risky behaviors)

- Operating from an ecological perspective that seeks to enhance young people's systems of support and social networks (e.g., caring adults, peers, family, community)

- All young people having the capacity for growth and healthy development when provided with opportunities for self-exploration and skill building

- Youth in these programs being equal participants with adults and actively involved in the design, delivery, and evaluation of the program's services (i.e., youth voice)

- Strong focus on community service and/or civic engagement and helping youth develop the skills and knowledge they need to successfully transition to adulthood

Social workers who work in these youth serving programs need to have a passion for supporting young people in their growth and development and the ability to work collaboratively with youth. These programs reject adultism—the belief that young people are ignorant and less important than (and even inferior) to adults.

School Social Work Practice

School social work is one of the oldest fields of practice within the profession of social work, dating back to 1906 when they were referred to as "visiting teachers." Over time, these employees were renamed "**school social workers**," and the field was increasingly professionalized by passing standards, regulations, and educational requirements to be a school social worker. As a result of the growth of clinical social work, school social workers were increasingly called on do therapeutic work with children and to assist children with disabilities

IMG 9.4

as new federal legislation (e.g., Education for All Handicapped Children Act of 1975) was passed to ensure that schools adequately addressed their needs (Allen-Meares, 2013). Today, **school social work** is a recognized field of practice, and many schools hire them because they understand the value they bring to the educational environment.

According to the U.S. Bureau of Labor Statistics (2021), of the 715,600 social workers in the United States in 2020, 45,960 worked in elementary and secondary schools. Unfortunately, not all schools have a school social worker though, oftentimes due to a lack of funding; thus, the vision of the **School Social Work Association of America** (SWAA) is to have a "school social worker in every school" (n.d.a.). The American Civil Liberties Union (Whitaker et al., n.d.) published a discouraging report titled, "Cops and No Counselors" to highlight data from 2015–2016 showing that 14 million children attend a school with a police officer but no social worker, nurse, counselor, or psychologist.

What School Social Workers Do

According to the SWAA (n.d.b.), social workers are the link between the school, the home, and the community, a unique role to play in a school. Teachers and other school personnel do not typically have the training and the bandwidth to support students who have emotional/behavioral difficulties and/or problems at home. Social workers are also experts on the available resources in the community and can refer families to these services. School social workers provide important services to the students, to their families, and to the school itself (SWAA, n.d.b.). Much of the work of school social workers in informed by **trauma-informed** and **culturally responsive approaches** to their work. For more on trauma-informed care, see Chapters 3 and 7. Below is a summary of common services that are provided by school social workers to students, families, and schools.

Services Provided to Students

- Support students with mental health disorders
- Provide individual, group, and family counseling services
- Provide crisis intervention (e.g., suicidal ideation, sexual assault, children experiencing housing insecurity, death of a family member)
- Address barriers that negatively impact students' academic success
- Provide mediation and conflict resolution services (e.g., between youth, between children and school personnel)
- Help to increase social skills of children and youth
- Support students experiencing child maltreatment (i.e., school social workers are mandated reporters)
- Support students with disabilities (physical, cognitive, and/or sensory) who have individual education plans (IEPs)

Services Provided to Families

- Refer families to resources in the community (e.g., food, shelter, counseling, family violence shelter, substance abuse; services for children with disabilities, etc.)
- Act as a liaison for homeless children and their families (required by federal legislation—the McKinney-Vento Act)
- Assist families in how to support their child academically
- Advocate for families who are eligible for services from the school district

Services Provided to Schools

- Support teachers who have students with behavioral challenges in the classroom using positive behavioral intervention strategies
- Provide training to school personnel on a range of topics such as cultural competency, how to address bullying, behavior management strategies, and so on

- Develop specialized programs within the school to serve the various needs of at-risk youth (e.g., on-campus health center, substance abuse groups, support for undocumented youth, etc.)

Where School Social Workers Work

Social workers who want to do school social work can find positions in elementary schools, middle schools, and high schools, depending on which age group they prefer to work with. The nature of the job will vary somewhat based on the age group. For example, in high schools it will be common to focus on developmental and life issues that adolescents commonly experience such as drop-out prevention, safe and healthy relationships, support around issues of sexual violence, mental health challenges, and college preparation. Some schools will require a master's degree in social work and to be licensed (as a school social worker or a clinical social worker), while other schools may only require a bachelor's degree in social work. Additionally, some states have specific requirements for coursework you must have completed during your social work studies, and many social work programs have responded by offering a specialized track for school social work.

It has been increasingly common for social workers to find **employment at colleges and universities**, an exciting development for those who are interested in supporting college students. Many of today's college students are facing an array of challenges such as balancing college while working full-time, mental health struggles, financial stressors, and being a first-generation college student. Many universities have responded to these needs by offering case managers (sometimes referred to as care teams), mental health counseling, food pantries, writing centers and tutoring services, and other services and programs to help their students stay in college and graduate. Social workers are ideally suited for many of these types of positions.

School Social Work Case Study

Ana is a school social worker in a high school in your community, and one of the students she is working with is Juan. Juan is 16 years old. He is undocumented and describes himself as queer. His parents brought him to the United States from Mexico when he was 8 years old for a better life. Juan has two younger siblings who look up to him, and he loves being a supportive big brother. He has been experiencing anxiety and depression for the past 6 months due to the barriers he faces as an undocumented youth. He wants to attend college, but his family will not be able to afford it, and he will not qualify for federal student loans due to his immigration status. Juan is a talented artist (draws, paints), and he aspires to become a high school art teacher, but this will require an undergraduate degree in education. His parents both work (his mother as a housekeeper in a hotel and his father in construction), but there are times they struggle to meet basic needs due to low wages. They do not qualify for many social welfare programs due to their immigration status. Since his parents did not attend college, they are not able to help him navigate the complexities of applying to go to college and gaining access to financial aid.

Juan's mom accepts him being gay, but his father does not and wants him to "be a man." Juan does have a strong group of friends, some of whom are also undocumented youth whom he has met through his activism for the Dream Act. Juan has a couple of dedicated teachers who support and mentor him. He has friends at school but has also been bullied at times due to his race and socioeconomic status.

Questions

1. What are the strengths in this case?

2. How can Ana, the school social worker, assist Juan and his family at the micro level? Be very specific.

3. How can Ana, the school social worker, assist Juan and students like him at the macro level? Be very specific.

4. How can Ana be as culturally responsive as possible when working with Juan and his family?

5. What questions or feelings are raised for you as you imagine working with a family in this situation?

Racism and the Child Welfare System

For some time, concerns have been raised by those inside and outside of the child welfare system about the role that racism plays when families, particularly BIPOC (Black, Indigenous, and People of Color) families, become involved with state child protection systems. Due to hard data collected by government officials, it has not been a secret that low-income families and families of color are disproportionately impacted, yet this issue has been elevated in recent years, likely due to the role of the Black Lives Matter movement in focusing the nation's attention on the role of systemic racism in various segments of our society. Low-income families and families of color are reported more to child welfare officials, and as a result children of color are disproportionately represented in the foster care system. Even though some may argue that poverty and the resulting stressors that come along with living in poverty are major risk factors for child maltreatment, that alone cannot explain these racial and income disparities.

The child welfare system has a very long and troubling history with Native American and Indigenous communities, and as a result historically many Native children experienced serious trauma from being removed from their home and tribal community. A federal piece of legislation, the **Indian Child Welfare Act (ICWA)** was passed in 1978 to ensure that the child welfare system cannot continue these harmful practices. ICWA seeks to ensure that Native children are kept with Native families and outlines the rights and legal powers that tribes have when a child comes to the attention of child welfare authorities. Child protection caseworkers are trained about this law and the need to follow it carefully when they are working with a Native American family.

In June 2020, a new social movement, the **upEND Movement**, emerged in response to concerns about the impact of racism and White supremacy in state child welfare systems. This movement is spearheaded by the Center for the Study of Social Policy and the University of Houston's Graduate College of Social Work. The members of this movement are calling for the abolition of the child welfare system as it currently operates as they view it as family policing system. They describe their movement as

> an emerging, collaborative movement aimed at ending the surveillance and removal of Black, Native, and, in many jurisdictions, Latinx children and families by the child welfare system and increasing meaningful supports so families can care for their children. Currently, public systems by design hyper-surveil Black, Native, and Latinx families; community-based supports and basic safety net supports are minimal; and child welfare's response to "helping" families in need results in high rates of removal for Black and Native children. upEND seeks to end the practice of state sanctioned separation of children from their families as a response to social problems like food insecurity, poverty, lack of affordable and safe housing, and lack of meaningful prevention services. upEND also seeks to reimagine how we support and serve families and eliminate the root causes that create conditions for harm to occur. (Center for the Study of Social Policy, n.d.)

The upEND movement argues that instead of having a punitive child welfare system, families would be better served if they were provided with robust social supports and community services such as child allowances, affordable housing and childcare, jobs with livable wages, and mental health and substance abuse services.

Research Focus: Home Visiting Programs

One evidence-based intervention model that is used in work with children and families is **home visiting programs**. These models can vary somewhat by program, but the basic idea is that social workers, child development specialists, or nurses make home visits to pregnant moms and moms with newborns to provide them with support, parenting skills and knowledge, and other needed resources to promote infant health and parent–child bonding and reduce the risk of child maltreatment. Prominent examples of home visiting programs in the United States are Home Instruction for Parents of Preschool Youngsters (HIPPY), Nurse-Family Partnership, Healthy Families America, and Parents as Teachers. Some programs are targeted to families meeting certain requirements while others are more universally offered. Learning to be a parent is not easy, so this intervention is designed to assist new parents in supporting their child's healthy growth and development.

It is important that social workers evaluate their interventions to ensure that they are effective in meeting the program goals that have been identified. When social workers have strong evidence that their program is effective, they are in a stronger position to gain the support of lawmakers and funders in providing financial support for the program. Home visiting programs have been studied extensively by researchers and are referred to as an **evidence-based intervention** because researchers have found positive outcomes related to children's health, school readiness, parenting skills, and reducing child maltreatment. They have been shown to be an excellent return on investment as every dollar spent on a home visiting program can reduce costs in child protection, Temporary Assistance NF, K–12 special education, and criminal justice. The U.S. Department of Human Services currently recognizes 22 home visiting models as meeting the requirements for federal funding due to their effectiveness. Visit their website to learn more https://homvee.acf.hhs.gov/).

Chapter Summary

Children are a vulnerable population in our society, and many face challenges due to poverty, food insecurity, child maltreatment, school struggles, and other ACEs. Social work with children and families is one of the most prominent areas of social work practice. It is hard to find a practicing social worker whose work does not impact this population in some way, and many fields of practice serve children and their families such as health care, mental health care (including addictions), and juvenile justice, just to name a few. However, this chapter focused primarily on three fields of practice for social workers who have a passion for working with children and youth: child welfare, school social work, and positive youth development. Even though child protection is a critical area of social work practice, it is not for everyone, and many social workers choose to work with children and families in other settings such as schools, nonprofit organizations, child advocacy organizations, and foster care and adoption agencies. Child allowances are an important public policy focus, though the United States has been reluctant compared to other wealthy nations to make this a permanent part of the nation's social welfare system. It is important that social workers conduct research evaluating the effectiveness of their interventions. Research on home visiting programs indicates that this is a promising intervention to support pregnant moms and families with newborn infants.

Discussion Questions

1. After learning about social work in child protection, school social work, and positive youth development, which of these areas could you see yourself working in and not working in? Why so?

2. Child allowances were part of the Biden Administration's American Rescue Plan during the coronavirus pandemic, but lawmakers allowed the child allowance to expire and did not extend this policy. Compared to other wealthy nations, why do you think the United States has been hesitant to adopt child allowances as a policy to help combat child poverty?

3. This chapter highlighted the concept of ACEs and an intervention model, home visiting programs. How can these help social workers appeal to state and federal lawmakers for the need for enhanced government funding to support prevention strategies for children, a vulnerable population in our society?

4. Many social workers work with children and families at the micro level. But what *macro-level approaches* could be used to support children and families, particularly in the areas of child poverty and child maltreatment?

5. What did you learn about social work practice with children and youth that was most surprising to you?

References

Allen-Meares, P. (2013). School social work. In *Encyclopedia of social work*. NASW Press & Oxford University Press. https://oxfordre.com/socialwork/view/10.1093/acrefore/9780199975839.001.0001/acrefore-9780199975839-e-351

Centers for Disease Control and Prevention. (n.d.a.). *Risk and protective factors*. https://www.cdc.gov/violenceprevention/childabuseandneglect/riskprotectivefactors.html

Centers for Disease Control and Prevention. (n.d.b.). *Preventing adverse childhood experiences*. https://www.cdc.gov/violenceprevention/aces/fastfact.html

Center for the Study of Social Policy. (n.d.). *Frequently asked questions*. https://cssp.org/wp-content/uploads/2020/05/upEND-EXTERNAL-FAQ.pdf

Children's Bureau. (2021). *The AFCARS report, FY 2020 data*. Office of the Administration for Children and Families https://www.acf.hhs.gov/sites/default/files/documents/cb/afcarsreport28.pdf

Children's Defense Fund. (2021). *The state of America's children 2021*. https://www.childrensdefense.org/state-of-americas-children/

Child Welfare Information Gateway. (2019). *What is child abuse and neglect? Recognizing the signs and symptoms*. U.S. Department of Health and Human Services, Children's Bureau. https://www.childwelfare.gov/pubs/factsheets/whatiscan/

Child Welfare Information Gateway. (2021). *Foster care statistics 2019*. U.S. Department of Health and Human Services, Administration for Children and Families, Children's Bureau. https://www.childwelfare.gov/pubs/ factsheets/foster/

Mervosh, S. (2021, July 28). The pandemic hurt these students the most. *The New York Times*. https://www.nytimes.com/2021/07/28/us/covid-schools-at-home-learning-study.html

Parolin, Z., Collyer, S., & Curran, M.A. (2022). *Sixth child tax credit payment kept 3.7 million children out of poverty in December*. Poverty and Social Policy Brief. Vol. 6, No.1. Center on Poverty and Social Policy, Columbia University. https://www.povertycenter.columbia.edu/publication/montly-poverty-december-2021

Pew Research Center. (2015). *Parenting in America: Outlook, worries, and aspirations are strongly linked to financial situation*. https://www.pewresearch.org/social-trends/2015/12/17/1-the-american-family-today/

School Social Work Association of America (n.d.a.). *Who we are*. https://www.sswaa.org/about

School Social Work Association of America. (n.d.b.). *Role of school social worker*. https://www.sswaa.org/school-social-work

U.S. Bureau of Labor Statistics. (2021). Occupational employment and wages, child, family, and school social workers, May 2020. https://www.bls.gov/oes/current/oes211021.htm

U.S. Department of Health & Human Services, Administration for Children and Families, Administration on Children, Youth and Families, Children's Bureau. (2021). *Child maltreatment 2019*. https://www.acf.hhs.gov/cb/report/child-maltreatment-2019

Whitaker, A., Torres-Guillen, S., Morten, M., Jordan, H., Coyle, S., Mann, A., & Sun, W. (n.d.). *Cops and no counselors: How the lack of school mental health staff is harming students.* ACLU. https://www.aclu.org/report/cops-and-no-counselors

Youth.Gov. (n.d.). Positive youth development. https://youth.gov/youth-topics/positive-youth-development

Zippel, C. (October 21, 2021). *9 in 10 Families with low incomes are using child tax credits to pay for necessities, education.* Center on Budget and Policy Priorities. https://www.cbpp.org/blog/9-in-10-families-with-low-incomes-are-using-child-tax-credits-to-pay-for-necessities-education

Credits

CHAPTER 10

Social Work Practice With Older Adults

Jess Retrum

Learning Objectives

After reading this chapter, students will be able to do the following:

- Summarize the biggest social issues facing our aging population

- Describe why it is essential to consider diversity and culture when working with older people

- Explain what is imperative for social workers to understand about late life as a developmental stage

- Identify three major career path options for social workers who want to work with older people

- Evaluate modifications to affordable housing and Medicaid as a potential public policy solution for lack of affordable, accessible housing and poor quality of residential care

- Summarize research findings on social isolation and older people

- Explain the goals of various social work interventions and seeking to address negative outcomes of social isolation among older adults

- Evaluate goodness of fit with social work practice with older people and their support systems as a potential future career option

IMG 10.1

SOCIAL WORKER SPOTLIGHT:
Early Career Gerontological Social Worker, Florence Onabolu, MSW

My name is Florence Onabolu, and my passion to work with older adults started back in Nigeria, West Africa. I grew up mostly around older adults and witnessed a lot of injustices in the practices of people geared toward older folks. The lack of care, respect, and good policies that foster aging gracefully were nowhere to be found. I knew almost immediately I wanted to be a part of the change that accentuates better living conditions for older adults.

Once I got an opportunity to pursue a social work education at the Metropolitan State University of Denver, my determination to serve the older population was put to the test. During the 1st year of my undergraduate studies, I was a volunteer intern with the social services team at Someren Glen Christian Living Community. I got firsthand exposure to what working with older adults entails. Monitoring care plans, keeping older folks company during recess hours, and playing bingo games was hardly a simple task but was so refreshing. Looking at the faces of the older folks as they laid in bed in the nursing home as if waiting for someone to come rescue them is one image I can hardly get rid of.

In the final year of my undergraduate studies, I was an intern at Senior Support Services—an agency serving older adults 55 and older facing homelessness. I was an intake coordinator, asking questions and seeking answers as every individual coming in told their stories of how they ended up homeless. Each valid story made me realize just how much society underestimates the problems older adults face in terms of housing. Many older folks lose their housing during natural and man-made disasters like hurricanes and wildfires. Some can find shelters while others are displaced with nowhere to go. I felt heartbroken for every person who walked through the doors and was unable to find housing because they were not qualified. After graduation, I became a caregiver to gain hands-on knowledge about elder care. Working with Hoyer lifts, mobility assistance, monitoring medications, and incontinence care are just some of the duties I performed. The gratitude extended by family members and clients made my determination worth it. Being a caregiver has been one of my most rewarding identities.

Eventually, I decided to pursue my master's degree so I could gain more knowledge and skills to better serve the older population. During my graduate degree, I served as a therapist intern with the older adult team at the Aurora Mental Health Center (AuMHC). The agency provides a holistic approach to mental health care, including outpatient care, general treatment, prevention, and recovery services. Conducting mental health assessments, giving diagnosis, providing care plans, and maintaining a therapeutic alliance with my clients were my sole responsibilities. I would not trade the time I spent with the team because I worked with a lot of supportive coworkers.

Being a therapist made me realize the importance of self-care. Many people perceive the concept of self-care as foreign, but it cannot be overemphasized. Paying attention to the symptoms of being burnt out helped me figure out I was almost falling prey. I became aware that my bottle was half empty every time I met with a client, and I wasn't doing enough to make sure it became full again. I was almost emptied out! I started taking out more time for myself at the start and end of the day to decompress alone before attending to other personal issues. That was the refueling I needed to keep showing up for my clients.

As I continue moving forward in my social work career and look back at each landmark, I remember what brought me into the profession. My determination and desire to make a difference in the lives of older adults is paying off because when duty calls for me, I am ready. I put on my helping hat, and every smile I discover in the eyes of the people I serve makes me long for nothing more. I know I still have a long way to go, but I'll get there!

Older adults are often portrayed as slow, tired, or stubborn, but what people don't realize is that people over 65, 75, and even 85 are often energetic, intelligent, funny, innovative, complicated, and interesting people. During this development stage of life, many changes occur that require adaptation and/or support, and sometimes these changes lead to vulnerabilities. People are living so much longer these days; it is changing our social landscape and creates an increased need for social work expertise in working with this population. There are many settings in which social workers support older adults in their work. The demand for social workers that serve older people and their social supports is high. The need for social workers trained to work with older people, particularly in health care, is expected to grow by almost 20% in the next 10 years (U.S. Bureau of Labor Statistics, 2020). Since the U.S. population and worldwide is aging, most helping professionals and health care professionals will face aging or aging-related issues in their practice on a regular basis (World Health Organization [WHO], 2023).

What Is Aging?

In Atul Gawande's (2014) best-selling book, *Being Mortal*, he states that one of the tragedies of life is that we are all aging beginning the day that we are born. From the purely biological point of view, **aging** is a result of increased buildup of different types of molecular and cellular damage over time in the human body. This leads to a natural, slow decline in physical and mental capacity, an increasing risk of disease, and ultimately death. Aging in every aspect of human functioning naturally occurs to all of us. It will happen differently for everyone physically and cognitively. How and when changes occur are related to the number of years someone has been alive, but that is only one factor in many that determine aging. Beyond biological changes and genetics, aging effects are related to many other social factors such as one's social and physical environment. It is true the human body becomes more susceptible to health challenges through the normal aging process and that the older someone is increases the risk of having one or more chronic conditions. However, there is a great deal a variability among older adults on how they are impacted by and their adaptability to health and mental health changes. This difference exists within and between groups of older people from racial and ethnic, geographic locations, and socioeconomic backgrounds.

Social work practitioners who work with older individuals work in a wide variety of settings and must see the potential strengths and positive aspects of growing old in addition to the health declines and inevitable changes seen as negative. Social workers need to learn the skills and have knowledge of the psychological, social, and cultural factors influencing older people and their supports' ability to adapt to changes. They must learn what is and is not part of the **normal aging process** and to assess and analyze the related social and psychological benefits in addition to needs and problems. Older populations are often at risk due to poverty; mental or physical illness; family problems; discrimination and oppression related to cultural and racial diversity, gender, sexual orientation, and disability; and other factors. While a broad overview of **gerontological social work** will be provided, it would be impossible to cover all areas in which social workers work with older adults and their support services. Therefore, this chapter will only give specific examples of a few important fields of practice that have older adults as the primary focus of the work: geriatric care management in community services and long-term care and hospice and palliative care.

> **10.1   PRACTICE ACTIVITY**
>
> Describe who you would like to be and some of the characteristics that you would like to have at age 75. Imagine you are that person and a 5-year-old child passes you on the street. What would they see?

Our Aging World: Challenges Facing Older People

All over the world, people are living longer, in a massive way. Between 2015 and 2050, the proportion of the world's population over 60 years will nearly double from 12% to 22% (WHO, 2023). In the United States the number of older adults was 3 million in 1900 and grew to 52 million in 2018. Those in the oldest category (over 85) was 100,000 in 1900 but is now over 7 million (Federal Interagency Forum on Aging-Related Statistics, 2020). The demographic changes in the United States that are leading to a significantly larger share of the population being over age 65 is sometimes referred to as the "graying of America." What does this mean for our world? The **biggest challenges facing older people** are health inequities, economic security and work, adapting to health changes, access to health, and mental health care. Important barriers to quality of life and a livable environment exist for many older people, and often their needs aren't reflected in policies that impact these issues. As the population ages and people live longer, the needs that already face our vulnerable older people for economic security, health care (including mental and behavioral health), housing, and transportation will continue to increase, but many speculate that our systems are not adapting to accommodate these needs. The most common **mental health challenges** facing older people are depression, anxiety, and dementia.

Ageism is a major challenge and has a negative impact on how we approach the challenges and solutions facing older people. There are deeply harmful impacts that ageism, paired with racism and other forms of oppression, have on society's ability to support older people in ways they need. "Ageism refers to the stereotypes (how we think), prejudice (how we feel) and discrimination (how we act) towards others or oneself based on age" (WHO, 2023, para. 1). **Ageist stereotypes** often frame older people as frail, boring, dependent, vulnerable, and a burden on our families, social programs, and health systems. These are not only largely untrue and unhelpful, but also have hurtful and costly impacts on older people and their families (Ayalon et al., 2021; Levy et al., 2020).

Revisioning Aging, Wellness, and Healthy Aging Through an Anti-Oppressive Lens

While society tends to focus on the problems related to aging, it is important to combat alarmist and ageist approaches. Aging is a very natural part of being human, which in and of itself should not be viewed as negative and problematic. From a societal or macro-level point of view, a negative perspective on what will happen due to our aging population has been called **apocalyptic demography** (Robertson, 1991), with disastrous, inevitable predictions of what will happen to health and social systems (Gee, 2002). While it is important to advocate for policies that will embrace the changing demographics, we have learned it is better to focus on the setting goals for wellness and healthy aging to assist older people and their supports from all walks for life to achieve healthy aging. Gerontologic social workers aspire to work through an anti-oppressive and trauma-informed lens by using life span approaches to assessment and interventions and recognizing social determinants of health and the importance of culturally responsive care (Hulko et al., 2019).

Aging and Diversity

When you think about someone who is older, who comes to mind? A parent or grandparent? Family member? Community member? Service provider? Indeed, our views of older people are influenced by our personal experiences with them. The truth is, those experiencing their later stages of life have so many differences among them, it is impossible to provide good social work services based on a narrow profile. It is essential to recognize the immense variation that exists among the older population social workers will encounter in their career pathways. Social and geographical location and **intersectional identities of older individuals** will drastically impact who they are and what they will need. For example, race/ethnicity, culture, gender, sexual orientation, gender identity, social class, rural versus urban living environment, and any combination of these will reveal different people who also vary in family and social support composition, temperament, interests, beliefs, values, and upbringing. In addition to these important differentiating characteristics, there are also very distinct differences between subgroups of those who are between the ages of 65 and 110. Some differentiate between young old (65–75 years old), middle old (76–85 years old), and the oldest old (86-plus years old). That's a lot of variety!

The demographic shifts of the older population are becoming progressively more racially diverse. Table 10.1 (Federal Interagency Forum on Aging-Related Statistics, 2020) describes projected shifts we will be between 2018 and 2060.

TABLE 10.1   Population Age 65 and Over, by Race and Hispanic origin, 2018 and Projected 2060

	2018	2060
Non-Hispanic White alone	77%	55%
Non-Hispanic Black alone	9%	13%
Non-Hispanic Asian alone	5%	8%
Hispanic (of any race)	8%	21%
Non-Hispanic all other races alone or in combination	1%	3%

Source: Federal Interagency Forum on Aging-Related Statistics, Older Americans 2020: Key Indicators of Well-Being, https://agingstats.gov/docs/LatestReport/OA20_508_10142020.pdf, 2020.

SOCIAL JUSTICE SPOTLIGHT:
Health Inequities Among the Older Adult Population

The United States is among the wealthiest nations in the world and spends far more per person on health care than any other industrialized nation, yet the health of its people does not reflect this. Over the last 35 years, the U.S. population has been dying at younger ages than those of the populations in countries like ours and has experienced poorer health throughout the life course, from birth to old age (Institute of Medicine, 2013). Older people face health inequities beyond those related to natural aging. What's more, populations within the general older adults from different socioeconomic status, racial/ ethical background, gender, LGBTQI+ community status, disability status, and geographic location experience different health outcomes. These are often referred to as **social determinants of health**.

According to the National Institute on Minority Health and Health Disparities (2022), "Many populations in America, whether defined by race, ethnicity, immigrant status, disability, sex, gender, or geography, experience higher rates of certain diseases and more deaths and suffering from them compared with the general population. While the diversity of the American population is one of the nation's greatest assets, one of its greatest challenges is reducing the profound disparity in health status of its racial and ethnic minority, rural, low-income, and other underserved populations" (para. 1). In addition to the biological factors causing disease progression, the National Institute on Minority Health and Health Disparities sharpens the scientific community's focus on nonbiological factors that impact **health disparities** such as socioeconomics, politics, discrimination, culture, and environment. There is indisputable evidence that health inequalities (or health disparities) exist broadly, beyond individual behaviors or isolated communities. These inequities are a matter of social injustice as often they are avoidable and due to systemic failures. Extensive research has shown that socioeconomic status, race/ethnicity, sex, and other factors play a role in common health and mental health issues facing older people disproportionately impact minority subgroups in more negative and often more lethal ways (Mehrotra & Wagner, 2018).

Socioeconomic status is often measured be examining educational attainment and poverty. Older adults have lower socioeconomic status than the rest of the population due to the challenges of losing income after retirement. Within that, subgroups among older populations have much larger disparities. As of 2018, 85% of people over 65 years of age are a high school graduate, and 28% have a bachelor's degree or more. Educational attainment for White older adults is higher than average (much lower for) and lower Black older adults (76% high school [HS] grad, 17% bachelor's degree [BD] or more) and much lower for Hispanic (of any race; 54% HS grad, 12% BD or more). For Asian older adults, high school attainment is lower than national average, but of those, the percent of those attaining a bachelor's degree is higher than the national average (74% HS grad, 17% BD or more). Poverty rates are associated with being older, unfortunately, with 9% of individuals ages 65–74 and 14% for those age 85 and over. Within those, women have higher rates, as do Asian alone (12%) and both Hispanic and Black alone, above 19%.

The experiences of older adults who are members of the **lesbian, gay, bisexual, and transgender** (LGBT) community also face unique challenges. According to SAGE and the National Resource Center on LGBT Aging, while Census surveys have not measured how many LGBT people live in the United States, other studies and reports help us estimate that currently there are around 3 million LGBT adults over age 50 with growth expectation to around 7 million by 2030.

"LGBT older people face unique challenges as they age:

- Twice as likely to be single and live alone

- Four times less likely to have children

- Far more likely than our heterosexual peers to have faced discrimination, social stigma, and the effects of prejudice

- More likely, therefore, to face poverty and homelessness, and to have poor physical and mental health" (SAGE & National Resource Center on LGBT Aging, 2020, p. 1)

Gerontological social workers are taking this on as it relates to one chronic illness commonly impacting older people: diabetes. In a trend study over 20 years, found an increase in the disparity between White and Black older adults in the development, but more significantly in the disease burdens, of diabetes in the United States (Odlum et al., 2020). Social workers who want to work on a macro level to make changes to improve the lives of other people can take on roles such as becoming a leader in their organization or doing policy advocacy work.

Consequences of the COVID-19 Pandemic

In early 2020, the United States began to experience the devastating effects of the **coronavirus** (COVID-19), which had and continues to have a unique and more consequential impact on older adults for a variety of reasons. These include but are not limited to more severe complications, higher death rate, lower activity levels (Oliveira, et al., 2021), as well as increased risks for the known negative effects of **social isolation** such as access to social supports and health care and exacerbation to existing mental health conditions. Although some studies indicate the effects of the disease have varying impacts of different populations, indicating certain characteristics in older populations minimized and created more resiliency for some older people (Parlapani et al., 2021).

A population of older adults hit very hard by COVID-19 are those living in **skilled care and residential facilities**. The death rate for COVID-19 in these settings was higher than the general population (Center for Disease Control, 2022). Social determinants of COVID-19 have largely been older age, race and ethnicity, poverty, and chronic conditions and social work interventions that integrate/advocate for technology, reduce caregiver stress, and lessen isolation could enable more persons to remain in the community. A rapid increase of telehealth services aimed at both physical and mental health care was experienced in urban and rural communities across the country (Cox, 2020). Access for lower income and rural communities due to limited access to internet were particularly concerning.

Additionally, the COVID-19 pandemic had a disproportionate health and socio-economic impact on **older members of communities of color**. Social workers from across the country needed to adapt. For example, one project focused on social work with an older African American community to receive maximum support and services through faith-based community approaches (Shelton et al., 2021). There is no doubt social works focused on older populations, sometimes called **gerontological social workers**, are on the frontlines of the significant challenges the COVID-19 pandemic. These practitioners were relied heavily upon to support the biopsychosocial needs of older adults in hospitals, communities, and long-term care settings. A recent research area focused on whether social workers are trained to meet the emerging needs of older adults during the pandemic. This focus has taught us that more training on disaster preparedness, telehealth, and coordination of scarce resources is important (Beltran & Miller, 2021). The recent COVID-19 pandemic has made an enormous impact on the way social workers care for the geriatric population. Since it has only been 2 years since its onset, COVID-19 is only just beginning to be inserted formally in the social work education. We seek to understand and teach that the way needs have changed for older people from all walks of life amidst a pandemic.

The **social isolation** necessary to keep older people at lower risk often increases their risk for loneliness, and social workers recommended new, alternatives to quality of contacts to lessen the negative effects (Teater et al., 2021). There was also an increase in complicated **grief** and **bereavement** as partners, families, and friends across the country suffered the loss of loved ones but often were unable to be physically present during the death and/or services to mourn their loss due to the need to minimize the spread of the highly contagious disease. There are lasting impacts from COVID-19 on older adults and their families that we are only beginning to understand.

Important Public Policies and Programs Impacting Older People

In 2025, the United States will celebrate the 60th anniversary of the **Older Americans Act** (OAA), which funds programs and services aimed at assisting older people to have independent, healthy, and productive lives in their homes and communities (Colello & Napili, 2021). Programs related to OAA serve over 11 million seniors. Social workers provide many of these services and have long played leadership roles in various aging-related organizations at the local, state, and federal levels. Services authorized by the OAA include but are not limited to health and wellness promotion, job training, family caregiver support, long-term care ombudsmen, nutrition programs, transportation, tribal assistance programs, and programs to prevent and address elder abuse, neglect, and exploitation. The aging network of services includes 56 state and territorial agencies, over 600 **area agencies on aging** (AAAs), over 260 Title VI Native American aging programs, and more than 20,000 community service providers. OAA also dictates some policies and programs that underpin the long-term care support systems across the country (Colello & Napili, 2021). The OAA has historically been widely supported by members of both major political parties, although there is often debate about how much funding to invest.

Social Security is another program housed within and facilitated by the federal government. The program works by using taxes paid into a trust fund to provide benefits to people who are eligible. Social Security is the key source of income for most older people. Almost nine out of 10 people aged 65 and older were receiving a Social Security benefit as of June 30, 2022 (Dushi & Trenkamp, 2021). In 1935 **President Roosevelt** signed the **Social Security Act** as part of the New Deal during a time of deep despair in our country as we recovered from the economic crisis of Great Depression in the 1930s. Social Security was designed to pay retired workers age 65 or older a continuing income after retirement and has evolved over the years. This has been recognized as one of the most successful social programs

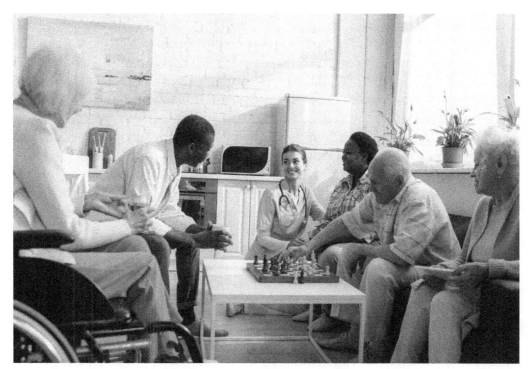

IMG 10.2

addressing poverty in the United States, particular for older people and those experiencing disability. In 2022, an average of 66 million Americans per month will receive a Social Security benefit, and,

- "Social Security benefits represent about 30% of the income of the elderly.

- Among elderly Social Security beneficiaries, 37% of men and 42% of women receive 50% or more of their income from Social Security.

- Among elderly Social Security beneficiaries, 12% of men and 15% of women rely on Social Security for 90% or more of their income" (Dushi & Trenkamp, 2021, Fact Sheet, para. 1).

Medicare and Medicaid are the two public health insurance programs. **Medicare** is national health insurance program for people 65 or older, and some people under 65 with certain disabilities or conditions. The Centers for Medicare & Medicaid Services, which is a federal agency, runs Medicare and has set standards for costs and what can be coverage. (For more information, visit Medicare.gov.). An individual's Medicare coverage will be the same no matter what state they live in. **Medicaid** is program funded and administered at the federal and state level that helps cover medical costs for a certain portion of individuals with low income and restricted resources. Each state runs their own Medicaid program, but the federal government dictates certain rules that all state Medicaid programs must follow.

The eligibility scope varies from state to state. (For more information, visit Medicaid.gov; U.S. Department of Health and Human Services, 2023). The **Affordable Care Act (ACA)**, formally known as the Patient Protection and Affordable Care Act and informally known as Obamacare, is another important law that is covered in more detail in a different chapter (see Chapter 8). This landmark U.S. federal statute was enacted by the 111th U.S. Congress and signed into law by President Barack Obama on March 23, 2010. The ACA impacted older people by expanding coverage in several ways, including protecting older people from being banned from coverage because of preexisting conditions. According to the Centers for Medicare & Medicaid Services (2023), over 16 million adults purchase insurance through the individual market, so this was a significant benefit for older people.

Gerontological Social Work Practice

Gerontological social workers help older clients manage **psychological**, **emotional**, and **social challenges** by providing counseling and therapy and advising clients' families about how to best support aging loved ones. Additionally, they ensure communication between the older individual they serve and the rest of the providers they work with. They often assist with referrals or communication for clients to receive the services they need if or when they move between inpatient and outpatient care, in-home care, day treatment programs, and so on.

Gerontological social workers interface with older adults in broad variety of ways. The roles of social workers vary a great deal because older people are diverse in their needs related to biological, psychological, spiritual, and social needs at various points during their many phases of life. Older people may need support with short-term or long-term challenges. The needs also vary depending on the geographical area they live in, the families and supports they are nestled within, and the communities they belong to. Gerontological social workers are **employed in different settings** such as community social and human services agencies, organizations considered part of the continuum of long-term care system, adult protective services, geriatric care management organizations, and geriatric mental health care organizations, providing services including advanced psychotherapy with older people, substance misuse, and dementia-related care. A large portion of the patients in most **health care settings** such as hospitals providing inpatient acute care, home care, and hospices are older people. Most of these health care settings will have some if not many social workers on staff. Finally, there are many **legal and retirement planning services** who serve a large proportion of older clients that also employ social workers.

As you can see, working with older adults can mean many things. There are a wide variety of needs, and older adult cases can range from simple to extremely complex medically, psychologically, and/or socially. Social workers pursing a successful career working with older people require the following:

- a high level of skill, more than many of the more popular fields of practice

- a broad knowledgebase of human behavior

- ability to become a specialist and generalist

- ability to interact with all age groups

- interest in complexity

- expertise in preserving self-determination

- highly developed assessment, intervention, and family work skills

- ability to integrate alternative interventions (McInnis-Dittrich, 2020)

In summary, **the range of settings** in which social workers will serve older people include social service agencies, health care–focused settings with medical and skilled care provision (e.g., home health care, hospitals, hospice, palliative care) and settings considered part of the long-term care system (e.g., assisted living, nursing homes, adult day care), as well as in roles that assist older people across these settings such as integrated care and geriatric care management. In addition, specialty areas in which social workers are often needed to provide expertise include assessment and intervention with individuals experiencing depression and anxiety, dementia, substance use and misuse, and elder abuse. This chapter focuses closely on a few common areas that serve older people in which you will always find social workers: geriatric care management in community services and long-term care and hospice and palliative care.

| 10.3 | **PRACTICE ACTIVITY** |

Reflect on some of the most common stereotypes and biases that people have about older adults and list them.

1. Where do you think these come from?

2. Why do most people tend to have negative feelings about life as an older adult after age 65?

3. What can we do as a society to have a more positive and strengths-based view of aging and moving into older age?

What Is a Biopsychosocial and Spiritual Assessment?

It is important to realize that while social workers are often called on to help older people address a problem they are facing, they must first obtain a clear picture of all the aspects of a person. A clear understanding includes what is and what has not been going well. All people have strengths and challenges. **Strengths** are aspects of older people and their surroundings that have carried them through each phase of life, helped them accomplish their successes, and overcome obstacles. **Challenges** are the problems they may face that can originate within their body or mind or from the social environmental context in which they grew up or are currently living in. To develop an accurate, comprehensive picture of an older person and, therefore clues about the best ways to help them, social workers need tools to guide them. Regardless of the setting a social worker is in, an important first step in working with older people is to develop a positive, respectful rapport and conduct a **biopsychosocial spiritual assessment.**

The purpose of a biopsychosocial and spiritual assessment is to help determine a **holistic picture** of an older adult, their social supports, and their social environment. Individuals in later life have a long history that includes overcoming challenges and risks. Conducting a thorough assessment will provide indications for the social worker that will help them address the immediate problem or concern. This is often referred to as using a **strengths-based**, or **holistic approach** to assessment of needs. The domains of any assessment are broad: personal information, presenting problem or issue, the historical context of the individual, their social network, and their environment. Based on these, the social worker can develop their assessment and plan for intervention. The level of detail a social worker will need to assess within these domains, or use additional and more specific assessment or diagnostic tools, will vary based on the setting in which the social worker is assisting and the specific problem or issues the older individual is facing. The following is an example of categories that might be seen in a comprehensive biopsychosocial spiritual assessment.

I. **Identifying Information**

a. Demographic information: age, sex, ethnic group, current employment, marital or partner status, physical environment/housing: nature of living circumstances (house, apartment, group home or other shared living arrangement, unhoused); neighborhood

b. Physical health, psychological or mental health, and cognitive functioning (typical and current), social and spiritual status (typical and current)

c. Referral information: referral source (self or other), reason for referral. Other professionals or Indigenous helpers currently involved

d. Data sources used in writing this assessment: interviews with others involved (list of dates and persons), tests performed, other data used

II. **Presenting Problem**

a. Individual's thoughts and feelings about illness, treatment, and care

    b. Description of the problem and situation for which help is sought as stated by the client. Here's an example:

        1. What do we need to know about the client and family to give them the best care?

        2. How do the client and family best receive information?

        3. What is most important to the client right now and in the future? Is this different from what they perceive as important to their family?

        4. Are their past experiences related to the current challenge they are facing? How was this handled in the past?

III. Background

    a. Developmental history: from early life to present (if obtainable)

    b. Family background: description of family of origin and current family. Extent of support. Family perspective on client and client's perspective on family. Family communication patterns. Family's influence on client and intergenerational factors

    c. Cultural background

    d. Spiritual and/or religious background

    e. Health care power of attorney and supporting documents

    f. Intimate relationship history

    g. Educational and/or vocational training

    h. Employment history

    i. Military history (if applicable)

    j. Use or misuse of alcohol or drugs, self, and family

    k. Medical history (e.g., birth information, illnesses, accidents, surgery, allergies, disabilities, health problems in family, nutrition, exercise, sleep)

    l. Mental health history (e.g., previous mental health issues and treatment, hospitalizations, outcome of treatment, family mental health issues)

    m. Nodal events: specifically, deaths of significant others, serious losses or traumas, significant life achievements

IV. Assessment

    a. Primary domains when working with older clients: cognitive, emotional, social support network, functional (activities of daily living)

b. Key issue or problem from the client's perspective; from the worker's perspective

c. Client and family functioning

d. The factors, including thoughts, behaviors, personality, environmental circumstances, stressors, vulnerabilities, and needs, that seem to be contributing to the problem(s). Systems theory with the ecological perspective as a framework when identifying these factors

e. Strengths, sources of meaning, coping ability, and resources that can be mobilized to help the client

f. Client's motivation and potential to benefit from intervention

V. **Recommendations to Consider in Planning Intervention**

a. Short-term and long-term goals

b. Areas of special attention

c. Interprofessional team involvement or communication

d. Possible obstacles and approaches

Assessing an older client is the first step in providing quality care. There are certain strategies on how to assess the functioning of an older adult in greater detail than a general biopsychosocial–spiritual assessment, depending on the specific area of practice. For example, the **Handbook of Geriatric Assessment** offers extensive coverage of all areas of an older person's life that may need assessing, including physical, cognitive, mental health, substance abuse, neglect and abuse, socialness, spirituality, ability to perform daily activities, and pain assessment strategies (Gallo et al., 2006). There are also resources for advanced assessments focused on other common needs of older people such as mental health, decision-making, cognitive function, economics, and legal and future planning issues for older people. **Common assessment tool examples** from the primary domains when working with older clients include the Mini-Mental Status Exam (Folstein et al., 1975) for cognitive function, the Geriatric Depression Scale (GDS; Brink et al., 1982) for emotional function, the Lubben Social Network Scale (Lubben et al., 2006) for social support network, and the Katz Index of Activities of Daily Living (Katz, 1983) for functional assessment. In a similar vein, social work interventions greatly depend on the presenting problem when it comes to caring for older adults. At this stage of life, there are many difficulties, and focusing on the strengths of the individual can help empower them (McInnis-Dittrich, 2020). There are many resources that showcase common interventions for many geriatric challenges, including dementia and Alzheimer's, Parkinson's disease, and lack of social and emotional support (Youdin, 2014).

IMG 10.3

The Importance of Culturally Relevant Practice

Social workers who work with older adults must be familiar with the impact of **discrimination** and **oppression of older people** and their caregivers, support systems, and communities. They must understand the **intersectionality** of multiple identities and characteristics beyond age that occur due to diversity and structural inequalities throughout the life course. Social workers must show competence in the ability to do the following:

- Appraise their own values related to diversity and aging

- Analyze how social determinants of health, diversity and oppression impact older clients and supports

- Address social, cultural, and spiritual histories, values, and beliefs of older clients and supports

- Explain and defend the impact of structural inequalities and value of diversity of older people within the interprofessional teams, communities, and organizations that they work (Council on Social Work Education Specialized Practice Curricular Guide for Gero Social Work Practice, 2015)

Community Social Services

Community social service agencies provide a wide range of counseling, advocacy, case management, and preventative- and protective-related services to older people. They are often considered part of the aging network encouraged by funding from the OAA and its area agencies on aging. These are often housed in either government-established organizations or nonprofit organizations or in sectarian organizations such as Lutheran Social Services, Jewish Family Services, Catholic Social Services, and so on. Older people can be referred to social service agencies in several ways but typically because of a concern for an older person's health, mental health, or physical safety. Services provided at social service agencies address a wide variety of needs—for example, nutritional programs (meal delivery or meals provided at a site), housing (emergency or low income), employment services, care management, counseling on benefit and eligibility for insurance and services, veteran focused services, and mental health therapy.

Long-Term Care

Long-term care describes the broad array of services designed to meet a person's health or personal care needs for a short or long period of time. The intent is for older individuals to live as **safely and independently** as is feasible when they can no longer conduct everyday activities on their own. Long-term care services can be provided in one's home, a community-based setting, or in a facility, such as nursing home. According to NASW (2003), "The principal components of social work services in long-term care settings are designed to provide assessment, treatment, rehabilitation, and supportive care, and to preserve and enhance social functioning. Service provision requires a unique combination of physical, psychological, and social interventions and family support, the goal of which is to promote an optimal level of psychological, physical, and social functioning" (page 5, para. 2).

The role of social workers supporting the care of older adults leads to unique opportunities, which often involve the creation of meaningful and supportive connections with clients and their families and/or families of choice, facilitating change in problematic systems at both the individual and community levels. In **residential care settings**, social workers conduct intake assessments to determine patients' mental, emotional, and social needs; work in partnership with a team of medical doctors, nurses, psychologists, case managers, and other health care staff to create, implement, and regularly update patient treatment plans as needs change over time. They also involve, as appropriate, older adults' families, partners, and/or friends in discussing treatment plan options, such as a plan to eventually transition to a new setting, such as return home. Social workers in residential care settings are often in charge of coordinating transitions related to planning a successful discharge and ensuring a sustainable plan post discharge.

Caregivers, both formal and informal, are an essential aspect of the long-term care system. They are an important focus of assessment and treatment for gerontological social workers. Formal caregivers refer to those who provide care through an agency. **Informal care givers** are those who are not paid and provide care out of a social relationship and are most often a family member, most commonly a partner/spouse or adult child. Family caregivers have been referred to as "the backbone" of the long-term care support system (Office of the Assistant Secretary for Planning and Evaluation, n.d.), because they are typically the reason older adults are able to remain at home, which prevents physical and mental health challenges and contributes to higher quality of life. If it wasn't for informal caregivers, costs of care would skyrocket to an inordinate amount. Many resources exist for family caregivers, such as the National Family Caregiver Support Program (https://acl. gov/programs/support-caregivers/national-family-caregiver-support-program), the National Alliance for Caregiving (https://www.caregiving.org/), and family caregiving resources at the AARP

What Does a Day in the Life of a Geriatric Care Manager Look Like?

By Roslyn Paine, a geriatric care manager for Rocky Mountain Senior Solutions, LLC (https://rmseniorsolutions.com/)

Imagine walking into a situation in which an older adult can no longer live on their own but does not want to give up their independence. This is one of many typical scenarios encountered in my job. The older adult client has their own opinion of where they want to live, and the family often has another. So, what is my role? I must listen to both sides, assess the situation, and advocate for the client. Of course, safety is the most important thing to consider. Can they live safely in their own home? Do they need supplemental home care services? Are they still driving? Do they have family or other support systems living close by?

Many geriatric care managers have a social work or nursing background. They often have a master's-level education and have become specialized in the field of gerontology, either through work experience or certification. The services geriatric care managers provide include the following:

- providing an in-home assessment and care plan

- assisting families with long distance care management

- crisis intervention

- collaborating with hospice and other medical professionals to manage patient care

- monitoring client's care in a facility

- assisting with moving an older adult from their home to assisted living/memory care

- providing referrals to other agencies (i.e., Meals on Wheels, adult day centers, home care agencies, hospice, support groups, etc.)

Caregiver stress and family conflict are issues that come up frequently. Often by the time a family consults a geriatric care manager they are overwhelmed. Consultations are frequently the result of a fall or recent hospital visit, and the family realizes their loved one can no longer continue to live independently. Becoming familiar with the challenges of Alzheimer's or other dementia is also important as many clients in the moderate to advanced stages of dementia cannot live independently. In addition to the initial assessment and care plan, geriatric care managers often provide ongoing support and reevaluation as the client's needs can change with time.

Geriatric care managers can work independently, be employed with home care agencies, or be part of a larger group of care managers. Many geriatric care managers belong to the Aging Life Care Association (https://www.aginglifecare.org//). This organization provides continuing education, conferences, business, and marketing resources for care managers and publications so that its members stay informed of the most relevant news and information for the profession.

Geriatric care management services are not covered by insurance and are mostly private pay. On occasion long-term care insurance may cover care coordination, but it is much more common for the family and client to pay for services. There is often one fee for the initial assessment and then an hourly rate is charged for ongoing support needs.

A geriatric care manager should be detail oriented, knowledgeable of resources for older adults in their community, and be a strong advocate for their client. They should also work well under pressure during a crisis and have a calm approach when family conflicts arise. Working with older adults is very rewarding. There is so much that can be done to improve their quality of life and provide peace of mind to their families.

Palliative and Hospice Social Work

Palliative care is specialized health care and therapeutic interventions for people living with a serious illness. It is focused on providing relief from the symptoms and stress of the illness rather than treatments focused on cure. The goal is to improve quality of life for both the patient and the family. **Palliative care social workers** support individuals and their supports, including families coping with serious illness and facing mortality, the dying process, and bereavement. Palliative care social workers have a distinctive role to help people identify and address changes that come with serious and life-limiting illnesses and existential questions and contemplations about relationships and life meaning. **Hospice social workers** focus on palliative care that is specialized to support individuals and their supports at the end of life. **End-of-life care** refers to a multidimensional assessment and interventions provided to assist individuals and their supports as they approach end of life. Whether sudden or expected, the end of a person's life is a unique experience that has a great impact on the person, social and family systems with whom that are connected, and their legacy. The scope of social work in palliative and end of-life care extends across many practice settings and populations and requires intervention at the individual, family, group, community, and organizational levels. While palliative and hospice care are widely available to people at any age, the largest portion of the people served are over the age of 65 years old.

Beyond the regular engagement, assessments, and interventions that all gerontological social workers might perform, "essential skills for effective palliative and end of life care include:

- the ability to recognize signs and symptoms of impending death and prepare family
- members in a manner that is guided by clinical assessment
- competence in facilitating communication among clients, family members, and members
- of the care team
- competence in integrating grief theories into practice
- competence in determining appropriate interventions based on the assessment
- competence in advocating for clients, family members, and caregivers for needed services, including pain management
- competence in navigating a complex network of resources and making appropriate linkages for clients and family members
- competence in supporting clients, families, and caregivers including anticipatory mourning, grief, bereavement, and follow-up services.

Interventions commonly provided by social workers in palliative and end of life care include:

- individual counseling and psychotherapy (including addressing the cognitive behavioral interventions)
- family counseling
- family-team conferencing
- crisis counseling
- information and education
- multidimensional interventions regarding symptom management

---

10.4   PRACTICE ACTIVITY

A lot of people have fears about dying and being at the end of their life. As described, an important area of practice for social workers who work with older adults is providing end-of-life care in hospice and palliative care settings.

1. Is this an area of practice that you could see yourself working in? Why or why not?

2. Do some research on Death with Dignity laws, which allow critically ill people to end their life with the assistance of a physician under certain circumstances. Learn how many states currently have these laws. Do you support laws like this? Why or why not?

- support groups, bereavement groups
- case management and discharge planning
- decision making and the implications of various treatment alternatives
- resource counseling (including caregiving resources; alternate level of care options such as long-term care or hospice care; financial and legal needs; advance directives; and permanency planning for dependents)
- client advocacy/navigation of systems." (NASW, 2004, para. page 20-21)

Gerontological Case Study

Mr. Howard is an 82-year-old Black male who was diagnosed with Parkinson's disease 3 years ago. He lives with his wife independently in a retirement community, where they've owned a condo for over 10 years and live close to some of their lifelong friends. Mr. Howard is a retired professor from a well-respected university in a city not far from where they live. Mrs. Howard is a retired schoolteacher and is in good health, as she manages her diabetes carefully. They have three children in their late 50s and early 60s, seven grandchildren, and four great-grandchildren. Since his diagnosis with Parkinson's, Mr. Howard has experienced worsening of symptoms and has trouble managing his pain. Mrs. Howard reports to the Parkinson's doctor that Mr. Howard needs more assistance with walking, has more frequent episodes of uncontrolled shaking, and has grown more forgetful. She worries about him falling but is very concerned about talking with him about this because he is very proud. Mr. Howard often resists telling his children about his changing symptoms, stating he doesn't want to be a disruption to their very busy, successful careers and social lives. The Parkinson's care team has asked the social worker to meet with Mr. Howard after some recent tests reveal more decline, indicating the couple may need to plan for additional specialized care for Mr. Howard to properly manage his symptoms and to function safely and successfully at home.

Questions

1. What are the strengths of this situation?

2. What are the initial steps the palliative care social worker could take to better understand this older person's and their family members' needs at the micro or clinical practice level? Be very specific.

3. How can the palliative care social worker be culturally responsive in this case?

4. What questions or feelings are raised for you as you imagine working with this older person and his family?

▌ Policy Focus: Affordable Housing and Medicaid

For many decades, **long-term support services (LTSS)** and **affordable housing programs** for older people have largely been separate programs. There is an enormous gap in housing needs for both older people who receive LTSS and the need for senior housing. A new initiative is taking hold in which a few states are testing a transformation in how LTSS and housing programs are provided. This initiative tackles some of the major challenges facing older adults, namely health inequities, economic security and work, adapting to health changes, access to a livable environment, health, and mental health care. As is well known in the literature, addressing the housing, nutrition, transportation, and other social needs of older people can significantly affect health outcomes. The Center on Budget and Policy Priorities notes that even though Medicaid can't pay for these types of services directly, they can support enrollees in other innovative ways (Katch, 2020). States seeking to improve Medicaid beneficiaries' health and limit unnecessary health care spending are increasingly focusing on how they can ensure that beneficiaries can obtain these services. One public policy paper examined how three states have implemented programs that address the needs of Medicaid and state funded beneficiaries by intentionally integrating housing with home and community-based services (HCBS), thus providing a streamlined processes for addressing needs. This has, in most cases, reduced the frequency of moving

IMG 10.4

to a higher cost environment. Some observations contributing to the success of these shifts were better efficiency and effectiveness of care coordination, collaboration and better communication among housing and support service providers, increased opportunities for aging in place, and resident participation in high rates. One downside was with less concentration of skilled need, providers may not be as likely to provide services on site. Innovative new approaches like these can lead to a "win-win" by increasing quality of life for older adults and decreasing higher skilled needs and costs (Stone et al., 2022). In this case a macro-level social worker may be employed at a public policy institute and work with lobbyists to advocate for additional policies that remove barriers and create financial incentives for other states to replicate these programs and evaluate the outcomes.

Research Focus: Social Isolation and Older People

Gerontological social work researchers study many aspects of the issues facing older adults and their supports today. From **dementia research** that examines the best ways to support individuals and supports throughout disease progression to **policy research** that explores the best way to transform the long-term care system to address health disparities in older populations, social work researchers can be found contributing to the knowledge base that guides our profession. **Aging research organizations** employing social work researchers can be found in schools and colleges of social work, health systems, and nationwide institutes such as the National Institute on Aging (https://www.nia.nih.gov/) and Gerontological Society of America (https://www.geron.org/). There are also private grant funders invested in researching and implementing programming for vulnerable older adults, such as the AARP Foundation.

An important topic relevant to older people is **social isolation**. It is estimated that between 10% and 17% of older adults over 65 are socially isolated (Dickens et al., 2011; Findlay & Cartwright, 2002; Iliffe et al., 2007). Social isolation is a known risk factor for poor physical and mental health (Berg & Cassells, 1992; Cacioppo & Hawkley, 2003; Crooks et al., 2008; Findlay & Cartwright, 2002; Iliffe et al., 2007). These negative effects are most pronounced among older adults and poor and minority populations—the fastest growing groups in the country. Although the health risks are known, less is known about how to identify those who become socially isolated, why, and the best ways to prevent isolation and the related negative effects (Retrum & Elder, 2012).

Social isolation and loneliness for older adults occurs due to a variety of inter-related factors that exist at the individual, community, and societal levels. The relationship between **risk factors** (e.g., living alone) and **protective factors** (e.g., a strong social network), along with an individual's social context and history, can help pinpoint how and why isolation occurs. It is essential that social workers understand the distinction between social isolation as it relates to social connections and resources as opposed the perception of feeling lonely. There are many older people who have very few social connections who are happy, content, and healthy, while there are many older adults who don't fit the definition of being social isolated yet feel desperately alone and unhappy and experience health risks.

The National Academies of Sciences, Engineering, and Medicine are three academies that work together to organize and fuel research and recognize outstanding knowledge development. They engage in independent, objective analysis and provide advice to the United States to address complex problems and determine promising policy solutions. The National Academies formed a **Committee on Health and Medical Dimensions of Social Isolation and Loneliness in Older Adults** in fall 2018. The committee was charged with summarizing the known evidence for the social isolation and loneliness impact on health and quality of life in individuals over 50. They were particularly interested in vulnerable groups such as low-income, underserved, and at-risk populations due to health inequities. The committee also was tasked with identifying opportunities for health care clinical settings to reduce the **negative impacts of social isolation and loneliness**. After the work of the committee was complete, the National Academies published *Consensus Study Report, Social Isolation and Loneliness in Older Adults, Opportunities of the Health Care System* that makes recommendations based on five overarching "Goals for Enhancing the Roles of the Health Care Sector in Addressing the Impacts of Social Isolation and Loneliness in Older Adults:

1. **Develop a more robust evidence base** for effectives assessment, prevention, and intervention strategies for social isolation and loneliness;

2. **Translate current research into health care practices** in order to reduce the negative impacts of social isolation and loneliness;

3. **Improve awareness** of the health and medical impacts of social isolation and loneliness across the health care workforce and among members of the public;

4. **Strengthen ongoing education and training** related to social isolation and loneliness in older adults for the health care workforce; and

5. **Strengthen ties between the health care system and community-based networks and resources** that address social isolation and loneliness in older adults." (National Academies of Sciences, Engineering, and Medicine, 2020, p. 5)

In sum, detailed recommendations included increasing funding from government and private grant making entities to invest in research on the relationship between **social connectivity** and mortality, health (accounting for risk factors), and clinical and public health interventions, with a close eye on use of distinct and quality measures of different types of isolation and diverse populations, unique risk factors, replicability, and scalability (National Academies of Sciences, Engineering, and Medicine, 2020). The hope is that social work researchers will continue to engage with health care systems and communities across the country to follow these recommendations. An example of how social worker clinicians have taken this forward was work on a team that tested a new **telehealth intervention** addressing COVID-19, which was found to be effective and indicated areas of needed improvements for an older population of veterans (Weiskittle et al., 2022).

Chapter Summary

People are living so much longer these days; it is changing our social landscape and creates an increased need for social work expertise in working with this population. Social work practitioners who work with older individuals work in a wide variety of settings and must see the potential strengths and positive aspects of growing old in addition to the health declines and inevitable changes seen as negative. Social workers need to learn the skills and have knowledge of the psychological, social, and cultural factors influencing older people and their ability to adapt to changes. There is a great deal a variability among older adults on how they are impacted by and their adaptability to health and mental health changes. This difference exists within and between groups of older people from racial, ethnic, and geographic locations and socioeconomic backgrounds. At the heart of all gerontological social work practice is conducting a thorough and thoughtful biopsychosocial–spiritual assessment upon which to determine ways to support older adults in the ways they seek support. This chapter focuses closely on a few common areas that serve older people in which you will always find social workers: geriatric care management in community services and long-term care and hospice and palliative care. There are important competencies social workers must strive for to be successful in working with older people, and the work with this population can be extremely rewarding, interesting, challenging, and fun.

Discussion Questions

1. Describe ageism and the consequences it has for society and older people. Provide examples of how ageist perspectives can negatively impact the individual and family as well as the community.

2. Explore your values and beliefs about aging. How could this impact your approach to working with a variety of older people experiencing challenges?

3. We are facing an aging society that has effects for social workers in the United States and across the world. What are some things micro-level social workers need to think about to prepare? What macro-level approaches are needed?

4. When you read about statistics related to aging trends, what was your initial reaction? Were these reactions of fear, curiosity, or elation? Or something different?

5. What aspects of social work with older adults in this chapter surprised you? What aspects do you think you may enjoy the most? What aspects are you not so sure of?

References

Ayalon, L., Chasteen, A., Diehl, M., Levy, B. R., Neupert, S. D., Rothermund, K., Tesch-Römer, C. & Wahl, H. W. (2021). Aging in times of the COVID-19 pandemic: Avoiding ageism and fostering intergenerational solidarity. *The Journals of Gerontology: Series B, 76*(2), e49–e52.

Beltran, S., & Miller, C. (2021). Social work graduates entering the field of gerontology during COVID-19: Exploring perceived readiness and needs. *Innovation in Aging, 5*(1), 390.

Berg, R. L., & Cassells, J. S. (1992). Social Isolation Among Older Individuals The Relationship to Mortality and Morbidity The Second Fifty Years: Promoting Health and Preventing Disability: The National Academies Press, Division of Health Promotion Disease Prevention Institute of Medicine.

Brink, T. L., Yesavage, J. A., Lum, O., Heersema, P. H., Adey, M., & Rose, T. L. (1982). Screening tests for geriatric depression. *Clinical Gerontologist, 1*(1), 37–43.

Cacioppo, J. T., & Hawkley, L. C. (2003). Social isolation and health, with an emphasis on underlying mechanisms. Perspectives in Biology and Medicine, 46(3), S39-S52.

Centers for Medicare & Medicaid Services (2023). Marketplace 2023 Open Enrollment Period Report: National Snapshot #3. https://www.cms.gov/newsroom/press-releases/nearly-16-million-people-have-signed-affordable-health-coverage-aca-marketplaces-start-open

Colello, K. J., & Napili, A. (2021). *Older Americans Act: Overview and funding.* Congressional Research Service. https://crsreports.congress.gov/product/pdf/R/R43414

Council on Social Work Education Specialized Practice Curricular Guide for Gero Social Work Practice (2015) EPAS Curricular Guide Resource Series ISBN 978-0-87293-186-2,

https://www.cswe.org/CSWE/media/GeroEdResources/Gero_Guide_WEB_final_
NewSite.pdf

Cox, C. (2020). Older adults and COVID 19: Social justice, disparities, and social work practice. *Journal of Gerontological Social Work, 63*(6–7), 611–624.

Crooks, V. C., Lubben, J., Petitti, D. B., Little, D., & Chiu, V. (2008). Social network, cognitive function, and dementia incidence among elderly women. American Journal of Public Health, 98(7), 1221.

Dickens, A. P., Richards, S. H., Greaves, C. J., & Campbell, J. L. (2011). Interventions targeting social isolation in older people: a systematic review.

Dushi, I., & Trenkamp, B. (2021). *Improving the measurement of retirement income of the aged population* (ORES Working Paper No. 116). Social Security Administration. https://www.ssa.gov/policy/docs/workingpapers/wp116.html, https://www.ssa.gov/news/press/factsheets/basicfact-alt.pdf

Federal Interagency Forum on Aging-Related Statistics. (2020). *Older Americans 2020: Key indicators of well-being.* https://agingstats.gov

Findlay, R. A., & Cartwright, C. (2002). Social Isolation & Older People: A Literature Review Report for Seniors Interest Branch & Ministerial Advisory Council on Older People, Queensland Government: The University of Queensland, Australian Centre On Ageing.

Folstein, M. F., Folstein, S. E., & McHugh, P. R. (1975). "Mini-mental state": A practical method for grading the cognitive state of patients for the clinician. *Journal of Psychiatric Research, 12*(3), 189–198.

Gallo, J. J., Fulmer, T., Bogner, H. R., & Paveza, G. J. (2006). *Handbook of Geriatric Assessment.* Jones and Bartlett Publishers.

Gawande, A. (2014). *Being mortal: Medicine and what matters in the end.* Metropolitan Books.

Gee, E. M. (2002). Misconceptions and misapprehensions about population ageing. *International Journal of Epidemiology, 31*, 750–753. https://doi.org/10.1093/ije/31.4.750

Hulko, W., Brotman, S., Stern, L., & Ferrer, I. (2019). *Gerontological social work in action: Anti-oppressive practice with older adults, their families, and communities.* Taylor & Francis.

Iliffe, S., Kharicha, K., Harari, D., Swift, C., Gillmann, G., & Stuck, A. E. (2007). Health risk appraisal in older people 2: the implications for clinicians and commissioners of social isolation risk in older people. British Journal of General Practice, 57(537), 277-282.

Institute of Medicine. (2013, January). U.S. health in international perspective: Shorter lives, poorer health (Institute of Medicine Report Brief). Retrieved from http://www.nationalacademies.org/hmd/Reports /2013/US-Health-in-International-Perspective-Shorter-Lives-Poorer-Health.aspx

Katch, H. (2020). *Medicaid can partner with housing providers and others to address enrollees' social needs.* Center on Budget and Policy Priorities. https://www.cbpp.org/research/health/medicaid-can-partner-with-housing-providers-and-others-to-address-enrollees-social

Katz, S. (1983). Assessing self-maintenance: Activities of daily living, mobility, and instrumental activities of daily living. *Journal of the American Geriatrics Society*, 31(12), 721–727. https://doi.org/10.1111/j.1532-5415.1983.tb03391.x

Levy, B. R., Slade, M. D., Chang, E. S., Kannoth, S., & Wang, S. Y. (2020). Ageism amplifies cost and prevalence of health conditions. *The Gerontologist*, 60(1), 174–181.

Lubben, J., Blozik, E., Gillmann, G., Iliffe, S., von Renteln Kruse, W., Beck, J. C., & Stuck, A. E. (2006). Performance of an abbreviated version of the Lubben Social Network Scale among three European community-dwelling older adult populations. *The Gerontologist*, 46(4), 503–513.

McInnis-Dittrich, K. (2020). *Social work with older adults: A biopsychosocial approach to assessment and intervention* (5th ed.). Allyn & Bacon.

Mehrotra, C. M., & Wagner, L. S. (2018). *Aging and diversity: An active learning experience.* Routledge.

National Academies of Sciences, Engineering, and Medicine. (2020). *Social isolation and loneliness in older adults: Opportunities for the health care system*. National Academies Press.

National Association of Social Workers. (2003). NASW standards for social work services in long-term care facilities. National Association of Social Workers. https://www.socialworkers.org/LinkClick.aspx?fileticket=cwW7lzBfYxg%3D&portalid=0

National Association of Social Workers. (2004). *Standards for palliative & end of life care.* https://www.socialworkers.org/LinkClick.aspx?fileticket=xBMd58VwEhk%3D&portalid=0

National Institute on Minority Health and Health Disparities. (2022, September 30). Minority health and health disparities: Definitions and parameters. https://www.nimhd.nih.gov/about/overview/

Odlum, M., Moise, N., Kronish, I. M., Broadwell, P., Alcántara, C., Davis, N. J., Cheung, Y.K.K., Perotte, A, and & Yoon, S. (2020). Trends in poor health indicators among Black and Hispanic middle-aged and older adults in the United States, 1999–2018. *JAMA Network Open*, 3(11), e2025134.

Office of the Assistant Secretary for Planning and Evaluation. (n.d.). *Family caregivers: Our heroes on the frontlines of long-term care.* https://aspe.hhs.gov/family-caregivers-our-heroes-frontlines-long-term-care#:~:text=Family%20and%20informal%20caregivers%20are,care%20for%20millions%20of%20Americans

Oliveira, M. R., Sudati, I. P., Konzen, V. D. M., de Campos, A. C., Wibelinger, L. M., Correa, C., Moraes Miguel, F, Nunes Silva, R., & Borghi-Silva, A. (2021). COVID-19 and the impact on the physical activity level of elderly people: A systematic review. *Experimental Gerontology*, 159, 111675.

Parlapani, E., Holeva, V., Nikopoulou, V. A., Kaprinis, S., Nouskas, I., & Diakogiannis, I. (2021). A review on the COVID-19-related psychological impact on older adults: Vulnerable or not? *Aging Clinical and Experimental Research*, 33(6), 1729–1743.

Retrum, J. H., & Elder, K. (2012). Framework for Isolation in Adults Over 50: AARP Foundation.

Robertson, A. (1991). The politics of Alzheimer's disease: A case study in apocalyptic demography. In M. Minkler & C. Estes (Eds.), *Critical perspectives on aging: The political and moral economy of growing old* (pp. 135–152). Baywood.

Shelton, R. L., Hall, M., Ford, S., & Cosby, R. L. (2021). Telehealth in a Washington, DC African American religious community at the onset of COVID-19: showcasing a virtual health ministry project. *Social Work in Health Care, 60*(2), 208–223.SAGE & National Resource Center on LGBT Aging. (2023). Facts on LGBT aging. https://www.sageusa.org/wp-content/uploads/2021/03/sage-lgbt-aging-facts-final.pdf

Stone, R., Sanders, A., Harrell, R., and Guzman, S. (2022) *Increasing independent living choices through coordinating affordable housing and Medicaid: Housing as an indicator in the 2020 long-term services and supports state scorecard.* AARP Public Policy Institute, https://www.aarp.org/content/dam/aarp/ppi/2022/10/increasing-independent-living-choices-through-coordinating-affordable-housing-medicaid-2020-long-term-services-supports-state-scorecard.doi.10.26419-2fppi.-%2000173.001.pdf

Teater, B., Chonody, J. M., & Davis, N. (2021). Risk and protective factors of loneliness among older adults: The significance of social isolation and quality and type of contact. *Social Work in Public Health, 36*(2), 128–141. U.S. Department of Health & Human Services. (2023). *Home page.* www.hhs.gov

U.S. Bureau of Labor Statistics. (2023). *Occupational Outlook Handbook, social workers.* https://www.bls.gov/ooh/community-and-social-service/social-workers.htm

U.S. Department of Health & Human Services, Centers for Disease Control and Prevention. (2022). *Social determinants of health at CDC.* https://www.cdc.gov/about/sdoh/index.html

Weiskittle, R., Tsang, W., Schwabenbauer, A., Andrew, N., & Mlinac, M. (2022). Feasibility of a COVID-19 rapid response telehealth group addressing older adult worry and social isolation. *Clinical Gerontologist, 45*(1), 129–143.

World Health Organization. (2023). Ageing. Overview. https://www.who.int/health-topics/ageing#tab=tab_1

Youdin, R. (2014). Clinical Gerontological Social Work Practice, Springer Publishing Company.

Credits

CHAPTER 11

Social Work Practice in Criminal Justice and Legal Settings

Learning Objectives

After reading this chapter, students will be able to do the following:

- Summarize the biggest social problems involving crime and violence in the United States

- Define forensic social work and describe the tensions that exist between the criminal justice and social work fields due to differences in professional values

- Describe the criminal justice system, including the three main components

- Identify three major career path options for social workers who want to work in criminal justice and legal settings

- Evaluate federal public policies that seek to reduce hate crimes in the United States

- Summarize research findings on restorative justice practices that are used in the field of criminal justice

- Explain the various ways that systemic racism in the criminal justice system has impacted communities of color and the impact of the Black Lives Matter social movement in creating change regarding this social problem

- Evaluate goodness of fit with social work practice with children and families as a potential future career option

Natasha Mitchell, MSW

My name is Natasha Mitchell, and I have a 25-year career working in the criminal justice system—specifically the juvenile justice system. I was drawn to the field as a result of my upbringing, as is the case with most social workers. I was raised in a particular background that most social scientists considered "high risk" (i.e., single-mother household, low income, latchkey kid, urban neighborhood). Given the "high-risk" label that was attached to me, I beat the odds but witnessed some of my family and friends fall prey. It was my goal very early on to work with kids from similar backgrounds in some capacity.

I obtained an undergraduate degree in sociology with an emphasis in crime and delinquency. My first job after earning my undergraduate was a counselor at an all-girls treatment facility. It was an entry-level direct care position with the responsibility to oversee their structured programming (e.g., education, recreation, treatment groups, etc.) and engage them in activities (e.g., reading, writing, watching television, playing board games). I continued my career in similar positions at a variety of detention and treatment facilities working with male and female youth. Eventually, my career transitioned away from direct care services to managerial positions that involved supervising programs and employees, which I found just as rewarding as working with the youth. I ended my tenure within criminal justice institutions in a role that was further removed from the youth and required implementing programming and policies intended to prevent incidents of sexual abuse and sexual harassment, ensuring there was an appropriate response if the facility/agency received allegations of sexual abuse or sexual harassment and advocating on behalf of the youth if they were involved in an incident that violated the sexual safety policies.

It is my opinion that a criminal justice social worker offers the person compassion, has the ability to view the individual holistically, understands the impact that life experiences and trauma has on an individual, and has the ability to develop a relationship on a heart level to propel the individual to recognize their own strengths. In the past, the presence of criminal justice social workers was limited to providing group and individual treatment. More recently there has been an increase in the number of criminal justice social workers who are beginning to influence policies and programs. These recent changes can be attributed to the call from social workers and social justice advocates for a move away from a correctional or punitive model to a more therapeutic and rehabilitative model criminal justice system.

I returned to school 15 years after working in the field to obtain a master's degree in social work. Once I obtained my master's degree, I intended to remain within the juvenile justice system as a therapist; however, life had other plans, and I'm so thankful for that! I am currently involved in very interesting and rewarding work as a forensic social worker. Forensic social work was initially introduced to the field as part of death penalty mitigation teams (e.g., defense attorney, paralegal, legal researcher, investigator, social worker). The forensic social worker provides expertise in collecting complete social histories and providing support for people under the threat of execution. However, the work has expanded to all criminal cases (felony and misdemeanor) that involve minors and adults. The forensic social worker participates on the multidisciplinary mitigation team to achieve a fair sentence if there is a conviction/adjudication. The social worker's primary role is to develop the person's story and make the story a part of the defense.

I love being a social worker for so many reasons, but the main reason is the limitless opportunities that we have to influence the world. If you are interested in a career as a forensic social worker, check with your local public defender's office for internship opportunities.

Criminal justice is one of the oldest fields of practice for social workers in the United States, despite the tensions that have existed between the social work profession and the criminal justice system due to differences in values and ideology. Social workers who work in this field must sort out the tension between being an **agent of social control** versus an **agent of social support**. Despite these challenges, social workers bring vital skills, values, and knowledge to this field in their efforts to facilitate change with client systems at the micro and mezzo level and systemic change at the macro level. Social workers interested in this area of practice, which is more commonly referred to as **forensic social work**, can choose to work with offenders or victims of crime, children or adults, and throughout various parts of the criminal justice system, which includes law enforcement, corrections, and the courts.

At a macro level, social workers have been focused on a number of disturbing problems that involve the criminal justice system such as **police brutality** against communities of color and **mass shootings**, which have prompted serious debate over the need for federal gun control legislation to address the high prevalence of gun violence in the United States. The U.S. criminal justice system is a controversial system that has faced serious criticisms over the years due to its practice of **mass incarceration**, allegations of **systemic racism** and unequal treatment toward Black, Indigenous, and People of Color (BIPOC), the criminalization of those with mental illness, and its emphasis on punishment over rehabilitation. Calls for criminal justice reform have been taken more seriously by lawmakers of both parties in recent years to address these systemic challenges. One emerging model is to imbed social workers in police departments to help police officers better respond to cases of family violence, suicidal ideation, and cases in which law enforcement responds to persons with serious mental illness, though some argue that this should be carefully considered to ensure that social workers who work with police stay true to their primary mission and values.

IMG 11.1

Overview of the U.S. Criminal Justice System

As shown in Table 11.1, there are three major components of the criminal justice system: law enforcement (federal, state, and local), the judiciary (federal and state courts), and corrections (state and federal correctional systems; prisons, probation, parole).

TABLE 11.1   Three Major Components of the Adult Criminal Justice System

Law enforcement	When someone breaks the law, they typically encounter law enforcement officers first. This includes police officers, sheriffs, detectives, deputies, state troopers, and federal government agents (e.g., Federal Bureau of Investigations [FBI], Drug Enforcement Agency [DEA], border patrol)
Judiciary	It is the role of the court system to decide whether a defendant is guilty or innocent of the charges brought against them. Those involved in this system are judges, prosecutors, defense attorneys, and juries.
Corrections	This part of the system is charged with punishment and sentencing and includes prisons (incarceration), probation, and parole. Those who work in this system include corrections officers, parole officers, and probation officers.

Due to differing views and ideological positions regarding crime and punishment in our society, not everyone agrees on what the overall goals or purpose of the criminal justice system should be. But they usually include some combination of the following:

- preventing crime

- protecting public safety

- promoting social order

- punishing those who commit crimes (i.e., justice for victims)

- rehabilitating offenders so that they can become safe and contributing members of society after they are released from the criminal justice system

There has always been tension between whether the primary goal of the criminal justice should be punishment or rehabilitation, or some combination of both. Political conservatives have typically fallen on the "tough on crime" side of the spectrum with a primary emphasis on punishment, while those on the left have typically supported an approach that includes treatment for offenders. Social workers also strongly support rehabilitation for offenders who can be rehabilitated as well as funding to support preventative programs.

- **Punishment**: This approach relies on the idea that the best way to prevent crime is through punishment.

- **Rehabilitation**: This approach relies on the perspective that the best way to prevent crime is to offer treatment (e.g., therapy, substance abuse treatment, job skills, life skills, education) that allows offenders to change their behavior with the goal of preventing recidivism (i.e., reoffending).

11.1   PRACTICE ACTIVITY

Visit the website of one of the following organizations: The Sentencing Project, the National Institute for Criminal Justice Reform, The Innocence Project, the Equal Justice Initiative, Sandy Hook Promise, Everytown for Gun Safety, or the Southern Poverty Law Center.

1.   What issues are they working to address currently?

2.   Would you be interested in working for one of these organizations? Why or why not?

3.   What organizations in your city or state are working on issues such as police brutality, gun violence, and/or efforts to decrease mass incarceration?

Overview of the Larger Social Problem: Criminal Behavior and Violence

Americans typically think about crime in two major categories—**violent crime** and **nonviolent crime**, and for obvious reasons, most people have heightened concerns over acts of violent crime. Table 11.2 highlights four major categories of crime. Based on crime statistics from the FBI and the Bureau of Justice Statistics (BJS), we know that both violent crime and property crime fell significantly between 1993 and 2019. FBI data shows that violent crime decreased by 49% while property crime decreased by 55%. The data from BJS showed even starker decreases during this same time period—74% and 71%, respectively (Gramlich, 2020). It is important to note that these sources collect their data using different methods. However, despite this data most Americans tend to perceive that crime is up even when the data shows the opposite is true (Gramlich, 2020). According to FBI data, we also know that property crime is much more common than violent crime; in 2019, there were a total of 2,109.9 property crimes per 100,000 people, compared with 379.4 violent crimes per 100,000 people (Gramlich, 2020).

However, concerning crime data reported by the Centers for Disease Control and Prevention (CDC; and aligned with FBI data) emerged during the pandemic, which showed that the murder rate in the United States rose 30% between 2019 and 2020, and that this was the highest increase in a single year in more than a century. FBI data showed that aggravated assault rose 12% during this same time period (Gramlich, 2021b). According to Gramlich (2021b), "Experts have pointed to a variety of potential causes, including the economic and societal changes brought on by the coronavirus pandemic and changes in police-community relations after the murder of George Floyd in Minnesota last year. But the exact reasons remain unclear" (para. 9). To put this data in a larger context, Gramlich (2021b) explains that though the serious spike in the murder rate occurred from 2019–2020, the murder rate was still lower than the murder rate in the early 1990s and that Americans are significantly more likely to die from suicide or a drug overdose than homicide.

TABLE 11.2   Major Categories of Crime

Type of Crime	Description	Examples
Violent crimes	Crimes that cause bodily (and often emotional) harm to another person	Homicide, assault, sexual violence, family violence, violent hate crimes, robbery, gun violence
Property crimes	Taking of money or property without the threat of force	Burglary; theft, including auto theft; larceny; arson
Consensual crimes or crimes against morality	These are often thought of as "victimless crimes" since there is a complainant, though this point could be up for debate	Prostitution, gambling, illegal drug use, pornography
White-collar crimes	Crimes that are committed in the context of one's place of employment	Fraud, embezzlement, money laundering

Gun Violence in the United States

Gun violence has been a hot-button political issue in the United States for many years, in part because of the high number of disturbing mass shootings in recent years such as the racist attack at a grocery store in Buffalo, New York, on May 14, 2022, during which a White 18-year-old gunman murdered 10 people, most of them Black. Ten days later another 18-year-old gunman killed 19 fourth-grade children and two teachers and injured 17 people at an elementary school in Uvalde, Texas. This was the deadliest **school shooting** since the mass shooting at Sandy Hook Elementary School in Newtown, Connecticut, during which 20 children and six staff members were killed on December 14, 2012. On June 5, 2022, National Public Radio published an article titled, "22 weeks into the year, America has already seen at least 246 mass shootings," an average of 11 mass shootings a week in 2022. This compares to 692 mass shootings in 2021 and 610 in 2020 (Ahmed, 2022). While there is no single definition of a **mass shooting**, most experts, such as the Gun Violence Archive, consider a mass shooting to involve an incident where at least four people are shot or killed, not including the shooter.

IMG 11.2

According to the Pew Research Center (Gramlich, 2022), which did an analysis of FBI and CDC data, 45,222 Americans died in 2020 from **gun-related injuries**, more than any other year on record and an increase of 43% from a decade prior. This figure includes fatalities from murder and suicide as well as those that involved law enforcement, those that were unintentional, and those with circumstances that could not be determined. The largest proportion of gun deaths were suicides (54%), while 43% were murders. Nearly 80% of murders involved a firearm (Gramlich, 2022).

According to this report, "**Gun murders**, in particular, have climbed sharply in recent years. The 19,384 gun murders that took place in 2020 were the most since at least 1968, exceeding the previous peak of 18,253 recorded by the CDC in 1993. The 2020 total represented a 34% increase from the year before, a 49% increase over five years and a 75% increase over 10 years" (Gramlich, 2022, para. 7). There has been a lot of commentary that the **gun death rate** in the United States is much higher than other advanced nations that we get compared to, and the data bears this out. In 2016, the most recent data available for comparison purposes, the gun death rate in the United States. was 10.6 per 100,000 people compared to 2.7 in France, 2.1 in Canada, 1.0 in Australia, 0.9 in Germany, and 0.6 in Spain (Gramlich, 2022).

The need for stronger **gun control legislation** has been a politically divisive topic in the United States, with many passionate supporters of gun rights on one side and gun control advocates on the other. Many of the most ardent advocates for stronger gun control legislation are those who have been impacted by mass shootings, such as the parents of children killed in school shootings such as Sandy Hook and the high school students from Parkland, Florida, who have engaged in various forms of activism, including lobbying lawmakers, organizing March for our Lives political rallies and marches, and raising awareness social media (#NeverAgain).

According to a survey conducted by the Pew Research Center in April 2021, roughly half of Americans see gun violence as a significant problem in the United States, and 53% favor stricter gun laws (Schaeffer, 2021). However, when it comes to the specifics, some laws have wide support from people from both political parties (e.g., preventing those with mental illnesses from purchasing guns, background checks for private gun sales and gun shows), while other laws are much more divisive (e.g., federal database to track all gun sales, banning assault-style weapons; Schaeffer, 2021).

However, on June 25, 2022, President Biden signed a gun control bill into law that would expand background checks for gun buyers who are under the age of 21, provide funding to states' fund intervention programs focused on school safety and mental health, provide incentives for states to pass red flag laws that enable courts to remove a gun from those who are considered dangerous, and close the "boyfriend loophole" so that dating partners who are convicted of domestic violence cannot purchase a firearm (not just spouses). Many federal lawmakers were hoping to pass a stronger bill, but many applauded the fact that bill that was able to pass after 3 decades of gridlock in the U.S. Congress. The bill was signed into law a month after the mass shooting at an elementary school in Uvalde, Texas.

Theories of Criminal Behavior

A burning research topic for social science researchers is to better understand why some people engage in criminal behavior, and this has been studied by experts in various disciplines such as sociology, criminology, and psychology. Some refer to this as the scientific study of **deviance**, which refers to the study of people who violate the social norms, rules, and laws of society. There are two primary groupings for the theories that attempt to explain criminal behavior: individual and environmental causes.

Individual Causes

Biological theories of crime assert that the cause of criminal behavior is one's biology (e.g., genetic, hormonal, or neurological), whereas psychological theories of criminal behavior focus on one's psychological makeup as the cause (e.g., intelligence, personality, mental health disorders, and the impact of childhood trauma). This approach has been more commonly embraced in the United States by lawmakers, criminal justice professionals, and citizens, in part due to the strong societal value of individualism. Those who believe that the causes of criminal behavior are rooted in the individual focus on solutions such as punishment, substance abuse treatment, and mental health therapy.

Environmental Causes

These theories, many developed by sociologists, posit that criminal behavior is due to particular kinds of social circumstances and the impact of one's social environment. The theories would argue that those vulnerable to committing crimes are more likely to live in high poverty, high-crime neighborhoods and single-parent homes. One famous example is **Merton's strain theory of deviance**, which says that some engage in criminal behavior because this is the only way they are able to achieve society's goals of wealth and success. This theory is based on the idea that the social structure is the problem since not all members of society are given equal means to achieve societal goals due to their race and/or socioeconomic status. Solutions for those who believe that crime is caused primarily by the larger social environment include reducing poverty, instituting universal health care, and providing access to opportunity such as quality K–12 and higher education and job opportunities that pay a living wage.

SOCIAL JUSTICE SPOTLIGHT:
Racism in the U.S. Criminal Justice System

The unequal treatment of people in the criminal justice system, primarily based on race and class, has been a troubling social problem for some time and has been well documented with social science data. Two well-known and widely read books by experts have focused on **systemic racism** and the disparate treatment of People of Color in the criminal justice system. In 2014, attorney and founder of the Equal Justice Initiative, Bryan Stevenson, published a book titled *Just Mercy*, which was later made into a movie. The book tells the true story of Stevenson's work to free innocent people on death row who were wrongly convicted and address many of the problems in the criminal justice system such as children who are prosecuted as adults, system racism, various forms of abuse that prisoners endure while incarcerated, and excessive and unfair sentencing practices.

The New Jim Crow was published in 2010 by legal scholar Michelle Alexander. Recall that the Jim Crow laws that were enacted in southern states after the Civil War ended were a form a racial apartheid that sought to segregate White people from Black people, preserve White supremacy, and subjugate the rights of Black people. They were not dismantled until he 1960s when federal legislation (e.g., Civil Rights Act of 1964 and Voting Rights Act of 1965) was passed by the Lyndon Johnson administration. Ritter (2022) summarizes the primary argument that Alexander makes in her book, which is that:

> the new way that Black and Brown people are systematically subjugated in U.S. society is through the criminal justice system. She cites mounds of social science data that shows that African Americans and Latinos are incarcerated at higher rates than Whites and are given harsher sentences than Whites for the same crimes. She argues that this relegates Blacks and Latinos to a permanent second-class status because many felons find it impossible to secure employment and have basic rights taken away from them, such as voting and receiving certain social welfare benefits after they have served their time. (p. 267)

Alexander and other social scientists have documented the disproportionate impact that the **war on drugs** has had on communities of color in the United States. The federal government's war on drugs began under President Richard Nixon in the 1970s and escalated greatly under President Ronald Reagan in the 1980s. The result was a host of legislation that was passed by the U.S. Congress and state legislatures that focused on more severe punishment for drug-related crimes. Not surprisingly, this led to a huge increase in incarcerations for nonviolent drug crimes.

The United States has faced increasing criticisms over its practice of **mass incarceration**, and state and federal lawmakers have made this a public policy priority in recent years. After decades of lawmakers from both political parties being "tough in crime," today there is more bipartisan agreement that the focus should be on violent criminals, not those committing nonviolent drug offenses. The United States has the highest incarceration rate in the world and has the highest number of people behind bars (2.1 million people at the end of 2019). As a point of comparison in 2018, the United States incarcerated 639 inmates per 100,000 people compared to 131 in England and Wales, 93 in France, and 69 in Germany. However, in 2019 the incarceration rate fell to its lowest level since 1995, according to BJS data. A variety of factors explain the decrease such as a decline in violent and property crimes rates, a decline in arrests, and changes in laws and sentencing designed to decrease the number of people who are incarcerated (Gramlich, 2021a).

Capital punishment, or the death penalty, has been a hotly debated issue in the United States for many decades, and one of the main criticisms of this practice (other than the morality of the practice) is that it is racially biased. The Death Penalty Information Center (DPIC) reports data showing that defendants of color are disproportionately given a death sentence and that the vast majority of death penalty cases involve a White victim despite the fact that White and Black people are equally likely to be victims of crime. According to the author of a 2020 report by the DPIC, "The death penalty has been used to enforce racial hierarchies throughout United States history, beginning with the colonial period and continuing to this day" (Ndulue, 2020, para. 8). As of July 2022, 23 states have abolished the death penalty, many replacing it with life imprisonment with no possibility of parole. The National Association of Social Workers (NASW) does not support the practice of capital punishment.

The problem of **police brutality** that communities of color have had to endure for decades came to light in a significant way as a result of the **Black Lives Matter** social movement. Though BIPOC have experienced this for a very long time, a number of high-profile cases (e.g., Michael Brown, Eric Garner, George Floyd, Breonna Taylor, Tamir Rice) in which unarmed Black men and women were shot and killed by police officers brought this issue into the mainstream and forced Americans to confront it. After George Floyd was murdered, massive marches and protests emerged all around the world demanding changes in laws and practices by law enforcement officers.

Overview of the Juvenile Justice System

Before social work was a recognized discipline in the United States, social reformers during the progressive era began to advocate for children and attempt to convince the lawmakers of the day that children should not be served in the same criminal justice system as adults based on their vulnerable status. The settlement house workers in Chicago worked with the Chicago Bar Association and the Illinois Conference of Charities and Corrections to convince the Illinois State Legislature to create the **nation's first juvenile court in 1898** (Brownell & Roberts, 2002). This was an historic achievement. In the ensuing years, all states developed their own juvenile system.

Though there are some similarities to the adult criminal justice system, the **juvenile justice system** is distinct in both practice and philosophy. Due to the science that demonstrates that juveniles are fundamentally different from adults due to their brain development, they are not held to the same level of responsibility for their actions. This system is also much more focused on treatment and rehabilitation due to the belief that many young people can be rehabilitated and that future involvement with the criminal justice system

> **11.2   PRACTICE ACTIVITY**
>
> After reading about the argument that systemic racism is a significant problem in the criminal justice system, reflect on the following questions:
>
> 1. Should this be an issue of importance to the social work profession? How are social work ethics connected to this issue?
>
> 2. What role can social workers play in addressing this problem?
>
> 3. How has reading about this changed your views about the war on drugs, mass incarceration, and/or capital punishment?

can be prevented with the proper supports. When a young person becomes formally involved with the juvenile system, there are several potential outcomes, as shown in Table 11.3.

IMG 11.3

TABLE 11.3   Possible Outcomes for a Youth Involved With the Juvenile Justice System

Diversion or case dismissal	Diversion approaches are used when professionals feel it would be best to hold a youth accountable for their actions, but outside of the formal legal system so they can avoid having a criminal record. Empirical research supports the efficacy of this approach in reducing recidivism for many youth (Annie E. Casey Foundation, 2020b). A youth's case can be dismissed before or after adjudication (e.g., prosecutor decides not to move forward with the case; youth is found to be innocent of the charges).
Probation	When a youth is found to be guilty of their charges by the juvenile court, or enters a plea agreement, one outcome is to be placed on probation, and they must follow the requirements of their probation agreement (e.g., mandatory treatment, pay restitution, community service, etc.).
Residential placement	According to the Annie E. Casey Foundation (2020c), residential facilities for juveniles vary widely: "Some are large (100 beds or more) and some small (15 beds or fewer); some feature correctional designs that closely mirror adult prisons and some are group homes or residential treatment centers akin to the child welfare and mental health systems; some are locked and/or fenced, while some are secured only by staff; and some are operated by states, while others are operated by local governments or by private businesses or nonprofit organizations" (para. 16).

Juvenile Justice Statistics

The Office of Juvenile Justice and Delinquency Prevention collects data on juveniles who are charged with criminal law violations. In 2019, juvenile courts handled 722,600 delinquency cases. Person offense cases accounted for the largest proportion (33%), followed by property offense cases (30%), public order offense cases (24%), and drug offense cases (13%). Their data shows the number of delinquency cases declined 56% between 2005 and 2019, with decreases in all four offense categories: property offense cases (down 65%), public order offense cases (down 59%), drug law violation cases (down 47%), and person offense cases (down 45%; Hockenberry, 2022).

In 2019, three quarters of these juvenile cases involved males. For a breakdown on race, the data shows that 43% involved White youth, 35% Black youth, 19% Hispanic youth, 2% American Indian youth (including Alaska Natives), and 1% Asian youth (including Native Hawaiians and Other Pacific Islanders). For comparison purposes, in 2019, the U.S. juvenile population consisted of 53% White youth, 15% Black youth, 24% Hispanic youth, 2% American Indian youth, and 6% Asian youth; thus, Asian youth and Black youth were over-represented. Juveniles younger than age 16 accounted for 54% of cases (Hockenberry, 2022).

At intake, authorities decide whether to dismiss the case, handle it informally (without filing a petition), or file a petition to formally request an adjudicatory hearing or waiver hearing. In 2019,

- 19% of all delinquency cases (136,800 cases) were dismissed at intake, generally for lack of legal sufficiency;

- an additional 28% (199,200 cases) were handled informally, with the juvenile agreeing to some type of voluntary sanction (e.g., restitution); and

- in more than half of all delinquency cases (54% or 386,600 cases), authorities filed a petition and handled the case formally (Hockenberry, 2022).

In 2019, juveniles were adjudicated delinquent in 53% (203,600) of cases, meaning that they were found to be responsible for committing the charges brought against them. For these youth, a hearing is held to decide which sanctions will be imposed. In 2019, formal probation was the most severe disposition ordered in 65% of cases, and residential placement was the most severe disposition in 27% of cases (Hockenberry, 2022).

A Controversy Within Juvenile Justice System: Trying Children as Adults

The National Center for Juvenile Justice (2021) estimates that roughly 53,000 children were **prosecuted in an adult criminal court** in 2019 (an 80% drop from 2000 when 250,000 youth a year were charged as adults). This happens when a youth commits a very serious crime and a judge or prosecutor transfers the case to a criminal court, where they will be tried as an adult. Some states have laws that will automatically transfer a juvenile case for any young person who commits certain offenses. Advocacy organizations such as the American Civil Liberties Union (ACLU), The Sentencing Project, and the Southern Poverty Law Center (SPLC) are critical of this practice due to racial disparities primarily impacting Black youth and harmful outcomes for youth as a result of spending time in solitary confinement and being housed in adult jails and prisons where they are often subjected to physical and sexual violence (ACLU, n.d.; Fatherree, 2022; Mistrett & Espinoza, 2021). In 2005 the U.S. Supreme Court banned the death penalty for children.

Social Work Practice in Criminal Justice and Legal Settings

Social workers were in criminal justice settings from the very beginning of the profession. During the progressive era, early women social reformers (before there were professional social workers) were primarily concerned with women and children who were vulnerable to abuse and exploitation. The first organization in the United States to assist abused women was founded in 1885 when the Chicago Women's Club created the Chicago Protective Agency for Women and Children to provide advocacy and legal aid services to poor and working-class women who were vulnerable to various forms of abuse, including sexual violence and battering (Batlan, 2015; Brownell & Roberts, 2002). As stated earlier in the chapter, the early settlement house workers in Chicago helped to create the nation's first juvenile court in 1898, arguing that vulnerable children need to be served in a separate and more supportive system based on their age and vulnerable status. According to scholars, "In the 1800s, social work was identified with corrections and other forms of social welfare institutions. During this time, many social reformers were involved with prisons, juvenile delinquency and reformatories (Gibelman, 1995, as cited in Brownell & Roberts, 2002, p. 3).

Forensic Social Work

Over time, social workers' work on criminal justice became more professionalized and formalized into what is now referred to as **forensic social work**. Forensic social work is unfamiliar to many people despite the fact that many social workers engage in this field of practice. When most people hear the word *forensic* they tend to think about crime scene investigators whose job is collect and analyze physical evidence at a crime scene. However, the term is broader than this. Merriam-Webster (n.d.) defines **forensic** as "relating to or dealing with the application of scientific knowledge to legal problems." In simple terms, when a social worker

IMG 11.4

has a job that intersects with the legal system in some way, they are doing forensic social work!

Brownell and Roberts (2002) define forensic social work as "policies, practices and social work roles with juvenile and adult offenders and victims of crimes" (p. 3). They go on to explain that, "throughout the 20th century, forensic social workers have been on the front lines completing pre-sentence reports, risk assessments, mental health and substance abuse counseling, group therapy, community outreach, and social service and employment advocacy for juvenile delinquents, adult offenders, and sexual assault and domestic violence victims" (p. 1).

The **National Organization of Forensic Social Work** (NOFSW, 2020) is a membership organization that supports the advancement of forensic social work, and they have six core values that guide their work: justice, equity, lawfulness, competence/accountability, integrity, and transdisciplinary collaboration. They define forensic social work as

> the application of social work to questions and issues relating to law and legal systems. This specialty of our profession goes far beyond clinics and psychiatric hospitals for criminal defendants being evaluated and treated on issues of competency and responsibility. A broader definition includes social work practice which in any way is related to legal issues and litigation, both criminal and civil. Child custody issues,

involving separation, divorce, neglect, termination of parental rights, the implications of child and spouse abuse, juvenile and adult justice services, corrections, and mandated treatment all fall under this definition. (NOFSW, n.d.)

In their work with individuals at the micro level, forensic social workers provide a thorough assessment and then share their knowledge and expertise with various actors in the legal arena, such as attorneys and judges. This work requires that social workers become knowledgeable of the law and legal concepts and become skilled in providing testimony in court proceedings and other legal meetings using language that those outside of social work can understand. Some social workers engage in **arbitration** and **mediation** to help opposing parties resolve a dispute and avoid lengthy litigation. At a macro level, forensic social workers can provide training for those in legal settings and engage in program and policy development.

It is important to keep in mind that forensic social work is performed by social workers in many different fields of practice such as child protection, gerontology, and psychiatric social work, which are profiled in other chapters of this book. This chapter will profile six work settings for social workers who work in the field of criminal justice: correctional facilities, community corrections, juvenile justice, the courts, victim's services programs, and sexual assault and family violence programs.

Social Work in Correctional Facilities

The vast majority of social workers who work in **correctional facilities** such as jails and prisons are licensed clinical social workers (LCSWs) who perform a range of case management and clinical roles for those who are incarcerated. There is a popular phrase that has been used in recent years to describe the criminalization of those with mental illness: "Prisons are the new asylums." See Chapter 7 for more of this history. In early U.S. history, those with mental illness were routinely housed in jails and prisons in terrible conditions, but thanks to advocacy efforts by social reformers such as **Dorothea Dix**, this practice ended and those who needed treatment were treated in specialized mental health facilities. So, it is a sad situation that today many people with mental health disorders receive treatment in jails and prisons since they have no other option.

Social workers in correctional settings provide intakes and psychosocial assessments and develop treatment plans for those who are incarcerated. They provide counseling and individual and group therapy for those who are incarcerated, and this can include serving men, women, or youth, depending on the facility. Various focuses of counseling/therapy can include substance abuse treatment, intimate partner violence, sex offender treatment, and life skills classes to help prisoners successfully reintegrate into the community after they are released.

Social workers in this setting have the opportunity to draw on the social work core value of "dignity and worth of the person" and assist a population that many in society have a difficult time finding compassion for based on their actions.

Social Work in Community Corrections

When offenders are supervised by the criminal justice system while residing in the community, instead of being incarcerated in a facility, this is referred to as **community corrections**, otherwise known as **probation** and **parole**. A social work degree is not required for probation and parole officers. The typical requirement is a bachelor's degree in criminal justice, sociology, psychology, social work, or a related field. Social workers in these roles make recommendations to the court regarding sentencing recommendations after conducting a thorough assessment of an offender. Social workers who work in probation and parole have a dual role of (a) monitoring whether their clients are complying with the court-ordered conditions of their parole or probation (e.g., drug testing, substance abuse treatment), and (b) supporting their clients in leading a more successful life, free from reoffending. Social workers can tap into their case management and broker role as they develop treatment plans and connect their clients with needed services and community supports.

Social workers can also work in **reentry programs** that support formerly incarcerated individuals in making a successful transition back to the community where they will be living, which is not an easy task. Inmates with a criminal record often find it difficult to get employers to hire them and to resist the negative influences that led them to commit crimes unless they have a strong support system. Reentry programs often focus on connecting offenders with supportive services such as housing, job training, job placement, and substance abuse treatment.

Social Workers in the Court System

Forensic social workers intersect with the court system in a variety of ways. They can serve as expert witnesses in civil and criminal cases, for example. It is important to understand the difference between civil and criminal cases. **Criminal cases** involve situations during which someone caused harm to another person (e.g., bodily harm, harm to one's property) and thus are a threat to public safety. **Civil cases** involve private disputes between individuals and/or organizations (e.g., when someone sues another person or business, divorces, custody cases). There are a variety of work settings, such as child protective services and adult protective services, for which social workers must write a report to the court and update the judge on the progress of their cases, including their assessment and recommendations.

A very interesting and innovative development is the creation of **specialty** or **specialized courts**. There are three main types of specialized courts: drug courts, veteran's courts, and mental health courts. The purpose of these courts is to divert nonviolent offenders from the criminal court system by providing them support from an interdisciplinary team of professionals who have specialized training in these areas (e.g., substance abuse, mental health disorders, and veterans). Social workers are heavily utilized in these specialized courts based on their professional knowledge and expertise. The ultimate goal of these courts is to reduce recidivism by connecting the offender with needed treatment and rehabilitation, often focused on substance abuse and mental health treatment. This model meshes very well with the philosophy and practice of social work.

Victim's Services Programs

Being a victim of a crime, especially a violent crime, is a traumatic experience for the victim and their loved ones, and most victims typically need emotional support and assistance in navigating the complexities of the legal system. In the 1970s a **victim's rights movement** emerged in the United States due to frustrations by victims regarding their lack of power and legal status in the criminal cases in which they were a victim. As a result, all 50 states have enacted various policies to provide more protections for victims and to operate from a more "victim-centric" approach (National Crime Victim Law Institute, 2011).

Two important developments because of this increasing focus on the rights of crime victims are the development and proliferation of **victim services programs** and the Crime Victims Fund. In 1984 a federal law passed titled the "Victims of Crime Act," or VOCA. VOCA established the **Crime Victims Fund**, which sends funding to states and localities to support victims in the immediate aftermath of a crime. It is important to know that this fund is not supported by tax dollars but instead is financed by fines and penalties paid by convicted federal offenders, as well as gifts and donations. All of this is administered by the Office for Victims of Crime, a program within the U.S. Department of Justice.

Dollars from the Crime Victims Fund are used to support both victim compensation and victim assistance. Compensation programs reimburse victims for expenses such as medical costs, mental health counseling, funeral and burial costs, and lost wages. These monies also support victim assistance programs (e.g., rape crisis centers, family violence shelters, child abuse treatment programs) that provide a range of services such as counseling, crisis intervention, emergency housing, advocacy, and transportation. Social workers who have a strong desire to support victims of crime can find positions that are titled **victim witness coordinators** or **victim advocates**, which can be housed in district attorney offices, county attorney offices, police departments, and nonprofit organizations.

IMG 11.5

Sexual Assault and Family Violence Programs

According to data collected by the CDC, both **sexual violence** and **intimate partner violence** (IPV) is very prevalent in the United States. In 2016–2017, 54% of women and 31% of men reported experiencing sexual violence that includes rape, being made to penetrate someone else (only men were asked this), sexual coercion, and unwanted sexual contact. Just counting rape, one in four women and one in 26 men report being a survivor of completed or attempted rape at some point in their lifetime (Basile et al., 2022). Additionally, one in three women and one in three men report experiencing IPV in their lifetime, which includes physical violence, sexual violence, and stalking by an intimate partner (Smith et al., 2018).

In response to these distressing social problems, there are nonprofit organizations across the country that support survivors of sexual violence and IPV. These organizations include a variety of services such as mental health counseling, group therapy, emergency shelters, victim advocacy within the legal system, transitional housing, childcare, and support with education and employment. Social workers in these organizations will often intersect with the legal system since some survivors will be involved with the court when there is a criminal case against the perpetrator of the abuse. Social workers in this field of practice assist survivors in healing and recovering from the trauma they experienced and serve in an advocate role to support them in their dealings with the legal system.

Social Workers in the Juvenile Justice System

Many social workers who work in the field of criminal justice are drawn to the juvenile system based on their desire to work with youth who have engaged in risky behaviors and to support them in getting on a better path so they do not continue to offend. Social workers typically work in probation or in residential facilities and perform case management, counseling, and therapeutic services. Because of the strong focus on treatment and rehabilitation, social workers have the opportunity to work with the whole family.

Diversion approaches are commonly used in the juvenile system as a method of "diverting" young people away from the formal legal system while still finding ways to hold them accountable for their actions. Many child advocates who focus on juvenile justice reform argue that these approaches are superior to punitive policies and practices that contribute to the "**school-to-prison pipeline**" for many youth of color, for example. Diversion options can include warn and release, community service, restorative justice practices that bring the youth together with the persons they caused harm to, and referral to other services and community supports such as mental health/substance abuse treatment, family counseling, education support, and job training. The Annie E. Casey Foundation (2020b) recommends that at least 60% of juvenile cases should be diverted and that other approaches such as probation should be used with youth who have committed serious offenses or are a threat to public safety.

Restorative justice approaches are also commonly used by many who work in the juvenile justice system. Facilitators who are trained in this approach facilitate a meeting between the youth who caused the harm with the parties who have been harmed to come up with a solution. The process looks like the following (Annie E. Casey Foundation, 2022a):

- **"The person harmed** has an opportunity to share how they were affected and what they need to heal.

- **The young person** assumes responsibility for causing harm and articulates what they need to reduce the likelihood of it happening again.

- **The facilitator** helps participants reach an agreement that meets everyone's needs. Solutions might include financial restitution, replacing items that were broken or lost or completing certain chores on behalf of the person or community harmed" (para. 7).

Juvenile Justice Case Study

Melvin is a social worker who works in the juvenile justice system and thoroughly enjoys working with these youth and helping support them in getting on the right track in life. Many of the youth he works with are young men of color who face a number of systemic challenges in life such as living in poverty and neighborhoods that have under-resourced schools and high levels of crime, violence, and drug use.

Melvin has become particularly discouraged by a number of recent cases in which juveniles have been charged and prosecuted in the adult criminal justice system, which goes against his personal and professional values. He is also disheartened by the racial disparities that he sees in terms of juvenile arrests. Even though some of the youth that he works with have engaged in behaviors that have caused harm to others, he also feels strongly that young people are different than adults due to their social development and developing brains and are not well served in an adult system where they are at high risk for abuse and victimization. He has seen firsthand how young people can turn their lives around when they have support from caring adults and needed resources.

Questions

1. What thoughts and feelings come up for you as you imagine being in this social worker's shoes? Do you agree with Melvin's perspective? Why or why not?

2. Putting on your "macro social work hat," what can Melvin do to try to change these problems that he is witnessing in his state?

3. How can Melvin use his social work expertise to try to change the laws in his state? What would be a good first step?

4. How comfortable would you be to step into an advocacy role to try to change policies that you find unjust?

5. What questions does this case example raise for you?

Research Focus: Restorative Justice

In social work, there is a strong value and emphasis on evaluating social work interventions to ensure they are helping and not harming client systems. Once a specific intervention is shown to be supported by research evidence it can be considered a "best practice" or an evidence-based intervention since there is evidence to support its efficacy. **Restorative justice practices** have been studied by researchers in various disciplines. The Office of Juvenile Justice and Delinquency Prevention (2021) conducted a literature review in which they examined the results of various research studies that evaluated this practice and found

11.3 **PRACTICE ACTIVITY**

After reading about social work practice in these various work settings, what skills do you think are important to excel in this field? Since social workers work in a host setting with people from different professional backgrounds, how can they work collaboratively with others while still bringing their social work values and ethics into their work?

promising, though somewhat mixed, results for both the offender and the victim. The aim of most studies is to evaluate whether this practice helps to reduce recidivism better than more traditional approaches and to assess whether it was a positive experience for those involved.

Though outcomes vary somewhat based on race, gender, prior offending history, and type of offense committed, overall this review found that compared with juveniles who are processed traditionally in the juvenile justice system, youths who participate in restorative justice programs are less likely to reoffend—a very positive finding! Research shows, for example, that youth offenders who participate in restorative justice programs are more likely to express satisfaction with how their cases were handled, accept responsibility for their actions, and complete restitution agreements, compared with participants who received the traditional approach (Development Services Group, 2021).

Results are also positive for victims, though there is one important caveat. According to the authors of the literature review,

> Numerous studies have found that victims who participated in restorative justice programs had greater perceptions of fairness, compared with victims who were processed by the traditional juvenile justice system. This may be due to the perception that justice-involved youths in restorative justice programs are more likely to repair the harm they caused (for example, by writing an apology letter or apologizing to the victim directly and accepting culpability for their actions) and complete restitution, compared with justice-involved youths processed through the traditional justice system. Despite these promising findings, some studies have found that victims are not always satisfied after participating in restorative justice programs, and some programs tend to emphasize the justice-involved youth's needs more than the victim's needs For example, victims who participated in victim–offender mediation reported at times that they felt pressured to participate and to accept the justice-involved youth's apology, and that they also experienced anxiety at the thought of facing the justice-involved youth. Victims have also reported feelings of revictimization during the mediation process (Development Services Group, 2021, Outcome Evidence, para. 7 and 8).

The authors noted that while there has been some good research studying this practice approach, more rigorous research, using randomized control group designs, is needed to more accurately evaluate the true effectiveness of restorative justice models.

Policy Focus: Federal Hate Crime Legislation

Social workers working at the macro level in criminal justice can find work in advocacy organizations that attempt to change policies and work on criminal justice reform. Prominent examples of organizations doing this work are The Sentencing Project, the National Institute for Criminal Justice Reform, The Innocence Project, the Equal Justice Initiative, Sandy Hook Promise, Everytown for Gun Safety, and the Southern Poverty Law Center. There are many examples of policies that have been passed into law to make changes in the criminal justice system, but this section will focus on federal hate crime legislation.

The United States has a long history of people who commit acts of violence against certain groups of people as an act of hatred and a tool of oppression. The lynching of African Americans is one example of this. In recent years, there have been a number of high-profile cases in which someone was assaulted or killed based on their race, gender identity, or other aspect of their identity. Recent examples include cases where Asian Americans were assaulted based on their race and the man who shot and killed 10 Black people in a mass shooting at a grocery store in Buffalo, New York. This man is now facing multiple counts of federal hate crimes in charges filed by the Department of Justice. In 2021, the Southern Poverty Law Center documented 1,221 hate groups and antigovernment extremist groups operating in the United States (Miller & Rivas, 2022).

The FBI (n.d.) defines a **hate crime** as a "criminal offense against a person or property motivated in whole or in part by an offender's bias against a race, religion, disability, sexual orientation, ethnicity, gender, or gender identity" (para. 4). The FBI reported that in 2021 there were 10,530 hate crime incidents involving 12,411 victims. The hate crime incident was motivated by race or ethnicity in 65% of cases, sexual orientation (16%), religion (14%), gender identity (3%), disability (1%), and gender (1%) (U.S. Department of Justice, 2023).

In 1968, President Lyndon Johnson signed the first federal hate crimes statute into law, which was focused on targeting people based on their race, color, religion, or national origin. This was an historic achievement as it recognized for the first time that some citizens can be victimized solely based on their identity and need special protections from this type of violent crime. However, after this first law was passed, there was growing recognition that hate crimes laws needed to be strengthened and needed to protect other groups of people, namely women, LGBTQ+ individuals, and those with disabilities.

After 10 years of advocacy by organizations such as the Human Rights Campaign and the mother of Matthew Shepard, Judy Shepard, the **Matthew Shepard and James Byrd, Jr. Hate Crimes Prevention Act** was signed into law by President Obama on October 28, 2009. This law was prompted by the hate crimes of two men, both of whom were killed in 1998. Matthew Shepard was a young college student who was tortured and killed in Laramie, Wyoming, for being gay, and James Byrd, Jr. was a Black man who was chained to the back of a pickup truck by three White men and dragged to his death in Jasper, Texas.

The new law expanded the federal definition of hate crime laws to include gender, sexual orientation, gender identity, and disability and gave more tools to prosecutors and federal law enforcement in their efforts to enforce and respond to these crimes. Shockingly, the U.S. Congress did not pass a **federal antilynching bill** until 2022, when the Emmett Till Anti-Lynching Act was signed into law by President Biden, making lynching a federal hate crime for the first time in the United States. The bill was named after Emmett Till, a 14-year-old boy who was lynched in Mississippi in 1955. The bill was sponsored by three African American U.S. senators—Kamala Harris, Cory Booker, and Tim Scott—and was able to gain momentum and support in the aftermath of the murder of George Floyd by a police officer. The first antilynching bill was introduced in the U.S. Congress in 1900 and was introduced more than 240 times, failing each time. It was blocked over the years by a minority of U.S. senators who were determined to maintain the Jim Crow system in the South (Jenkins & Peck, 2022).

▌ Chapter Summary

There are a multitude of opportunities for social workers who want to impact change in the field of criminal justice and other legal settings at the micro, mezzo, and macro levels. Social workers interested in this area of practice can work with offenders or victims of crime, children or adults, and throughout various parts of the criminal justice system, which includes law enforcement, corrections, and the courts. When a social worker has a job that intersects with the legal system in some way, they are doing forensic social work. Forensic social workers work in many different fields of practice such as child protection, gerontology, and psychiatric social work. However, this chapter focused on six work settings for social workers who work in the field of criminal justice and other legal settings: correctional facilities, community corrections, juvenile justice, the courts, victim's services programs, and sexual assault and family violence programs.

Social workers who work in this field are often employed in host settings with professionals from other disciplines such as criminal justice and the law; thus, they must sort out professional tensions due to differences in values, ethics, and ideology. The NOFSW has six core values that guide their work: justice, equity, lawfulness, competence/accountability, integrity, and transdisciplinary collaboration. Getting hate crimes legislation passed into law at the federal level has been an important public policy focus for many advocacy organizations. The Matthew Shepard and James Byrd, Jr. Hate Crimes Prevention Act was signed into law by President Obama in 2009. Shockingly, the U.S. Congress did not pass a federal antilynching bill until 2022, when the Emmett Till Anti-Lynching Act was signed into law by President Biden, making lynching a federal hate crime for the first time in the United States. Research on restorative justice practices, an approach that brings the victim and offender together, indicates that this is a promising intervention to support both victims and offenders.

Discussion Questions

1. After learning about forensic social work and the six major career paths outlined in this chapter, which of these areas feel like they could be a good fit, and which are not appealing? Why?

2. A number of issues were highlighted in this chapter that some view as examples of social injustices that have serious negative consequences for certain groups. Summarize them here. Which ones concern you the most?

3. After reading this chapter, what are the biggest ethical tensions you can imagine that arise for social workers in this field who work with professionals from other disciplines?

4. Do some research on the Matthew Shepard and James Byrd, Jr. Hate Crimes Prevention Act or the Emmett Till Anti-Lynching Act. What obstacles did advocates and supporters of these policies face, and why did it take so long to get them passed into law by the U.S. Congress?

5. This chapter highlighted interventions in the field that use restorative justice and diversion approaches. How would you explain how these approaches are different from the more traditional approaches used in the criminal justice field? How do these approaches align with social work values and ethics?

References

Alexander, M. (2010). The new Jim Crow: Mass incarceration in the age of colorblindness. New York: New Press.

American Civil Liberties Union. (n.d.). *Youth solitary confinement.* https://www.aclu.org/issues/juvenile-justice/youth-incarceration/youth-solitary-confinement

Ahmed, S. (2022, November 20). *22 weeks into the year, America has already seen at least 246 mass shootings.* National Public Radio. https://www.npr.org/2022/05/15/1099008586/mass-shootings-us-2022-tally-number

Annie E. Casey Foundation. (2020a, May 24). *What is restorative justice for young people?* https://www.aecf.org/blog/what-is-restorative-justice-for-young-people?gclid=CjwKCA-jw-8qVBhANEiwAfjXLrlZkXgESOaHFbmbv7TN9P32Eshg6lAkHYXpDuBAwIAXATj6egH-po6xoCV7wQAvD_BwE

Annie E. Casey Foundation. (2020b, October 22). *What is diversion in juvenile justice?* https://www.aecf.org/blog/what-is-juvenile-diversion

Annie E. Casey (2020c, December 12). *What is juvenile justice?* https://www.aecf.org/blog/what-is-juvenile-justice#:~:text=Juvenile%20justice%20in%20the%20United,accused%20of%20breaking%20the%20law

Basile, K. C., Smith, S. G., Kresnow, M., Khatiwada S., & Leemis, R.W. (2022). *The National Intimate Partner and Sexual Violence Survey: 2016/2017 report on sexual violence.* National Center for Injury Prevention and Control, Centers for Disease Control and Prevention. https://www.cdc.gov/violenceprevention/pdf/nisvs/nisvsReportonSexualViolence.pdf

Batlan, F. (2015). *Women and justice for the poor: A history of legal aid, 1863–1945.* Cambridge University Press.

Brownell, P., & Roberts, A. R. (2002). A century of social work in criminal justice and correctional settings. *Journal of Offender Rehabilitation, 35*(2), 1–17.

Development Services Group. (2021). *Restorative justice for juveniles.* Office of Juvenile Justice and Delinquency Prevention. https://ojjdp.ojp.gov/model-programs-guide/literature-reviews/restorative-justice-for-juveniles

Fatherree, D. (2022). *Criminal injustice: States unfairly prosecute children as adults.* Southern Poverty Law Center. https://www.splcenter.org/news/2022/01/21/criminal-injustice-states-unfairly-prosecute-children-adults

Federal Bureau of Investigation. (n.d.). *Defining a hate crime.* https://www.fbi.gov/investigate/civil-rights/hate-crimes#Definition

Gramlich, J. (2020, November 20). *What the data says (and doesn't say) about crime in the United States.* Pew Research Center. https://www.pewresearch.org/fact-tank/2020/11/20/facts-about-crime-in-the-u-s/

Gramlich, J. (2021a, August 16). *America's incarceration rate falls to lowest level since 1995.* Pew Research Center. https://www.pewresearch.org/fact-tank/2021/08/16/americas-incarceration-rate-lowest-since-1995/

Gramlich, J. (2021b, October 27). *What we know about the increase in U.S. murders in 2020.* Pew Research Center. https://www.pewresearch.org/fact-tank/2021/10/27/what-we-know-about-the-increase-in-u-s-murders-in-2020/

Gramlich, J. (2022, February 3). *What the data says about gun deaths in the U.S.* Pew Research Center. https://www.pewresearch.org/fact-tank/2022/02/03/what-the-data-says-about-gun-deaths-in-the-u-s/

Hockenberry, S. (2022, February). *Delinquency cases in juvenile court, 2019.* Office of Juvenile Justice and Delinquency Prevention. https://ojjdp.ojp.gov/library/publications/delinquency-cases-juvenile-court-2019

Jenkins, J. A., & Peck, J. (2022, March 9). Congress finally passed a federal anti-lynching bill—after 120 years of failure. *The Washington Post*. https://www.washingtonpost.com/politics/2022/03/09/congress-finally-passed-federal-anti-lynching-law-after-120-years-failure/

Merriam-Webster. (n.d.). *Forensic*. https://www.merriam-webster.com/dictionary/forensic

Miller, C., & Rivas, R. C. (2022). The year in hate and extremism report 2021. Southern Poverty Law Center. https://www.splcenter.org/20220309/year-hate-extremism-report-2021

Mistrett, M., & Espinoza, M (2021, December 16). *Youth in adult courts, jails, & prisons*. The Sentencing Project. https://www.sentencingproject.org/publications/youth-in-adult-courts-jails-and-prisons/

National Center for Juvenile Justice. (2021). *Youth younger than 18 prosecuted in criminal court: National Estimate, 2019 cases*. http://www.ncjj.org/Publication/Youth-Younger-than-18-Prosecuted-in-Criminal-Court-National-Estimate-2019-Cases.aspx

National Crime Victim Law Institute. (2011). *Fundamentals of victims' rights: A brief history of crime victims' rights in the United States*. Office of Justice Programs. https://www.ojp.gov/ncjrs/virtual-library/abstracts/fundamentals-victims-rights-brief-history-crime-victims-rights

National Organization of Forensic Social Work. (n.d.). *What is forensic social work?* https://www.nofsw.org/what-is-forensic-social-work-1

National Organization of Forensic Social Work. (2020). *Specialty guidelines for values and ethics*. https://www.nofsw.org/_files/ugd/f468b9_20e60b0830ed4a51808154902b7e9f20.pdf

Ndulue, N. (2020, September 15). *Enduring injustice: The persistence of racial discrimination in the U.S. death penalty*. Death Penalty Information Center. https://deathpenaltyinfo.org/news/dpic-releases-major-new-report-on-race-and-the-u-s-death-penalty

Ritter, J. A. (2022). *Social work policy practice: Changing our community, nation, and the world* (3rd ed.). Cognella.

Schaeffer, K. (2021, September 13). *Key facts about Americans and guns*. Pew Research Center. https://www.pewresearch.org/fact-tank/2021/09/13/key-facts-about-americans-and-guns/

Smith, S. G., Zhang, X., Basile, K. C., Merrick, M. T., Wang, J., Kresnow, M., Chen, J. (2018). *The National Intimate Partner and Sexual Violence Survey (NISVS): 2015 data brief—updated release*. National Center for Injury Prevention and Control, Centers for Disease Control and Prevention. https://www.cdc.gov/violenceprevention/pdf/2015data-brief508.pdf

Stevenson, B. (2015). *Just mercy: A story of justice and redemption*. New York: Spiegel & Grau.

U.S. Department of Justice. (2023). *2021 hate crime statistics*. https://www.justice.gov/hatecrimes/hate-crime-statistics

▐ Credits

CHAPTER 12

International Social Work and Human Rights

Learning Objectives

After reading this chapter, students will be able to do the following:

- Summarize the biggest challenges facing migrants in the United States and around the world and the unique challenges facing those who are undocumented or without legal status

- Explain the role and purpose of the United Nations and UN human rights treaties such as the UN Declaration of Human Rights

- Differentiate between cultural competence and cultural humility

- Describe the process of immigrating to the United States and the four federal government agencies that are charged with overseeing immigration and enforcing immigration laws in this country

- Highlight current pressing social problems that impact vulnerable people across the globe such as human trafficking, gender inequality, and climate change

- Evaluate the role of the Pew Research Center in conducting research on immigration in the United States

- Identify three major career path options for social workers who want to work with immigrants and refugees in the United States

- Identify three major career path options for social workers who want to work with immigrants and refugees in another country

- Explain the goals of comprehensive immigration reform legislation and why the U.S. Congress has failed to pass this legislation over the past few decades

- Evaluate goodness of fit with social work practice with immigrant and refugee populations as a potential future career option

IMG 12.1

Even though most social workers in the United States work at the local level, it is critical that social workers have a global perspective since the nations of the world are increasingly interconnected and interdependent due to the increased **globalization** of our world. It is vital that we care about the well-being of humans across our borders as much as those who reside within our borders. Every day there are **migrants** who leave their home country to live in another country, and people do this for a wide variety of reasons, such as to seek a better or different life for themselves and their family members; for better employment and/or educational opportunities; to join relatives and loved ones; or to escape a natural disaster, war, or other forms of violence in their home country. It can be a stressful and treacherous journey for some migrants depending on their circumstances. A 2022 report from the United Nations High Commissioner for Refugees (UNHCR) reported that at the end of 2021 there were 89.3 million **forcibly displaced people** in the world who were driven to flee their home due to conflicts, violence, fear of persecution, and human rights violations, and this number doubled over the previous decade. This shocking figure means that one in every 78 people on the planet has had to deal with the trauma of being forced to leave their home. Many displaced people had to leave their homes due to war and conflicts in their region, for example in Ukraine, Syria, Afghanistan, South Sudan, and Myanmar.

The United States is often touted as a "nation of immigrants," and part of this country's story is that it is a place where people around the world can move to in order to live "the American dream." The **American dream** refers to the idea that if you are willing to work hard, people of all backgrounds and socioeconomic statuses can get a good education, make a good living, own their own home, and raise a family. The United States has had numerous waves of immigration since the nation was founded, and many different cultural groups have become part of the social fabric of this nation by sharing their culture via their family customs, religious/spiritual beliefs, food, art, music, and so on. Many who visit the country are struck by how racially and ethnically heterogeneous the population is and the rich **cultural diversity** that exists in many areas of the country, such as Los Angeles, California; Houston, Texas; Miami, Florida; and New York City, just to name a few. According to the Pew Research Center, the United States has more immigrants that any other nation in the world! According to their data, in 2018, 44.8 million people living in the United States were born in another country, accounting for roughly 20% of the world's migrants. And nearly every nation in the world is represented by those who have immigrated to the United States (Budiman, 2020).

However, there is also another side to this story as immigration is one of the most politically divisive issues in the United States. From the beginning, the United States has had an uneasy and contradictory relationship with newly arriving immigrant groups as they are feared and resented by some segments of the American population. Many immigrants face challenges that include discrimination, being exploited for their labor, experiencing violent hate crimes, and facing intense pressure to fully assimilate to the dominant culture. And the obstacles are even more dire for people living in the United States who are **undocumented** (i.e., being without legal status).

This chapter will provide important information on career options for social workers who are interested in working with immigrant and refugee populations in the United States and abroad. Social workers who work abroad are employed by governmental and nongovernmental organizations (NGOs) that focus on human rights, social development, and economic development. However, due to the high numbers of immigrants living in the country, an exciting feature of international social work is that social workers can engage in this work right here at home.

SOCIAL WORKER SPOTLIGHT:
Megan Hope, LMSW

My Social Work Career With Immigrant and Refugee Communities

My odyssey toward a professional social work career—one focused on working with immigrants and refugees—began in my hometown of Garden City, Kansas. As I was growing up in the 1980s and 1990s, our rural community was transformed by the arrival of new Latin American immigrants and resettled Southeast Asian refugees, the primary workforce for two meat-packing plants. Since my childhood was the picture of stability (we lived in the house where my dad was born), it was both fascinating and frightening to me to imagine people being so far from home, separated from family, and met with suspicion, xenophobia, and racism. But my parents and other progressive community leaders, including newcomers themselves, believed that "our" town belonged to anyone who wanted to make a go of it there. They worked for equitable access to economic opportunity, education, and participation in civic life. By the time I left home, about 49% of the town was foreign born, and all our horizons had expanded.

In college I majored in English and anthropology, studied Spanish, and learned more about immigration. After graduation I spent a year as a full-time, live-in volunteer at Annunciation House in El Paso, Texas. I began at the organization's emergency house of hospitality for newly arrived immigrant adults and children. Soon I was asked to help run Casa Vides, the house for Latin American, African, Eastern European, and other guests with prolonged immigration legal cases and other long-term needs. The experience at both houses was intense, requiring simultaneous attention to meal prep, intakes of new guests at any hour of the day or night, and counseling about individuals' plans and needed lengths of stay. There were also frequent crises to attend to involving survivors of interpersonal violence, torture, and war; recent border crossers beaten by human smugglers or otherwise injured during their journeys; unaccompanied children; people with AIDS, tuberculosis, and other illnesses; and others representative of the dangers that motivate migration and are encountered during it.

The hours I spent sharing meals and a home with immigrant guests politicized me. I became more poignantly aware of the macro forces shaping their circumstances and of my responsibility for unjust policies, structures, and ways of living. And although I didn't know it at the time, I also learned some principles helpful to social work practice: Making realistic commitments and keeping them is important, especially for people whose reasonable expectations for safety and justice have so often been betrayed. In a mainstream culture that prizes personal comfort, we must be willingly inconvenienced by the needs of others. You can hold people accountable without judging them. As Annunciation House's philosophy states, direct service is done with "imperfections, errors, fears, moments of doubt, and with an ever-present sense of [our] humanity." Everyone carries with them their strengths and vulnerabilities, and the wisdom and knowledge of how they have survived until now. And sometimes we all just need to have our stories heard.

After another year of work in human services—coordinating social and immigration legal services for migrant farmworkers in western Missouri and helping Spanish-speaking immigrants and other legal aid clients apply for public benefits—I decided to go to back to school. I wanted to learn more about the history, politics, and cultures of Latin America. Although I've often joked that my resulting master's degree in Latin American studies perhaps best qualified me to be a bilingual waitress, it did complement and inform my subsequent work.

Since the United States has decided to define immigration primarily as a legal issue—as opposed to an economic or humanitarian one—and since so many aspects of immigrants' lives are dictated by their immigration status, I realized I needed to have a basic understanding of immigration legal processes. I began to gain that at Legal Aid of Western Missouri and its Migrant Farmworker Project, where I worked as a paralegal on family-based immigration processes and wrote grant proposals to support legal services for immigrant survivors of crime. I soon learned about another pervasive legal problem experienced by immigrant workers: wage theft. With the Kansas City Worker Justice Center, I coordinated monthly free legal clinics to help workers file claims for unpaid and underpaid wages. In other volunteer work, I tried to address some of the economic and political situations that drive many immigrants to the United States and that often kept them poor after arrival. I worked with groups that advocated for the rights of workers in *maquiladoras* (foreign-owned export factories) in Mexico and Central America and lobbied for better state-level legislation for immigrants, refugees, and all working people.

Through study, personal travel, and work, I've been lucky to go to more than 30 countries, including 21 in the "developing" world. For several years I had an occasional job doing program reviews for two international child sponsorship organizations that provided educational benefits, health care, youth development, and job training for families in developing countries. Often, the in-country program staff I interviewed and shadowed were social workers, as were many of the people in the United States whose careers I most admired. Looking further into the academic study of social work, I realized that nearly everything I'd tried my hand at fit within the profession's wide tent. I figured I might as well make it official.

I began my Master's of Social Work program at the University of Denver as more of a community practice person but didn't like the idea of having to choose one concentration over another. Our sympathetic academic dean helped me design more of a mix of classes than ordinarily prescribed so that I could take mental health assessment and family therapy classes alongside policy advocacy and theories of organizational leadership. I also earned a certificate in social work practice with Latinx populations.

As a 2nd-year student, I was captivated by the description of a field placement with a pilot project offering mental health and other support to adults in immigration detention. I became the first intern of the Social Service Project at the Rocky Mountain

Immigrant Advocacy Network, a nonprofit provider of immigration legal services. I was later hired onto the staff and eventually became the director of the Social Service Project, now a permanent program. During my 12 years of involvement, our team grew to as many as five MSWs providing therapeutic conversations, health care and other detention conditions advocacy, postrelease planning, coordination of forensic health evaluations, affidavits for habeas petitions, discernment of immigrant eligibility for public benefits, and many other forms of advocacy and accompaniment for adults in immigration detention, certain unaccompanied youth in the custody of the Office of Refugee Resettlement, and nondetained children and families. We became a model of interdisciplinary collaboration between social workers and legal professionals, a concept that's grown increasingly popular in the immigration legal services realm.

Particularly important, many Social Service Project interns and staff have been social workers with recent personal or family immigration experiences. I am privileged to have had so many particular opportunities to develop the career I have. But nothing I've learned or done is equal to the lived experiences of people who have immigrated themselves or accompanied loved ones through immigration processes, and it is critical that more social workers who reflect the diversity of immigrant clients be meaningfully supported to join this field of practice.

To have been allowed into the rooms—in homes around the world, houses of hospitality, courts, detention centers—and lives of the people I've worked with, and to be a small receptacle for and amplifier of their worries and deferred dreams, is humbling and sacred. I wholeheartedly recommend it.

Overview of Immigration in the United States

Over the past few decades, **immigration** has been one of the most politically divisive issues in the United States. After the September 11th attacks in 2001, immigration rose to the top of the political agenda as concerns over homeland security were heightened. Recent data from the Pew Research Center shows that while a majority of Americans have positive views about immigrants (e.g., 66% of Americans feel that immigrants strengthen the country "because of their hard work and talents"), about a quarter believe that immigrants burden the country by taking jobs, housing and health care (Budiman, 2020, para. 33). Budiman (2020) notes that these views vary greatly by political party affiliation:

> Among Democrats and Democratic-leaning independents, 88% think immigrants strengthen the country with their hard work and talents, and just 8% say they are a burden. Among Republicans and Republican-leaning independents, 41% say immigrants strengthen the country, while 44% say they burden it. (para. 34)

These varying political views have led to different policy positions by the Democratic and Republican parties in recent years. Generally speaking, the Republican party has embraced a "tough on immigration" approach that includes restricting immigration, including for those who are refugees, supporting strict deportation polices for those who are in the country illegally, and advocating strategies such as "building a wall" on the southern border to keep people from coming into the country. The Democratic party, on the other hand, has supported comprehensive immigration reform policies that would provide a path to citizenship for undocumented people residing in the United States as well as policies such as the DREAM Act that support undocumented youth who have grown up in the country and wish to become legal citizens.

All countries must come up with immigration policies and practices that govern how people can immigrate to their country. Government officials must decide who can enter, in what numbers, and under which circumstances. Countries vary in how strict their policies are in allowing newcomers from other nations. As Ritter (2022) notes, "Some countries are fairly welcoming, while others take great care to preserve their country's homogeneity when it comes to race, religion, and culture. In the United States, the pendulum swings back and forth between immigration policies that restrict immigration (e.g., Chinese Exclusion Act, Emergency Quota Act of 1921, Immigration Act of 1924, Operation Wetback in the 1950s) and policies that ease quota restrictions (e.g., Immigration and Nationality Act of 1965, Refugee Act of 1980, Immigration Act of 1990)" (p. 271).

Government Immigration Agencies

The federal government is generally responsible for immigration laws and policies, though some duties are delegated to states and localities. As a result, states vary greatly in how supportive they are of immigrants, including those who are undocumented. There are four federal government agencies heavily involved with immigration:

- **Department of Homeland Security**: This agency, which was created after the 9/11 attacks in 2001, has as a mission of protecting the United States from domestic and foreign threats and both man-made and natural disasters.

- **U.S. Citizenship and Immigration Services (USCIS):** This is the main government agency that processes immigration applications and is managed by the Department of Homeland Security. They process applications from family members and employers who sponsor foreign nationals; conduct interviews and English and civics tests to those who are in the process of becoming a citizen; process refugee applications and grant asylum; and manage the E-verify system to help ensure that employers are hiring those who are eligible to work in the United States.

- **U.S. Department of State**: This organization has the primary responsibility of issuing visas (both temporary and permanent visas) and determining who can obtain a visa.

- **Immigrant and Customs Enforcement (ICE)**: This agency enforces immigration laws and has the investigatory power to detain and remove/deport those who are in the country without legal status. Even though they have the power to deport anyone who is in the country illegally, they are supposed to prioritize those who have been convicted of a crime or are deemed a threat to national security.

- **Customs and Border Protection**: Managed by the Department of Homeland Security, this agency is charged with protecting the nation's borders and not allowing people to enter the country illegally.

What Is the Process of Immigrating to the United States?

In most cases, people can immigrate to the United States in one of four ways: (a) family-based immigration (they have an immediate relative here); (b) employment-based immigration for those with valuable skills (an employer sponsors them to work here); (c) as a refugee or asylum seeker; or (d) through the Diversity Visa Program, which is designated for immigrants from countries with low rates of immigration to the United States (55,000 visas each year through a computer-generated lottery). According to many immigration experts and attorneys, the immigration system is broken and needs to be overhauled, and it takes much too long for people to immigrate using the current legal channels.

IMG 12.2

According to the American Immigration Council (2021),

> The body of law governing U.S. immigration policy is called the Immigration and Nationality Act (INA). The INA allows the United States to grant up to 675,000 permanent immigrant visas each year across various visa categories. On top of those 675,000 visas, the INA sets no limit on the annual admission of U.S. citizens' spouses, parents, and children under the age of 21. In addition, each year the president is required to consult with Congress and set an annual number of refugees to be admitted to the United States through the U.S. Refugee Admissions Program. … The INA also places a limit on how many immigrants can come to the United States from any one country. (para. 2,15)

Once a person obtains an immigrant **visa** and arrives in the United States they become a **lawful permanent resident**, which means that they can apply for jobs and remain in the country on a permanent basis. After 3–5 years, depending on the circumstances, they can then apply to become a U.S. citizen. Applicants for **U.S. citizenship** must be at least 18 years old, demonstrate continuous residency, demonstrate "good moral character," pass English and U.S. history and civics exams (with certain exceptions), and pay an application fee, among other requirements. The United States also has a process for granting temporary visas, which allow people to live in the country on a temporary basis, for example tourists, students, and those who are here to work temporarily.

Defining Terms: Immigration

Migrants: Migrants are people who leave their home country for a better or different life for themselves and their family members. They leave their home country to seek employment and/or education opportunities. Migrants also sometimes come to a new country to join relatives or to escape a natural disaster.

Refugees: According to the American Immigration Council (2021), **refugees** "are admitted to the United States based upon an inability to return to their home countries because of a well-founded fear of persecution due to their race, membership in a particular social group, political opinion, religion, or national origin. Refugees apply for admission from outside of the United States. The admission of refugees turns on numerous factors, such as the degree of risk they face, membership in a group that is of special concern to the United States (designated yearly by the president and Congress), and whether or not they have family members in the United States" (para. 16). In 2019, 30,000 refugees were resettled in the United States (Budiman, 2020).

Asylum seekers: While a refugee is granted refugee status while outside the United States, an asylum seeker is granted asylee status (based on the same five protected grounds upon which refugees rely) after already being in the country or when arriving at a port of entry. There is no limit to the number of individuals who may be granted asylum each year. Both refugees and asylees are eligible to become lawful permanent residents 1 year after admission to the United States as a refugee or 1 year after receiving asylum.

Internally displaced person: This refers to people who have had to flee their home due to violence, armed conflict, human rights violations, or a natural or man-made disaster, but they are still living within the borders of their home country.

Undocumented or unauthorized immigrants: Those who are in the country without legal status. Some use the terms *illegal immigrants*, *illegals*, or *illegal aliens* when referring to those who have entered the United States with no legal status. However, many find these terms offensive and assert that no human being should be described as "illegal."

How Many People in the United States Are Immigrants?

Data from the Pew Research Center (Budiman, 2020) shows that in 2018 there were a record 44.8 million people in the United States (13.7% of the U.S. population) who were born in another country, and this number quadrupled since 1965. Three U.S. states house nearly half of the immigrants: California (24%), Texas (11%), and Florida (10%). In terms of geographic region, the majority of immigrants come from Asia (28%) and Mexico (25%), and the other regions are as follows: Europe, Canada, and other nations in North America (13%), the Caribbean (10%), Central America (8%), South America (7%), the Middle East and North Africa (4%), and sub-Saharan Africa (5%).

Research Focus: The Pew Research Center

The Pew Research Center, a nonprofit and nonpartisan research organization, is one of the most famous and important research organizations in the United States. Pew (n.d.) gathers data on a host of important topics, including "politics and policy; news habits and media; the internet and technology; religion; race and ethnicity; international affairs; social, demographic and economic trends; science; research methodology and data science; and **immigration and migration** (para. 3). They gather macro-level social science data using public polling and demographic research methods in order to help inform sound decision-making in our society by lawmakers and other decision-makers. Much of the data on immigration in this chapter was pulled from the Pew Research Center (e.g., Budiman, 2020). Visit their website to learn more about their work (www.pewresearch.org).

What Are the Biggest Challenges Facing Immigrants and Refugees in the United States?

Social workers have a long history of working to support those who immigrate to the United States at both the micro and the macro level. Recall the early settlement house workers and the settlement house movement that were highlighted in Chapter 2. Even though immigrants make substantial contributions to this country, the transition of settling into a new country is challenging, and there are often significant barriers to overcome.

Discrimination and Hate Crimes

Many immigrants in the United States experience discrimination due to their skin color, social customs, and immigration status. This can include being treated differently in the workplace, having unequal access to health care and other human services, experiencing differential treatment by law enforcement, and experiencing hate crimes. Many immigrants know well the experience of "**othering**" that can happen within a society when a group of people are viewed as part of the "outgroup" rather than the "ingroup." Individuals whose immigration status is more obvious (e.g., the way they dress, having a strong accent, etc.) tend to face more discrimination in larger society.

Acculturation or **assimilation** is the process of adaptation that results when two cultural groups interact and/or when or the extent to which an individual assumes the norms and values of the host culture. There is a strong expectation and pressure that many immigrants feel to quickly assimilate to the dominant American culture, which includes learning to speak English, adopting the larger culture's social norms, and embracing American values. Though immigrants do have the desire to assimilate, they also often have a desire to preserve elements from their own cultural background that have significant meaning for them, and many experience some stress or tension due to the lived experience of having to navigate between two cultures.

Hate crimes against those who are immigrants, or are perceived to be immigrants, include verbal assaults and acts of physical harm. Increased discrimination and hate crimes sometimes occur because of events that happen in the larger culture, for example when Americans witnessed the treatment of Muslim Americans deteriorate after the 9/11 attacks and when President Trump signed an executive order banning people from six Muslim-majority nations from entering the country, referred to as the "Muslim ban." Additionally, there was an increase of hate crimes against people of Asian descent living in the United States, which some experts attribute to President Trump's rhetoric where he constantly referred to the COVID-19 pandemic as the "Chinese virus."

Poverty and Income Insecurity

Many are familiar with **Maslow's hierarchy of needs**, the famous theory by psychologist Abraham Maslow. At the bottom of the pyramid is physiological needs, which includes our most basic needs of food, water, clothing, shelter, rest, and basic health. There is a lot of variability in terms of the level of financial security that people have when they immigrate to the United States, with some having adequate financial resources and a family support system when they arrive and others who arrive with little more than the clothes on their back after making a traumatic and treacherous journey. In 2018, 14.6% of immigrants were living in poverty, and almost one in five did not have health insurance (Budiman et al., 2018). There are many organizations in the United States that are set up to assist newly arriving immigrants and refugees with these basic needs.

One of the most pressing goals of many arriving immigrants is to find employment so they can support themselves, and their families, financially. However, this can be a challenging task when one is new to the country due to discrimination, language barriers, lack of a professional network, and required educational and other professional requirements that are specific to the United States. It can take many years before first-generation immigrants feel that they are financially secure, and the dream of many immigrants is that their children will have a much better life than they do. Research by the Pew Research Center (2013) bears this out:

> Second-generation Americans—the 20 million adult U.S.-born children of immigrants—are substantially better off than immigrants themselves on key measures of socioeconomic attainment. … They have higher incomes; more are college graduates and homeowners; and fewer live in poverty. In all of these measures, their characteristics resemble those of the full U.S. adult population. (para. 1)

Special Barriers Facing Undocumented Immigrants

Though the vast majority of immigrants (77%) are in the country legally, a significant minority (roughly 23%) are **undocumented**, meaning they have no legal status (Budiman, 2020). In recent years, there have been roughly 10–11 million people living in the United States who are undocumented, which is about 3% of the population. Unless you have the lived experience of being an undocumented immigrant, it is hard to fathom what it feels like to "live in the shadows." Historically, undocumented immigrants have been unable to obtain a driver's license, gain eligibility for many social service programs, work legally, and attend higher education due to financial barriers and not having access to federal financial aid. Those who are undocumented must find a way to work despite not having any legal status or work permit. For this reason, some undocumented immigrants are exploited for their labor since their employer knows that they can get away with it since undocumented workers often have no legal recourse and would face **deportation**.

Undocumented individuals live with the fear of being caught by law enforcement or immigration officials and deported, which means being separated from their family members. Federal lawmakers (primarily those from the Democratic party) have been unsuccessful in passing federal legislation that would help undocumented people get onto a path to citizenship due to stark political divisions over this issue (see "Policy Focus: Immigration Legislation in the United States", later in this chapter).

Problems Affecting the Most Vulnerable Populations in the Global World

When we take a global perspective, we see vast inequalities and troubling human rights abuses and violations that disproportionately impact the most vulnerable people in the world such as women, children, migrants, and those living in extreme poverty.

Human Rights

The concept of **human rights** is one of the most important frameworks that we have and has helped to clarify our thinking around the inherent rights and freedoms that all humans should have no matter what country they live in or the various social identities that they hold. These basic rights are outlined in one of the most famous written documents of all time, the **U.N. Declaration of Human Rights**, which was adopted by the United Nations General Assembly in 1948 in the aftermath of World War II and the genocide of 6 million Jews. **Eleanor Roosevelt**, the widow of the former president Franklin Delano Roosevelt, was the chair of the commission that was charged with drafting this now sacred human rights document. The Declaration of Human Rights is the most translated document in the world and outlines two broad categories of universal human rights:

Economic, social, and cultural rights:

- adequate standard of living
- education

339 of 448 International Social Work and Human Rights

- health care
- housing
- water, food, and sanitation
- social security
- decent work, fair wage, and safe working conditions
- to take part in cultural life and enjoy one's culture

Civil and political rights:

- right to a life free from torture, slavery, forced labor, or cruel or degrading treatment
- freedom of movement
- liberty and privacy
- equal treatment before the law, fair trial, and presumption of innocence
- freedom of thought, opinion, and expression
- freedom of religion
- freedom from discrimination
- freedom of association and peaceful assembly
- ability to vote and participate in public and civic life

Summary of the Rights in the U.N. Declaration of Human Rights

Article 1: All human beings are born free and equal in dignity and rights.

Article 2: Everyone is entitled to all the rights and freedoms set forth in this Declaration, without distinction of any kind, such as race, colour, sex, language, religion, political or other opinion, national or social origin, property, birth or other status.

Article 3: Right to life, liberty and security of person.

Article 4: No one shall be held in slavery or servitude; slavery and the slave trade shall be prohibited in all their forms.

Article 5: No one shall be subjected to torture or to cruel, inhuman or degrading treatment or punishment.

Article 6: Right to recognition everywhere as a person before the law.

Article 7: All are equal before the law and are entitled without any discrimination to equal protection of the law.

Article 8: Right to an effective remedy by the competent national tribunals for acts violating the fundamental rights granted him by the constitution or by law.

Article 9: No one shall be subjected to arbitrary arrest, detention or exile.

Article 10: Right to a fair trial.

Article 11: Right to be presumed innocent until proved guilty.

Article 12: No one shall be subjected to arbitrary interference with one's privacy.

Article 13: Right to freedom of movement (within one's borders; to leave and return to one's home country).

Article 14: Right to seek asylum.

Article 15: Right to a nationality.

Article 16: Right to marry and have a family (requires consent from all parties).

Article 17: Right to own property.

Article 18: Right to freedom of thought, conscience and religion.

Article 19: Right to freedom of opinion and expression.

Article 20: Right to freedom of peaceful assembly and association.

Article 21: Right to take part in the government of his country, directly or through freely chosen representatives.

Article 22: Right to social security and to the economic, social and cultural rights indispensable for his dignity and the free development of one's personality.

Article 23: Right to work and to just and equal compensation.

Article 24: Right to rest and leisure.

Article 25: Right to adequate standard of living, including food, clothing, housing, and medical care and necessary social services, and the right to security in the event of unemployment, sickness, disability, widowhood, old age or other lack of livelihood in circumstances beyond one's control.

Article 26: Right to education.

Article 27: Right to freely participate in the cultural life of one's community and to benefit from scientific advancements.

Article 28: Everyone is entitled to a social and international order in which the rights and freedoms set forth in this Declaration can be fully realized.

Article 29: Everyone has duties to the community; one's rights can only be limited when meeting the just requirements of morality, public order and the general welfare in a democratic society.

Article 30: Nothing in this Declaration may be interpreted as allowing any State, group, or person to engage in any acts aimed at the destruction of any of the rights and freedoms set forth in this document.

Source: Adapted from United Nations (n.d.a.). Universal Declaration of Human Rights. https://www.un.org/ en/about-us/universal-declaration-of-human-rights

IMG 12.3

The Role of the United Nations

The **United Nations** is a world-famous international organization that most people are familiar with. For some social workers with a strong passion for doing work in the international arena, the United Nations is a dream job to have after gaining much experience in the field. It was founded in 1945 by 51 nations who believed it was important to have an organization that could bring the nations of the world together to address common problems and identify solutions as a global community. Today 193 nations are members. The four main purposes of the are as follows:

- to keep peace throughout the world

- to develop friendly relations among nations

- to help nations work together to improve the lives of poor people, to conquer hunger, disease and illiteracy, and to encourage respect for each other's rights and freedoms

- to be a centre for harmonizing the actions of nations to achieve these goals (United Nations, n.d.b., para. 4)

The United Nations has a strong humanitarian focus, and because of this they do important work to try to remedy the direst social problems in the world. The **2030 Agenda for Sustainable Development** was adopted by all U.N. member states in 2015. According to the U.N. Department of Economic and Social Affairs (n.d.), the 2030 agenda

> provides a shared blueprint for peace and prosperity for people and the planet, now and into the future. At its heart are the 17 Sustainable Development Goals (SDGs), which are an urgent call for action by all countries—developed and developing—in a global partnership. They recognize that ending poverty and other deprivations must go hand-in-hand with strategies that improve health and education, reduce inequality, and spur economic growth—all while tackling climate change and working to preserve our oceans and forests. (para. 1)

Much of the work of the United Nations in recent years has focused heavily on the following issues, which are all embedded in the 17 goals in the 2030 Agenda for Sustainable Development (visit https://www.un.org/sustainabledevelopment/ to read these goals in more detail):

- alleviating extreme poverty and hunger

- improving health and life expectancy, with a strong focus on decreasing child and maternal mortality

- the need for employment opportunities for all people while decreasing the number of people experiencing labor exploitation and human trafficking

- ensuring that all children have access to education

- promoting gender equality

- promoting public health initiatives with a strong focus on clean water and sanitation

- focusing on strategies needed to address climate change and environmental justice and to support clean and affordable energy

Social Work Practice in the International Arena

For social workers who work with groups of people from different cultural backgrounds, the concepts of cultural responsiveness, cultural competency, and cultural humility are crucial to understand. Social workers are taught that the interventions and practices that they use need to be "**culturally responsive**." This means that interventions need to be tailored in such a way so that the client's culture is respected and taken into account. Interventions designed for individuals from the dominant culture might not be effective for those from different cultural backgrounds. The concept of **cultural competency** refers to the idea that social workers should strive to learn as much as they can about the cultural backgrounds of those they serve such as a group's history, language, customs, practices, values, and belief systems. However, some have come to critique this approach, arguing that it leads to overgeneralizations, stereotyping, and "othering" of those from nondominant groups by predominately White social workers and overlooks the complexity and diversity of people within cultural groups (Morgaine & Capous-Desyllas, 2015). These critics argue that **cultural humility**, or "coming from a place of not knowing about people's cultures, histories, and experiences in life" is preferred since it emphasizes a commitment by social workers to engage in lifelong learning and understanding about the lived experiences of those from other cultures and supports the idea of the client being the expert of their life, not the social worker (Morgaine & Capous-Desyllas, 2015, p. 151). The National

IMG 12.4

Association of Social Workers (NASW) uses both terms in their Code of Ethics. Social workers who have a strong interest and desire to work with immigrants and refugees can work in government organizations or NGOs within the United States, or they can choose to work abroad.

Nonprofit and Governmental Organizations in the United States

Social workers who have a strong desire to specialize in international social work have an array of options when it comes to finding work in the United States.

- **Organizations that support immigrants and refugees:** There are a vast array of organizations in the United States that exist to support those who have immigrated to the country, such as refugee resettlement programs, organizations in border areas where people are trying to enter (e.g., seeking asylum), and organizations that are set up to provide specialized supports to specific immigrant groups that focus on help with basic needs (e.g., food, shelter, clothing, medical care, etc.), education, job training, employment, and spaces for connection and belonging with other people who share their cultural background. The Office of Refugee Resettlement (under the U.S. Department of Health and Human Services) is a government agency that provides services and benefits for refugees in the United States.

- **International adoption agencies:** Social workers with a passion for supporting people in adding to their family through adoption can find employment working in adoption agencies that focus on international adoption. Social workers in this area of practice gain crucial knowledge and expertise in the international adoption world, including important laws and policies that govern this area of practice. Families who adopt internationally need specialized support and training so that they can provide a safe and nurturing home for a child from another country, some of whom have had an unstable beginning to their life such as spending time in an orphanage.

- **Environmental justice organizations:** There has been a growing recognition that social workers need to become more engaged in issues of **environmental justice** because poor environmental conditions directly affect the health and mental health of people. In recent years, more and more social workers have become interested in working in organizations that are focused on protecting earth's physical environment and addressing threats to the sustainability of life on this planet due to the exploitation of our natural resources for corporate profit, the negative impacts of climate change, and the pollution of our air, water, and soil. This area of practice has been termed by some as "**climate justice work,**" "**green social work,**" or "**environmental social work.**" Social workers who practice in this area argue that social work's mission of social justice requires the profession to be involved due to the inequalities that impact many people. For example, the wealthiest people in the world use the majority of the world's resources, and the communities with the least financial and political capital suffer most from the negative effects of poor environmental conditions, which some refer to as **environmental racism**. Social workers who want to work in this area can find employment in environmental justice organizations at the local, state, and national levels.

- **Advocacy organizations**: Social workers working at the macro level can find employment in advocacy organizations that attempt to enact humane policies that impact immigrants and refugees at the local, state, national, and even international level. Prominent examples of organizations doing this work are the National Alliance for Immigrant Rights, UnidosUS, National Immigration Law Center, and many organizations at the state level such as New York Immigrant Coalition.

12.1   PRACTICE ACTIVITY

What Is the Best Terminology to Use?

Morgaine and Capous-Desyllas (2015) explain that different terminology has been used over the years to describe and categorize the nations of the world. At one time it was common to group nations into one of the following categories: *first world*, *second world*, and *third world* depending in large part on the country's wealth and political status. These terms became criticized over time as they implied a hierarchy, with *first-world* countries considered to be superior. Later, those in the international arena began to distinguish between countries that are *developed* versus *developing*, and this is still used commonly today. However, some do not like these terms because "they assume a desire to develop along the traditional 'western' model of economic development" (p. 394). Some prefer to use the terms *Global North* and *Global South* to indicate nations that are north and south of the equator. This can be a useful framework because, generally speaking, nations that are located in the Global North are better developed, while countries in the Global South are in the earlier stages of social, economic, and political development. However, this is not a perfect model as a few countries, such as Australia, are located in the Global South but are considered developed nations.

Questions

1.   What thoughts come up for you as you read this?

2.   Is the terminology that we use important?

3.   Which one of these do you prefer to use?

NGOs Outside of the United States

It can be an exciting and daunting endeavor for American social workers to move to another country to live and work with individuals facing a wide variety of needs. Americans who have lived or traveled abroad often describe it as "life-changing experience" because they are able to gain a broader view of the world and have a new appreciation for how people around the world do things differently and think differently than we do at home. It helps Americans to be less **ethnocentric**, which refers to the tendency for people to believe that their culture is superior to other cultures. When people think about working or volunteering for various organizations abroad, there are a few famous examples, such as the United Nations, the Peace Corps, and Amnesty International. These are all incredible organizations doing important work, but there are countless opportunities to do social work abroad. Morgaine and Capous-Desyllas (2015) highlight two primary focuses for social workers who work abroad: (a) social development work and (b) disaster management and international relief work. Human rights work is another important focus for some who are involved in working internationally.

Social Development Work

There are countless programs and organizations that operate in developing nations around the world and are focused on what has been termed **social development**, including many criticisms based on how well-intentioned people from developed nations have sometimes gone about this work in a way that is not sensitive to the needs and desires of the local people. Morgaine and Capous-Desyllas (2015) explain that international social development work involves projects that are geared towards "helping developing countries create the necessary capacity needed for sustainable solutions to issues that arise, with the goal of developing a greater quality of life for individuals, families, groups, and communities" (p. 407). They highlight five different domains of social development work that these projects fall under:

- **Democracy building:** Helping a nation to build systems and processes that support civic engagement and involvement in government, including the right to elect their leaders through free and fair elections.

- **Economic development:** Projects that focus on supporting the development of industries (e.g., agriculture) and local business (e.g., programs that allow low-income people access to a small and affordable loan to start a business)

- **Environmental development:** Projects that focus on wildlife preservation and ecology and mitigating the negative impacts of industrialization and pollution.

- **Human development:** Any projects that support people's development in society such as access to education; early childhood development; health programs; gender equality; poverty reduction; reducing child and maternal mortality, etc.

- **Infrastructure development**: Projects that focus on water systems, waste disposal, irrigation, etc. (p. 408)

Though there have been many successful programs and efforts in the world of social development, it is imperative that those who work in these programs work in collaboration with the local people in the development of solutions to allow them to share in the decision-making and that "the local communities' perceived needs and desires are what drives the development rather than the needs perceived by others" (Morgaine & Capous-Desyllas, 2015, p. 409).

Disaster Management and International Relief Work

A second important category of international work has to do with assisting individuals and communities in the aftermath of a **disaster** under emergency circumstances, which can be from man-made or natural causes. Many people can relate to the helplessness that they feel when they witness a horrific disaster and the impact that it has on people who are in the aftermath of a traumatic event or crisis. Examples of **natural disasters** include droughts, earthquakes, floods, hurricanes, tsunamis, tornados, wildfires, and winter storms. Examples of **man-made disasters** include war or genocide, terrorism, explosions, transportation

IMG 12.5

accidents, fires, epidemics, and hazardous materials exposures. Some projects are prevention focused and assist nations in developing preparedness plans and procedures that can be followed to assist people when a disaster occurs and to minimize suffering and causalities. **Relief work**, on the other hand, is focused on providing immediate assistance to those who have been impacted (e.g., basic human needs such as food, water, clothing, shelter, and family reunification) as well as mental health professionals who provide emotional and psychological support via crisis intervention.

Human Rights Work

A third prominent category of international work includes organizations, such as Amnesty International and Human Rights Watch, that draw attention to **human rights abuses or violations** that impact various groups of people around the world. When a country's government does not uphold the list of rights that are included in the Declaration of Human Rights, they are at risk of violating **international law**. An exhaustive list of examples of human rights abuses would be quite long but includes genocide; sexual violence; torture; violations of free speech and freedom of expression, including persecuting those who speak out against their government; war crimes; unfair trials; slavery; and human trafficking. The main role of human rights organizations is

- to publicize and draw attention to current human rights abuses around the globe;
- to pressure governments and businesses to intervene and stop human rights violations;
- to get justice for victims; and
- to punish those who committed human rights violations or atrocities.

Human trafficking, which is also referred to as "modern-day slavery," is a serious human rights violation that occurs across the globe, including in the United States. It is strongly opposed by a number of human rights organizations such as the United Nations. **Human trafficking** occurs when human beings are exploited for their labor by means of force, threat, coercion, deception, or abduction. Major types of human trafficking include domestic servitude (i.e., employees who coerced and/or forced to work in private homes and are convinced that they cannot leave), sex trafficking (i.e., forced into the commercial sex industry), forced labor (i.e. forced to work under the threat of violence for no pay), bonded labor (i.e., forced to work until a debt is paid off), child labor (i.e., enslavement of a child), and forced marriage (i.e., women and children who are forced to marry against their will; End Slavery Now, n.d.). Shocking data from 2016 gather by the International

Labour Organization, Walk Free Foundation, and the International Organization for Migration revealed the extent of human trafficking—40 million people were victims of modern slavery, and 152 million children between ages 5 and 17 were subjected to child labor (International Labor Organization, 2017).

International Social Work Case Study

You are a social worker working in a community-based organization that provides physical and mental health services for many low-income people in the community. The vast majority of your clients are Latinx, many from Mexico and Central America. Many of your clients are documented, but some are undocumented, meaning they have no legal status. Over the years, you have learned much about the plight and experiences of those who come to this country without legal status—the trauma many endured in their home country due to war and violence and the obstacles they face once they arrive in the United States and have to find a way to live and work and raise a family while having no legal papers to be here. You are often overcome by the courage it took for these families to come here for better opportunities and a better life for themselves and their children. You run several groups with undocumented youth who have been raised in the United States but who need support as they navigate how they will attend college, obtain employment, and raise a family one day considering the obstacles they face with not being a U.S. citizen. You love working with these youth and want to support them in achieving their goals and dreams. You have witnessed many of these youth become activists as they work through various immigrant rights organizations to try to get legislation passed at the state and national level such as in-state tuition for undocumented youth, the DREAM Act, and comprehensive immigration reform.

You live in a border state where the politics surrounding illegal immigration are very politically divisive, and some of the people, including some state lawmakers, in your state support passing laws that focus on catching and deporting those who are in the country illegally. Even though you are working at the micro level in a clinical role, you have been trying to figure out what else you might be able to do.

Questions

1. What thoughts and feelings come up for you as you read this case study?

2. What are the arguments on both sides of this political issue, and which side aligns more with your personal and professional values?

3. Review the NASW Code of Ethics. What guidance can it provide you as to how you might position on this issue?

4. Based on your professional experience and expertise, how could you get involved in a macro role to possibly influence legislation in your state?

5. What questions or feelings are raised for you as you imagine yourself in this situation?

Policy Focus: Immigration Legislation in the United States

For many decades, immigration has been one of the most divisive political issues in the United States. Generally speaking, Democrats and moderate Republicans have been in support of legislation that would create a path to citizenship for the roughly 10–11 million undocumented immigrants currently residing in the United States, referred to as **comprehensive immigration legislation**, while conservative Republicans have strongly opposed this. Most of the comprehensive immigration bills that have been proposed over the years outline a process that would create a **path to legalization** for undocumented immigrants, and some of the bills include penalties (e.g., paying a fine and/or back taxes). Many of these bills also include increased border security, verification requirements for employers to ensure they are not hiring undocumented workers, and changing the visa system to bring in more high-skilled workers. Under most comprehensive plans, immigrants would have to pass a background check and prove they can speak or are studying English, among other requirements. Even though this legislation has the support of most Democrats and some Republican lawmakers, a minority of conservative federal lawmakers have been successful in defeating these measures.

Because lawmakers in the U.S. Congress have been unable to find a way to compromise on this issue and meaningful policy change has stalled at the federal level, many states have decided to take matters into their own hands. Conservative lawmakers in right-leaning states, such as Arizona, have taken a more punitive approach that focuses on catching and deporting those who are here without legal status. Meanwhile, lawmakers in left-leaning states have passed legislation to try to make some progress, though they admit that these efforts fall short of the progress that could be made with a strong comprehensive bill at the federal level. For example, lawmakers in some states have passed state laws to better support the undocumented residents in their state. Some states, for example, allow undocumented immigrants to obtain a driver's license, pay in-state tuition at state colleges or universities, and obtain some social service benefits. Additionally, some states and cities have become **"sanctuaries"** for undocumented immigrants, which means that they are not willing to cooperate with federal immigration officials in turning in undocumented immigrants so they can be deported (unless they have engaged in serious criminal activity).

Unfortunately, the **DREAM Act**, which would create a pathway to citizenship for some young undocumented people who have been raised in the United States, has not been successfully passed into law at the federal level despite efforts to pass it since 2001. Because of this, President Obama created the **DACA program**

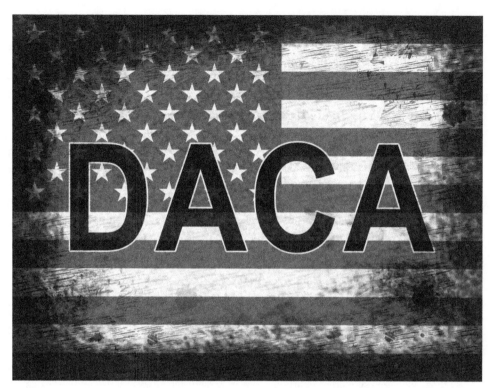

IMG 12.6

(i.e., Deferred Action for Childhood Arrivals) via an executive order in 2012. As a result of this executive order, the Department of Homeland Security would not have the authority to deport young undocumented immigrants who come forward and qualify for this program. Homeland Security officials now have the authority to grant deferred action, a reprieve that has to be renewed every 2 years. These young people will then be able to obtain work permits so they can work legally as well as obtain a driver's license. However, it is important to note that DACA is a temporary measure and is not a path to permanent citizenship as laid out in the DREAM Act. It is also at risk of being overturned since it was passed into law by President Obama's executive order. Opponents of DACA (such as former President Trump and conservative lawmakers who are challenging it in the courts), have attempted to abolish the DACA program. So, while the future of the DACA program hangs in the balance, many Americans continue to wait for federal lawmakers to finally take some needed action so that the 10–11 million undocumented people living in the United States do not have to remain living in the shadows.

Gender Inequality and Human Trafficking

One of the biggest priorities for those who work in the international arena, including those who work at the United Nations, is to work toward **gender equality** so that women have the same opportunities and rights under the law as men. Though conditions for girls and women continue to improve, they are still disproportionately impacted by discrimination, poverty, and violence. Unfortunately, the United States is one of only a handful of nations that has failed to ratify **the Convention on the Elimination Against All Forms of Discrimination Against Women**, or CEDAW. CEDAW is a human rights treaty that outlines the rights for all women across the globe. The following problems impact many women around the world (Mapp, 2014; Ritter 2022:

- **Violence against women, including femicide:** There are various forms of **sexual violence** that many women are subjected to such as sexual harassment, sexual assault, and rape. **Intimate partner violence** is also a serious social problem in many societies where women are subjected to violent and aggressive acts by an intimate partner, dating partner, or former spouse that can include physical abuse, psychological abuse, and sexual violence. **Femicide** is the intentional killing of women, because they are women, by intimate partners or those who are not intimate partners. It is truly disturbing how many women are killed at the hands of men.

- **Honor killings and female genital mutilation:** In some countries, predominantly Muslim nations, women are subjected to **honor killings** when family members believe that a women has brought dishonor among the family. This can happen when a family believes that a woman in the family has engaged in an extramarital affair, wants to choose who she wants to marry against the wishes of her family, or even after being raped. According to Mapp (2014), honor killings are against the law but are frequently not punished severely. According to the World Health Organization (WHO, 2023a), more than 200 million girls and women have been subjected to female genital cutting in 30 countries, including Asia, Africa, and the Middle East. WHO considers this a human rights violation that is unacceptable and should not be practiced. **Female genital mutilation** involves "the partial or total removal of external female genitalia or other injury to the female genital organs for non-medical reasons" (WHO, 2023a, para. 1) and can cause serious complications and prevent enjoyment of sexual activity. Female genital cutting is rooted in societal beliefs that seek to preserve a women's chastity and to ensure premarital virginity and marital fidelity.

- **Feminization of poverty:** The feminization of poverty refers to social science data and statistics that document that women are disproportionately impacted by living in poverty. One of the biggest risk factors to living in poverty is being a woman due to lack of access to education, gender discrimination, unequal access to opportunity in the workplace, and the gender wage gap, meaning that women are often paid less than men in the workplace. Various organizations such as the United Nations have worked hard to change cultural norms and beliefs that that girls and women have the right to primary and postsecondary education and to fight against the idea that it is not a good use of resources to educate girls due to the belief that their only option is to marry and have children.

- **Early marriage:** Though it is against the law in many countries for women to be married under the age of 18, these laws are not always enforced. Poverty is one reason for this practice since families do not have to bear the expense of raising girls in the family. Mapp (2014) notes that young girls who marry early are at risk for domestic violence, early pregnancy, and not finishing their education, which results in a lack of employment opportunities and maternal death and injury.

- **Government representation by women:** Though progress has been made, many women are denied the opportunity to hold public office and to be involved in the civic and political affairs of their community and nation. Even in the United States, there has never been a woman president and roughly 20–25%% of the U.S. Congress is made up of women.

- **Women's health and maternal mortality:** In many countries, women do not have the same access to quality health care as men do, and some nations have high rates of **maternity mortality,** which means that a woman dies in childbirth. The good news is that between 2000 and 2077, the number of maternal deaths per 100,000 live deaths dropped by 38% worldwide. However, every day in 2017, roughly 810 women died from preventable causes related to pregnancy and childbirth (WHOb, 2023).

- **Reproductive rights and family planning:** Women in many countries across the globe are not provided with access to **contraception and abortion rights** due to strong cultural and religious beliefs that limit their right to control their bodies in this regard. According to the Center for Reproductive Rights (n.d.), "970 million women, representing 59% of women of reproductive age, live in countries that broadly allow abortion. While a majority of women live in countries where they can exercise their right to abortion, 41 percent of women live under restrictive laws. The inability to access safe and legal abortion care impacts 700 million women of reproductive age. According to the World Health Organization, 23,000 women die of unsafe abortion each year and tens of thousands more experience significant health complications" (para. 7).

PRACTICE ACTIVITY

Human Rights Treaties

International human rights treaties, organized through the United Nations, are important human rights instruments that are used to improve the lives of groups of people who face oppression around the world no matter what country they live in. The United States has ratified some of these treaties yet has not ratified others, such as the U.N. Convention on the Rights of the Child and the U.N. Convention on the Elimination of All Forms of Discrimination Against Women. Do some research to better understand why the United States is an outlier in the world in failing to ratify these two international treaties that are set up to protect the rights of children and women.

1. Who supports ratification, and who does not?

2. What are the arguments on both sides of this debate?

3. Do you think the United States should ratify them? Why or why not?

Chapter Summary

The United States is one of the most diverse nations in the world, and nearly every nation is represented by those who have immigrated to the United States (Budiman, 2020). Social work practice with immigrants is one of the oldest areas of social work practice in the country, as we recall from the early social workers in the settlement house movement who served newly arriving immigrants attempting to settle into many large cities in the north and northeast part of the country, such as Chicago, Boston, and New York City. One of the major themes of this chapter was the contradictory attitudes that exist with regard to immigrants who move to the United States. Some welcome them and believe they make our country stronger and richer in cultural diversity, while others fear and resent them. Beginning a new life and starting over in a new country is not an easy path; thus, there are many opportunities for social workers to support individuals and families who are on this journey. This chapter described career path options for social workers who wish to work with immigrants and refugees here in the United States as well as abroad primarily in areas such as political advocacy, addressing income insecurity and basic needs, providing access to education and employment, social development work, protecting human rights, and disaster management international relief work.

There has been a wide range of advocacy work at the state and federal level led by immigration activists and advocacy organizations in attempts to pass various policies to support immigrant populations. Some of these policies have been successful such as state-level policies that allow undocumented immigrants to obtain a driver's license, pay in-state tuition at state colleges or universities, and obtain some social service benefits. President Obama created the DACA program via an executive order to protect undocumented youth from deportation. But federal legislation such as the DREAM Act and comprehensive immigration reform policies have failed to pass due to the divisive politics surrounding the topic of immigration in recent years. Social workers who are interested in working as researchers can work for an organization such as Pew Research Center, which gathers macro-level social science data using public polling and demographic research methods to help inform sound decision-making by lawmakers and other decision-makers. Current global challenges demand that social workers be involved in change efforts that are focused on human trafficking, gender inequality, and environmental justice.

Discussion Questions

1. After learning about social work practice in the international arena, could you see yourself working with immigrants and refugees in the United States or abroad? Why or why not?

2. Over the past few decades, lawmakers in both parties have tried to get comprehensive immigration legislation passed at the federal level, which would create a path to citizenship for the 10–11 million undocumented people who live in the United States, but these efforts have been unsuccessful. Why has this been such a tough and divisive political issue that has prevented lawmakers in finding enough areas of compromise?

3. This chapter highlighted a number of social problems facing women around the globe that are rooted in the problem of gender inequality. What was most surprising to you, and how can nations continue to work together to improve conditions for women and young girls?

4. After learning about the difference between cultural competence and cultural humility, which one resonates with you more? How can you work to enhance this ability when working with future clients who will come from diverse and different backgrounds?

5. What did you learn about social work practice with immigrants and refugees that was most surprising to you?

References

American Immigration Council. (2021, September 14). *How the United States immigration system works.* https://www.americanimmigrationcouncil.org/research/how-united-states-immigration-system-works

Budiman, A. (2020, August 20). *Key findings about U.S. immigrants.* Pew Research Center. https://www.pewresearch.org/fact-tank/2020/08/20/key-findings-about-u-s-immigrants/

Budiman, A., Tamir, C., Mora, L., & Noe-Bustamante, L. (2018, August 20). *Facts on U. S. immigrants, 2018.* Pew Research Center. https://www.pewresearch.org/hispanic/2020/08/20/facts-on-u-s-immigrants-current-data/

Center for Reproductive Rights. (n.d.). *The world's abortion laws.* https://reproductiverights.org/maps/worlds-abortion-laws/

End Slavery Now. (n.d.). *Slavery today.* http://www.endslaverynow.org/learn/slavery-today

International Labor Organization. (2017). *40 million in modern slavery and 152 million in child labour around the world.* https://www.ilo.org/global/about-the-ilo/newsroom/news/WCMS_574717/lang--en/index.htm

Mapp, S. C. (2014). *Human rights and social justice.* Oxford University Press.

Morgaine, K., & Capous-Desyllas, M. (2015). *Anti-oppressive social work practice.* SAGE.

Pew Research Center. (n.d.). *About Pew Research Center.* https://www.pewresearch.org/about/

Pew Research Center. (2013, February 7). *Second-generation Americans: A portrait of the adult children of immigrants.* https://www.pewresearch.org/social-trends/2013/02/07/second-generation-americans/

Ritter, J. A. (2022). *Social work policy practice: Changing our community, nation, and the world* (3rd ed.). Cognella.

United Nations. (n.d.a.). *Universal declaration of human rights.* https://www.un.org/en/about-us/universal-declaration-of-human-rights

United Nations. (n.d.b.). *History of the UN.* https://www.un.org/un70/en/content/history/index.html

United Nations Department of Economic and Social Affairs. (n.d.). *Do you know all 17 SDGs?* https://sdgs.un.org/goals

United Nations High Commissioner for Refugees. (2022). *Global trends: Forced displacement in 2021.* https://www.unhcr.org/62a9d1494/global-trends-report-2021

World Health Organization. (2023a, January 31). *Female genital mutilation.* https://www.who.int/news-room/fact-sheets/detail/female-genital-mutilation#:~:text=More%20than%20200%20million%20girls,rights%20of%20girls%20and%20women.

World Health Organization. (2023b, February 22). *Maternal mortality.* https://www.who.int/news-room/fact-sheets/detail/maternal-mortality

Credits

CHAPTER 13

Social Work Practice in Substance Abuse and Addiction

▐ Learning Objectives

After reading this chapter, students will be able to do the following:

- Summarize the various impacts of substance use disorders (SUDs) on individuals, families, and communities, including its prevalence in the United States

- Define SUDs and differentiate between substance abuse and substance addiction

- Describe the primary treatment settings and treatment approaches for those with a SUD

- Identify career path options and roles for social workers who want to work in the field of substance addiction

- Explain why using a harm-reduction approach is important in SUD practice and summarize the research findings on programs that use harm-reduction values and practices

- Evaluate state and federal policies that seek to legalize marijuana and other substances

- Describe the opioid epidemic and the troubling rise in overdose deaths in the United States over the past decade, including racial disparities

- Explain why the war on drugs is a racial justice issue of concern for social workers

- Evaluate goodness of fit with substance abuse and addictions as a potential future career option

SOCIAL WORKER SPOTLIGHT:
Perri Corvino, LCSW, MA, LAC (They/Them)

Some of us knew from early on that we wanted to be social workers. Some of us followed a winding path toward social work and discovered that social work is just right for us! When I decided to go to college, I pursued a bachelor's degree in psychology (SUNY Potsdam) because I hadn't heard of social work. But as I was looking for graduate programs, I stumbled across social work. As I read about the field, I quickly realized that social work was more aligned with my progressive values and politics than psychology. So, I entered a Master of Social Work (MSW) program at Loyola University Chicago, and I am currently writing my dissertation to fulfill the requirements of my PhD in social work at Smith College.

I have a passion for working with people recovering from substance addiction. Ironically, I avoided all materials during graduate school about addiction because I was raised in an addictive family system and didn't want to learn more about it! I continued to follow my winding path and found my first job at a residential facility for addiction recovery. While there, I quickly found that I was shaped by my history to do this work. At this first job, I thought that all addictive processes were due to a chemical imbalance. However, I soon learned that trauma played a major role in problematic substance use: Almost all the people I have treated for addiction had a history of trauma and were using substances to escape from their distressing memories and intense symptoms.

While I knew that addiction affected people across all social identities, I didn't realize how people embodying marginalized identities were affected in harsher and crueler ways. Here are some examples: I have seen a disproportionate number of People of Color imprisoned for minor drug offenses, especially Black people. I have seen poor people involved with child welfare solely because they use substances recreationally. I have seen queer youth use substances to ease the pain of daily discrimination and rejection. I have seen fellow social workers struggle with substances because they were feeling burned out from hearing these injustices.

As I recognized the bigger, more complex picture of substance use, I knew that I had to shift my social work practice to fully embrace all people who use substances. I attended trainings and workshops on treatment methods. I sought out supervisors who were innovative and creative in their practice approach. Through my exploration, I identified three frameworks that are the foundation of my social work practice: trauma-informed care (TIC), anti-oppressive practice (AOP), and harm reduction. TIC encouraged me to acknowledge the universality of trauma and the deep effects trauma has on a person and society. AOP encouraged me to acknowledge the far reach of oppression, especially for People of Color. Harm reduction taught me to embrace all people by respecting their autonomy and choices.

TIC, AOP, and harm reduction are buzzwords these days. I'd like to give you a sense of what it's like to view the world and our experiences through these perspectives on the macro and micro level. Consider my macro vision of a society that works diligently to support and embrace people who use substances. First, we could reduce the stigma surrounding substance use to relieve people of shame and open a pathway to treatment. Second, we could confront our racism, sexism, cisgenderism, and so on, because these -isms lead to institutional policies that incarcerate people instead of treating them. Third, we could change our federal and state drug policies to favor treatment over incarceration. Fourth, we could provide every person with health care, reproductive freedom, universal income, and expanded access to food assistance programs to unburden people from financial burdens that cause undue stress and hardship. In other words, when our basic financial needs are attended to and met, we have the option to connect with others instead of medicating ourselves with substances.

On the micro level, we social workers can make meaningful changes to our values, beliefs, and perspectives by integrating TIC, AOP, and harm reduction into our practice. At this moment, I have a set of principles that guide me that I would like to share with you. I strive to create a comfortable-enough treatment environment that supports learning, retention, integration, and eventually, recovery. I am responsive, transparent, and open to feedback. I offer time for us to have thoughtful and intentional conversations about identity and culture. I partner with clients to ensure that their treatment needs are being addressed. I welcome the expertise of the client's lived experience. I strive to use inclusive language to reduce the chances of stigmatizing or shaming a client. And at the core of my practice is my dedication to lifelong learning, connecting genuinely with others, acting through my integrity, and striving for liberation for all.

My beautiful, winding path toward and through social work has been marked by serendipitous occurrences, intentional shifts, trust in the process of discovery, and a willingness to embrace new perspectives. If you're like me, you might sometimes feel lost, totally confident at other times, and an amalgamation of emotions in between. And while the lost times can be lonely and despairing, I remind myself to apply TIC, AOP, and harm reduction to my life. In other words, my social work practice not only supports the people I serve, but my social work practice supports me.

Unfortunately, most people are affected by **drug and alcohol addiction**, whether they have experienced it firsthand or have witnessed the devastating impact on a friend or loved one. During the pandemic, numerous news articles emerged with alarming data about the rise in deaths due to **drug overdoses**, the majority caused by synthetic opioids, such as fentanyl. Between April 2020 and 2021, more than 100,000 Americans died of overdoses, and according to a piece in *The New York Times*, "The figure marks the first time the number of overdose deaths in the United States has exceeded 100,000 a year, more than the toll of car crashes and gun fatalities combined. Overdose deaths have more than doubled since 2015"

(Rabin, 2021, para. 2). In response, local and federal government agencies and lawmakers have come up with a variety of policies and programs to help address this growing social problem in U.S. society.

Because of the high prevalence of SUDs in our society, the chances are very low that any practicing social worker will avoid encountering this issue. Some social workers choose to make this their primary area of focus, while others work in settings, such as child protection, criminal justice, and mental health, in which some clients are suffering with addiction as one of their presenting challenges. Thus, it is vital that all social workers gain important knowledge and experience in this field and are aware of substance abuse services in their community. Though there are a variety of addictions that people can have, such as food, shopping, gambling, and sex addiction, this chapter will focus on addiction to the following **substances**, some that are legal and some that are illegal:

- Alcohol (e.g., beer, wine, distilled liquors)
- Nicotine (e.g., cigarettes, cigars, chewing tobacco)
- Cannabinoids (e.g., marijuana)
- Hallucinogens (e.g., LSD; methylenedioxy-methamphetamine, or MDMA)
- Opioids, including synthetic opioids (e.g., heroin, methadone, oxycodone, morphine, Vicodin, fentanyl)
- Depressants (e.g., benzodiazepines such as Valium and Xanax and barbiturates)
- Stimulants (e.g., cocaine, methamphetamine)

While there is still much to learn about both the causes and treatment of addiction, researchers have come a long way in their knowledge and understanding. Gone are the days when alcohol and drug addiction were viewed as an individual failing by those who simply lacked the will power to stop abusing. Today, we understand that addiction is a **mental health disorder** with harmful consequences for individual and their loved ones as well as society at large. We also know that recovery is possible with the right support. One of the positive benefits of this new understanding is that people are more compassionate toward those who suffer from addiction and there is less social stigma than in the past. However, despite this advancing knowledge, some in our society still debate the best way to address this social problem and whether the focus should be on punishment (e.g., via the criminal justice system) or treatment (i.e., rehabilitation). This chapter provides a current and topical examination of SUDs in the three important domains of practice, policy, and research.

IMG 13.1

Overview of the Larger Social Problem: Substance Abuse in the United States

According to the National Institute on Drug Abuse (NIDA, 2020), people take drugs for a variety of reasons, such as curiosity; how it makes them feel; to lessen their social anxieties; to improve their performance at school, work, and in sports; and because of social pressure. It is important to understand the distinction between **substance abuse** and **substance addiction** or **substance use disorder (SUD)**. When someone abuses substances, they take it more often or use it in higher doses than they are supposed to but are able to change and/or stop this behavior—unlike those who suffer from addiction. The National Institute of Mental Health (NIMH, 2021) defines a substance abuse disorder as "a mental disorder that affects a person's brain and behavior, leading to a person's inability to control their use of substances such as legal or illegal drugs, alcohol, or medications. Symptoms can range from moderate to severe, with addiction being the most severe form of SUDs" (para. 1). NIDA (2020) defines **drug addiction** as "a chronic, relapsing disorder characterized by compulsive drug seeking and use despite adverse consequences. It is considered a brain disorder, because it involves functional changes to brain circuits involved in reward, stress, and self-control. Those changes may last a long time after a person has stopped taking drugs" (p. 4).

Social workers sometimes work with individuals who have a SUD along with a **co-occurring mental health disorder** (e.g., anxiety disorder, major depression, bipolar disorder, PTSD, etc.), meaning that they coexist at the same time. One often comes before the other. For example, someone with a mental health disorder might turn to substances to alleviate their symptoms. In other cases, the use of drugs or alcohol might worsen or trigger a mental health condition. But experts agree that both should be treated at the same time.

Prevalence

Even though we hear a lot about SUDs in our society, it is helpful to understand how many people are impacted by it. The **Substance Abuse and Mental Health Services Administration (SAMHSA)** collects yearly data on the percentage of the population who have a SUD. According to their latest report, in 2021, 46.3 million people aged 12 or older (or 16.5% of the population) had a SUD in the past year. This includes 29.5 million who had an alcohol use disorder, 24 million who had a drug use disorder, and 7.3 million people who had both an alcohol use disorder and a drug use disorder (SAMHSA, 2022). In terms of age, the percentage was highest for those aged 18–25 (25.6%), followed by adults aged 26 and older (16.1%), then by adolescents aged 12–17 (8.5%) (SAMHSA, 2022).

Causes of Substance Addiction

Many of us wonder why some people who use drugs and alcohol develop an addiction, while others do not. Today, experts agree that there is no one cause of a SUD; rather, the causes are multifaceted and are often a combination of **risk factors** (both biological and environmental) and **protective factors** (McLellan, 2017; NIDA, 2020). The more risk factors someone has increases the chances that taking drugs will lead to addiction, while having more protective factors can reduce a person's risk. NIDA (2020) reports that genes account for between 40% and 60% of a person's risk of addiction (2020):

Personal risk factors

- Genes (family history of substance abuse or mental disorders)
- History of child maltreatment
- Aggressive behavior in childhood
- Age/stage of development, gender, and ethnicity
- Having a current mental health disorder
- Struggles at school (i.e., low academic achievement)
- Poor social skills and peer refusal skills
- Drug use at an early age (harmful effects on the developing brain)

Environmental risk factors

- High conflict and chaotic home environment; violence in the home
- Having parents who use substances
- Living in a neighborhood with high poverty, high prevalence of drug and alcohol misuse, and easy access to inexpensive substances
- Being exposed to heavy advertising of drug and alcohol products
- Availability of drugs at school
- Peer influences to use substances

Protective factors

- Involvement in healthy recreational and social activities
- Supportive monitoring by parents
- Positive relationships in general
- Involvement in school
- Antidrug policies at school
- Development of healthy coping skills
- Self-efficacy (belief in one's self-control)

McLellan (2017) hits home the importance of understanding both risk factors and protective factors as well as **how critical adolescence is** for determining whether many people develop a SUD:

> Prevention science has concluded that there are three important points regarding vulnerability. First, no single personal or environmental factor determines whether an individual will have a substance misuse problem or disorder. Second, most risk and protective factors can be modified through preventive policies and programs to reduce vulnerability. Finally, although substance misuse problems and disorders may occur at any age, adolescence and young adulthood are particularly critical at-risk periods.
>
> With regard to substance use disorders, research now indicates that more than 85% of those who meet criteria for a substance use disorder sometime in their lifetime do so during adolescence Put differently, young adults who transition the adolescent years without meeting criteria for a substance use disorder are not likely to ever develop one. (para. 29, 30)

PRACTICE ACTIVITY

When you imagine working with individuals who have a severe SUD, what thoughts, feelings, and images come up for you? Do you notice any resistance to working with this population? If so, where do you think this resistance stems from?

Impact of SUD on Individuals, Families, and Larger Society

When experts explain the negative consequences of substance use addiction, they point to the multiple impacts on the individual user, their loved ones, and society at large.

Consequences to the Individual User

There is a long list of health consequences to drug and alcohol addiction that can cause serious impacts to one's health and well-being, such as lung and heart disease, stroke, cancer, and mental health disorders. Methamphetamines can cause serious dental problems, and some drugs can damage or destroy nerve cells. Drug users who share equipment when injecting drugs can contract diseases such as HIV and hepatitis C. And of course, some cause overdoses and even heartbreaking fatalities. For example, each year, illicit and prescription drug overdoses cause tens of thousands of people to die (over 100,000 in 2021), alcohol contributes to the annual deaths of more than 140,000 Americans (Centers for Disease Control and Prevention [CDC], 2022a), and smoking tobacco and exposure to secondhand smoke is linked to an estimated 500,000 casualties each year (CDC, 2022c).

Consequences to Family Members and Loved Ones

There are a number of ways that a SUD can impact other people in the drug-addicted individual's life, such as friends, family, and loved ones. First there is the emotional impact on loved ones who have to witness someone they love suffer the devastating impacts of addiction. It can be particularly traumatic for children who have a parent with a SUD, and in some cases child protection authorities must become involved if there is a serious risk to the children's health and safety. Some children have to be separated from parents who end up being incarcerated and, in some cases, might have to live with a relative or foster family.

Secondhand tobacco smoke can increase the risk of heart disease and lung cancer in people who have never smoked, which is why we have so many laws today prohibiting people from smoking in public spaces such as airplanes, bars and restaurants, and the workplace. Finally, there can be serious consequences when a pregnant woman uses substances while pregnant. Some exposed children can experience withdrawal symptoms after birth, and some can have problems with their development. Children who were exposed to alcohol before birth can have **fetal alcohol spectrum disorder**, which can include physical problems as well as problems with their behavior and learning.

Consequences to Larger Society

According to NIDA (2020), Americans pay more than $700 billion a year in increased health care costs, crime, and lost productivity due to the use and misuse of alcohol, nicotine, illicit drugs, and prescription drugs. Therefore, many experts point to the importance of investing in efforts focused on the **prevention of SUDs**. One concrete example of a consequence to larger society is motor vehicle accidents as a result of people who drive under the influence and cause injuries and even death to other drivers on the road. The CDC (2022b) reports that in 2020, 11,654 people were killed in motor vehicle crashes involving alcohol-impaired drivers, which accounted for 30% of all traffic-related deaths in that year. This translates to 32 people in the United States being killed every day in crashes involving an alcohol-impaired driver—one death every 45 minutes.

The Opioid Epidemic

It has been alarming to witness the rising number of deaths in the United States that are caused by **drug overdoses** over the past decade, with many experts labeling it as a public health crisis and epidemic. In 2021, news headlines around the country reported data from the CDC that for the first time in U.S. history, deaths caused by drug overdoses had topped 100,000 (the actual figure being 106,699) and that the majority of these deaths in 2021 (80,411) were caused by opioids; this figure was 21,089 in 2010 (NIDA, 2023). The majority of deaths due to overdoses are caused by **opioids**, which includes prescription opioids, heroin, and synthetic opioids (primarily fentanyl). However, overdose deaths caused by stimulants such as cocaine and methamphetamine are also significant, with 32,537 deaths in 2021 (NIDA, 2023). As a result of this troubling trend, multiple government agencies and lawmakers at the federal and state level have responded to help address this social problem in our society. See Practice Activity 13.2.

Fentanyl is a synthetic prescription drug that is used by doctors to help patients with pain after a surgery or for chronic pain management. However, fentanyl is also illegally made in labs and sold as pills, in powder form, or put on blotter paper to be placed under the tongue. Fentanyl is so dangerous and lethal because it is like morphine, but is 50–100 times more powerful, and it is often mixed in with other drugs such as heroin, cocaine, methamphetamine, and MDMA (which consumers are often unaware of). It is cheap to produce, making it an attractive option for those who produce and sell drugs illegally. Fentanyl is highly addictive based on its potency and the effect that it has on the brain, which leads to an intense and euphoric high. There is a medicine called Naloxone that can be given to a person to reverse a fentanyl overdose (see "Research Focus: Efficacy of Harm-Reduction Programs" later in this chapter). And while medications like methadone and buprenorphine can significantly reduce deaths among opioid addiction patients, only about a quarter of people who could benefit from these treatments receive them, according to multiple barriers (Lopez, 2023).

IMG 13.2

In 2022, the CDC reported data that showed troubling **racial disparities** when examining race and ethnicity among those who overdosed between 2019 and 2020 (Kariisa, et al., 2022). Researchers reported a disproportionate increase in overdose deaths among Black persons (44%) and American Indian and Alaska Native persons (39%) compared to White persons (22%). And the rate among Black males 65 years and over increased to nearly seven times that of White males of the same age. They found that overdose deaths were associated with living in counties with high economic inequality, and the researchers recommended the need to prioritize prevention and SUD treatment in these areas. Finally, this data revealed that previous substance use treatment was lowest among Black decedents and approximately one half that of White decedents, which reveals racial inequities regarding access to treatment. One of the recommendations in their report was as follows:

> Prevention efforts must rapidly incorporate existing, evidence-based, culturally responsive interventions that address polysubstance use and social determinants of health to reduce inequities around prevention, treatment, and harm reduction. Integration of evidence-based substance use disorder treatment with culturally tailored traditional practices, spirituality, and religion might improve treatment acceptance among Black and AI/AN populations. Culturally specific awareness campaigns,

employment in nontraditional and community settings, and trusted community prevention messengers to assist with linkages to treatment and harm reduction services could reduce stigma and mistrust as well as improve access and provision of care. (Kariisa et al., 2022, para. 21)

13.2   PRACTICE ACTIVITY

When the data reported by government agencies such as NIDA and the CDC showed the astronomic rise of deaths in the United States due to drug overdoses (over 100,000 in 2021) over the past decade, the government began to act as this became viewed as a public health crisis and an epidemic that required swift government action and funding. Visit a few of the following websites to learn more:

- Actions taken by the Biden Administration:

  https://www.whitehouse.gov/ondcp/briefing-room/2022/08/31/actions-taken-by-the-biden-harris-administration-to-address-addiction-and-the-overdose-epidemic/

  https://www.whitehouse.gov/briefing-room/statements-releases/2022/09/23/fact-sheet-biden-harris-administration-announces-new-actions-and-funding-to-address-the-overdose-epidemic-and-support-recovery/

- The CDC plays an important role in collecting and reporting data, educating the public, and supporting states with effective strategies:

  https://www.cdc.gov/opioids/overdoseprevention/cdc-role.html

  https://www.cdc.gov/stopoverdose/

- The U.S. Department of Health and Human Services developed an overdose prevention strategy:

  https://www.hhs.gov/overdose-prevention/background#strategy

- The federal government passed three pieces of legislation in recent years to address the epidemic by expanding prevention efforts, expanding access to treatment and overdose reversal drugs, increasing the oversight of prescription opioids, and curbing the supply of illegally produced opioids—the Comprehensive Addiction and Recovery Act of 2016 (CARA); the 21st Century Cures Act; and the Substance Use-Disorder Prevention That Promotes Opioid Recovery and Treatment (SUPPORT) for Patients and Communities Act. (Google these bills to learn more.)

- The federal government has invested $10 million in grant funding between the years 2022 and 2025 to support the expansion of harm-reduction programs in order to reduce deaths due to overdoses (administered by SAMHSA):

  https://www.samhsa.gov/find-help/harm-reduction

- Legislation has been passed in many states and cities to address this problem at the local and state level. (Google your state to see what actions, if any, have been taken.)

The U.S. War on Drugs

Most Americans are familiar with the phrase "the war on drugs" but may not fully know its origins and history. Today, the **war on drugs** is viewed with controversy, and many have become critical of how the laws that were implemented as a result of this "war" tragically impacted many poverty-stricken communities of color (Alexander, 2010; Morrison, 2021). President Nixon declared a war on drugs in 1971 and stated that it was "public enemy number one" (NPR, 2007). Two years later, Nixon created the DEA, or **Drug Enforcement Agency**, to coordinate these efforts across various law enforcement agencies. Years later, one of Nixon's policy aides, John Ehrlichman, admitted in an interview that Nixon's tough-on-crime laws were a mechanism for them to target two groups that were against the Nixon administration, namely leftist activists and Black people (Baum, 2016). But many think about the 1980s as the time period when the war on drugs rapidly accelerated during the presidency of Ronald Reagan.

During the 1980s, crack cocaine became a significant public health and public safety concern and was commonly referred to as the "**crack cocaine epidemic**." First Lady Nancy Reagan began her "Just Say No" to drugs campaign, and Americans during this time watched commercials on television warning them about the dangers of drug use. Then in 1986, President Reagan signed a piece of legislation into law, the **Anti-Drug Abuse Act of 1986**, which allocated $1.7 billion to fight the drug war. One of the major features of this law was to create **mandatory minimum sentences** (anywhere from 20 years to life) for drug offenses, which social scientists later discovered led to mass incarceration and stark racial disparities in the prison system. An example of racial bias in Reagan's 1986 law is revealed by differences between how people were sentenced for **crack cocaine versus powder cocaine**. Possession of crack cocaine, which was used more by low-income People of Color, resulted in harsher penalties than possession of powder cocaine, which was used by more affluent people. These get tough-on-crime policies were continued by later U.S. presidents George H.W. Bush and Bill Clinton.

The United States incarcerates a larger share of its population than any other nation in the world—2.1 million people at the end of 2019 (Gramlich, 2021), sometimes referred to as **mass incarceration**. A review of federal and state incarceration data by the Associated Press shows that, between 1975 and 2019, the U.S. prison population went from 240,593 to 1.43 million Americans; and about 20% of people who were incarcerated listed a drug offense as their most serious crime (Morrison, 2021). Today, many social scientists and criminologists report with dismay the impact that these laws have had on poverty-stricken communities of color, as many nonviolent drug offenders became entangled with the criminal justice system instead of being offered drug treatment:

The racial disparities reveal the war's uneven toll. Following the passage of stiffer penalties for crack cocaine and other drugs, the Black incarceration rate in America exploded from about 600 per 100,000 people in 1970 to 1,808 in 2000. In the same time span, the rate for the Latino population grew from 208 per 100,000 people to 615, while the white incarceration rate grew from 103 per 100,000 people to 242. (Morrison, 2021, para. 11)

Michelle Alexander's best-selling book, published in 2010, *The New Jim Crow: Mass Incarceration in the Age of Colorblindness*, has been a very influential book that raised people's awareness of the role of structural racism in the criminal justice system. The thesis of the book, which is supported by social science data, is that since the 1970s, the criminal justice system has been used to subjugate and marginalize communities of color and to preserve the racial caste system in the United States—thus, **"the new Jim Crow."** Alexander documents how states replicated the federal government's mandatory minimum drug sentencing laws and other features that grew out of this movement such as the rise of private prisons, the explosion of the prison population, the militarization of the police, and new laws that take basic rights away from those who have been convicted of felonies (e.g., right to vote, right to secure employment, right to access social welfare benefits, etc.). While racial disparities still exist when it comes to drug sentencing, the **Equal Justice Initiative** (2019) notes that there was a different response from the government and the media when it came to the opioid epidemic (which impacts more White people) compared to the crack cocaine epidemic. For example, the victims of opioids were portrayed more compassionately, and the government responded with legislation and funding to combat the opioid epidemic.

Treatment for Drug and Alcohol Addiction

Addiction is treatable, but like other chronic diseases, it cannot be totally cured. The goal of treatment is to support people in ending their use of substances and to regain control over their life, a process that is known as **being in recovery**. There are **11 diagnostic criteria** in the *Diagnostic Manual of Mental Disorders*, 5th edition, text revision (or DSM 5-TR; American Psychological Association, 2022) that help guide mental health practitioners in diagnosing people with a SUD. Having two or three of these indicates a mild disorder, four or five a moderate disorder, and six or more a severe disorder:

- Using the substance in larger amounts or for longer than intended
- Not managing to cut down or stop using the substance despite wanting to

- Spending a lot of time getting, using, or recovering from use of the substance
- Cravings and urges to use the substance
- Inability to manage commitments (e.g., work, home, or school) due to substance use
- Continuing to use, even when it causes problems in relationships
- Giving up important activities (e.g., social, occupational, or recreational) because of use
- Continuing to use, even when it puts you in danger
- Continuing to use, even when physical or psychological problems may be made worse by the substance
- Experiencing drug tolerance meaning you need more to get the effect you want
- Experiencing withdrawal symptoms

According to NIDA, experiencing a **relapse**, which means returning to using drugs or alcohol after a period of sobriety, can be a normal part of the recovery process for some people and does not necessarily mean that treatment has failed. Rather, it is proof that recovery involves changing behaviors that are deeply rooted and is an indication that treatment needs to be resumed or modified or that another approach is needed. However, NIDA (2020) does point out that even though it is normal for people to relapse, it can also be very dangerous and even deadly due to the risk of overdose. They explain that "if a person uses as much of the drug as they did before quitting, they can easily overdose because their bodies are no longer adapted to their previous level of drug exposure" (p. 23).

Addiction experts and researchers have studied why it is so difficult for many people to stop using drugs and alcohol. First, nearly all addicted individuals believe that they can stop using on their own without any help, particularly at the outset of the disease. Second, due to the ways that drugs interact with parts of the brain, the high that people feel from using drugs produces feelings of great pleasure and euphoria, which then leads to repeating this pleasurable activity. NIDA (2020) explains why drug rewards are so much more powerful than natural rewards in life:

> This is why a person who misuses drugs eventually feels flat, without motivation, lifeless, and/or depressed, and is unable to enjoy things that were previously pleasurable. Now, the person needs to keep taking drugs to experience even a normal level of reward—which only makes the problem worse, like a vicious cycle. Also, the person will often need to take larger amounts of the drug to produce the familiar high—an effect known as *tolerance*. (p. 18)

IMG 13.3

Third, long-term drug use produces changes in the brain that have behavioral consequences that make it difficult to stop, such as an inability to control one's impulses to use drugs and alcohol despite knowing the negative consequences of this behavior.

Primary Treatment Approaches

There are four primary approaches to treatment for those with a SUD—medication, behavioral therapies, 12-step support groups, and programs that use harm-reduction practices. One of the hallmarks of treatment is understanding that no single treatment is right for everyone.

Medication Approaches and Detoxification

For some people, such as those who are addicted to opioids, medication is considered the first line of treatment, in combination with behavioral therapies. Medication can be used to treat withdrawal symptoms and/or to help the brain to gradually adapt to the absence of the drug, which can help people focus on treatment and prevent relapse. Medications can also be used to help some people to **detoxify from drugs**, though if someone wants to recover, this is just the first step in the recovery process and is not sufficient alone. Examples of medications that are commonly used include methadone for those addicted to opioids, nicotine replacement therapies, and a few that are used with those experiencing alcohol withdrawal.

Behavioral Therapies

Various forms of behavioral therapy are commonly used to help treat those with a SUD. Prominent examples include cognitive behavioral therapies (CBT), family therapy, and counseling approaches such as motivational interviewing. **CBT** is a very effective therapy for people experiencing certain mental health disorders, such as a SUD. It focuses on helping people understand how their thoughts and thought patterns impact their mood and behaviors. This therapy helps people to identify their dysfunctional automatic thoughts, ways of thinking that are inaccurate or distorted, and underlying core beliefs that shape how they view the world. The goal is to help people become aware of their thought patterns and develop healthier and more positive behaviors and coping skills. **Family therapy** can be helpful in providing support to the whole family that has been impacted by a family member's addiction. Family therapy can help members learn how to best support someone who is in recovery, to deal with unhealthy family dynamics, and to strengthen the health and functioning of the family.

Motivational interviewing (MI) has been found to be a successful approach when working with people in recovery who often struggle with finding the motivation to stop using and are thus resistant to changing their behavior. This is a strengths-based approach that uses empathy, compassion, and reflective listening in its approach. MI acknowledges that resistance is part of the change process and that the counselor's role is to support the individual in recognizing and resolving the ambivalence they are experiencing throughout the recovery process.

Twelve-Step Groups

The most famous and well known 12-step group is **Alcoholics Anonymous (AA)**, which was founded in 1938 by Bill Wilson, author of the Big Book that is used heavily in AA. **Narcotics Anonymous** is set up to serve those in recovery from drug addiction. Twelve-step groups are not run by professionals; rather, they are an example of a peer support group model in which members of this community support each other in recovering from drug and/or alcohol addiction. Important aspects of the 12-step model are attending meetings regularly (members come to share their experiences with each other), selecting a sponsor to help them work through the 12 steps, and engaging in service to the organization by helping other alcoholics or drug-addicted individuals in the organization. There are several AA phrases that have become commonplace in our society such as "one day at a time," "making amends," "surrendering to a higher power," and "first things first." The **12 steps of AA** (n.d.) are as follows:

1. We admitted we were powerless over alcohol—that our lives had become unmanageable.

2. Came to believe that a Power greater than ourselves could restore us to sanity.

3. Made a decision to turn our will and our lives over to the care of God as we understood Him.

4. Made a searching and fearless moral inventory of ourselves.

5. Admitted to God, to ourselves, and to another human being the exact nature of our wrongs.

6. Were entirely ready to have God remove all these defects of character.

7. Humbly asked Him to remove our shortcomings.

8. Made a list of all persons we had harmed, and became willing to make amends to them all.

9. Made direct amends to such people wherever possible, except when to do so would injure them or others.

10. Continued to take personal inventory and when we were wrong promptly admitted it.

11. Sought through prayer and meditation to improve our conscious contact with God as we understood Him, praying only for knowledge of His will for us and the power to carry that out.

12. Having had a spiritual awakening as the result of these Steps, we tried to carry this message to alcoholics, and to practice these principles in all our affairs.

IMG 13.4

At one time the zero-tolerance approach to addictions was viewed as the only valid approach, and many were initially skeptical of harm-reduction approaches (e.g., facilities that distributed clean syringes to those using drugs) as they viewed them as encouraging or approving of substance abuse. What was once considered a controversial practice has now become accepted as an evidence-based practice. What thoughts and feelings come up for you as you learn about the values, philosophy, and practices behind harm-reduction programs? Would you feel comfortable working in a program that utilizes these practices? Why or why not?

There are also 12-step groups for family members and friends of people in recovery, such as **Al-Anon** and **Alateen**. Al-Anon and Alateen provide support to those who have been impacted by someone else's drinking. Al-Anon (n.d.) explains that

> alcoholism is a family disease. The disease affects all those who have a relationship with a problem drinker. Those of us closest to the alcoholic suffer the most, and those who care the most can easily get caught up in the behavior of another person. We react to the alcoholic's behavior. We focus on them, what they do, where they are, how much they drink. We try to control their drinking for them. We take on the blame, guilt, and shame that really belong to the drinker. We can become as addicted to the alcoholic, as the alcoholic is to alcohol. We, too, can become ill. (Frequently asked questions: How do alcoholics affect family and friends?)

Overview of Treatment Settings for Those With SUDs

There are a range of settings in which treatment is provided for those who seek support with recovering from substance use addiction, as shown in Table 13.1. The continuum of care includes medical detoxification centers, inpatient treatment options, outpatient treatment options, and services provided to those who become involved with the criminal justice and child welfare systems.

Principles of Effective Treatment

NIDA is a federal agency that is considered one of the leading experts on the science of addiction. They produce a report titled *Principles of Drug Addiction Treatment: A Research Based Guide* that is in its third edition (revised in 2018). In this guide, they outline **13 principles of effective treatment** for substance abuse disorders:

- Addiction is a complex but treatable disease that affects brain function and behavior.

- No single treatment is appropriate for everyone.

TABLE 13.1   Treatment Settings for Those With SUDs

Medical detox centers	Detox centers seek to medically stabilize patients, minimize their withdrawal symptoms, prevent the potentially harmful effects of withdrawal, and help them transition into a substance abuse rehabilitation program or other form of continued care.
Long-term residential treatment	In this setting, individuals with a SUD live in a residential setting for 24 hours a day in a therapeutic community with other residents and staff, usually between 6–12 months, or longer. This is a nonhospital setting where treatment is highly structured and individualized. The range of services provided can include individual and group counseling/therapy, medication, family counseling, and vocational and legal support. It is also referred to as "long-term rehab" or "in-patient care."
Short-term residential treatment	Also known as "short-term rehab," this setting is similar to long-term residential treatment except that the stay is much shorter; it can be less than 30 days but most always less than 90 days. Short-term rehab is the only option for some people due to financial reasons and/or only being able to be away from work and family for a shorter time. It is highly recommended to continue to stay engaged in treatment afterward, for example in outpatient treatment and/or a 12-step program.
Outpatient treatment programs	Outpatient programs do not require overnight stays and thus provide a less intensive and less expensive form of treatment, but one that can afford more flexibility for those with job and family responsibilities. Individuals visit a clinic or treatment center during specific days and hours each week, and similar to residential treatment, a variety of counseling and therapeutic services are provided. There are various levels of intensity (e.g., less than 9 hours a week to 20 hours a week). Some who start out inpatient treatment later transition to outpatient services.
Treating people with a SUD who are involved with the criminal justice and/or child welfare system; drug courts	In each state, there are programs and services that are offered to people with a SUD who become involved with the criminal justice system and/or the child welfare system. Licensed addictions counselors and other mental health professionals who work in these systems, or are contracted by these systems, provide substance abuse treatment within correctional facilities and other settings. It is vital that treatment continue upon release from these systems to ensure continued progress in recovery. The purpose of **drug courts** is to divert nonviolent offenders from the criminal court system by providing them support from an interdisciplinary team of professionals who have specialized training in substance abuse. Social workers are heavily utilized in these specialized courts based on their professional knowledge and expertise. The ultimate goal is to reduce recidivism by connecting the offender with needed substance abuse treatment.

- Treatment needs to be readily available.

- Effective treatment attends to multiple needs of the individual, not just their drug abuse.

- Remaining in treatment for an adequate period of time is critical. Research indicates that most addicted individuals need at least 3 months in treatment to significantly reduce or stop their drug use and that the best outcomes occur with longer durations of treatment.

- Behavioral therapies—including individual, family, or group counseling—are the most commonly used forms of drug abuse treatment.

- Medications are an important element of treatment for many patients, especially when combined with counseling and other behavioral therapies.

- An individual's treatment and services plan must be assessed continually and modified as necessary to ensure that it meets their changing needs.

- Many drug-addicted individuals also have other mental disorders. When these problems co-occur, treatment should address both (or all).

- Medically assisted detoxification is only the first stage of addiction treatment and by itself does little to change long-term drug abuse.

- Treatment does not need to be voluntary to be effective.

- Drug use during treatment must be monitored continuously, as lapses during treatment do occur.

- Treatment programs should test patients for the presence of HIV/AIDS, hepatitis B and C, tuberculosis, and other infectious diseases as well as provide targeted risk-reduction counseling, linking patients to treatment if necessary.

Major Barriers to Treatment

There are numerous barriers that prevent many people with a SUD from accessing treatment. A recent article in *The New York Times* pointed out that "if it's easier to get high than get treatment, people who are addicted will get high. The U.S. has effectively made it easy to get high and hard to get help" (Lopez, 2022, para. 5). While it is frustrating to see these barriers, it is helpful to know what they are so they can be addressed by policy makers and leaders in this field:

- *Stigma*: Even though we have come a long way in reducing the stigma surrounding addiction since there is more understanding that it is a disease and a mental health disorder, there are still many people who feel ashamed and do not want their family members, friends, and coworkers to know they suffer from a SUD. In other cases, some cannot yet see that they have a problem and/or do not believe that treatment can help them. People with a SUD and another mental health disorder (i.e., a co-occurring disorder) are also less likely to seek help.

- *Treatment remains inaccessible to many*: Many people cannot afford out-patient or inpatient treatment, particularly if they do not have health insurance that provides adequate coverage for it. Federal legislation such as the Mental Health Parity Act and the Affordable Care Act expanded access to many people by expanding who qualifies for Medicaid and by requiring health insurance companies to provide equal coverage for mental disorders and other physical health disorders, but unfortunately there are still many people who go without, and many families still have to fight with their health insurance company to get access to needed treatment. However, 12-step programs, such as AA and NA, which are free of cost, are important options.

- *They live in an area with a shortage of SUD treatment providers*: There are some areas of the country, particularly in rural states and communities, that have a shortage of mental health providers and treatment centers to provide substance abuse treatment; thus, people must get on a wait list until a space opens up and may have to travel long distances to receive care.

- *Difficulty navigating the complex system for SUDs*: The health care and mental health care systems in the United States are complex and not very well coordinated, which many people find overwhelming to navigate unless they have a lot of support.

- *Barriers related to gender and racial discrimination*: When women try to access treatment, they often find services that are designed more for men and do not take into consideration their lived experiences and needs, such as the need for childcare. And there are racial disparities due to a number of factors such as BIPOC being (a) more likely to be punished by the criminal justice system; (b) more likely to be lower income, which limits access to treatment; (c) more likely to live in an under-resourced community with fewer treatment options; (d) more likely to be offered treatment options that are designed for White people and are not culturally responsive; and (e) the impact of racism and racial discrimination.

Research Focus: Harm Reduction Programs

At one time, **harm-reduction practices** were considered controversial, but today they are widely supported by experts and practitioners in the field and are considered an evidence-based practice. Many credit people who use drugs with coming up with the ideas and values behind harm-reduction programs. This approach developed in response to those who became critical of the "zero-tolerance" approach to drugs and alcohol, which does not work for everyone who struggles with using abusing substances.

The philosophy behind **harm reduction** centers on the idea that you need to meet people with a SUD where they are and that whether someone is in recovery or not, they can still be supported and provided with important information about how to stay as safe and healthy as possible while they are using substances. The values that inform this approach include nonjudgment; treating individuals with dignity, compassion, and respect; accepting that behavior change is often an incremental process; and respecting people's autonomy and self-determination. It is a public health strategy that acknowledges that drugs and alcohol are a part of society and that certain practices can help people to use them as safely as possible; abstinence is one option among many others. Examples of harm-reduction practices include the following:

- Providing free syringes to prevent the transmission of diseases like HIV and hepatitis

- Overdose prevention sites where people can consume drugs in a monitored center and staff can intervene when there is an overdose

- Fentanyl test strips that can detect the presence of fentanyl in other drugs such as cocaine, meth, and heroine

- Naloxone kits, which are portable pouches that contain an opioid antidote that can be administered to revive someone who is overdosing and provide a short window of time to get them to access emergency medical services

- Taking prescription medication before being exposed to HIV to decrease the chances of getting it (pre-exposure prophylaxis, or PrEP)

- Addiction treatment and 12-step support groups

- Sex education and testing and treatment for sexually transmitted infections (STIs)

According to NIDA (n.d.), researchers who have studied harm-reduction strategies have concluded that they lead to significant benefits such as preventing deaths from overdoses as well as the transmission of infectious diseases among people who use drugs. Other benefits include reducing emergency department visits and costly health care services and offering people who use drugs opportunities to connect to addictions treatment and other health care services in settings with less stigma. Additionally, a recent article in the *Journal of the American Medical Association* (JAMA) stated, "Decades of robust research on harm reduction strategies, specifically syringe services and naloxone distribution, demonstrate that these strategies are associated with reduced morbidity, mortality, and transmission of infectious diseases and improved individual health outcomes and services engagement and that they have high cost-effectiveness" (Samuels et al., 2022, p. 1).

Because the research evidence has shown the benefits of this approach to individuals and larger society, the federal government has invested $10 million in grant funding between the years 2022 and 2025 to support the expansion of harm-reduction programs in the nation in its efforts to reduce deaths due to overdoses. These funds are administered though SAMHSA, the Substance Abuse and Mental Health Services Administration.

Social Work Practice in Substance Abuse and Addictions

As described in Chapter 7, the mental health workforce is made up of professionals from various disciplines and professional backgrounds such as social work, psychology, psychiatry, and counseling, though licensed clinical social workers (LCSWs) are the largest group of mental health providers in the United States. The U.S. Bureau of Labor Statistics (BLS, 2022) reports that in 2021 there were 119,800 social workers who worked in mental health and substance abuse and that employment in this field of practice is expected to grow 11% between 2021 and 2031, showing a continuing demand for these services.

Those with a Bachelor of Social Work (BSW) can work as case managers and care coordinators in a setting that provides substance abuse services, and they can also work in prevention and education programs. According to NIDA (2022), there are **prevention programs** that are backed up by research evidence that can significantly reduce early use of tobacco, alcohol, and drugs by helping them to perceive the use of these substances as harmful. There are three types of prevention programs: universal programs (provided to all youth in a school or other setting), selective programs (focused on youth who have specific factors that place them at increased risk), and indicated programs (designed for youth who have begun using substances).

However, a MSW and obtaining licensure as a LCSW is generally recommended since this is what is needed to diagnose, treat, and provide counseling and therapy to those who suffer with addiction. Though it is not required, some social workers who work in this field decide to gain further education by getting certified or licensed as an **addictions counselor** as this provides additional specialized knowledge about the science and practice of drug and alcohol addiction. The requirements for this type of licensure and/or certification vary state to state. Those with a PhD in social work can work as researchers to evaluate interventions and add to the knowledge base in efforts to help us better understand substance abuse and addiction.

Drug Court Case Study

Olivia is a social worker who works in a drug court and supports men and women suffering from substance abuse addiction and because of this have gotten into trouble with the law. One of her clients is Monica, who has just successfully completed drug court and probation after achieving 2 years of sobriety. She began using drugs and alcohol at age 16 and eventually found herself addicted to meth and heroin. She became involved with the criminal justice system after being charged with a DUI and drug distribution. She lost her kids and her home and spent some time being homeless and living on the street. Despite the stereotypes of people who are drug addicted, Monica says that she came from "a good family" with a mother who was a teacher and a father who owned a local business. She describes them as good parents and feels guilty for all that she has put them through.

After some serious "soul searching," Monica decided to dedicate herself to the drug court program, to get sober, and to turn her life around. Though she describes the drug court program as "super demanding," she explains that the weekly therapy, 12-step program, and case management support helped her to get sober for the first time in 14 years. Her children are back living with her, she has stable housing, and she is about to begin a program to become a drug and alcohol counselor. Monica cannot say enough about the drug court program and how much the various professionals supported her in her recovery. She states, "I would not be here today without their support and belief in me. I feel excited and hopeful for my future, which I never thought would be possible."

Questions

1. What feelings come up for you as you imagine working with a client like Monica in a program like this?

2. What are the strengths in this case?

3. What kinds of supportive services would you recommend to continue to support Monica and her family and to help her prevent relapsing?

4. What kind of work can social workers like Olivia engage in since drug courts have been shown to be very successful for many program participants?

5. What questions does this case raise for you?

Policy Focus: Policies to Legalize Marijuana (and Other Drugs)

Social workers working at the macro level can find work in various organizations that shape public policies focused on substance use and addiction in society. Prominent examples of organizations doing this work are the Partnership to End Addiction, the Drug Policy Alliance, and organizations that support marijuana legalization, such as the American Civil Liberties Union (ACLU) and the National Organization for the Reform of Marijuana Laws (NORML). Historically, one of the biggest political debates in the United States has been whether the use and sale of recreational marijuana (and other drugs) should be legal. In the past, **marijuana legalization** was a very controversial position, but today it enjoys much wider support and acceptance from the general public, and the country has seen a growing number of states that have moved to legalize it. There has been a sea change in the majority of Americans' opinions on this issue as 2022 data from the Pew Research Center shows that 88% of Americans support marijuana legalization for medical or recreational use. Only 10% say it should not be legal at all (Green, 2022).

In 2012, Colorado and Washington state became the first U.S. states to legalize the recreational use of marijuana when voters in those two states supported statewide ballot measures to do so. Over the next 10 years, 19 other states would

IMG 13.5

follow suit, as well as Washington, DC, and Guam, bringing the total number of U.S. states to 21 (as of February 2023).

Those who argue against marijuana legalization are opposed to drug use for moral reasons and believe that it is harmful to people and to society at large. They worry that drug legalization leads to more people becoming addicted and developing a SUD. Supporters, on the other hand, argue that marijuana has medicinal benefits, that people have the right to use drugs as long as they are not harming other people, and that marijuana is less dangerous than alcohol, which is legal. They maintain that when drugs are legalized and regulated by the government, the criminal element is removed and marijuana can be taxed like other goods and services, which brings in more tax revenue. Furthermore, many organizations point out that drug enforcement laws are racist and have contributed to the mass incarceration of People of Color who are punished more harshly than White people for the same drug crimes (see "Social Justice Spotlight: The War on Drugs" earlier in this chapter). In their statement supporting federal legislation to decriminalize cannabis, the ACLU (2022) reports that over 400,000 people are arrested each year for possession of marijuana and that a Black person is 3.64 times more likely to be arrested even though Black and White people use marijuana at similar rates.

In the U.S. Congress, recent efforts have been made, primarily by Democratic lawmakers, to **decriminalize marijuana** and remove it from the list of federally controlled substances. In 2022, two pieces of federal legislation were introduced to achieve this, the *Marijuana Opportunity and Reinvestment and Expungement Act* and the *Cannabis Administration and Opportunity Act.* However, they have been unable to pass the U.S. Congress due to not having enough votes from Republican lawmakers. President Biden has called on all state governors to offer pardons to all people who have been convicted of simple marijuana possession. Even though some argue that drugs other than marijuana should be legalized, this does not currently have the same level of support as marijuana legalization.

Chapter Summary

The NIMH (2021) defines a SUD as "a mental disorder that affects a person's brain and behavior, leading to a person's inability to control their use of substances such as legal or illegal drugs, alcohol, or medications. Symptoms can range from moderate to severe, with addiction being the most severe form of SUDs" (para. 1). In the past, addiction was viewed as a moral failing that people lacked the willpower to control, but now it is understood that it is a mental health disorder that is not curable, but that people can recover from with the right support. In 2021, news headlines around the country reported data from the CDC that for the first time in U.S. history, deaths caused by drug overdoses had topped 100,000 and that the vast majority of these deaths were caused by synthetic opioids, primarily fentanyl. This has resulted in people viewing this as an urgent public health crisis, which prompted a variety of responses from state and federal lawmakers, including dedicated federal funding and government investments in programs that embrace harm-reduction values and practices. A number of advocacy organizations have also been focused on laws that decriminalize marijuana and dismantle the war on drugs, which has resulted in the mass incarceration of a disproportionate number of People of Color since the 1980s.

There are a multitude of employment opportunities for social workers who want to impact change in the field of addictions at the micro, mezzo, and macro levels. Those with a BSW can work as case managers and case coordinators and in education and prevention programs. LCSWs can work in a variety of treatment settings such as detox centers, inpatient treatment centers, and outpatient treatment centers, and they can treat those who become involved with the criminal justice and child welfare systems. Some social workers choose to get licensed or certified in addictions counseling to gain more skills and knowledge for working in this field of practice, though it is not required. Those with a PhD in social work can choose this as an area of research. It is highly recommended that social workers gain experience with harm-reduction practices since this is a major feature of working in this field. There is a shortage of substance abuse treatment facilities and providers in many areas of the country, and social workers who work in this field will continue to be in high demand over the next decade, according to the BLS. At the macro level, social workers are needed to help remove the barriers that prevent so many people from getting access to needed substance abuse treatment and to advocate for policies at the state and federal level that are informed by the research evidence and are free from racial bias.

Discussion Questions

1. After learning about social work practice in the field of substance addiction and the major career paths outlined in this chapter, which of these settings feel like they could be a good fit for you? Which ones do not feel like a good fit?

2. A number of criticisms were highlighted in this chapter related to racial inequities that result in some serious negative consequences for certain groups. Summarize them here. Which ones concern you the most?

3. What is your opinion on state laws that have legalized marijuana over the past decade? Do you support federal legislation that would decriminalize

marijuana use in the United States? Defend your position citing arguments on both sides of this debate.

4. This chapter discusses the role of social stigma for people who struggle with a SUD. Do you feel we have made significant progress in reducing stigma? Is there still more work to do?

5. This chapter highlighted some promising interventions in this field, such as harm-reduction approaches, efforts to reduce deaths due to overdose, prevention programs, and drug courts. How do these approaches align with social work values and ethics? What more would you like to learn about these interventions to have a more informed opinion about them?

References

American Civil Liberties Union. (2022). *ACLU comment on Senate introduction of the Cannabis Administration and Opportunity Act.* https://www.aclu.org/press-releases/aclu-comment-senate-introduction-cannabis-administration-and-opportunity-act

Al-Anon. (n.d.). *Frequently asked questions: How do alcoholics affect families and friends?* https://al-anon.org/newcomers/faq/

Alcoholics Anonymous. (n.d.). *The twelve steps.* https://www.aa.org/the-twelve-steps

Alexander, M. (2010). *The new Jim Crow: Mass incarceration in the age of colorblindness.* The New Press.

American Psychiatric Association. (2022). *Diagnostic and statistical manual of mental disorders* (5th ed., text revision). https://doi.org/10.1176/appi.books.9780890425787

Baum, D. (2016). Legalize it all: How to win the war on drugs. *Harper's Magazine.* https://harpers.org/archive/2016/04/legalize-it-all/

Centers for Disease Control and Prevention. (2022a). *Deaths from excessive alcohol use in the Unites States.* https://www.cdc.gov/alcohol/features/excessive-alcohol-deaths.html#:~:text=More%20than%20140%2C000%20people%20die,how%20you%20can%20take%20action.

Centers for Disease Control and Prevention. (2022b). *Impaired driving: Get the facts.* https://www.cdc.gov/transportationsafety/impaired_driving/impaired-drv_factsheet.html

Centers for Disease Control and Prevention. (2022c). *Tobacco use: Data and statistics.* https://www.cdc.gov/tobacco/data_statistics/index.htm

Equal Justice Initiative. (2019, December 9). *Racial double standard in drug laws persists today.* https://eji.org/news/racial-double-standard-in-drug-laws-persists-today/

Gramlich, J. (2021, August 16). *America's incarceration rate falls to lowest level since 1995.* Pew Research Center. https://www.pewresearch.org/fact-tank/2021/08/16/americas-incarceration-rate-lowest-since-1995/

Green, T. V. (2022, November 22). *Americans overwhelmingly say marijuana should be legal for medical or recreational use*. Pew Research Center. https://www.pewresearch.org/fact-tank/2022/11/22/americans-overwhelmingly-say-marijuana-should-be-legal-for-medical-or-recreational-use/

Kariisa, M., Davis, N. L., Kumar, S., Seth, P., Mattson, C. L., Chowdhury, F., & Jones, C. M. (2022). Vital signs*:* Drug overdose deaths, by selected sociodemographic and social determinants of health characteristics—25 states and the District of Columbia, 2019–2020. *Morbidity & Mortality Weekly Report, 71*, 940–947. http://dx.doi.org/10.15585/mmwr.mm7129e2

Lopez, G. (2022). A rising death toll: Overdoses are increasing at a troubling rate. *The New York Times*. https://www.nytimes.com/2022/02/13/briefing/opioids-drug-overdose-death-toll.html

Lopez, G. (2023). Lives we can save: The opioid crisis doesn't need to be this bad. It's another example of America's surprising resistance to effective treatments. *The New York Times*. https://www.nytimes.com/2023/02/21/briefing/opioids.html

McLellan A. T. (2017). Substance misuse and substance use disorders: Why do they matter in healthcare? *Transactions of the American Clinical and Climatological Association, 128*, 112–130. https://www.ncbi.nlm.nih.gov/pmc/articles/PMC5525418/

Morrison, A. (2021). *50 year war on drugs imprisoned millions of Black Americans*. Associated Press. https://apnews.com/article/war-on-drugs-75e61c224de3a394235df80de7d70b70

National Institute on Drug Abuse. (n.d.). *Harm reduction*. https://nida.nih.gov/research-topics/harm-reduction

National Institute on Drug Abuse. (2018). *Principles of drug addiction treatment: A research-based guide* (3rd ed.). https://nida.nih.gov/publications/principles-drug-addiction-treatment-research-based-guide-third-edition/preface

National Institute on Drug Abuse. (2020). *Drugs, brain & behavior: The science of addiction*. https://nida.nih.gov/publications/drugs-brains-behavior-science-addiction/drug-misuse-addiction

National Institute on Drug Abuse. (2023). *Drug overdose death rates*. https://nida.nih.gov/research-topics/trends-statistics/overdose-death-rates#:~:text=Opioid%2Dinvolved%20overdose%20deaths%20rose,with%2080%2C411%20reported%20overdose%20deaths

National Institute of Mental Health. (2021). *Substance use and co-occurring mental disorders*. https://www.nimh.nih.gov/health/topics/substance-use-and-mental-health#part_2423

National Public Radio. (2007, April 2). *Timeline: America's war on drugs*. https://www.npr.org/templates/story/story.php?storyId=9252490

Rabin, R. C. (2021, November 17). Overdose deaths reached record high as the pandemic spread. *The New York Times*. https://www.nytimes.com/2021/11/17/health/drug-overdoses-fentanyl-deaths.html

Samuels, E. A., Bailer, D. A., & Yolken, A. (2022). Overdose prevention centers: An essential strategy to address the overdose crisis. *JAMA Network Open*. https://jamanetwork.

com/journals/jamanetworkopen/fullarticle/2794326?utm_campaign=articlePD-F&utm_medium=articlePDFlink&utm_source=articlePDF&utm_content=jamanet-workopen.2022.22153

Substance Abuse and Mental Health Services Administration. (2022). *Key substance use and mental health indicators in the United States: Results from the 2021 National Survey on Drug Use and Health* (HHS Publication No. PEP22-07-01-005, NSDUH Series H-57). Center for Behavioral Health Statistics and Quality. https://www.samhsa.gov/data/report/2021-nsduh-annual-national-report

U.S. Bureau of Labor Statistics. (2022, September 8). *Social workers*. Occupational Outlook Handbook. https://www.bls.gov/ooh/community-and-social-service/social-workers.htm#tab-6

Credits

CHAPTER 14

Looking Forward

Learning Objectives

After reading this chapter, students will be able to do the following:

- Evaluate goodness of fit with social work as a potential future career option

- Summarize important social issues that need be a strong area of focus for the social work profession looking forward

- Clarify the significance of the 12 grand challenges of social work

- Differentiate between burnout, compassion fatigue, and vicarious traumatization

- Define and differentiate between environmental justice, environmental racism, and green social work

- Describe key challenges facing social workers in the workplace, along with potential solutions to better support them

- Explain both the challenges and benefits of social work unifying around needed political change in the United States

- Provide two examples of workplace trends that are occurring within social work

t is important for the social work profession to think ahead; anticipate future human needs based on social, political, economic, and technological changes in our society; and be nimble in planning for how to be responsive and meet those needs. Due to the many pressing social and political issues facing our country, this is an important time to become a social worker and effect change with individuals, families, organizations, communities, and society at large. In recent years, Americans have witnessed a global health pandemic, rising income inequality between the rich and poor, economic recessions that have resulted in economic hardship for many, high levels of gun violence, rising political divisions between those on the left and the right, and troubling social justice issues affecting women, communities of color, and LGBTQ+ individuals. As described in this book, there are **several hallmarks of a social work education** that make social workers uniquely qualified to serve as change agents and to address many of the nation's most pressing social problems:

- Social workers have a strong value base that is outlined in the NASW Code of Ethics.

- Social work has a mission of social justice focused on the groups in society who are oppressed and/or marginalized.

- Social workers impact change with client systems at the micro, mezzo, and macro level.

- The three key domains of social work include practice, policy, and research.

- Unlike many other professions, social work is unique in the wide variety of work settings they can be employed in; the generalized skill set and knowledge base they acquire enables them to contribute to a broad array of workplaces.

- Social workers utilize a wide variety of theoretical perspectives and practice frameworks to guide their work (e.g., trauma-informed care, ecological systems perspective, strengths-based perspective, anti-oppressive social work practice).

IMG 14.1

Critical Social Issues on the Horizon

There are a number of pressing social and political issues that the social work profession will need to confront in the coming years if the profession wishes to continue to be relevant and live up to its **mission of social justice**, and this chapter will highlight five: poverty and income/wealth inequality, racial justice, environmental justice, unifying the social work profession for needed political action, and embracing a global perspective. As a reminder, Chapter 5 provided the following ways to conceptualize social justice:

- the distribution of wealth, opportunities, and privileges within a society
- the ability people have to realize their potential in the society in which they live
- promoting a just society by challenging social injustice
- equal access to opportunity in a society
- having the same rights as others to participate fully in all realms of private and public life
- the right to be treated equally under the law
- justice as fairness

Poverty and Income/Wealth Inequality

Chapter 6 provided an overview of poverty in the United States, including some important data and statistics to document this social problem. It is a sad irony that the wealthiest nation in the world has such a high poverty rate and high level of income/wealth inequality. **Income inequality** is the income gap between those who are very wealthy and everyone else, while **wealth inequality** is the wealth gap between the rich and everyone else. This is considered a justice issue because certain groups or populations are disproportionately affected by poverty and income/wealth inequality such as People of Color, women, and children. Though poverty and income inequality may seem like intractable social problems that are impossible to solve, this is not true.

Other nations that the United States gets compared to (e.g., those in Scandinavia and Europe) have found ways to create a more level playing field to citizens of all social classes via their social welfare programs and policies. Scandinavia, in particular, is famous for its generous tax-funded social welfare system that provides universal cradle-to-grave social welfare benefits to all citizens regardless of income level in order to provide more equal access to opportunity. These benefits include free health care, a monthly child allowance until the child is 16–18 years old, paid sick leave, paid family leave after the birth of a child (480 days in

Sweden), 4–5 weeks paid vacation per year, government-subsidized childcare, free college or vocational training, housing subsidies, and very generous benefits for senior citizens after retirement. As a result, people in Scandinavia are among the healthiest, happiest, and most educated in the world and live in nations with the lowest poverty rates.

NASW supports programs and policies that seek to decrease the poverty rate and create an economic system that operates fairly so that working- and middle-class families are able to prosper just as much as those at the top of the economic ladder. The NASW's (2018-2020) policy position on **economic justice** is as follows:

> NASW has been a champion of economic justice and equity since its inception. The social work profession was founded on the notion that those living in poverty are often politically marginalized and in need of advocates to help mitigate their plight. NASW believes that America must fully use and develop available, productive, and creative human resources and capacities. We reject any suggestions that the United States cannot achieve economic reforms that lead to economic justice and end economic disparities based on race, ethnicity, and gender. (pp. 87)

Racial Justice

The topic of racism and racial justice was emphasized in every chapter of this book and was heavily covered in Chapter 4. Despite the fact that the United States has cherished societal values that include freedom, happiness, and equality *for all*, the roots of **White supremacy** run deep, and our nation continues to strive to make progress with regard to social justice and equality for People of Color who face systemic barriers and violence. Like **Dr. Martin Luther King Jr.** famously stated, "The arc of the moral universe is long, but it bends towards justice." The social work profession is being called on by those both inside and outside the profession to **decolonize the profession** and examine more deeply its role in perpetuating White supremacy and using practices that are oppressive to some groups.

The social work profession has historically operated based on White, Western, Eurocentric practices, frameworks, and values. Social work education programs need to be committed to reaching students from diverse backgrounds in order to have a more diverse social work workforce that represents the individuals and communities it serves in terms of race/ethnicity, socioeconomic status, and lived experiences. The **decolonize social work movement** originated from Indigenous people and scholars and is often referred to as **Indigenous social work** but over time has generalized to the idea that social workers need to use practices that respect the customs, beliefs, and worldviews of the diverse and non-Western populations they work with and create less oppressive ways of delivering services.

In 2020, NASW published a news release expressing the social work profession's commitment to addressing racism both outside and inside the profession:

> Like our nation, the history of social work is complicated. Racism and white supremacy are ingrained within American institutions and systems and have therefore affected social work ideology and practice for generations.
>
> The mission of social work is to enhance human well-being and help meet the basic needs of all people, with particular attention to those who are vulnerable, oppressed, and living in poverty. We cannot maximize this mission and fully actualize our core professional values without advocating to reform, dismantle, or even abolish the racist and oppressive systems we may work within and beside.
>
> While the national conversation remains focused on ending police brutality, racism persists in many other institutions. The child welfare system has often more rigorously regulated and castigated Black, Brown, and Indigenous families. Medical racism, which has origins in slavery and eugenics, has led to modern day health disparities and inequities in health care access and treatment. The oppressive collateral consequences resulting from mass incarceration, the War on Drugs, and the school-to-prison pipeline have exacerbated economic inequalities in Black, Brown, and Indigenous communities.
>
> Social workers have had roles in perpetuating these harmful social systems, and this history cannot be ignored.
>
> Social work also has a major role to play in creating an antiracist society. As many professions and organizations are doing, we must pause to look inward and use that knowledge to propel us toward action for meaningful social change. We must build upon the good social workers have done in the fight for civil rights, health care access, child protection, the War on Poverty and marriage equality by working more intentionally to elevate Black, Brown, and Indigenous lives in the communities we serve.
>
> We have certainly made mistakes, but we are also a group of professionals committed to helping, lifting up, and advocating for oppressed and marginalized groups of people and fighting injustice in society. Social workers have an ethical duty to dismantle racism, both personally and professionally, and to demonstrate what it means to be antiracist.
>
> Directly confronting racism at the individual, agency, and institutional levels is the antiracist mandate we all must embrace. By using the NASW Code of Ethics as a guidepost, social workers can help dismantle systems of oppression, take action against white supremacy culture, and be leaders in the movement for racial justice. (para. 1–7)

IMG 14.2

Environmental Justice

Chapters 4 and 12 discussed how many communities of color in the United States are disproportionately impacted by **climate change** and why this is a social justice issue of importance to the social work profession. There is a clear and wide consensus from climate scientists that the warming of the planet is caused by humans, that it has reached a crisis point that must be addressed by policy makers across the world, and that if immediate action is not taken we will continue to witness human suffering due to disturbing weather patterns and the destruction of the planet's ecosystems. The U.S. Environmental Protection Agency (n.d.) defines **environmental justice** as

> the fair treatment and meaningful involvement of all people regardless of race, color, national origin, or income, with respect to the development, implementation, and enforcement of environmental laws, regulations, and policies. This goal will be achieved when everyone enjoys:
>
> - The same degree of protection from environmental and health hazards, and
> - Equal access to the decision-making process to have a healthy environment in which to live, learn, and work. (para. 1)

At one time, the topic of climate change and environmentalism was considered outside of the scope and expertise of the social work profession and was left to other disciplines to focus on. However, in recent years more social workers at all levels, including social work scholars and leaders, began calling on the profession to include this as an important focus of concern for social workers due to the disproportionate effects that climate change has on poor and marginalized communities in the United States and around the world. In fact, NASW (2018b) stated in their policy statement on environmental policy, "Social work, with its focus on political advocacy, can be an important force in addressing environmental issues. Social workers can engage in strategizing to organize and confront environmental justice through grassroots organizing, political action, and collaboration with communities, including indigenous leaders" (pp. 115–116).

Beltran et al. (2016) argue that content on environmental justice and environmental racism needs to be incorporated into social work curriculum within social work programs. The term **environmental racism** was coined to describe the fact that race is the most reliable variable in predicting which communities bear the burden of toxic environmental pollution (Beltran et al., 2016) as sewage treatment plants, landfills, and hazardous waste sites are typically located in areas where communities of color live.

Dominelli (2013) coined the term **green social work** to describe social workers who focus on environmental issues in their professional work. According to Dominelli (2013):

> Green social workers aim to promote environmental justice and resist environmental injustice by helping people mobilise and organise activities that protect their physical environment. Consequently, green social work practice affirms human rights and social justice to enhance the well-being of people and the environment for today and the future. Its concern to deal with forms of environmental degradation that undermine people's well-being provides the rationale that justifies social workers' involvement in environmental issues. (p. 437)

Meeting the Needs of Children and Older Adults

Both children and older adults are vulnerable populations that require strong social policies and programs to help them thrive in our society. **Older adults** face a number of challenges in society such as lack of income security; deteriorating health, including mental health; the need for affordable housing and caregiver support; elder abuse; discrimination in the workplace; and issues surrounding death and dying. As discussed in Chapter 10, the "graying of America" refers to a demographic shift in which a higher proportion of the U.S. population consists of older adults, in part due to longer life expectancy, decreasing fertility rates,

IMG 14.3

and the high number of baby boomers who are retiring. According to the Administration for Community Living (2021), in 2019 the number of adults age 65 and older was 54.1 million, approximately 1 in 7 Americans. This was an increase of 36% over the previous decade. Current estimates indicate that in 2040, there will be about 80.8 million older persons, more than twice as many as in 2000. And the number of older adults will reach 94.7 million by 2060. Additionally, those who are 85 and older are projected to more than double by 2040 (Administration for Community Living, 2021).

It is crucial that social workers engage in advocacy efforts to ensure that we provide adequate care and support to older adults and that federal programs such as Social Security and Medicare continue to be strong and solvent to keep older Americans out of poverty and as healthy as possible into old age.

However, it is equally important that social workers focus on the needs of children and to be a supporter of **children's rights**. Because children do not have the opportunity to vote and engage in other forms of political participation, they have a tougher time advocating for their needs in society compared to groups that have benefitted from social movements on their behalf. Chapter 9 highlighted adverse childhood experiences that children experience such as poverty, child maltreatment, and lack of educational opportunities and how children of color face even greater obstacles. According to Ritter (2022), children get the short end of the stick when it comes to federal spending:

Children are not a budget priority despite decades of solid research showing the importance of investing in children ages 0 to 5 years, because these are critical years for brain development. Spending on older adults is higher due to the expensive social programs that are devoted to serving them, such as Social Security and Medicare, and because of the growing aging population. However, children are just as vulnerable as older adults and require strong social programs to ensure that their developmental, health, and mental health needs are addressed, particularly in the first 5 years of life when their brains are developing. (p. 324)

Unifying the Social Work Profession for Needed Political Action

In its policy statement on the role of government and social policy, the NASW (2018c) expresses their position very clearly that government at all levels has a major role and responsibility to meet human needs through policies that support universal social welfare benefits and services: "It is the position of NASW that federal, state, and local governments must have a role in developing policies and programs that expand opportunities; address social and economic justice; improve the quality of life of all people in this country, with special emphasis on oppressed groups; and enhance the social conditions of the nation's communities" (p. 281).

One of the best things about the social work profession is the broad array of work settings where social workers can work after earning a degree in social work. Indeed, social work likely has the broadest scope of practice of any profession out there! However, this creates a challenge when the profession needs to come together and unify around important social and political issues, sometimes referred to as the "silo effect." For example, in recent years nurses and teachers in various states have been politically active around various policy issues that affect their workforce and those they serve. But because social workers labor in different fields of practice, this is a barrier that the profession needs to work to overcome.

Some people are surprised to learn that NASW takes political stands on various political issues that are published in their book *Social Work Speaks*. NASW hires lobbyists to help pass policies that support the rights, health, and well-being of the individuals, families, and communities that social workers serve. Finally, NASW has a political action committee that donated funding to political candidates who support social work values and priorities. Social work is nonpartisan but supports policies and lawmakers who support the values and ethics of the social work profession.

The importance of **voting** and **voter registration** has been elevated as an important issue in social work at the highest levels. In 2016, the Voting Is Social Work website (votingissocialwork.org) was launched to mobilize efforts by social workers to get more Americans registered to vote. Social work leaders who have spearheaded this effort argue that there is a strong connection between political participation by citizens who advocate for the needs of their communities (i.e., making your voices heard) and policies that advance social justice.

Embracing a Global Perspective to Social Work

Chapter 12 provides an in-depth overview of **international social work**. A number of social workers and social work scholars who specialize in international social work are calling on the social work profession to embrace a **global human rights perspective** and focus on concerning social problems that people experience in all parts of the world, particularly women, children, and migrants. Social work scholar Mapp (2014) argues,

> While it is easier to prioritize the needs of those who are close to us over those who are further away, this approach is damaging in the long run. First, social work's ethic of care requires that no distinction be drawn between "our" poor and "their" poor. Second, with the globalization of our world, social, economic, and political forces in one region of the world can affect other regions of the world, and injustices experienced in local communities can emanate from forces beyond national borders. Thus, the struggles of those who live half a world away can affect us locally. (p. Preface vii–viii)

It is vital that social workers who work with groups of people from different cultural backgrounds are **culturally competent**, use interventions that are **culturally responsive**, and embrace the concept of cultural humility. Interventions need to be tailored in such a way so that the client's culture is respected and taken into account. Social workers should strive to learn as much as they can about the cultural backgrounds of those they serve, such as a group's history, language, customs, practices, values, and belief systems. **Cultural humility**, or "coming from a place of not knowing about people's cultures, histories, and experiences in life" is preferred since it emphasizes a commitment by social workers to engage in lifelong learning and understanding about the lived experiences of those from other cultures and supports the idea of the client being the expert of their life, not the social worker (Morgaine & Capous-Desyllas, 2015, p. 151).

Social work programs have a responsibility to offer coursework in international or global social work and to provide opportunities, including field internships, for students to learn about both the

---

14.1   PRACTICE ACTIVITY

1. Of the issues that were highlighted under "Critical Social Issues on the Horizon to Social Work," which ones resonated most with you, and why?

2. Which one of these issues would you like to get involved with as a social worker?

3. Are there any issues that were *not* included that you think should?

strengths and challenges of people and cultural groups from other nations. Finally, U.S. social workers should be open to learning about, and sometimes borrowing, the innovative policies and practice approaches used by social workers in other nations.

The Grand Challenges for Social Work

Following the tradition of other disciplines, in 2013 the American Academy of Social Work & Social Welfare (AASWSW) set out to develop a list of "grand challenges" that need to be addressed in our society, guided by a social work perspective. After a lengthy process in which numerous social work interest groups and organizations were consulted and allowed to provide input, **12 grand challenges** were outlined and published under three broad categories (Grand Challenges for Social Work, n.d.).

TABLE 14.1   The 12 Grand Challenges for Social Work

I. Individual and family well-being
Ensure healthy development for youth
Close the health gap
Build healthy relationships to end violence
Advance long and productive lives

II. Stronger social fabric
Eradicate social isolation
End homelessness
Create social responses to a changing environment
Harness technology for social good

III. Just society
Eliminate racism
Promote smart decarceration
Build financial capability and assets for all
Reduce extreme economic inequality
Achieve equal opportunity and justice

In a published article about the grand challenges, authors point to previous periods in U.S. history in which social workers "played a powerful role in lifting the nation out of the distress that accompanied industrial and social transformation, rapid urbanization, and economic instability" (Uehara et al., 2013, p. 165), for example, social workers who worked at the Children's Bureau (from 1910–1921) whose work cut the child mortality rate in half as well as social workers who worked to pass a number of important social policies and programs during the Great Depression that prevented millions of families from severe economic devastation. These authors go on to say,

> If we are to maximize social work's contribution to society, we must attract the world's most passionate and gifted individuals to the profession. We must bridge the gap between the science and the practice of social work, and between social work and other disciplines and fields. We must develop effective interventions and bring those programs to scale with sustainability. In addition, we must dramatically increase the public understanding of why the science and practice of social work is crucial not only to the quality of life but also to the sustainability of our lives. (p. 166)

Today's Social Work Workplace

As has been noted in this book, social workers work in a wide array of workplace settings due to social work's broad scope of practice. The work environment varies widely from setting to setting on factors related to the size of the organization, how structured the setting is, the type of supervision provided, the level of predictability, and the amount of stress that employees experience. However, the workplace is constantly changing and evolving. A good recent example is the **impact that the coronavirus pandemic** has had on how Americans work since many workers transitioned to working from home and meeting with coworkers and clients over virtual platforms such as Zoom and Microsoft Teams. And even though the worst of the pandemic seems to be behind us, employees are now asking their employers to continue these flexible work practices as they now enjoy splitting their time between working at home and the office. Many employees are demanding more from their employers so that they can create a healthy work–life balance, particularly social workers who have jobs that are stressful and emotionally demanding. This section will highlight a few key areas that are especially relevant for today's social work workforce.

The Importance of Wellness and Self-Care

Self-care is important for everyone, but particularly for those who work in a helping profession due to the emotional labor that is required. When social workers do not prioritize taking care of their own physical and emotional well-being, they are not able to provide clients with the support and level of service

IMG 14.4

that they deserve. There have been some interesting conversations by experts of this topic on whether **self-care** is an individual or societal responsibility, and the answer appears to be both! Even though self-care needs to be a personal practice, it is equally important to demand structural changes (i.e., policies and practices) in our workplaces and society at large that strike a healthy balance between wellness and productivity and to promote values that support a healthy work–life balance.

However, this requires intention if emotional well-being is to be truly prioritized. When self-care takes a back seat to other priorities, social workers can experience **burnout**, **compassion fatigue**, and **vicarious traumatization**, and it is important to distinguish between these related though conceptually distinct phenomena. The U.S. Department of Justice, Office for Victims of Crime (n.d.) defines these terms as follows:

- **Burnout:** A state of physical, emotional, and mental exhaustion caused by long-term involvement in emotionally demanding situations. Symptoms may include depression, cynicism, boredom, loss of compassion, and discouragement.

- **Compassion Fatigue:** A combination of physical, emotional, and spiritual depletion associated with caring for others who are in significant emotional pain and physical distress.

- **Vicarious Trauma**: An occupational challenge for people working and volunteering in the fields of victim services, law enforcement, emergency medical services, fire services, and other allied professions, due to their continuous exposure to victims of trauma and violence. Exposure to the trauma of others has been shown to change the world-view of these responders and can put people and organizations at risk for a range of negative consequences. (para. 1, 2, 12)

On the positive side, social workers can experience **compassion satisfaction** and **vicarious resilience** as a result of the meaningful and purposeful work that they carry out with individuals, families, and communities. The U.S. Department of Justice, Office for Victims of Crime (n.d.) offers the following definitions for these important concepts:

- **Compassion satisfaction** refers to the pleasure derived from work, including feeling positively about the meaningfulness of one's contribution to the work and/or to the greater good of society.

- **Vicarious resilience** is a process of learning about overcoming adversity from a trauma survivor and the resulting positive transformation and empowerment experienced through witnessing the survivor's empathy and interaction. (para. 3, 10)

Prioritizing Anti-Oppressive Social Work Practice

Social work's mission of social justice requires that social workers work to dismantle oppression that is systemic and structural by looking both inside and outside the profession. **Anti-oppressive social work practice** is covered in several chapters of this book, most notably in Chapters 3 and 4. And Chapter 2 highlights the history of the social work profession and how the historic contributions of many social workers of color have been deemphasized and ignored. Even though social work has long supported the goals and vision of social movements that have worked tirelessly for social, economic, and political equality, it has also been complicit and has used harmful practices that have replicated the discrimination and oppression found in the larger society (as reflected in the news release by NASW that is included earlier in this chapter). It is important for the profession to be able to celebrate its successes and contributions to society while also acknowledging when it has fallen short of its mission and failed to live up to its values. This is a healthy practice for any profession.

Groups that have been impacted by oppression include communities of color, women, LGBTQ+ individuals, religious minorities, those with low socioeconomic status, those with disabilities, those with mental illness, immigrants, children, and older adults. The social work profession is being called on to engage in **anti-racism work** and to use **culturally responsive social work practices** that respect the cultural diversity of those we serve. Finally, because the social work workforce is overwhelmingly female, White, and middle class, the profession should work toward having a workforce that more accurately reflects the diversity and lived experiences of those who live in this country.

Fair Compensation and Good Working Conditions

Even though social work is a career of service, some social workers work in fields in which the pay is not commensurate with the social worker's knowledge, skills, and experience. More work needs to be done to raise awareness about the value that social workers bring to the lives of individuals and communities across the nation. According to the U.S. Bureau of Labor Statistics (n.d.), the employment of social workers is expected to increase by 12% from 2020 to 2030, which is faster than average for all occupations. The employment of child, family, and school social workers is expected to grow by 13%; mental health and substance abuse social workers by 15%; and health care social workers by 13%. However, NASW is projecting a shortage of social work professionals to meet the need for social work services in the coming years due to various barriers that make it difficult for people to enter the field of social work and because of the numbers of retiring social workers who need to be replaced.

Both the **recruitment and retention of social workers** are issues that deserve attention. Unfortunately, many students do not consider a career in social work due to low starting salaries and fears that they will be unable to pay off their student loans, despite the demand for their services. The Council on Social Work Education (CSWE) reports that in their 2020 annual survey of social work programs, 70% of Bachelor of Social Work (BSW) graduates and 73% of Master of Social Work (MSW) graduates had student loan debt. The average loan debt was $27,264 for BSW gradates and $47,965 for MSW graduates (CSWE, 2021). Meanwhile, the median pay for social workers in 2021, according to the U.S. Bureau of Labor Statistics (n.d.), was $50,390 a year. NASW advocates for social workers to receive adequate pay and reimbursement that is comparable to other similar helping professions and has made **college student loan forgiveness** for social workers one of their main advocacy

| 14.2 | **PRACTICE ACTIVITY** |

Google the Dorothy I. Height and Whitney M. Young, Jr. Social Work Reinvestment Act to learn more about this piece of federal legislation that NASW has worked to get passed into law for many years.

1. What problem is this bill trying to address?

2. Who is this bill named after?

3. What would this bill do exactly?

4. If this bill were to be passed into law, what impact would it have on the social work profession, in your opinion?

priorities due to the challenges that many social workers face in paying off their student loans.

Finally, to retain social workers, we must ensure that they have a safe working environment and have manageable workloads so they do not burn out. This requires that social services organizations have sufficient funding to employ to cover their staffing needs. Having a sustainable workforce requires employers who do not exploit their employees' labor but rather create an environment that is supportive of their health and well-being.

Current Social Work Career Trends

It is always fascinating to witness how the social work profession evolves over time and the new career opportunities that develop for those with a degree in social work. Even though many of the traditional career paths for social workers are still in place, such as mental health, health care, child welfare, and settings that provide care for older adults, the field is constantly changing and evolving, and a few key trends are highlighted:

- *Delivering social work services virtually*: The proliferation of telehealth and **telemental health services** began before the coronavirus pandemic but expanded rapidly during this time out of necessity in order to keep everyone

IMG 14.5

safe and healthy. However, services delivered in this format will continue as it is a very convenient way for many to receive services and allows access for some people who ordinarily do not have access such as those who live in rural areas and other areas that are underserved.

- *Macro-level social justice work*: Over the past decade, more social workers have been interested in working in macro-level social work, particularly in the political arena, to focus on a number of pressing social problems our country faces such as poverty and income inequality, access to health care and mental health care, gun violence, climate change, and police brutality, just to name a few. More and more social workers are working in advocacy organizations, working as lobbyists, and even running for political office at the local, state, and national levels.

- *Research and evaluation*: There is a significant need for social workers who are interested in conducting qualitative and quantitative research to help the profession further its knowledge base, evaluate interventions in order to develop best practices, and help organizations engage in program evaluation to help them evaluate the services they are providing to ensure that they are helping and not harming. Social workers with an MSW degree can do some of this work, while some research positions require an earned doctorate degree. Social workers who earn a doctorate in social work and pursue a career in academia teach social work in a university setting while engaging in scholarly work.

- *Private sector opportunities*: Many people believe that all social workers work for the government, but this is a myth as over half of social workers work in the private sector, either in nonprofit organizations or for-profit settings. Many corporate settings like to hire social workers in jobs that require strong skills in management, conflict resolution, training, counseling, and communication. Social workers are encouraged to think outside of the box when they consider the skill set they can contribute to a wide array of organizations.

- *Creative approaches to change*: Finally, many social workers bring creative approaches to their work, particularly through the use of art. At the micro level, some social workers use therapeutic approaches such as art therapy, music therapy, and theater. Body work is also a thriving area of practice as social workers use approaches with clients that include yoga, mindfulness, and meditation. Animal-assisted therapy is a growing practice used by social workers in some settings. At the macro level, social workers can also use **creativity** in their social change work by making documentary films and using other artforms (e.g., music, painting, photography) to raise awareness of social issues in society.

Is Social Work for You?

As stated in Chapter 1 of this book, social work is not for everyone, and it is important to carefully assess whether you have the passion and skills necessary for this career of service to others. For those who do decide to enter social work, it is an opportunity for lifelong personal and professional growth, growing expertise on how to facilitate a planned change process with client systems of all sizes, lifelong learning regarding the personal human struggles that many people face, and the opportunity to work toward a more just and equal society. The questions that follow can help you to assess whether social work might be a good fit for you based on your skill set, personality, values, and passions. For each question, use the scale provided.

14.3   PRACTICE ACTIVITY

Assess Your Goodness of Fit

Answer the questions to help you assess your goodness of fit with a career in social work using the following scale:

Strongly agree: 5 points

Agree: 4 points

Neutral: 3 points

Disagree: 2 points

Strongly disagree: 1 point

- Do you have a strong desire to address social inequalities and social injustices in our society?
- Do you enjoy working collaboratively as a member of a team?
- Are you committed to self-awareness and being dedicated to continually assessing your strengths, limitations, and personal biases?
- Do you think of yourself as a problem solver and someone who enjoys facilitating change at the micro, mezzo, or macro level in society?
- Do you possess empathy/compassion toward others and genuinely care about people who struggle?
- Do you believe in the worth and dignity of all human beings (no matter their actions)?

- Do you have strong interpersonal and communication skills? Do you have the ability to build rapport with others that can lead to a positive trusting relationship?

- Do you have a strong interest, openness, and curiosity in working with individuals from diverse backgrounds that are different from your own background (e.g., age, gender, sexual orientation, culture, race/ethnicity, socioeconomic status, disability status)?

- Are you able to balance multiple responsibilities and maintain a healthy work–life balance? Can you keep yourself healthy so that you can be there for your clients?

- Are you professional in your interactions in the workplace, even during instances of conflict?

- Are you a good listener? Can you be fully present to someone sharing their personal struggles with you?

- Do your personal values align well with the six core values outlined in the NASW Code of Ethics?

If you score around a 45 or higher, this indicates a strong alignment with a potential future career in social work.

Chapter Summary

Social work is a wonderful career, but it is not for everyone. When considering any career, it is important to understand the values, skills, and knowledge that are needed to assess whether it would be a good fit for you. By the end of an Introduction to Social Work course, most students have a much better idea about this. If you discover that you get very excited and passionate as you learn about the concepts in this book, that might be an indication that this career is for you. When talking with those who chose to become a social worker, we learn that there are many different paths that brought people to this career path. For some, it is a calling, and for others, it is a deliberate choice to enter a career of service that they feel well suited for. Social work can be incredibly rewarding, but it can also be emotionally taxing, thus the need to take very good care of oneself. Days working as a social worker are rarely dull since every day is different, and this profession demands a commitment to continual personal growth, self-reflection, and new learning. For many social workers, it is a tremendous responsibility but also an honor and a gift to have the opportunity to work alongside others when they are struggling and in a time of need.

▌ Discussion Questions

1. This chapter highlighted the importance of wellness and self-care for social workers so they can avoid burnout, compassion fatigue, and vicarious traumatization. How can social workers advocate for themselves in the workplace to get support for policies and practices that support a healthy work–life balance for social workers?

2. Even though social workers fight for legislation that supports the individuals, families, and communities they serve, do you think it is also valid for them to fight for policies that support social workers in society, such as college loan forgiveness?

3. Review the 12 grand challenges for social work. Do you think that these 12 adequately capture the most important issues that the country, and the social work profession, should be focusing on? Is there anything missing, in your view?

4. Environmental justice was highlighted in this chapter as an issue that social workers should be actively involved in. Why do you think this issue was largely neglected by the profession for so long? Do you agree that this should be an issue of concern for social work?

5. What did your score in Practice Activity 14.3 reveal for you regarding your goodness of fit with social work? What did you learn about social work in this book that helped you clarify whether social work is a good fit for you? What other careers are you planning to explore?

▌ References

Administration for Community Living. (2021). *2020 profile of older Americans*. https://acl.gov/aging-and-disability-in-america/data-and-research/profile-older-americans

Beltran, R., Hacker, A., & Begun, S. (2016). Environmental justice is a social justice issue: Incorporating environmental justice into social work practice curricula. *Journal of Social Work Education, 52*(4), 493–502.

Council on Social Work Education. (2021). 2020 statistics on social work education in the United States. https://www.cswe.org/Research-Statistics/Research-Briefs-and-Publications/2020-Annual-Statistics-on-Social-Work-Education

Dominelli, L. (2013). Invited article environmental justice at the heart of social work practice: Greening the profession. *International Journal of Social Welfare, 22*, 431–439.

Grand Challenges for Social Work. (n.d.). *The challenges*. https://grandchallengesforsocialwork.org/#the-challenges

Mapp, S. C. (2014). *Human rights and social justice*. Oxford University Press.

Morgaine, K., & Capous-Desyllas, M. (2015). *Anti-oppressive social work practice*. SAGE.

National Association of Social Workers. (2018a). Economic Justice. In *Social Work Speaks* (11th ed., pp. 84–89. NASW Press.

National Association of Social Workers. (2018b). Environmental policy. In *Social Work Speaks* (11th ed., pp. 113–119. NASW Press.

National Association of Social Workers. (2018c). Role of government, social policy, and social work. In *Social work speaks* (11th ed., pp. 278–282). NASW Press.

National Association of Social Workers. (2020, August 21). *Social workers must help dismantle systems of oppression and fight racism within the social work profession*. https://www. socialworkers.org/News/News-Releases/ID/2219/Social-Workers-Must-Help-Dismantle-Systems-of-Oppression-and-Fight-Racism-Within-Social-Work-Profession

Ritter, J. (2022). *Social work policy practice: Changing our community, nation, and the world* (3rd ed.). Cognella.

Uehara, E., Flynn, M., Fong, R., Brekke, J., Barth, R. P., Coulton, C., Davis, K., DiNitto, D. J., Hawkins, D., Lubben, J., Manderscheid, R., Padilla, Y., Sherraden, M., & Walters, K. (2013). Grand challenges for social work. *Journal of the Society for Social Work and Research, 4*(3), 165–170.

U.S. Bureau of Labor Statistics. (2022, September 8). *Social workers*. Occupational Outlook Handbook. https://www.bls.gov/ooh/community-and-social-service/social-workers. htm

U.S. Department of Justice, Office of Victims of Crimes. (n.d.). *The vicarious trauma toolkit*. https://ovc.ojp.gov/program/vtt/glossary-terms

U.S. Environmental Protection Agency. (n.d.). *Environmental justice*. https://www.epa. gov/environmentaljustice

Credits

Index

About the Author

JESSICA RITTER is a full professor of social work in the Department of Social Work at Metropolitan State University of Denver. She earned her BSW, MSSW, and PhD in social work at the University of Texas at Austin. Prior to being on the faculty at MSU Denver, she was a full-time faculty member at George Mason University in the DC area and at Pacific University Oregon located just outside of Portland, Oregon. At Pacific University she served as the BSW program director and associate dean of social sciences. Ritter began her social work career in child protection due to her strong desire for working with children and families served by the child welfare system. Her career as a social worker and social work academic has been dedicated to child welfare and children's rights as well as political advocacy efforts focused on social and economic justice issues.

Dr. Ritter teaches a variety of social work courses, including Generalist Practice, Child Maltreatment, Research Methods, and Social Work Policy Practice. She has a special passion for teaching courses that focus on political advocacy with the goal of getting social work students excited about social policy, demystifying the political process, increasing students' levels of political efficacy, and inspiring them to be engaged politically. She has won teaching awards at multiple universities. Ritter is a Fulbright scholar and is the author of two other books—*101 Careers in Social Work* (3rd ed.) and *Social Work Policy Practice: Changing our Community, Nation, and the World* (3rd ed.). Being a social work educator is one of the great joys of her life!

www.ingramcontent.com/pod-product-compliance
Lightning Source LLC
Chambersburg PA
CBHW081057190125
20599CB00015B/1425